HOW SHARP IS
YOUR PENCIL?

How Sharp Is Your Pencil?

Edited by
Allen D. Bragdon
and
David Gamon

**Allen D. Bragdon
Publishers, Inc.**
CAPE COD & SAN FRANCISCO

BRAINWAVES BOOKS
a division of
Allen D. Bragdon Publishers, Inc.
252 Great Western Road
South Yarmouth, MA 02664

Earlier editions of this book were published by Harper & Row as *Can You Pass These Tests?*, by HarperCollins as *The Book of Tests*, and by Barnes & Noble Books as *What Do You Know?*

Copyright © 1987, 1989, 1997, 1999 by Allen D. Bragdon Publishers, Inc.

Library of Congress Catalog Card Number: 99-90520

ISBN 0-916410-64-1

BRAINWAVES® is a registered trademark of Allen D. Bragdon Publishers, Inc.

Cover design by Cindy Wood. Page formatting by Carolyn Zellers.

Printed in the United States of America

99 00 01 02 03   10 9 8 7 6 5 4 3 2 1

Acknowledgments

We would like to thank the following individuals who lent their good will and expertise to this project: Jennifer Terry and Warren Stallings at The Digital University who provided the battery of exam questions to establish computer competency; Toshio Ohori of the Department of Linguistics at the University of California, Berkeley, who translated *Kyotsu Ichiji*; Whitney Lowe of the Atlanta School of Massage, who gave unstintingly of his knowledge of massage therapy in formulating the questions and the informational introduction for that section; Pamela Blake of the Rutgers Office of TV and Radio, who was unwavering in her good humor despite the frustrations she was facing at the time; Ted Widmer, who graciously took time to explain the field of graphology to us.

Thanks, too, to Gabina Ivanova and A. Andreev, teacher and Principal, respectively, at the Soviet School to the Permanent Mission to the United Nations at Riverdale, NY, who prepared information about the history curriculum in Soviet elementary and secondary schools that appears in "U.S. History in the U.S.S.R." Liaison and translation were provided with skill and good will by Meredith Taylor, an editor and Russian language student, and by A. Korolkov, Attaché, and Nadia Nesterenko and Alla Dvornaya in the public relations office of the Soviet Permanent Mission to the U.N.

Arnulfo S. Rios, a student of government at Harvard University, dug into the Harvard archives on our behalf to come up with the examinations from pivotal years of U.S. History that appear in "U.S. History at Harvard." Kathleen O'Brien, a sociology student at the University of California, Santa Cruz, did the research in Washington, D.C., for "Voter Literacy."

Clifford R. Bragdon, Assistant Dean of the School of Architecture (and A.D.B.'s cousin), put us in touch with Professor Frank Bekum, who kindly prepared the questions and photos from his course there for "Architect."

Stephen Thernstrom, Winthrop Professor of History at Harvard University, was kind enough to let us use one of his older exams for "U.S. History at Harvard."

Kenneth Hoffman, Professor of Mathematics and Chair of the Committee on the Writing Requirement at M.I.T. provided us with the sample essay questions that appear in "Writing Competency."

Finally, a note regarding any variations the reader might notice in the style and content of the introductions to the chapters of the book: The amount of humor and arresting information included in each introduction stands in inverse proportion to the number of legal department personnel who took the opportunity to veto passages from the manuscript.

Allen D. Bragdon and David Gamon

Contents

Introduction

There are no rules here—no surprise spot-quizzes at the end of the lesson and no certification checkups later. *This is for fun*; it can also be a way to measure an avocational interest against a professional standard—or, if you have held in one of these jobs for a while, to check your knowledge of some of the specifics an entry—level applicant would have to know now. Someone looking for a compatible career opportunity or change can scan the questions in an area of interest to get a grasp on the knowledge, skills, and aptitudes that field requires. For this edition we have selected the most interesting exams from earlier collections published as *Can You Pass These Tests?*, *The Book of Tests* and *What Do You Know?* We have added two new exams of contemporary interest: Business Ethics and Computer Competency.

In many cases we have selected representative questions from a full-length examination because the complete version is so long it would become tedious; or the vocabulary is so technical the questions would be incomprehensible to someone not trained professionally in that field; or because the questions in the original are legally available only in small samplings or as similar questions used to train for the official version.

Yet all these questions are real. The information in them drives machines many of which we trust our lives to (Computer Competency, Air Traffic Controller, Nurse), and sometimes our reputations (Architect, Business Ethics: MBA students vs. incarcerated felons); others fuel an intense personal interest (Baseball, Dancing, Collecting, Food Skills). Unlike real life, each of the questions in these tests has one clear and correct answer. The answers follow each test and are isolated on paper tinted gray to reinforce the morals of the good. These pages are separated from the questions so readers with superior peripheral vision will not enjoy an advantage should their moral fiber relax for a moment.

The "Sidebar" material does not include answers. Sometimes it deals with essay questions; sometimes it relates to test situations for which no multiple-choice or fill-in formats with answers exists. (At times the sidebars may be more interesting than the tests themselves.) Since the test questions all have one correct answer, the performance of any given taker can be scored objectively. For example, if person A scores higher than person B, person A feels good and person B doesn't bring the subject up again.

There is nothing wrong with scanning the questions and looking up the answers as you go, either. It's amazing how much you can learn that way with no risk to your ego. Regard it as a convenient technique for accumulating enough esoteric facts to qualify you as a Renaissance Person and confound the packs of Trivial Pursuers nipping at your heels. We hope you will have a good time in these pages and maybe even learn something interesting enough to be useful.

Allen D. Bragdon
Bass River, MA
April 1999

AIR TRAFFIC CONTROLLER

Federal Aviation Administration

Frequent Flyers who might be considering a career change may occasionally admire the skills that a controller of air traffic must bring to bear on his or her chosen daily task. However, those F.F's are more likely than others to be aware of the downside. A.T.C.'s are the Saint Sebastians of flying, constantly pierced by the extra—sensory barbs of irritation from pilots and passengers. As an alternative career the job of usher in a movie theater presents a less threatening aspect, yet it has much in common with air traffic controller: big screen, semidark, limited options for placing the fundaments of the temporarily blind comfortably down onto a vacant spot, a repeated daily pattern involving an infinite variety of idiosyncratic moves, and ushers never have to cope with hijackings.

We selected one or more questions for this exam from each of the three sub-tests within the Federal Aviation Administration's exam used to test a trainee-applicant's ability to handle the job of air traffic controller. The first two are pure aptitude tests. The last one tests knowledge only, which is not required of a trainee, so incorrect answers do not reduce the overall test score but correct answers could add points to it. If an applicant has not finished college and has no job-specific experience, he or she would have to make a 75 percent total test score.

The first test consists of a number of drawings simulating a radar scope with patterns of air traffic, shown with heavy route lines, and a table of data about each numbered aircraft. (In reality, these data would appear on the screen next to the aircraft's position.) We have selected one such question. The drawing shows the flight paths that aircraft must follow, indicated by capital letters at each end. Changes in the route of flight can only occur at the intersection between the two routes. Each double slash displayed on the route of flight represents the aircraft traveling in the direction away from its trailing dots. Below or to the side of the problem you will be given a table containing critical flight information about each aircraft. The number by each slash on the drawing allows the matching of flight information to the correct aircraft. The flight information lists the altitude, speed in miles per hour, and the route of the aircraft. Compass directions are shown as compass points in 45-degree increments around the outside of the screen.

The second subtest contains two types of spatial relations questions; letter series (determine the logic in the sequence of letters and identify the pair that continues it), and symbol classification (you see two sets of symbols which share a rule of similarity and difference; pick the role-fitting choice that best replaces the question mark in the second set).

Should you become so encouraged by your performance on these tests to consider switching careers to air traffic controller, you should get in touch with the local U.S. Civil Service Commission office for forms and procedures. Before doing that, though, you might want to sleep on it. This strikes us as the quintessential no-flinch, no-duck job that could take its toll on a guilt-ridden personality requiring constant validation. Being right is routine, but if you're wrong it shows and the finger points. A less emotionally burdensome way to apply the same aptitudes to the task of instructing others wisely might be to direct your spouse and children in the most space-efficient method for packing the summer vacation paraphernalia into the back of the station wagon. That, too, has its perils, of course.

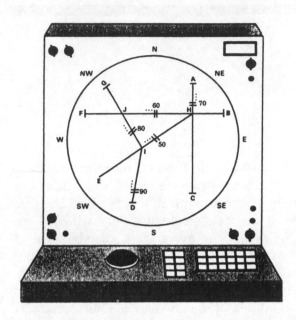

AIR TRAFFIC CONTROL FLIGHT INFORMATION			
Aircraft	Altitude	Speed	Route
50	28,000	500	DIHB
60	27,000	350	GJHB
70	29,000	500	AHB
80	27,000	500	FJI
90	28,000	500	BHID

MILEAGE 0 4 8 12

1. Approximately how many miles is Aircraft 50 from Point I?
    (A) 19
    (B) 16
    (C) 12
    (D) 10
    (E) 11

2. In approximately what direction is Aircraft 90 traveling?
    (A) East
    (B) Southeast
    (C) South
    (D) North
    (E) Northeast

3. What is the approximately number of miles from Point I to Point H?
    (A) 53
    (B) 30
    (C) 49
    (D) 35
    (E) 50

4. Which aircraft travels south, then directly east?
    (A) 90
    (B) 71
    (C) 50
    (D) 80
    (E) 60

5. Which aircraft will conflict?
    (A) 50 and 70
    (B) 70 and 90
    (C) 80 and 50
    (D) 60 and 80
    (E) None

6. Approximately how long will it take Aircraft 50 to go from Point I to Point H?
    (A) 4 minutes
    (B) 2 minutes
    (C) 12 minutes
    (D) 10 minutes
    (E) 15 minutes

7. Aircraft 70 flies a route south, then east; how many degrees will Aircraft 70 turn to go east?
    (A) 115
    (B) 60
    (C) 120
    (D) 90
    (E) 125

8. Which two aircraft travel over the same intersection at some point in their routes?
   (A) 50 and 70
   (B) 70 and 60
   (C) 60 and 80
   (D) 70 and 90
   (E) All of the preceding

9. Which aircraft begins its route traveling east then turns southeast?
   (A) 90
   (B) 50
   (C) 60
   (D) 80
   (E) 70

10. Which aircraft will conflict?
    (A) 50 and 60
    (B) 50 and 90
    (C) 70 AND 80
    (D) 80 AND 90
    (E) None

LETTER SERIES

DIRECTIONS: In these questions, you are given a series of letters that are arranged in some definite order. Below each question are five suggested answer choices; each answer choice consists of two sets of letters. You are to look at each letter series and determine what its order is and then from the suggested answers beneath select the set that gives the next two letters in the series in their correct order.

11. E E G I I K M

    (A) MN
    (B) OO
    (C) OQ
    (D) MO
    (E) NM

12. S H R I Q J P
    (A) KO
    (B) KL
    (C) OK
    (D) PK
    (E) ON

13. G N V H O W I
    (A) PJ
    (B) XJ
    (C) IP
    (D) PX
    (E) XG

14. P P G R R I T
    (A) TT
    (B) UV
    (C) UU
    (D) TU
    (E) TK

15. E E A E E B E
    (A) EE
    (B) EF
    (C) CE
    (D) FE
    (E) EC

16. A R C S E T G
    (A) HI
    (B) HU
    (C) UJ
    (D) UI
    (E) IV

17. A V A W A X A
    (A) ZA
    (B) YZ
    (C) YW
    (D) AZ
    (E) YA

18. X C X D X C X
    (A) XB
    (B) XA
    (C) XF
    (D) XG
    (E) DX

19. T G H U E F V
    (A) DC
    (B) DW
    (C) DE
    (D) CD
    (E) CW

20. D J H N L R
    (A) XT
    (B) OU
    (C) TX
    (D) PX
    (E) PV

21. J M K N L O M
    (A) PQ
    (B) PN
    (C) NM
    (D) NP
    (E) MM

22. C F I L O R
    (A) XW
    (B) UX
    (C) UU
    (D) UT
    (E) TU

23. B D F H J L
    (A) NP
    (B) OP
    (C) PN
    (D) PO
    (E) OP

24. A B Z C D Y E
    (A) XG
    (B) XW
    (C) FW
    (D) FX
    (E) FG

25. R L S M T N U
    (A) OV
    (B) UV
    (C) VW
    (D) OW
    (E) VO

26. L C D L E F L
    (A) LG
    (B) GH
    (C) LE
    (D) FG
    (E) GG

27. C E H L Q O L
    (A) QO
    (B) EC
    (C) NQ
    (D) GD
    (E) HC

28. F G D I B K L
    (A) IN
    (B) JH
    (C) AM
    (D) NJ
    (E) CF

29. Z X U Q O L H
    (A) FC
    (B) FB
    (C) DA
    (D) EB
    (E) GD

30. D F H H E G I I F H J
    (A) JG
    (B) GG
    (C) GI
    (D) JI
    (E) LL

31. C D F G J K O
    (A) PT
    (B) PU
    (C) TX
    (D) TZ
    (E) SX

32. A G L M L Q R
    (A) QR
    (B) QW
    (C) RW
    (D) QV
    (E) RQ

33. A C F H K M P
    (A) SV
    (B) RT
    (C) RU
    (D) SU
    (E) QR

34. M P N Q O R P
    (A) SQ
    (B) GR
    (C) TQ
    (D) QS
    (E) SR

35. F R H T J V L
    (A) MN
    (B) WY
    (C) XN
    (D) NW
    (E) XM

36. T G T H T I T
    (A) LT
    (B) JT
    (C) IM
    (D) TL
    (E) TJ

37. H G F K J I N
    (A) ML
    (B) PO
    (C) LM
    (D) OP
    (E) MO

38. S H R I Q J P
    (A) KO
    (B) KL
    (C) OK
    (D) PK
    (E) ON

39. J H N L R P V
    (A) TX
    (B) SZ
    (C) TZ
    (D) SY
    (E) ZT

40. M K H E K I F
    (A) MG
    (B) HI
    (C) JD
    (D) CM
    (E) CI

41. C E I O C F K
    (A) QC
    (B) RC
    (C) CP
    (D) RZ
    (E) CQ

42. Y X V T S Q O N L J I
    (A) HF
    (B) HG
    (C) GE
    (D) FE
    (E) GF

43. Y X V T S Q O N L J I
    (A) HF
    (B) HT
    (C) GE
    (D) FC
    (E) GI

44. E G T H J T K
    (A) LT
    (B) MT
    (C) LM
    (D) TL
    (E) MN

45. H G F K J I N
    (A) ML
    (B) PO
    (C) LM
    (D) OP
    (E) MO

46. Q G R I S K T
    (A) UL
    (B) MU
    (C) LU
    (D) MN
    (E) LM

47. A B Z C D Y E
    (A) XG
    (B) XW
    (C) FW
    (D) FX
    (E) IG

48. R L S M T N U
    (A) OV
    (B) UV
    (C) VW
    (D) OW
    (E) VO

49. L C D L C F L
    (A) LG
    (B) GH
    (C) LC
    (D) CH
    (E) GG

50. M N O M N O M
    (A) MN
    (B) NO
    (C) NM
    (D) ON
    (E) OM

51. A K B J C I D
    (A) EG
    (B) HE
    (C) EA
    (D) EH
    (E) GE

52. Y V W T U R S
    (A) PQ
    (B) PO
    (C) QO
    (D) QR
    (E) WU

53. M L N K O J P
    (A) IH
    (B) IQ
    (C) QH
    (D) QM
    (E) OP

54. F G I J L M O P
    (A) QR
    (B) PQ
    (C) PR
    (D) QS
    (E) RS

55. G I K J L N
    (A) HM
    (B) IK
    (C) LN
    (D) NM
    (E) MO

56. B C D E F G H
    (A) GI
    (B) IK
    (C) IJ
    (D) JL

(E) HL

57. R P N L J H F
    (A) R P N L J H F
    (B) DC
    (C) CB
    (D) DB
    (E) EP

58. T G H U E F V
    (A) DC
    (B) DW
    (C) DO
    (D) CD
    (E) CW

SYMBOL CLASSIFICATION
DIRECTIONS: Each question consists of two sets of symbols that are analogous to each other. That means the sets share a common characteristic while they differ in a specific aspect of that characteristic. In each question, the first set contains three symbols and the second set contains two symbols and a question mark. Following the symbol sets are five alternatives labeled A, B, C, D, and E. You must choose the one lettered symbol which can best be substituted for the question mark. The correct choice will have the characteristic common to both sets of symbols and yet maintain the same variation of that characteristic as the two symbols in the second set.

59.

60.

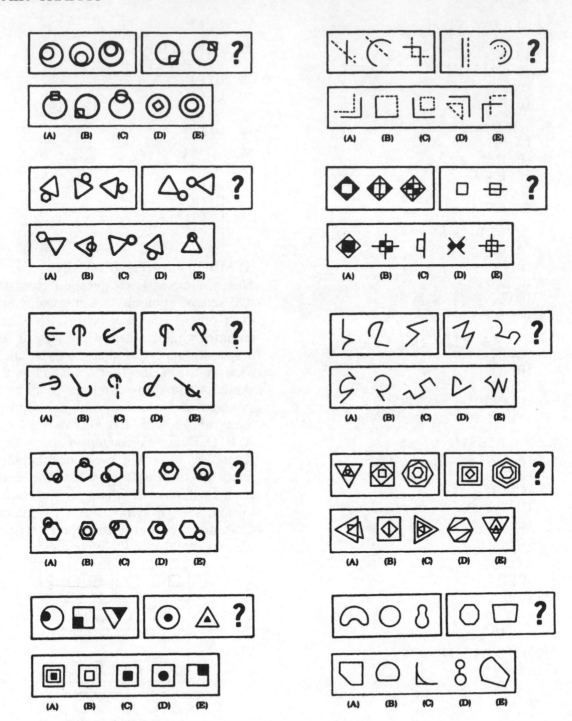

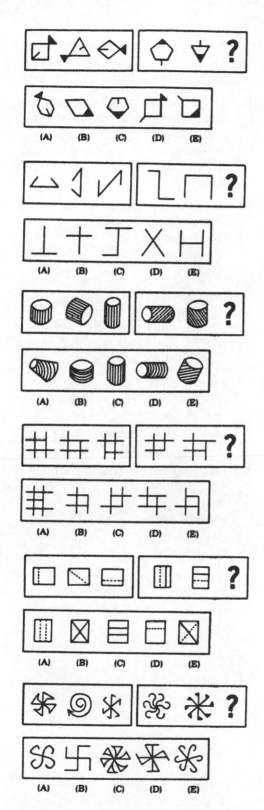

DIRECTIONS: This portion of the examination is designed to find out how much you already know about air traffic control. The questions deal with air traffic rules, air traffic procedures, in-flight traffic control procedures, air navigation and aids to navigation, and aviation weather. Remember, you can receive additional points on your score by answering questions in this text section correctly, but your total score on the exam will not be affected if you answer any questions in this section incorrectly.

77. What runway is used when the wind is less than 5 knots?
(A) Pilot choice
(B) Controller choice
(C) Calm wind
(D) Any

78. What runway is used when the wind is more than 5 knots?
(A) Most nearly aligned with the wind
(B) Any
(C) The one opposite the wind
(D) North runway

79. What is the VHF emergency frequency?
(A) 121.35
(B) 121.95
(C) 121.15
(D) 121.5

80. Transponder with no altitude encoding capability is
(A) /A
(B) /T
(C) /D
(D) /P

81. Pilots should discontinue position reporting over compulsory reporting points when informed by ATC that their aircraft is
(A) on the ground
(B) in radar contact
(C) above 14,000 feet
(D) in PCA

82. When may an aircraft discontinue reporting over compulsory reporting points?
    (A) Never
    (B) After the first fix
    (C) Any time
    (D) After receiving the statement "radar contact" from ATC

83. When using the broadband radar system, what is the separation minimum when less than 40 miles from the antenna?
    (A) 5 miles
    (B) 10 miles
    (C) 3 miles
    (D) 2 miles

84. Do not request speed adjustment of aircraft cleared for approach except when action is necessary to maintain or achieve desired or required spacing.
    (A) True
    (B) False

85. FAR 121 permits landing or takeoff by domestic scheduled air carriers where a local surface restriction to visibility is not less than _____, provided all turns after takeoff or before landing and all flights beyond _____ from the airport boundary can be accomplished above or outside the area so restricted.
    (A) 1/2 statute mile, 1 statute mile
    (B) 1 1/2 statute miles, 1 statue mile
    (C) 2 statute miles, 1 statute mile
    (D) 5 statute miles, 3 statute miles

86. This question pertains to number 85. Who is responsible for determining the nature of the visibility restriction that will permit compliance with the provisions of FAR 121?
    (A) Controller
    (B) Airport manager
    (C) Pilot
    (D) Supervisor

87. Clear aircraft to hold over different fixes whose holding pattern airspace areas

    (A) do not touch
    (B) do not overlap each other
    (C) have at least 7 miles between them
    (D) have at least 10 miles between them

88. The flight path parallel to the landing runway in the direction of landing is
    (A) downwind
    (B) base
    (C) upwind
    (D) final

89. Terminate interphone message with
    (A) operating initials
    (B) a goodbye
    (C) your name
    (D) SSN

90. State heading of 5 degrees as
    (A) "Heading, five degrees"
    (B) "Heading, zero zero five"
    (C) "Heading zero zero five degrees"
    (D) "Heading zero five"

91. Runway 27R is stated how?
    (A) "Runway twenty seven right"
    (B) "Runway twenty seven"
    (C) "Runway two seven right"
    (D) "Runway two seven"

92. Propeller aircraft within 20 miles of the airport should not be assigned a speed less than
    (A) 150 knots
    (B) 110 knots
    (C) 190 knots
    (D) 90 knots

93. Airspace within a horizontal radius of five statute miles from the graphical center of any airport at which a control tower is operating, extending from the surface up to but not including an altitude of 3000 feet above the elevation of the airport, is the
(A) airport control zone
(B) warning air
(C) restricted area
(D) airport traffic area

94. How many hours do you add to Central Standard Time to convert to Greenwich Mean Time?
(A) 5 hours
(B) 6 hours
(C) 4 hours
(D) 3 hours

95. How are nonradar environment aircraft in a holding pattern separated?
(A) Vertically
(B) Longitudinally
(C) By 2 miles
(D) By 5 miles

96. What is the phraseology for issuing a heading of thirty-two degrees?
(A) "Turn to heading of thirty-two degrees?
(B) "Fly thirty-two degrees"
(C) "Turn to heading zero three two"
(D) "Fly heading zero three two"

97. What is the international radio telephone distress signal?
(A) Three dots and one dash
(B) Help
(C) Dot, dash, dot, dot, dash
(D) Mayday

ANSWERS! ☛

1.	D	33.	C	65.	C
2.	C	34.	A	66.	A
3.	B	35.	C	67.	B
4.	B	36.	B	68.	A
5.	D	37.	A	69.	C
6.	A	38.	A	70.	A
7.	D	39.	C	71.	E
8.	C	40.	E	72.	A
9.	D	41.	B	73.	E
10.	B	42.	C	74.	D
11.	D	43.	C	75.	E
12.	A	44.	B	76.	C
13.	D	45.	A	77.	C
14.	E	46.	B	78.	A
15.	E	47.	D	79.	D
16.	D	48.	A	80.	B
17.	E	49.	D	81.	B
18.	E	50.	B	82.	D
19.	D	51.	B	83.	C
20.	E	52.	A	84.	A
21.	B	53.	B	85.	A
22.	B	54.	E	86.	C
23.	A	55.	E	87.	B
24.	D	56.	C	88.	C
25.	A	57.	D	89.	A
26.	B	58.	D	90.	B
27.	E	59.	A	91.	C
28.	A	60.	A	92.	A
29.	A	61.	B	93.	D
30.	A	62.	C	94.	B
31.	B	63.	D	95.	A
32.	D	64.	D	96.	D
				97.	D

ARCHITECT

Georgia Institute of Technology

"I'm a rambling wreck from Georgia Tech, and a helluvan engineer, er, ah, architect." Somehow that line loses some of the bravo ring inherent in the College of Engineering's version

T he College of Architecture at the Georgia Institute of Technology offers three courses, each one quarter in length, surveying man's architectural heritage from the beginnings of recorded history through the Middle Ages. The dates defining the limits of that period are (and this will help you with the second portion of the following test) c. 10,000 B.C. to c. A.D. 1400.

The first of these courses consists of two one-hour lectures and a one-hour recitation each week totaling three credit hours. It is an introductory course open to all students.

Students taking the final exam for this course would have three hours to complete it. During the first hour they sit with pencils poised in a semi-darkened room and watch 20 to 25 color slides flash onto a screen for 30 to 45 seconds each. For that group they are required only to identify the style of each monument. We have reproduced ten from that first group.

A second group of 10 to 15 slides presented in the same way poses a sterner task. The students must identify not only the style, but also the date(s) it was built (see earlier hint), the city and country in which it was built, and the name of the monument. We have reproduced six from that group. The source for the correct date is Sir Banister Fletcher's History of Architecture, 18th Edition.

At the end of the hour all the slides are flashed again for ten brief, agonizing seconds as eyes seek and frontal lobes throb silently in the semi-dark. So be fair; allow yourself to look at each photograph for half a minute, then cover it and go on to the next. After half an hour your time is up since there are half as many monuments pictured here as are shown in the actual exam.

We are grateful to Professor Arthur F. Beckum, Jr., who teaches this course at Georgia Tech, for selecting the following sixteen subjects, so don't blame us if they are too difficult for you.

I. Identify the following architectural monuments as to their *style* only: Sumerian, Assyrian, Neo-Mabylonian, Persian, Egyptian, Mioan, Mycenean, Greek, Etruscan, Roman, Early Christian, Myzantine, Carolingian/Ottonian, Romanesque, or Goth.

Ia

Ic

Ib

Id

Ie

Ig

If

Ih

II. Give the information requested for *each* of the pictures shown (use styles listed in I): NAME of monument; LOCATION (city/country); DATE(S); STYLE.

Ii

IIa

Ij

IId

IIc

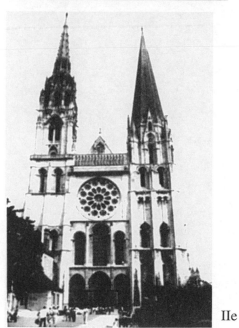

IIb

IIf

IIe

ANSWERS!☞

II. a.   Romanesque (Abby aux Hommes, Caen, France)

b.   Egyptian (Tomb of Mentuhotep, Dir-el-Bahari, Egypt)

c.   Roman (Basilica of Constantine, Rome, Italy)

d.   Gothic (Gargoyles)

e.   Greek (Ionic Order)

f.   Gothic (House of Jacques Cour, Bourges, France)

g.   Roman (Corinthian Order, From a temple in Rome)

h.   Gothic (Palazzo Cavalli, Venice, Italy)

i.   Greek (Parthenon, Athens, Greece)

j.   Romanesque (Cathedral, Bonn, Germany)

II. a.   Lysicrates monument; Athens, Greece;
334 B.C.; Greek

b.   S. Miniato al Monte; Florence, Italy;
A.D. 1018–62

c.   Pisa Cathedral; Pisa., Italy; A.D.
1063–1118; Romanesque

d.   Colosseum; Rome, Italy; A.D. 70–82;
Roman

e.   Chartres Cathedral; Chartres, France;
A.D. 1194–1260; Gothic

f.   Speyer Cathedral; Speyer, Germany;
A.D. 1031–61; Romanesque

AUTO MECHANICS

National Institute for Automotive Service Excellence

*Time was, a mechanic could cock his ear to an idling
engine, sniff the fluid leaks, finger the residue inside
the exhaust pipe, and tell you what was wrong. Then
he'd take out the faulty part, rebuild it, and put it back
in. Now it's dial-reading and "R&R" (remove and
replace). Before yearning for the old days though,
bear in mind that in the 16th century, Johann Hautach
produced a vehicle propelled only by coil springs and
nobody had yet invented full-color wall calendars.*

Auto mechanics, according to the Automotive Information Council's definition,
repair, service, and adjust mechanical and electrical parts of automobiles,
trucks, recreational vehicles, buses, tractors, and other gasoline-powered
equipment. They perform preventive maintenance, diagnose trouble, make
adjustments, estimate costs, repair or replace defective parts, rebuild assemblies, and test
all repairs to ensure proper operation. Some mechanics perform all kinds of repair work;
others specialize in one or two types of repair, such as engine repair (gasoline or diesel),
turbo-charging, fuel injection, front-wheel drive, transaxles, automatic transmission,
drive-train and rear axle, front end, brakes, electrical systems, heating and air conditioning, engine tune-ups, electronics, and auto body.

Probably the best way to get training in the field is from a trade, technical, or vocational school offering courses in automotive repair. It used to be that apprenticeship programs and informal on-the-job training were readily available, but with ever-higher levels
of technological complexity manufactured into vehicles, such opportunities are rare these
days. The Denver Automotive and Diesel College is one of the country's leading training
centers in the automotive and diesel mechanics, collision repair, and paint fields. For information about their programs, call them at 1-800-347-3232, or write to 460 South Lipan,
Denver CO 80223.

We've included sample test questions from ASE, or the National Institute for Automotive Service Excellence. ASE was established in 1972 to provide a standard of competence
in the automotive service industry. Through a voluntary competency testing and certification program, ASE measures and recognizes the diagnostic and repair skills and knowl-

edge of automobile and heavy-duty truck technicians, body repairers, and painters. It also encourages and assists in the development of effective training programs.

According to the 1992 Department of Labor census, there are approximately 864,000 individuals working as automobile mechanics in the United States. Additionally, there are over 306,000 men and women employed as truck or bus mechanics.

Until the early 1970s, consumers had no way to distinguish between incompetent and competent automotive mechanics. In response to this need, the independent, non-profit National Institute for Automotive Service Excellence (ASE) was established in 1972. At present there are about 397,000 technicians with current certification by ASE's rosters. They work in every segment of the automotive service industry: car and truck dealerships, independent garages, fleets, service stations, franchises, and more. ASE's mission is to improve the quality of vehicle repair and service through the voluntary testing and certification of automotive technicians. ASE has emerged as the only automotive certification program that is both industry-wide and national in scope. ASE, the recognized leader in automotive technician testing and certification, has been endorsed by over forty professional associations and trade groups.

Here's how ASE certification works: Prospective candidates register for and take one or more of ASE's twenty seven exams. (There are seven additional exams in development at present that will be introduced in the near future.) The tests are grouped into specialties for automobile, medium/heavy truck, school bus, and collision repair technicians as well as engine machinists, alternate fuels technicians, and parts specialists.

Upon passing at least one exam *and* after providing proof of two years of relevant work experience, the mechanic becomes an ASE-certified Technician. A mechanic who passes a designated battery of tests earns ASE Master Technician status; automobile technicians, for example, must pass eight exams. To remain certified, technicians must be retested every five years.

The tests, which are conducted twice a year at over 700 locations around the country, are administered by American College Testing (ACT). The exams stress real-world diagnostic and repair problems, not theory. They are no cinch to pass; approximately one out of three test-takers fails.

Consumers and employers use ASE certification as a valuable yard stick by which to measure the knowledge and skills of individual technicians as well as the commitment to quality of the repair facility employing ASE-certified technicians. For more information about ASE or the certification process, contact ASE at 13505 Dulles Technology Drive, Suite 2, Herndon, Virginia 20171-3421, or call 703-713-3800.

Automobile

1. An engine is using too much oil. Technician A says that worn valve guides could be the cause. Technician B says that tapered cylinder walls could be the cause. Who is right?
   (A) A only
   (B) B only
   (C) Both A and B
   (D) Neither A nor B

2. A vehicle with an automatic transaxle and a properly tuned engine accelerates poorly from a stop. Acceleration is normal above 35 mph. Which of these could be the cause?
   (A) A bad torque converter
   (B) A worn front pump
   (C) A bad governor valve
   (D) A low fluid level

3. A vehicle with a manual transaxle makes a clunking noise on acceleration and deceleration. Technician A says that play between the differential case and its pinion shaft could be the cause. Technician B says that worn drive axle u-joints could be the cause. Who is right?
   (A) A only
   (B) B only
   (C) Both A and B
   (D) Neither A nor B

4. During a wheel alignment, a technician finds the toe-out-on-turns (turning radius) to be incorrect. This could be caused by a bent:
   (A) pitman arm.
   (B) tie rod.
   (C) idler arm.
   (D) steering arm.

5. The brake pedal on a vehicle with power-assisted disc/drum brakes moves slowly to the floor during braking. Which of these could be the cause?
   (A) A leaking master cylinder primary cup
   (B) A leaking power brake booster
   (C) A leaking master cylinder residual check valve
   (D) An internal leak in the combination valve

6. If a charging system check shows a fully charged battery and a high charging rate, the technician should test the:
   (A) alternator diodes.
   (B) stator windings.
   (C) voltage regulator.
   (D) field current draw.

7. There is a growling (rumbling) noise at the air conditioning compressor when the system is OFF and the engine is running. Technician A says that a bad compressor clutch bearing could be the cause. Technician B says that a bad compressor bearing could be the cause. Who is right?
   (A) A only
   (B) B only
   (C) Both A and B
   (D) Neither A nor B

8. A warm, fuel injected engine has a high idle speed. Technician A says that an open cold start injector could be the cause. Technician B says that an open auxiliary-air regulator (valve) could be the cause. Who is right?
   (A) A only
   (B) B only
   (C) Both A and B
   (D) Neither A nor B

Alternative Fuels

1. A compressed natural gas fuel supply container has been installed inside a vehicle. The pressure relief valve should be vented to the outside using:
   (A) ½" rubber fuel line.
   (B) metallic tubing.
   (C) wire-braided flex line.
   (D) PCV pipe.

2. When running at idle speed, a NGV has a buzzing noise under the hood. The noise stops when the engine RPM is increased. Which of these could be the cause?
   (A) Natural gas entering the engine
   (B) First stage regular pressure drop
   (C) The vacuum stitch on/off controller
   (D) The automatic fuel selector switch

Medium/Heavy Truck

1. While performing a cylinder leakage test on an engine, the technician sees air bubbles in the upper radiator tank. Technician A says that a cracked head could be the cause. Technician B says that a cracked block could be the cause. Who is right?
   (A) A only
   (B) B only
   (C) Both A and B
   (D) Neither A nor B

2. A diesel engine with wet sleeves has been running too hot, and there is water in the crankcase. The most likely cause is:
   (A) a cracked block.
   (B) cracked liners.
   (C) leaking liner seals.
   (D) a leaking injector seal.

3. A two-plate pull-type clutch engages ok, but the transmission grinds when going into first gear from neutral. Technician A says that a worn clutch brake could be the cause. Technician B says that too little free play could be the cause. Who is right?

(A) A only
(B) B only
(C) Both A and B
(D) Neither A nor B

4. All the wheels on a truck with air brakes lock up when a small amount of pressure is applied to the treadle (foot) valve. Which of these could be the cause?
   (A) The application valve is bad.
   (B) The limiting valve is leaking.
   (C) The compressor regulator is sct too high.
   (D) The brakes are adjusted too tight.

5. There is too much lateral runout (wobble) on a pair of truck tires (duals) with spoke-type wheels. Which of these is the most likely cause'?
   (A) The spoke hub is out-of-round.
   (B) One or both wheels are bent.
   (C) The rim clamp nuts are torqued incorrectly.
   (D) The outside tire has a sidewall bulge.

6. A truck's battery discharges after sitting overnight. Technician A says that a bad alternator could be the cause. Technician B says that a bad starter could be the cause. Who is right?
   (A) A only
   (B) B only
   (C) Both A and B
   (D) Neither A nor B

7. A PM technician finds that the radiator coolant level is low, but that the coolant recovery tank is full. This could be caused by a:
   (A) stuck-closed thermostat.
   (B) stuck-open thermostat.
   (C) low protection level.
   (D) bad radiator cap.

School Bus

1. All the brakes drag on a school bus with hydraulic brakes. This is most likely caused by:
   (A) air in the hydraulic system.
   (B) excessive vacuum supply to the power brake booster.
   (C) a leaking secondary cup in the master cylinder.
   (D) no brake pedal free travel.

2. A school bus has a history of springs breaking at the center bolt holes. Technician A says that loose u-bolts could be the cause. Technician B says that look spring shackles could be the cause. Who is right?
   (A) A only
   (B) B only
   (C) Both A and B
   (D) Neither A nor B

3. When the door is opened and the amber lights cancel, the red lights do not illuminate on a school bus with an electronic 8-lamp warning system. Technician A says that a bad relay could be the cause. Technician B says that a bad master switch could be the cause. Who is right?
   (A) A only
   (B) B only
   (C) Both A and B
   (D) Neither A nor B

4. The windshield wipers on a school bus will not park. Which of these is the most likely cause?
   (A) The worm gear is out-of-adjustment
   (B) A bad parking switch assembly
   (C) A binding wiper transmission
   (D) A poor ground at the wiper motor

Collision Repair

1. Painter A says that primer-surfacer will dry faster if it is sprayed in several coats with flash time between coats. Painter B says that there will be less bridging if all the primer-surfacer is sprayed in one application. Who is right?
   (A) A only
   (B) B only
   (C) Both A and B
   (D) Neither A nor B

2. Which of these can be done to make metallic colors lighter?
   (A) Add more thinner/reducer to the paint.
   (B) Apply the finish in cooler shop temperatures.
   (C) Apply the finish with lower air pressure.
   (D) Apply more wet coats.

3. After high-strength steel is heated, it should be cooled by:
   (A) spraying it with cold water.
   (B) air hosing it.
   (C) letting it cool naturally.
   (D) wiping it with oil.

4. Technician A says that center-line frame gauges are used to check for sag. Technician B says that center-line frame gauges are used to check for sway. Who is right?
   (A) A only
   (B) B only
   (C) Both A and B
   (D) Neither A nor B

5. After a front-end collision repair, a front-wheel drive, unibody vehicle pulls to the left during hard acceleration. The most likely cause is:
   (A) drive train misalignment.
   (B) caster misalignment.
   (C) tracking misalignment.
   (D) camber misalignment.

Machinist

1. A loose valve seat must be:
   (A) staked.
   (B) spot welded.
   (C) bonded.
   (D) replaced.

2. Connecting rods for a piston assembly should not be heated above:
   (A) 250°F.
   (B) 450°F.
   (C) 650°F.
   (D) 850°F.

3. Machinist A says that I.D. tags and sensors should be removed before thermal cleaning (oven). Machinist B says that I.D. tags and sensors are safe when cleaned in a caustic solution. Who is right?
   (A) A only
   (B) B only
   (C) Both A and B
   (D) Neither A nor B

4. Material that is removed from the cylinder head or block can be compensated for by:
   (A) retarding the valve timing.
   (B) installing a thicker head gasket.
   (C) retarding ignition timing.
   (D) installing longer push rods.

Parts Specialist

1. Which of these related parts would be sold with a remanufactured differential?
   (A) Brake chamber
   (B) Torque arm
   (C) Spring bracket
   (D) End yoke

2. Which of these does a parts specialist need to know when locating a replacement ring and pinion gear assembly?
   (A) Tire size
   (B) Rear axle model
   (C) Axle shaft length
   (D) Drive line size

3. The special grease used between an ignition module and the distributor:
   (A) insulates the module from the distributor housing.
   (B) provides heat transfer between the module and the distributor
   (C) lubricates the module.
   (D) prevents corrosion.

4. Parts Specialist A says that heater hose should be used on a PCV system. Parts Specialist B says that fuel injection systems require a special design fuel hose. Who is right?
   (A) A only
   (B) B only
   (C) Both A and B
   (D) Neither A nor B

ANSWERS!☞

Automobile
1. C
2. A
3. C
4. D
5. A
6. C
7. A
8. B

Alternative Fuels
1. B
2. B

Medium/Heavy Truck
1. C
2. C
3. A
4. A
5. C
6. A
7. D

School Bus
1. D
2. A
3. A
4. B

Collision Repair
1. A
2. A
3. C
4. C
5. A

Machinist
1. D
2. B
3. A
4. B

Parts Specialist
1. D
2. B
3. B
4. B

BALLROOM DANCING INSTRUCTOR

Fred Astaire Dance Studios

"Me? A ballroom dancing instructor? Do you realize I was eight years old before I learned to tie my shoelaces, and now I have to sit down to reach them? They tell me I've a natural talent though. It's all in the hip rotation. When I get up to dance at a supper club, waiters walk into columns and husbands stop arguing with their wives. But teach it? Get a grip, Fred, I think a 'Cuban Walk' must be an escape route to Miami."

"You can do it, Ginger-baby, I know you can!"

T hose who are interested in becoming a ballroom dance studio instructor in the Fred Astaire franchise system attend a training class and study a manual prepared for its teachers. (The questions selected for this exam sometimes refer to these as "The American Style Dance Manuals.") Certification requires that the applicant must then pass an exam in one of three major ballroom dance styles: American Style, International Style (Ballroom Latin), and Theatre Arts Exhibition. The first level of skill is called "Bronze." The instructor may aspire to try his or her mettle on tests of ever more dizzying heights of skill and versatility called, exotically, "Silver," "Gold," and "Supreme Gold" levels. Generally, an instructor's income rises with each higher level.

After successfully getting into the profession as an instructor, the opportunities for advancement exist in the enrollment department as a specialist, in the teaching department as a supervisor, or – hold your hats, kids!—owning your *own* studio.

Licensed studio managers conduct periodic training classes for applicants who have no previous experience of formal training in ballroom dance instruction. The ones most likely to be employed show a natural talent for dancing, love to teach, and have a happy outgoing personality. Income is generally based on performance in the areas of hours taught, enrollment or re-enrollment of their students, and miscellaneous other studio activities, including studio parties and local, regional, or national dance competitions, showcases, or trips.

Once the instructor has attained a sufficient degree of proficiency, he or she may take a Professional Diploma examination. This exam may be taken in any or all of the three major styles of ballroom dancing. The Professional Diploma represents the most comprehensive qualification granted by the Dance Studio Organization. The succeeding levels of Professional Diploma exams from least to most difficult are as follows: Associate, Associate Major, Specialist, Specialist Major, Certified Dance Director, and Certified Adjudicator.

The questions that follow are from these of the Professional Diploma examination. They are therefore representative of an advanced degree of proficiency, which an instructor would normally have only after a considerable amount of teaching experience. For further information on becoming a Fred Astaire Dance Studio instructor, write Fred Astaire National Dance Association, Inc., Dept. BOT, P.O. Box 560367, Miami, FL 33256-0367.

1. Listed below are three group forms used to teach classes. Explain the purpose of each.
   (A) The circle
   (B) The line
   (C) The double line

2. Describe the four methods of "chant" teaching used to instruct classes, using a simple bronze figure to demonstrate each method.

3. Give a short history of the origin and background of the following American style dances:
   (A) Foxtrot
   (B) Waltz
   (C) Tango
   (D) Rumba
   (E) Cha cha
   (F) Mambo
   (G) Merengue
   (H) Samba
   (I) Eastern swing
   (J) Western swing
   (K) Disco-hustle

4. The first column in the description of figures section of the American Style Dance Manuals describes the measure, number of steps, and timing/rhythm. Give the definition of each, and illustrate how this column would be written for the gentleman's part of the progressive basic step in the bronze waltz. Also, give the abbreviations used to indicate the timing/rhythm of a figure.

5. The second column in the description of figures section of the American Style Dance Manuals describes the foot movements. Give the definition of the term "foot movements," and describe how they are indicated in the manuals.

6. The third column in the description of figures section of the American Style Dance Manuals describes alignment, in those dances where it is used. Define alignment. List the dances where it is used in the bronze syllabus, and explain the terms used to describe it.

7. The fifth column in the description of figures section of the American Style Dance Manuals describes the dance positions used in each figure. Define the term "dance position," name the thirteenth American style dance positions, and list the abbreviations used in the dance manuals to identify each.

8. List the eight facing ailments and the eight backing alignments, and the abbreviations used to describe each in the dance manuals.

9. Describe briefly the correct dance position hold as gentlemen, for the American style closed position (basic normal hold), in the smooth dances.

10. Briefly describe the normal sway and list the bronze dances in which it is used.

11. List the three types of forward and backward walks utilized in ballroom dancing.

12. Describe Latin hip movement-Cuban motion, and list the American style dances in which it is considered a basic technique of the dance.

13. Describe the line of dance (LOD) and tell why it is used in teaching.

14. When backing diagonally to the wall at a corner, what alignment in the new line of dance would be assumed upon taking a step forward?

15. Tell how the dance position hold for the Latin dances and swing differs from the basic normal hold for smooth dances.

16. Define rise and fall and list the American style bronze dances in which it is considered a basic technique of the dance.

17. Define samba pulse (or bounce action) and tell when it is used in the samba.

18. Define the following technical terminology:
    (A) Balance
    (B) Poise
    (C) Follow through
    (D) Styling
    (E) Impetus and momentum

19. Describe how you would count a selection of music to determine the measures per minute when it is not indicated on the record label.

20. Define the following musical terms:
    (A) Measures per minute (mpm)
    (B) Rhythm
    (C) Timing

21. List the meter(s)/time signatures for the American style bronze dances.

22. Define the following musical terms:
    (A) Bar or measure of music
    (B) 3/4 time, 4/4 time, 2/4 time
    (C) Syncopation
    (D) Tempo

23. Give a brief description of the differences between the three types of forward walks in ballroom dancing.

24. Explain the following terms used in the line of dance:
    (A) Down the line of dance
    (B) Across the line of dance
    (C) Against the line of dance
    (D) The new line of dance

25. List the variations for the 4th position of the feet.

26. Describe the four turning actions that utilize contrary body movement, or CBM, to initiate the turn.

27. Name the three types of lead used by the gentleman in ballroom dancing.

28. Describe counter sway (broken sway) and tell how it is used.

29. Explain what the term "no foot rise" indicates, and tell when it is used.

30. Describe the following leg or foot movements:
    (A) Heel pivot
    (B) Heel turn
    (C) Ronde and aerial ronde
    (D) Lunge
    (E) Hop

31. Give a short history of the origin and background of the following gold-supreme gold dances:
    (A) Bolero
    (B) Paso doble
    (C) Viennese waltz
    (D) peabody

32. Listed below are the four sections of the body used in ballroom dancing. Describe how each section of the body is used.
    (A) Upper and lower torso
    (B) Arms and hands
    (C) Legs and feet
    (D) Head

ANSWERS !☞

1. (A) In the circle, the teacher places the class around the room in a large circle indicating the starting alignment for the lady's part as well as the gentleman's part. This group form is excellent when teaching school figures that progress in the line of dance.

   (B) In the line, the teacher places the class in one or more lines, with everyone facing the same direction, normally facing the mirrors, and the teacher stands in front of the class. In this way the teacher can see every student in the mirror and the class merely has to follow the teacher's movements. This group form is effective when teaching school figures that do not progress around the room, and where the lady's part to a figure is the normal counterpart.

   (C) In the double line, the teacher places the ladies in one line and the gentlemen in another line, facing the ladies. The double line allows the partners actually to follow one another without being in dance position. This group form is excellent for teaching school figures where the lady's part is NOT the normal counterpart, and/or initially to teach progressive figures that cannot be danced in the circle form.

2. (A) Foot movements – lady's rumba box step. "Side-close-BACK-side-close-FORWARD." (B) Number of steps – lady's rumba box step. "One-two-THREE-four-five-SIX." (C) Timing or rhythm – tango promenade basic. SLOW, SLOW, QUICK, QUICK, SLOW. (D) Beats and bars – waltz progressive basic step. ONE-two-three-TWO-two-three-THREE-two-three-FOUR-two-three.

3. (A) Harry Fox was believed to be the first to use the "slow step," hence the birth of the foxtrot. The dance came into vogue around 1912 and was originated in the United States. It is a turning and progressive dance moving along the LOD.

   (B) The waltz dates back to the country folk dances of Bavaria but was not introduced into society until 1812. By 1840 it had become one of the most popular dances in the United States. It is a progressive and turning dance moving along the LOD.

   (C) The tango was introduced to the United States between 1910 and 1914. There is no clearly defined country of origin. It is claimed to have originated not only in Argentina but also in Brazil, Spain, Mexico, and France. It is a progressive dance moving along the LOD. A staccato movement of the feet and flexed knees highlight the dramatic style of the dance.

   (D) The rumba began with the African slaves of Cuba more than 400 years ago and was introduced to the United States in the early 1930s. It is a spot dance not moving along the LOD and is characterized by Latin hip movement, called Cuban motion.

   (E) The cha cha is a derivation of the mambo and the swing and has two geographical points of origin, the United States and Cuba. It is characterized by a syncopated timing and is a spot dance not moving along the LOD. Latin hip movement is a basic characteristic of the dance.

   (F) The mambo is of Cuban origin and was popularized by Perez Prado in his song "Mambo-Jambo," first introduced in Mexico City. It is characterized by its two-beat timing and Latin hip movement and is a spot dance not moving along the LOD.

(G) Both Haiti and the Dominican Republic claim to have originated the merengue. It was introduced to the United States in the early 1950s. It is characterized by Latin hip movement and is a spot dance not moving along the LOD.

(H) The samba was imported from Brazil in 1929. It is a spot dance, but there is some progression along the LOD. It is characterized by a springlike action called the samba pulse or bounce.

(I) Eastern swing was originally called the lindy hop and was originated in the southern area of the United States. It is the most famous of American folk dances. In the early 1940s it became most popular, and several timings developed, including single, double, and triple swing. It is a spot dance not moving along the LOD and is characterized by a relaxed, shuffling movement.

(J) Western swing was originally a regional style developed in the southwest and western states. It was introduced in the late 1950s and has gained popularity ever since, since it is so adaptable to today's rock music. It is a spot dance not moving along the LOD and is characterized by a slower tempo, "push" styling, and dancing in a "slot."

(K) Another American creation, the disco-hustle made its bid for popularity in the mid-1970s, with the release of the record "The Hustle." It has undergone many changes since and reflects the style and mood of today's popular disco music. It is a spot dance not moving along the LOD and is characterized by many styles and rhythmic timings, including the American hustle, the Latin hustle, and the Spanish hustle.

4. Measure—the number of bars of music used. Number of steps – the number of steps used to complete the figure. Timing/rhythm – the timing is the numbered beats (1, 2, 3- 1, 2, 3, etc.), or the rhythm is the SLOWS or QUICKS USED for each step. Gentleman's part of progressive basic step in the waltz:

1	1	1
2	2	
3	3	
2	4	1
5	2	
6	3	

Abbreviations used are:

S = a slow step given 2 beats of music

Q = a quick step given 1 beat of music

& = a syncopated step given 1/2 beat of music.

5. Foot movements – These refer to the position of one foot in relation to the other, i.e., forward, back, side, etc. They are indicated in this column by abbreviations, illustrating which foot is moving and in which direction it moves.

6. Alignment refers to the direction the foot (or feet) is pointed in relation to the room. Words used are "facing," "backing," "pointing," and "toward." It is used in the foxtrot, waltz, and tango. "Facing" and "backing" are used when the foot (or feet) has the same alignment as the body and on normal forward and back steps. "Pointing" is used on side steps when the direction of the foot is different from that of the body. "Toward" is used when no specific align-

ment is taken over a series of steps– but a finishing alignment is indicated.

7. Dance position definition: Dance position refers to the position of partners in relation to one another. The thirteen abbreviations and corresponding dance positions are:

(1) CL = CLOSED POSITION

(2) R SD = RIGHT SIDE POSITION

(3) L SD = LEFT SIDE POSITION

(4) PP = PROMENADE POSITION

(5) OPEN = OPEN POSITION

(6) CPP = COUNTER PROMENADE POSITION

(7) R OP = RIGHT OPEN POSITION

(8) L OP = LEFT OPEN POSITION

(9) APART = APART POSITION

(10)   FA = FALLAWAY POSITION

(11)PAR = PARALLEL POSITION

(12)   R PAR = RIGHT PARALLEL POSITION

(13)   L PAR = LEFT PARALLEL POSITION

8. FACING ALIGNMENTS

(1) Facing the Line of Dance (F LOD)

(2) Facing Diagonally to Center (F DC)

(3) Facing Center (F C)

(4) Facing Diagonally to Center against the Line of Dance (F DC A LOD)

(5) Facing against the Line of Dance (F A LOD)

(6) Facing Diagonally to Wall against the Line of Dance (F DW A LOD)

(7) Facing the Wall (F W)

(8) Facing Diagonally to Wall (F DW)

BACKING ALIGNMENTS

(1) Backing the Line of Dance (B LOD)

(2) Backing diagonally to Center (B DC)

(3) Backing Center (B C)

(4) Backing Diagonally to Center against the Line of Dance (B DC A LOD)

(5) Backing against the Line of Dance (B A LOD)

(6) Backing Diagonally to Wall against the Line of Dance (B DW A LOD)

(7) Backing the Wall (B W)

(8) Backing Diagonally to Wall (B DW)

9. Stand in an upright position with the feet close together, the body braced slightly at the waist, holding the head in a straight and upright position, looking directly forward. Do not raise the shoulders; they should remain at a normal level. Lift the left arm upward and to the side, bending it sharply at the elbow, the forearm pointing slightly upward with a slight forward slope from the elbow, which should be slightly lower than the shoulder.

The lady places the palm of her right hand into the palm of the gentleman's left hand, resting her fingers in the cradle between his thumb and forefinger. The gentleman closes the fingers on his left hand loosely around the side of the lady's right hand. Do not bend the hand downward from the wrist. The gentleman's right arm should be held as nearly as possible on the same line as his left arm. This will depend on the relative height of partners. The right hand should be placed approximately below the lady's left shoulder blade, striving to create a straight line at a downward slope from the elbow to the fingers of his right arm, slightly in advance of the body. Body contact is maintained between partners with the torso.

10. Sway is the sideward poise of the body which normally follows CBM in turning figures in the foxtrot and waltz. The side-

ward poise utilized in the normal sway results in a slight inclination of the upper body to the side in turning figures, toward the inside of the turn, as follows:

If CBM is taken with a step on the right foot, then sway to the right is achieved by an upward swinging of the hips into a side step with the left foot. If CMB is taken with a step on the left foot, then sway to the left is achieved by an upward swinging of the hips into a side step with the right foot. Normal sway does not follow CBM in pivots or spins.

On posed movements, if a step to the side is taken with the left foot, then sway to the right is achieved, and vice-versa.

11. (1) Forward and backwards walks for smooth dances with the exception of the tango.

(2) Forward and backward walks for the tango.

(3) Forward and backward walks for Latin and rhythm dances.

12. Latin hip movement, Cuban motion, is the authentic rolling, lateral motion of the hips which occurs as a result of the flexing and straightening of the knees and never by a conscious swing of the hips. It is a basic technique of the rumba, bolero, mambo, cha cha, and merengue.

13. The line of dance is an imaginary line along each side of the room, parallel to the wall, used to avoid confusion of couples and collision. The line of progression around the room is in a counterclockwise direction.

14. Facing diagonally to the center of the new line of dance.

15. In the Latin dances there is approximately six inches distance between partners, causing the elbows to curve. In the swing, a more casual position is assumed, with

partners partway between a closed and promenade position, causing the gentleman's left hand and arm to be lowered approximately at waist level.

16. Rise and fall refers to the use of the body, legs, ankles, and feet to achieve an upward stretching and soft lowering, causing variations of the level of the body. The softening of the knee(s) preceding and following an actual body rise is more important than the rise itself, which should occur naturally if the correct swing of the body and footwork technique have been used.

Rise and fall is a basic technique of the foxtrot and waltz.

17. Samba pulse, or bounce action, is a basic characteristic of the samba. The springlike action from the ankles cushioned by the slight flexing and straightening of the knees, can be danced smoothly with only a slight bounce, or with more spirit as the music directs. The springlike action is initiated by the ankles and emphasized by the flexing of the knees in all figures where the timing is:

"a,1,&,2- a,1,&,2." Bounce action is not used on figures with other timings.

18. (A) This term refers to the correct distribution of the weight of the body over the supporting foot (or feet).

(B) This term refers to the position of the upper body in relation to the feet and arms. Depending upon the dance and its characteristic style the body may be poised in an upright or slightly forward or backward position.

(C) The correct passing of the leg (foot ankle, calf, knee, thigh) under the body when moving from one position of the feet to another.

(D) The ability of the dancer to project his own interpretations of the characteristic style of the dances.

(E) These terms refer to. the force that. controls the dancers body flight i.e., the. rate of speed or intensity with which the body is driven to move.

19 Using a watch with a second hand, play the recording and count it in beats and bars. Counting aloud determine the number of "bars of music that were played over a 15-second period Multiply this number of. bars by 4 to arrive at the. total mpm.

20. (A) The actual number of measures played per minute determines the tempo or speed of the music; mpm is particularly important for competitions and examinations.

(B) In teaching rhythm denotes the use of the words "slow, quick," and "and" to describe. the value of the steps. In dancing, rhythm denotes the ability of the dancer to feel the beats and syncopations of the music and to correspond his dancing movements without losing the underlying beat.

(C) In teaching, timing denotes the use of a numerical count to describe the musical value of the steps. In dancing, timing denotes the ability of the dancer to correspond his steps and movements correctly to specific beats of the music or, more simply to keep time with the music.

21. (1.) Foxtrot—4/4 time

(2) Waltz—3/4 time

(3) Tango—4/4 or 2/4 time

(4) Rumba—4/4 time

(5) Cha cha—4/4 time

(6) Mambo—4/4 time

(7) Merengue—4/4 or 2/4 time

(8) Samba—4/4 or 2/4 time

(9) Eastern swing—4/4 time

(10)   Western swing—4/4 time

(11)Disco-hustle—4/4 time

22. (A) A bar is a separation of a series of beats of music. The bar tells the number of beats utilized in a measure of music.

(B) Three beats of music to the bar. Four beats of music to the bar. Two beats of music to the bar.

(C) Musically, steps that are given either a & beat or a 1/2 beat of music. These steps are identified by the use of the word "and" or "a" in teaching.

(D) Musically, the rate of speed at which the music is played. In teaching, the tempo of a dance is indicated by the mpm (measure per minute).

23. (A) Smooth dances (except tango). In smooth dances, except the tango, the moving leg is extended forward from the hip with the moving foot lightly skimming the floor. A normal stride is taken, and when at the extent of one's stride the weight is evenly distributed between the heel of the moving foot and the ball of the supporting foot, with. the. legs straight.

(B) In the tango the knees are more relaxed and the feet are picked up and placed in position instead of skimming over the floor, resulting in a more staccato action.

(C) In Latin and rhythm dances, more compact steps are taken and the extent of one's stride is never achieved. This results in the feet being placed into position rather than swinging from the hips.

24. (A) Used for steps that are normally taken in a forward direction in counterclockwise progression.

(B) Used for steps that are taken in any direction across the imaginary line of progression.

(C) Used for steps that are taken in any direction, moving clockwise (against the normal line of progression).

(D) The director parallel to the wall after turning a corner. The corner is the end of the old line of dance and the beginning of the new line of dance.

25. Forward with the toe turned out; forward in CBMP; diagonally forward; forward and across the CBMP; forward with the same shoulder leading; forward and leftward or rightward; back with the toe turned out; back with the toe turned in; back in CBMP; diagonally back; back with the same shoulder leading; back and leftward or rightward.

26. (1) Left foot forward—turning to the left. Turn the right side of the body forward, toward the moving left leg. CBM to the left.

(2) Right foot forward—turning to the right. Turn the left side of the body forward, toward the moving right leg. CBM to the right.

(3) Left foot back—turning to the right. Turn the right side of the body back, toward the moving left leg. CBM to the right.

(4) Right foot back—turning to the left. Turn the life side of the body back, toward the moving right leg. CBM to the left.

27. (1) Body lead (2) Hand and arm lead (3) Sight (visual) lead.

28. Counter sway is the sideward poise of the body which is achieved by inclining the upper torso toward the outside of the turn, sometimes used in the Viennese waltz. On posed movements, if a step to the side is taken with the left foot, then sway to the left is achieved, and vice-versa.

29. In describing rise and fall, the term "no foot rise" is used to denote a later rise in the foot on the inside of turns, and/or when the body is stretching upward without rising to the toes.

30. (A) In a heel pivot, the weight is retained on the foot that steps back. The turn is made on the heel with the foot flat. Pressure is felt on the ball of the other foot.

(B) In a heel turn, weight changes to the closing foot and the other foot moves for the next step. The turn is commenced on the ball of the foot as the other foot is drawn back with pressure on the heel. As the foot closes, both feet are flat, and turn is continued, with the feet close together and flat. Transfer weight at the end of the turn.

(C) The action of inscribing a circle on the floor with a toe of the extended moving leg. The aerial ronde refers to the same circular action with the leg raised off the floor. Ronde actions are taken from the hip.

(D) A pose taken by supporting the body weight on a bent leg while the free leg is extended outward to achieve a body line. Taken in any direction. Examples are the Corte, Same Foot Lunge, Fete Line, X Line, Throwaway, Oversway, and many more.

(E) The action of springing from and landing on the same foot, with or without progression.

31. (A) The bolero, the slowest form of the rumba, was introduced to the United

States in the mid-1930s. It was originally created in 1780 and is called the Cuban dance of love. It is a spot dance not moving along the LOD and is characterized by Latin hip movement.

(B) Paso doble dates back centuries to classical Flamenco dancing. Its music was originally intended for use at the bullfights when a toreador was victorious in the ring. It is characterized by both progression moving along the LOD and spot dancing, and utilities a staccato movement of the feet, pulled up torso, and dramatic movements of the head, arms, and hands.

(C) The Viennese waltz was first danced in the courts of European royalty during the early 1800s. It is a progressive and turning dance moving along the LOD.

(D) The Peabody is a variation of the foxtrot was named for Police Captain Frank Peabody, a New York dancer who created the dance steps. Due to his large frame and weight, he held his partners off to his right side, where he would sail around the room to this fast tempo. It is a progressive and turning dance moving along the LOD and is characterized by some bounce style. It is danced to Dixieland music.

32. (1) The torso. The upper torso includes the rib cage, chest, and shoulder region. It projects appearance and lead, and since it supports the arm and head, it is the basis for styling and lead through the dance hold. The shoulders are relaxed and should never be projected back of or forward of the prescribed normal hold.

The lower torso includes the hip region. It may be used independently of the upper torso for styling as in Latin hip movement, or as a focal point of lead and turning as in the samba roll. The lower torso should not be allowed to move out of line with the body, either backward or forward.

(2) The arms and hands. In the smooth dances, the arms and hands are used mainly as support and to create a smart appearance, relying on body momentum for lead. In the Latin/rhythm dances, and those smooth dances utilizing open work, the arms and hands are used for leading and style.

(3) The legs and feet. The legs and feet provide the dancer's movement. The legs should be relaxed and controlled as a complete unit. The feet should be extremely flexible and felt as consisting of three separate parts, the toe, ball, and heel.

(4) The head. The head is important for balance and styling. It should be carried by the neck, without dropping or lifting the chin.

BASEBALL UMPIRE

Joe Brinkman Umpire School

*Who said this first? "Who knows what evil lurks in
the heart of man?"*
  (A) Any ballplayer referring to any umpire
  (B) Any umpire referring to any fan
  *(C) A national leader referring to the leaders of
        an "Empire"*
  (D) The Shadow
*Hints: The Shadow was talking like that before
Ronnie and Joe, but not by much, and baseball was
invented in ...Er, um, did it really predate Ronnie?*

Every year, the Baseball Umpire Development Program evaluates the ability of amateur umpires hoping to enter this minefield professionally. The program passes on its recommendations to the various minor leagues, each of which employs its own staff of umpires. From there, it's a long ladder up to the majors. While in the minors, meanwhile, professional umpires in the Rookie, Class A, AA, and AAA leagues can expect to earn $1400 to $2000 a month. With luck and hard work, the minor-league umpire can eventually find himself face to face with the likes of Whitey Herzog in front of a national TV audience. Umpires in the majors earn $30,000 to $72,000 per season if their stomach linings can take it.

How do you get the chance to attend the B.U.D.P.'s Evaluation Course? First, you must complete a 5- to 6-week course of training at one of the three umpire-training schools in this country. In these courses, students are repeatedly tested on their knowledge of the rulebook, and the best students are chosen to participate in the Evaluation Course.

The test of highly technical knowledge on which you are about to score miserably, consists of questions from examinations given at the Joe Brinkman Umpire School in Cocoa, Florida. Anyone who wants more information about becoming an ump can write to them at Dept. BOT, 1021 Indian River Road, Cocoa, FL 32922.

1. A pitcher may attach a material of foreign color to his glove.
   [ ] True   [ ] False

2. A pitcher may wear a colored glove other than white or gray.
   [ ] True   [ ] False

3. A catcher may wear a first-baseman's mitt behind the plate.
   [ ] True   [ ] False

4. An outfielder may wear a first-baseman's mitt in the outfield.
   [ ] True   [ ] False

5. On a foul tip, the ball is dead.
   [ ] True   [ ] False

6. A batted ball goes sharply and directly off the catcher's mitt and is caught by him in his bare hand before touching the ground. This is a
   (A) foul tip
   (B) foul ball

7. On a foul tip, the runner from first base steals second; the umpire calls time and sends the runner back to first base. This ruling is correct.
   [ ] True   [ ] False

8. A batted ball goes sharply and directly from the bat off the catcher's mask and is caught by him before touching the ground. This is a
   (A) foul tip
   (B) foul ball

9. A batted ball goes sharply and directly from the bat off the catcher's mitt, hits him in the mask, and then is caught by him before touching the ground. This is a
   (A) foul tip
   (B) foul ball

10. A batted ball goes sharply and directly from the bat off the catcher's mitt, strikes the umpire in the mask, and is caught by the catcher before touching the ground. This is a
    (A) foul tip
    (B) foul ball

11. A pitched ball hits the sleeve of the batter's uniform but does not hit the batter himself. The umpire should award the batter first base.
    [ ] True   [ ] False

12. A balk can be called on a pitcher while no runners are on base.
    [ ] True   [ ] False

13. What are the two types of illegal pitches?

14. If no announcement of a substitution is made, the substitute shall be considered as having entered the game as follows:
    (A) Pitcher, when he takes his place on the pitcher's plate
    [ ] True   [ ] False
    (B) Batter, when he steps into the batter's box
    [ ] True   [ ]False
    (C) Fielder, when he reaches the position of the man replaced
    [ ] True   [ ] False
    (D) Runner, when he takes the place of the runner re placed
    [ ]True   [ ] False

15. In the top of the first inning, the visiting team jumps off to a six-run lead, when the pitcher is due to bat with a runner on second and one out. The manager feels that he wants to save his starting pitcher for another game, since he already has a comfortable lead, so he decides to pinch-hit for his pitcher. Is this legal? Why?

16. In the seventh inning at 9:00 P. M. a cloudburst occurs. In 15 minutes the field is completely under water. The groundskeepers and both managers tell the umpire that the field cannot be returned to playable condition today. At 9:20 P.M., the Umpire-in-Chief calls the game owing to wet grounds. Is he correct in doing this? Why?

17. A thrown ball strikes a photographer in the back while he is running away from the ball. The ball is dead.
     [ ] True   [ ] False

18. If the coach causes the pitcher to balk with a runner on third base by hollering "Time," the umpire should
    (A) ignore the balk and remove the coach from the game
    (B) allow the balk and remove the coach from the game
    (C) ignore the balk only

19. The score is 5 to 4 in favor of the visiting team in the middle of the seventh inning. In the bottom of the seventh inning, the home team scores two runs to take a 6 to 5 lead. Before the bottom of the seventh can be completed, rain forces the umpires to call the game. What is the final score?

20. It is legal to have four outfielders and only three infielders in addition to the pitcher and catcher.
     [ ] True   [ ]False

21. What is the penalty if a catcher stands with both feet out of the catcher's box before the pitcher releases the ball during an intentional base on balls?

22. To start the game, Baker comes to bat in place of proper batter Abel. The umpire cheeks his lineup card and, to avoid confusion before a pitch is thrown, tells the team's manager. The umpire has done the proper thing.
     [ ] True   [ ] False

23. Which of the following events would terminate a team's right to use the designated hitter for the remainder of the game?
    (A) Inserting a pinch hitter or pinch runner for the designated hitter
    (B) Putting the pitcher at another defensive position
    (C) The designated hitter is callcd out as a result of a batting-out-of-turn situation
    (D) The designated hitter enters the game as a pinch runner
    (E) A pinch hitter or pinch runner enters the game to pitch
    (F) The designated hitter is ejected
    (G) The pitcher bats for the designated bitter
    (H) The designated hitter enters the game defensively
    (I) A relief pitcher enters the game to pitch

24. If the pitcher is moved to another defensive position and a new pitcher enters the game to pitch,
    (A) the original pitcher bats for the replaced defensive player; the new pitcher's name is entered below the line, and the team retains its designated hitter
    (B) the original pitcher must bat in the designated hitter's spot, and the new pitcher in the replaced fielder's spot
    (C) the original pitcher must bat in the replaced fielder's spot, and the new pitcher in the designated hitter's spot
    (D) the manager has his choice of where he wants his two pitchers to bat

25. If the designated hitter enters the game to play left field, and at the same time a new catcher and first baseman enter the game,
    (A) the manager may put the pitcher in any one of the three spots in the lineup catcher, first baseman, or designated hitter (now the left fielder)
    (B) the designated hitter (left fielder) must occupy his original spot, but the pitcher could bat in either of the remaining vacant spots
    (C) the pitcher must bat in the designated hitter's spot, but the team loses the designated hitter for remainder of the game

26. If the umpire determines that the pitcher is intentionally pitching at a batter, the umpire should
    (A) first warn the pitcher and his manager, and remove the pitcher from the game if the offense is repeated
    (B) immediately remove the pitcher from the game

27. There is one out and a runner is on first base. From the rubber, the pitcher steps toward first base and feints a throw. This is a balk.
    [ ] True   [ ] False

28. There is one out and a runner is on first base. The pitcher balks as he attempts to pick the runner off first and throws the ball past the first baseman toward the right-field corner. The runner races all the way to third but misses second. The ball is thrown to second, where the shortstop appeals to the umpire, and he calls the runner out. The offensive manager protests the decision, claiming that the runner is entitled to second base because of the balk and that, because he never touched that base, he should be put back at second. Who is correct?

29. There are two outs, a runner on second, and it's the top of the ninth inning with the home team ahead two to one. The pitcher balks but pitches anyway. The batter singles to center field and the center fielder throws out the runner from second at the plate to apparently end the game. The visiting team's manager, however, informs the umpire that he wants the balk enforced, putting his runner at third base and bringing his batter back to bat. What should the umpire rule?

30. From a set position, a left-handed pitcher lifts his free foot past the plane of the front edge of the rubber, then steps and throws to first base. This is a balk.
    [ ] True   [ ] False

31. After his pitcher has walked two batters straight, the manager decides to go out to the mound to talk to him. The pitcher gets behind the next batter three to zero, when the manager decides to go out to the mound to bring in a relief pitcher
    (A) The manager can legally go out to the mound.
    [ ] True   [ ] False
    (B) The manager cannot legally go out to the mound, but he can change his pitcher from the dugout by informing the umpire.
    [ ] True   [ ] False

32. There are no outs, a runner is on second base, and there is a one-two count on the batter. On the next pitch, the umpire determines that the pitcher delivers a grease-ball, which the batter swings at and misses. The umpire should
    (A) warn the pitcher, move the runner to third, and call the batter out
    (B) eject the pitcher, leave the runner on second, and call a ball on the batter
    (C) warn the pitcher, leave the runner on second, and call a ball on the batter

(D) warn the pitcher, move the runner to third, and call a ball on the batter

(E) eject the pitcher, move the runner to third, and call a ball on the batter

33. There are no outs, a runner is on second base, and there is a one-two count on the batter. On the next pitch, the umpire determines that the pitcher delivers a spitball, but the batter hits the pitch for a single, which scores the runner. According to the rule book, the umpire should

(A) warn the pitcher and allow the single and the run

(B) eject the pitcher and allow the single and the run

(C) warn the pitcher, return the runner to second, and call a ball on the batter

(D) warn the pitcher, put the runner on third, and call the pitch a ball

(E) allow the single and the run and ignore the infraction since all runners advanced at least one base

34. What is the penalty for a pitcher who applies a foreign substance to the ball, expectorates on the ball, either of his hands, or his glove, defaces the ball, or delivers a shine ball, spitball, mud ball, or emery ball for the first time in the game?

35. When a pitcher holds the ball with both hands in front of his body and has one entire foot on, or in front of and touching (but not off the end of), the pitcher's plate and the other foot free, he will be considered to be in the

(A) wind-up position

(B) set position

Questions 36 through 39 refer to live- or dead-ball situations which may involve the placement of runners. In each situation,

(A) tell whether the ball remains alive or is ruled dead

(B) if the ball is ruled dead, place all runners including the batter

(C) if the ball is ruled dead, indicate who, if anyone, is called out on the play

36. There are two outs and a runner is on second base. The runner attempting to advance from second to third is unintentionally hit by a ground ball in the hole which the third baseman attempted to field but missed. The shortstop has no play on the ball.

(A) _____

(B) _____

(C) _____

37. There is one out and a runner is on second base. The batter hits a ground ball which the pitcher deflects and the ball hits the base umpire working in the infield. The second baseman picks up the ball and throws out the runner who had rounded third base.

(A) _____

(B) _____

(C) _____

38. The runner on second is attempting to steal third when the batter is hit with a pitched ball.

(A) _____

(B) _____

(C) _____

39. The bases are loaded, there are no outs, and the count is two-two. The runner on third attempts to steal home and is hit by the pitch, which is in the strike zone. The ball bounces six feet away. The catcher retrieves the ball and throws out the runner from second, who is attempting to advance on the play. The runner on first remains at first.

(A) _____

(B) _____

(C) _____

40. With a zero-two count on him, the batter steps back out of the batter's box while the pitcher is in his windup. The pitcher continues to pitch anyway, and throws a pitch which does not enter the strike zone. What should the umpire call?

41. The batter refuses to take his position in the batter's box. The umpire tells the pitcher to pitch. The pitcher throws an obvious ball. It is legal for the umpire to call it a strike even though he knows it is a ball.
    [ ] True   [ ] False

42. With a zero-two count on him, the batter refuses to take his position in the batter's box. The umpire tells the pitcher to pitch. The pitcher throws the pitch, which the umpire declares strike three. The pitch, however, eludes the catcher, and the batter runs to first base, beating the throw from the catcher. The umpire should
    (A) leave the batter-runner at first base
    (B) declare the batter-runner out

43. After bunting a fair ball, the batter-runner collides with the first baseman, who is attempting to catch the throw from the pitcher, who fielded the bunt. As a direct result of the collision, the first baseman drops the ball. The batter-runner was running entirely in fair territory but never got hit with the ball. The batter-runner is out for interference.
    True   False

44. There is one out, and runners are on first and third. The second baseman intentionally drops a line drive.
    The ball is dead.   [ ] True   [ ] False
    The batter is out.   [ ] True   [ ] False

45. There is one out, and a runner is on first. On the one-one pitch, the runner attempts to steal second. The batter swings and misses but interferes with the catcher's throw, which is too late to retire the runner at second. What should the umpire rule?

46. There are two outs, a runner is on second, and it is the ninth inning with the visiting team trailing five to four. The catcher interferes with the batter, who singles to center field, but the center fielder cuts down the runner attempting to score, which apparently ends the game. The visiting team manager informs the umpire that he wishes to accept the interference penalty, putting the runner back on second and the batter-runner at first with two outs. What should the umpire rule?

47. There are two outs, the bases are loaded, and there is a three-two count on the batter. With runners advancing on the pitch, the batter takes ball four. The runner from second touches and rounds third and is picked off by the catcher before the runner from third touches the plate. The run scores.
    [ ] True   [ ] False

48. The pitcher balks attempting to pick a runner off first and throws the ball into right field. The runner advances all the way to third but missed second. The defense throws the ball to second and appeals to the umpire.
    (A) The runner is out
    (B) The runner is returned to second since he was entitled to second without liability to be put out

49. There is one out and the runner is on first. The batter hits a fly ball to right field. The right fielder catches the ball and tries to double up the runner before he can return to first The ball gets by the first baseman and goes into the dugout. The runner is not yet back to first base when the ball enters the dugout.

(A) Place the runner.

(B) Must the runner retouch first base before advancing?

50. There is one out and runners are on second and third. The batter hits a ground ball to the third baseman, who gets the runner in a rundown between home and third. The runner eludes the rundown and gets back to third safely. Meanwhile, the runner from second advanced to third and is occupying third when the original runner returns. Both runners are tagged while on third base. Who is out?

51. A glove thrown at a fair batted ball has to touch the ball before the umpire awards bases.

[ ] True   [ ] False

Questions 52 through 54 refer to possible interference situations. In each situation:

(A) tell whether interference should be called.

(B) if interference should be called, tell who is declared out

(C) if interference should be called, place all runners

52. There is one out and a runner is on second. The catcher drops a third-strike pitch. On his way toward first base, the batter-runner unintentionally deflects the course of the ball, preventing the catcher from making a play on him. The runner winds up at third and the batter-runner at first.

(A) _____

(B) _____

(C) _____

53. There is one out and runners are on first and third. On the one-one pitch, the runners are double-stealing. The batter swings and misses, and his momentum causes him to step across home plate. Because of the batter's actions, the catcher is unable to make a play on either runner.

(A) _____

(B) _____

(C) _____

54. There is one out and a runner is on second. The batter hits a ground ball to shortstop. In running to first base, the batter-runner is running within the three-foot lane when he collides with the first baseman who was drawn off the bag by the shortstop's wild throw. The runner scores and the batter-runner winds up at second.

(A) _____

(B) _____

(C) _____

55. The three-two pitch to the batter is a wild pitch for ball four. The batter-runner sprints for first but sees he has no chance to advance to second, so he overruns first base. Is he allowed to overrun first in this situation, or can he be put out by being tagged?

ANSWERS!

1. False

2. True

3. True

4. False

5. False

6. A

7. False

8. B

9. A

10. B

11. True

12. False

13. Not in contact, quick pitch

14. (A) True
    (B) True
    (C) False
    (D) True

15. No. The starting pitcher must pitch to one complete batter.

16. No. He must wait 30 minutes.

17. False

18. A

19. Six to five

20. True

21. Balk

22. False

23 B, E, G, H

24 C

25. B

26. A

27. True

28. The umpire

29. The play stands; the game is over.

30. False

31. (A) False   (B) False

32. C

33. A

34. Call a ball, warn the pitcher, and announce the reason to the crowd.

35. A

36. (A) Alive

37. (A) Alive

38. (A) Dead
    (B) Batter to first
    (C) Runner returns

39. (A) Dead
    (B) Runner from third scores
    (C) Batter out on strike three—runners
    advance one base

40. Ball one

41. True

42. B

43. True

44. True, True

45. The batter is out; the runner returns to
    first.

46. The play stands; no option.

47. True

48. A

49. (A) Third base   (B) Yes

50. The runner from second base.

51. True

52. (A) No

53. (A) Yes
    (B) Runner from third is out
    (C) Runner from first returns.

54. (A) No

55. He is out by being tagged.

BIBLE
SCHOLAR

Presbyteries' Cooperative Committee

Is it possible that "In the beginning," "the Word"
was followed by a question mark?

The questions in this examination come from items used by the Presbyterian church (U.S.A.) to evaluate how well candidates for ministry know the Bible. Presbyteries Cooperative Committee has for a decade been building these instruments. ("Instruments" is a word that professional test makers and readers prefer to "tests" or "exams.") Each item is tested for fairness prior to its use on the actual exam. A passing grade for this examination is 70 items correct.

This is a multiple-choice examination. Five foils or choices are given for each item. Only one is correct. Questions are arranged by section of the Bible. Within each section, items progress from easier to more difficult. The answer page includes the correct response, and it cites the biblical reference. We also tell you the percentage of candidates getting each one correct at the last administration of that test question to candidates for the Presbyterian ministry, just in case you may be feeling competitive.

Entrance into ministry in the Presbyterian Church (U.S.A.) begins with membership in one of the local churches. Candidates must have degrees from a college and a seminary. They must then pass five denominational examinations, one of which will contain questions like the following ones, then pass an oral examination by a presbytery before being ordained. So if you answer 70 of these questions correctly, you have a right to a brief, warming sense of achievement.

Section 1: Pentateuch

1. The refrain, "And God saw that it was good.
   And there was evening and there was morn-
   ing . . . is found in
   (A) Exodus
   (B) Genesis
   (C) Numbers
   (D) Psalms
   (E) Song of Solomon

2. "The Lord saw that the wickedness of man
   was great in the earth, and that every imagination in the thoughts of his heart was only
   evil continually" refers to
   (A) God's reaction to the Fall
   (B) God's reaction to the murmuring of the
   children of Israel in the wilderness
   (C) God's reaction to the Tower of Babel
   (D) God's reasons for the Flood
   (E) God's reason for giving the Ten Com-
   mandments

3. Which wife first asked her husband to take a
   concubine, and then later cast her out?
   (A) Leah
   (B) Lot's wife
   (C) Rachel
   (D) Rebekah
   (E) Sarah

4. Caleb
   (A) opposed Joshua
   (B) tried to lead a revolt against Moses
   (C) was a spy who gave a good report of the
   Promised Land
   (D) was Isaac's third son
   (E) was killed by Pharaoh as Joseph pre-
   dicted

5. "Behold, I establish my covenant with you
   and your descendants after you, and with
   every living creature that is with you, the
   birds, the cattle, and every beast of the earth
   with you" was spoken to
   (A) Abraham
   (B) Jacob
   (C) Joseph

   (D) Noah
   (E) Seth

6. What was the purpose of the cities of
   refuge?
   (A) Cities where homeless people were wel-
   come
   (B) Cities where those accused of homicide
   could escape from the avenger
   (C) Fortresses guarding the borders of
   Canaan
   (D) Places where Canaanites could be safe
   (E) Places where widows and aliens were
   cared for

7. Melchizedek is first mentioned in connec-
   tion with
   (A) Abraham
   (B) David
   (C) Jacob
   (D) Joseph
   (E) Moses

8. "Be fruitful and multiply, and fill the
   earth . . . " was spoken to
   (A) Abraham
   (B) Adam
   (C) Joseph by Jacob
   (D) Joshua
   (E) The Children of Israel by Hosea

9. Rebekah was the wife of
   (A) Abraham
   (B) Isaac
   (C) Jacob
   (D) Joseph
   (E) Laban

10. "Sing to the Lord for he has triumphed glori-
    ously; the horse and his rider he has thrown
    into the sea" was sung by
    (A) Aaron
    (B) Balaam
    (C) Jacob
    (D) Joshua
    (E) Miriam

11. "Hear, 0 Israel: the Lord our God is one LORD: and you shall love the LORD your God with all your heart, and with all your soul, and with all your might" appears in
(A) Deuteronomy
(B) Exodus
(C) Joshua
(D) Leviticus
(E) Numbers

12. Which tribe was not allotted any territory in Canaan?
(A) Dan
(B) Ephraim
(C) Issachar
(D) Judah
(E) Levi

13. The conversation between Eve and the serpent was about
(A) Adam
(B) apples
(C) covenant
(D) death
(E) tilling the soil

14. Of the following persons, who was born the earliest?
(A) Benjamin
(B) Enoch
(C) Jacob
(D) Judah
(E) Moses

15. Israelite law demanded scrupulous care in the treatment of the blood of slain animals. The reason for this is that blood is
(A) the choicest part of the animal
(B) holy
(C) inedible
(D) life
(E) unclean

16. Moses was of the house of
(A) Benjamin
(B) Dan
(C) Judah
(D) Levi
(E) Simeon

17. The Pharaoh's order that the slaves had to provide their own straw for brickmaking was a reaction to
(A) Moses' act of murder and his flight
(B) the death of the first-born
(C) the high birthrate of the slaves
(D) the request to go into the wilderness for a feast day
(E) turning the water into blood

Section 2: Historical Books

1. David was associated with the prophet
(A) Barak
(B) Eli
(C) Elijah
(D) Michaiah
(E) Nathan

2. The king who is remembered for religious reform and reintroduction of the Book of Law was
(A) Amaziah
(B) Josiah
(C) Manassah
(D) Rehoboam
(E) Zedekiah

3. ". . . choose this day whom you will serve . . . : but as for me and my house we will serve the Lord" was said by
(A) Deborah
(B) Gideon
(C) Joshua
(D) Samson
(E) Saul

4. The king associated with the return of Judah from Exile was
(A) Ahasueras
(B) Alexander
(C) Cyrus
(D) Nebuchadnezzar
(E) Xerxes

5. Which enemy of the Hebrews did Samson fight?
(A) Edomites
(B) Egyptians
(C) Gibeonites
(D) Moabites
(E) Philistines

6. Which heir to the throne of David was supported by Bathsheba, Nathan, and Zadok?
(A) Adonijah
(B) Absalom
(C) Jereboam
(D) Rehoboam
(E) Solomon

7. David refused to take Saul's life, when he had the chance, because
(A) he did not believe in killing
(B) he was afraid the people would turn against him
(C) of gratitude to Saul
(D) of his respect for Jonathan
(E) Saul was the Lord's annointed

8. Which pair of people were important in Samuel's life?
(A) Barak and Sisera
(B) Eli and Nathan
(C) Hannah and Eli
(D) Hannah and Nathan
(E) Samson and Jephtha

9. Old Testament narratives about Rahab the harlot are found in
(A) Deuteronomy
(B) Exodus
(C) Genesis
(D) Joshua
(E) Samuel

10. The "judge" who rejected kingship was
(A) Abimelech
(B) Barak
(C) Ehud
(D) Gideon
(E) Samson

11. The recurring description, "In those days there was no king in Israel; every man did what was right in his own eyes," portrays the
(A) civil war between Saul and David
(B) period of the exile after the destruction of Jerusalem
(C) period of the Judges
(D) time of Samuel
(E) wilderness. wandering under Moses

12. What did Saul do to make Samuel turn against him?
(A) Claimed to be king despite Samuel's opposition
(B) Failed to destroy the Amelekites completely
(C) Refused to acknowledge David
(D) Refused to acknowledge Yahweh
(E) Was defeated in battle

13. The Canaanite army commander defeated by Deborah and Barak at the river Kishon was
(A) Anak
(B) Avath
(C) Cushan
(D) Ehud
(E) Sisera

Section 3: Prophets

1. "But he was wounded for our transgressions, he was bruised for our iniquities, upon him was the chastisement that made us whole, and with his stripes we are healed" is a servant song from the book of
(A) Daniel
(B) Ezekiel
(C) Isaiah
(D) Lamentations
(E) Obadiah

2. "Yet forty days and Ninevah shall be overthrown" is a warning from
(A) Amos
(B) Hosea
(C) Isaiah
(D) Jonah
(E) Micah

3. The autobiographical information, "I am no prophet, nor a prophet's son, but I am a herdsman, and a dresser of sycamore trees . . . and the Lord said to me, 'Go prophesy to my people Israel,'" is from the prophet
   (A) Amos
   (B) Hosea
   (C) Isaiah
   (D) Jonah
   (E) Micah

4. In which book do these characteristic lines appear? "Before I formed you in the womb I knew you," "Cursed be the day I was born," "Is there no balm in Gilead?"
   (A) Amos
   (B) Ezekiel
   (C) Hosea
   (D) Joel
   (E) Jeremiah

5. Which words from the LORD were spoken to Hosea the prophet?
   (A) "And he said to me, 'Son of Man, can these bones live?'"
   (B) "Go, take to yourself a wife of harlotry and have children of harlotry."
   (C) "I take no delight in your solemn assemblies."
   (D) "Seek the LORD while he may be found, call upon him while he is near."
   (E) "Yet I have loved Jacob, but I have hated Esau."

6. The vision of a new covenant to be written on the hearts of God's people is found in
   (A) Amos
   (B) Hosea
   (C) Jeremiah
   (D) Micah
   (E) Zephaniah

7. For an example of how God calls a prophet, one would turn to the book of
   (A) Ezekiel
   (B) Haggai
   (C) Joel

(D) Malachi
(E) Zechariah

8. "Come now, let us reason together, says the LORD: though your sins are like scarlet, they shall be white as snow; though they are red like crimson, they shall become like wool" is found in
   (A) Amos
   (B) Hosea
   (C) Isaiah
   (D) Jeremiah
   (E) Micah

9. "I saw in the night visions, and behold, with the clouds of heaven there came one like a son of man, and he came to the Ancient of Days" is found in the book of
   (A) Amos
   (B) Daniel
   (C) Ezekiel
   (D) Hosea
   (E) Nahum

10. The expressions "Call his name Not-my-people," "Call her name Not Pitied," "They made kings, but not through me" are typical of the prophet
    (A) Amos
    (B) Ezekiel
    (C) Hosea
    (D) Jonah
    (E) Zephaniah

11. Select the passage which comes from the book of Joel:
    (A) "Behold, a young woman shall conceive, and bear a son, and shall call his name Immanuel."
    (B) "Come now, let us reason together, says the Lord . . ."
    (C) "The earth shall be full of the knowledge of the Lord as the waters cover the sea."
    (D) "Woe to him who builds his house by unrighteousness, and his upper rooms by injustice."
    (E) "Your sons and daughters shall prophesy, your old men shall dream dreams, and your young men shall see visions."

12. The saying, "He has showed you, O man, what is good: and what does the LORD require of you but to do justice, and to love kindness, and to walk humbly with your God?" is found in
   (A) Ezekiel
   (B) Hosea
   (C) Jonah
   (D) Micah
   (E) Zechariah

13. Which prophet was commanded, "Son of man, eat what is offered to you; eat this scroll, and go, speak to the house of Israel"?
   (A) Ezekiel
   (B) Isaiah
   (C) Jeremiah
   (D) Jonah
   (E) Micah

14. These expressions are typical of which prophet? "Zion shall be plowed as a field." "But you, O Bethlehem Ephratha . . . from you shall come forth for me one who is to be ruler of Israel."
   (A) Habakkuk
   (B) Haggai
   (C) Joel
   (D) Micah
   (E) Zechariah

15. The prophet whose oracles were addressed primarily to Israel, although he was himself from Judah, was
   (A) Amos
   (B) Hosea
   (C) Jeremiah
   (D) Malachi
   (E) Obadiah

16. The prophet who wrote "But the righteous shall live by his faith" was
   (A) Hosea
   (B) Habakkuk
   (C) Jonah
   (D) Nahum
   (E) Malachi

17. The great image, which Nebuchadnezzar saw in his dream, represented
   (A) a series of empires
   (B) his own life history
   (C) Israel's history
   (D) the practice of idolatry
   (E) the whole of creation

Section 4: Psalms & Wisdom Literature

1. The line from the Psalms " . . . Thou pre-parest a table before me . . ." is completed by
   (A) "and I walk in faithfulness to thee"
   (B) "and in his temple all cry, 'Glory'"
   (C) "for I wait for thee"
   (D) "I shall never be moved"
   (E) "in the presence of my enemies"

2. "Her ways are ways of pleasantness and all her paths are peace" is said about
   (A) Bildad the Shuhite
   (B) Jerusalem
   (C) Job's wife
   (D) Queen of Sheba
   (E) Wisdom

3. God answers out of the whirlwind in response to which of the following characters?
   (A) David
   (B) Ecclesiastes
   (C) Job
   (D) Lemuel
   (E) Solomon

4. The last five Psalms all begin with
   (A) Come, bless the LORD
   (B) I cry with my voice to the Lord
   (C) I will call upon thee, O LORD
   (D) I will extol thee, my God and King
   (E) Praise the Lord

5. "O Lord, our Lord, how majestic is thy name in all the earth" begins and ends the Psalm that also states
   (A) "How long, O LORD, wilt thou forget me forever?"

(B) "May the Lord cut off all flattering lips"
(C) "The enemy have vanished in everlasting ruin"
(D) "The Lord is in his Holy Temple"
(E) "What is man that thou art mindful of him?"

6. In Psalm 150, God is praised with
(A) a call in his name
(B) a mighty army
(C) lute.and harp
(D) my whole heart
(E) new offerings

7. Which of the following words correctly completes the saying which occurs in Psalms 14 and 53: "The fool says in his heart, 'There is no
(A) God. '"
(B) justice.'"
(C) mercy. '"
(D) salvation.
(E) truth.'"

8 Who said, "Man that is born of woman is of few days, and full of trouble. He comes forth like a flower, and withers: he flees like a shadow, and continues not"?
(A) Bildad
(B) Elihu
(C) God
(D) Job
(E) Satan

9. The statement typical of Ecclesiastes is
(A) "All this I have tested by wisdom: I said, 'I will be wise'; but it was far from me."
(B) "Like a dog that returns to his vomit is a fool that repeats his folly."
(C) "Praise the Lord! Praise God in his sanctuary."
(D) "The Lord gave, and the Lord has taken away; blessed be the name of the Lord."
(E) "Zion stretches out her hands, but there is none to comfort her."

10. The book in which one finds "For I know that my Redeemer lives, and at last he will stand upon the earth; and after my skin has been thus destroyed, then from my flesh shall I see God" is
(A) Ecclesiastes
(B) Job
(C) Proverbs
(D) Psalms
(E) Song of Solomon

Section 5: Synoptic Gospels

1. "How hard it will be for those who have riches to enter the kingdom of God" comes at the conclusion of the
(A) cleansing of the Temple
(B) discourse on the end times in Mark 9
(C) Pharisees' efforts to get a sign from heaven
(D) restoration of sight to Bartimaeus
(E) story of the rich young ruler

2. The Word, a path, rocky ground are part of the parable of the
(A) candle
(B) growing grain
(C) lost sheep
(D) mustard seed
(E) sower

3. "I have not come to bring peace on earth" was said by
(A) Herod
(B) Jesus
(C) John the Baptist
(D) Philip
(E) Pilate

4. The Beatitudes are found in
(A) Mark and Luke
(B) Mark and Matthew
(C) Matthew and John
(D) Matthew and Luke
(E) Luke and John

5. The parables of leaven, wheat and tares, hidden treasures, the dragnet all relate to
   (A) instruction given to the Seventy
   (B) Jesus' opposition to the Pharisees
   (C) the end of the world
   (D) the kingdom of heaven
   (E) the second coming

6. "... and when they had sung a hymn they went out to the Mount of Olives" concludes
   (A) events at the home of Simon
   (B) Jesus' conversation with his disciples on the Mount of Olives
   (C) Jesus' experience in Gethsemane
   (D) the feeding of the five thousand
   (E) the story of the Last Supper

7. "Watch therefore, for you know neither the day nor the hour" is the conclusion to the parable of the
   (A) fig tree
   (B) marriage feast
   (C) talents
   (D) ten virgins
   (E) wicked tenants

8. Which of the following does NOT belong?
   (A) Baptism of Jesus
   (B) Camel-hair garment
   (C) Leather girdle
   (D) Locusts and wild honey
   (E) the Nazarene

9. "For many are called but few are chosen" comes at the conclusion of the parable of the
   (A) marriage feast
   (B) talents
   (C) ten virgins
   (D) two sons
   (E) wicked tenants

10. Which gospel begins with an introduction to the reader?
    (A) Matthew
    (B) Mark
    (C) Luke
    (D) John
    (E) None of the above

11. The only miracle of Jesus recorded in all four gospels is
    (A) cursing the fig tree
    (B) healing the paralytic
    (C) the feeding of the five thousand
    (D) the raising of Lazarus
    (E) the stilling of the storm at sea

12. Which of the following does NOT belong?
    (A) deafness
    (B) dumbness
    (C) Elizabeth
    (D) Gabriel
    (E) Zechariah

13. "Even the dust of your town that clings to our feet, we wipe off against you" is part of the story of the
    (A) disciples at Bethany
    (B) Gerasene demoniac
    (C) good Samaritan
    (D) mission of the Seventy
    (E) vineyard

Section 6: John's Writings: Gospel, Epistles, Revelation

1. "Behold the Lamb of God who takes away the sin of the world" is said of Jesus by whom?
   (A) John the Baptist
   (B) Man born blind
   (C) Martha
   (D) Mary of Bethany
   (E) Peter

2. "'I am the Alpha and the Omega,' says the Lord God, 'who is and who was and who is to come, the Almighty. '" These words occur in the
   (A) Gospel of John
   (B) First Epistle of John
   (C) Second Epistle of John
   (D) Third Epistle of John
   (E) Revelation of John

3. The woman at Jacob's well, from whom Jesus asked a drink, was a
   (A) Canaanite
   (B) Galilean
   (C) Samaritan
   (D) Syro-Phoenician
   (E) widow from Zarephath

4. The Book of the Revelation of John describes visions granted to the seer when he was in the Spirit on the Lord's day, while
   (A) praying on a high mountain
   (B) sorrowing over the earthly city of Jerusalem
   (C) staying on the island of Patmos
   (D) suffering persecution at Ephesus
   (E) worshipping in the temple

5. According to I John, to deny we have sinned makes God
   (A) angry
   (B) a liar
   (C) unfaithful
   (D) unrighteous
   (E) vengeful

6. In connection with the feeding of the five thousand as recorded by John, Jesus said
   (A) "Beware of the leaven of the Pharisees."
   (B) "I am the bread of life."
   (C) "I will make you fishers of men."
   (D) "My food is to do the will of him who sent me."
   (E) "Take, eat, this is my body."

Section 7: Acts and Writings of Paul

1. In Ephesians, Christ is said to have "broken down the dividing wall of hostility" between Jews and Gentiles because
   (A) anyone who hates his brother is a murderer
   (B) Gentiles are not children of the slave but of the free woman
   (C) Gentiles are the aroma of Christ to God
   (D) God has reconciled Jews and Gentiles in one body through the cross
   (E) the gifts and call of God are irrevocable

2. Which of these expressions is characteristic of I Corinthians?
   (A) "I have fought the good fight, I have finished the race."
   (B) "I through the law died to the law, that I might live to God."
   (C) "The brethren have been made confident in the Lord because of my imprisonment. "
   (D) "There are varieties of gifts but the same Spirit."
   (E) "Three times I have been shipwrecked."

3. "Since all have sinned and fall short of the glory of God, they are justified by his grace as a gift and through the redemption which is in Christ Jesus" is a theme from
   (A) Paul's letter to Rome
   (B) Paul's second letter to Corinth
   (C) Paul's sermon at Mars Hill
   (D) Peter's sermon at Pentecost
   (E) Stephen's sermon

4. "The grace of the Lord Jesus Christ and the love of God and the fellowship of the Holy Spirit be with you all" is a benediction given by
   (A) Jesus
   (B) John
   (C) Paul
   (D) Peter
   (E) Timothy

5. The Ethiopian eunuch met by Philip was reading from the prophet
   (A) Amos
   (B) Daniel
   (C) Ezekiel
   (D) Isaiah
   (E) Jeremiah

6. Peter's visit to Cornelius in Caesarea concerned the
   (A) appointment of a new disciple
   (B) Gentiles receiving the word of God
   (C) interpretation of Isaiah
   (D) preaching of the kingdom
   (E) stoning of Stephen

7. "For as often as you eat this bread and drink the cup, you proclaim the Lord's death until he comes" is found in
(A) Acts
(B) I Corinthians
(C) Ephesians
(D) Romans
(E) I Timothy

8. Peter's accusation to Ananias and Sapphira (who sold property while keeping back some of the proceeds) was that they
(A) dishonored the name of Jesus
(B) lied to God
(C) lied to Peter
(D) spoke blasphemous words
(E) were filled with new wine

9. Because the Corinthians had been reconciled to God through Christ and had been given the ministry of reconciliation, they were to consider themselves
(A) ambassadors of Christ
(B) contenders for the faith
(C) servants of the Lord
(D) shepherds of the flock
(E) soldiers of the cross

10. "Wretched man that I am! Who will deliver me from this body of death?" is a cry from
(A) Paul
(B) Peter
(C) Philemon
(D) Silas
(E) Titus

11. The book in which the expression "Rejoice in the LORD always; again I will say, Rejoice" is found is
(A) I Corinthians
(B) II Corinthians
(C) Ephesians
(D) Philippians
(E) Romans

12. The people gathered in the upper room after Jesus was lifted up into heaven included
(A) Barnabas
(B) Mary
(C) Nicodemus
(D) Saul
(E) Timothy

13. The Epistle to the Colossians describes Christ as
(A) the first-born from the dead
(B) the first-born of all creation
(C) the head of the body
(D) the image of the invisible God
(E) all of these

14. Paul's instruction, "If anyone is hungry, let him eat at home," pertains to
(A) conditioning for the trip to Corinth
(B) eating of food offered to idols
(C) preparations for a Jewish festival
(D) taking advantage of a host's generosity
(E) the Lord's Supper

15. Stephen's words before the council rehearse the part of Israel's history which includes the
(A) destruction of Jerusalem
(B) exile of Israel
(C) patriarchs and the exodus
(D) rebuilding of the temple
(E) return of Judah from exile

16. "Have this mind among yourselves, which is yours in Christ Jesus, who, though he was in the form of God, did not count equality with God a thing to be grasped," is found in
(A) II Corinthians
(B) Ephesians
(C) Philippians
(D) Romans
(E) Titus

17. Which of the following terms correctly fills in the blank? "For _____ Christ has set us free: stand fast therefore, and do not submit to the yoke of slavery."
(A) faith
(B) freedom
(C) justification
(D) love
(E) one another

Section 8: Other New Testament Books

1. "Now if perfection had been attainable through the Levitical priesthood . . . what further need would there have been for another priest to arise after the order of Melchizedek, rather than one named after the order of Aaron?" This is typical of the argument in
(A) Hebrews
(B) James
(C) Jude
(D) I Peter
(E) II Peter

2. The following quotation, ". . . show me your faith apart from your work and I by my works will show you my faith" is found in which of the following books?
(A) James
(B) I Peter
(C) Philemon
(D) Titus
(E) II Timothy

3. Which of the following statements is found in the Book of Hebrews?
(A) "Faith is the assurance of things hoped for, the conviction of things unseen."
(B) "For you have heard of my former life in Judaism, how I persecuted the church of God violently and tried to destroy it."
(C) "If anyone is in Christ, he is a new creation."

(D) "Practice hospitality ungrudgingly to one another."
(E) "With the Lord one day is as a thousand years, and a thousand years as one day.

4. A forest set ablaze by a small fire and the rudder of a ship are images for the
(A) emotions
(B) heart
(C) mind
(D) tongue
(E) will

5. The book which calls Jesus our faith's pioneer and perfecter is
(A) Hebrews
(B) James
(C) Jude
(D) I Peter
(E) II Peter

6. Which book speaks of the early Christian practice of praying over the sick and anointing them with oil?
(A) Hebrews
(B) James
(C) Jude
(D) I Peter
(E) II Peter

7. The book which says "Convince some who doubt, save some by snatching them out of the fire . . ." and speaks of Enoch as a prophet is
(A) Hebrews
(B) James
(C) Jude
(D) I Peter
(E) II Peter

ANSWERS!

Section 1: Pentateuch

1. (B); 99%; Genesis 1
2. (E); 95%; Genesis 6:5
3. (E); 86%; Genesis 16:1–6
4. (C); 83%; Numbers 13:30
5. (D); 83%; Genesis 9:9
6. (B); 80%; Numbers 35:6
7. (A); 79%; Genesis 14:18–22
8. (B); 77%; Genesis 1:28
9. (B); 79%; Genesis 24:67
10. (B); 76%; Exodus 15:21
11. (A); 76%; Deuteronomy 6:4
12. (E); 67%; Deuteronomy 10:9
13. (D); 61%; Genesis 3:2–4
14. (B); 63%; Genesis 5:19
15. (D); 67%; Leviticus 17:14
16. (D); 58%; Exodus 2:1
17. (D); 57%; Exodus 5:1–14

Section 2: Historical Books

1. (E); 93%; II Samuel 7:2
2. (B); 92%; II Kings 22
3. (C); 89%; Joshua 24:15
4. (C); 82%; II Chronicles 36:22
5. (E); 81%; Judges 15:14
6. (E); 79%; I Kings 1:11–12
7. (E); 77%; I Samuel 26:23
8. (C); 76%; I Samuel 1:9
9. (D); 75%; Joshua 6:15–25
10. (D); 65%; Judges 8:23
11. (C); 66%; Judges 17:6
12. (B); 60%; I Samuel 15:9
13. (E); 59%; Judges 4:15

Section 3 Prophets

1. (C); 92%; Isaiah 53:5
2. (D); 91%; Jonah 3:4
3. (A); 88%; Amos 7:14
4. (E); 88%; Jeremiah 1:5, 8:22
5. (B); 87%; Hosea 1:2
6. (C); 82%; Jeremiah 31:34
7. (A); 82%; Ezekiel 1–2
8. (C); 74%; Isaiah 1:18
9. (B); 74%; Daniel 7:13
10. (C); 75%; Hosea 1–2
11. (E); 78%; Joel 2:28
12. (D); 76%; Micah 6:8
13. (A); 65%; Ezekiel 3:1
14. (D); 64%; Micah
15. (A); 65%; Amos 1:1
16. (B); 54%; Habakkuk 2:4
17. (A); 51%; Daniel 2:36–45

Section 4: Psalms & Wisdom Literature

1. (E); 97%; Psalm 23
2. (E); 88%; Proverbs 3:17
3. (C); 85%; Job 38:1
4. (E); 81%; Psalms 145–150
5. (E); 77%; Psalm 8:4

6. (C); 74%; Psalm 150

7. (A); 76%; Psalms 14, 53

8. (D); 69%; Job 14:1–2

9. (A); 65%; Ecclesiastes 7:23

10. (B); 54%; Job 19:25

Section 5: Synoptic Gospels

1. (E); 96%; Mark 10:23

2. (E); 93%; Mark 4:26–32

3. (B); 87%; Matthew 10:34

4. (D); 85%; Matthew 5; Luke 6

5. (D); 83%; Synoptic refs

6. (E); 77%; Matthew 26:30

7. (D); 75%; Matthew 25:13

8. (E); 75%; Luke 3:7–16

9. (A); 71%; Matthew 22:14

10. (C); 69%; Luke 1:1–4

11. (C); 62%; Matthew 14, Mark 6, Luke 9, John 6

12. (A); 62%; Luke 1:5–38

13. (D); 59%; Luke 10:11

Section 6: John's Writings, Gospel, Epistles, Revelation

1. (A); 91%; John 1:29

2. (E); 86%; Revelation 1:8

3. (C); 85%; John 4:7

4. (C); 75%; Revelation 1:9

5. (B); 73%; I John 1:10

6. (B); 69%; John 6:35

Section 7: Acts and Writings of Paul

1. (D); 95%; Ephesians 2:14

2. (D); 94%; I Corinthians 12:4

3. (A); 87%; Romans

4. (C); 84%; II Corinthians 13:14

5. (D); 83%; Acts 8:30

6. (B); 82%; Acts 10

7. (B); 81%; I Corinthians 11:26

8. (B); 76%; Acts 5:4

9. (A); 76%; II Corinthians 5:20

10. (A); 74%; Romans 7:24

11. (D); 74%; Philippians 4:4

12. (B); 72%; Acts 1:14

13. (E); 68%; Colossians 1:15

14 (E); 62%; I Corinthians 11:34

15. (C); 60%; Acts 7

16. (C); 57%; Philippians 2:5–6

17. (B); 55%; Galatians 5:1

Section 8 Other New Testament Books

1. (A); 90%; Hebrews 7:11

2. (A); 86%; James 2:18

3. (A); 87%; Hebrews 11:1

4. (D); 72%; James 3:6

5. (A); 71%; Hebrews 12:2

6. (B); 62%; James 5:12

7. (C); 45%; Jude

BOOKKEEPER & ACCOUNTANT

N.Y. State Board of Regents

Why, in the name of sanity, would anyone want to take a bookkeeping exam for fun?! Because it can lull you into the illusion that a compelling force in your life, the flow of money, can be governed by orderly rules. Don't you find that comforting?

Every high school student in the state of New York is familiar with the Regents Exams. They test students on a mandatory syllabus created by the New York State Education Department, and thereby ensure that a minimum standard is met by all students in the state regardless of which high school they attend and how it grades them. Like the College Board's SAT, the Regents are meant to provide a consistent yardstick of the performance of students from different high schools.

The minimum passing grade is 65 percent. The scores are entered on the student's transcript. Some universities, like those in the State University of New York system, take the scores into consideration when evaluating an application for admission; others, especially out-of-state colleges, consider only the national standardized tests.

According to the most recent figures available, about 73 percent of the students who take the Bookkeeping/Accounting exam achieve the minimum passing grade.

We chose to select questions from the Accounting and Bookkeeping exam for this collection because almost everybody has to deal with some of these concepts along the cutting edge of practical existence if only to balance a checkbook. Well, *almost* balance a checkbook.

The numbers in brackets following each part and numbered question indicate the number of credit points allocated to each. These act like a bank account from which mistakes are deducted when the answers are scored.

DIRECTIONS (1–5): Base your answers on the statement of account shown below [5]

```
                    STATEMENT OF ACCOUNT

                      Liberty Products, Inc.
                         74 Spring Street
                         Ithaca, NY 14851

   TO: Bramar Industries          DATE:   March 31, 1986
       972 West Avenue
       Syracuse, NY 13219
```

DATE	ITEM	CHARGES	PAYMENTS AND CREDITS	BALANCE
	Previous Balance			785.35
March 8	Payment		785.35	
12	Invoice 17 – 582	550 –		550 –
17	Invoice 17 – 692	700 –		1250 –
31	Payment		550 –	700 –

```
     PAY LAST AMOUNT SHOWN IN BALANCE COLUMN
```

1. Which company is the customer?

2. What total amount was charged by the customer during March?

3. How much does the customer owe on March 31?

4. On which accounting schedule would Bramar Industries list Liberty Products, Inc.?

5. The terms on invoice 17-582 were 3/20, n/45. What was the correct amount for which the check should have been written when payment was made?

DIRECTIONS (6–35): Answer any 25 of the 30 questions in this part. For EACH statement or question, write in the separate answer section the LETTER preceding the word or expression that, of those given, best completes the statement or answers the question. [25]

6. Which item is NOT a source document?
    (A) an invoice
    (B) a magnetic tape
    (C) a punched card
    (D) a telephone conversation

7. What is double-entry accounting?
    (A) journalizing and posting
    (B) recording debit and credit parts for a transaction
    (C) using carbon paper when preparing a source document
    (D) posting a debit or credit and computing the new account balance

8. The balance in the asset account Supplies is $600. An ending inventory shows $200 of supplies on hand. The adjusting entry should be
    (A) debit Supplies Expense for $200, credit Supplies for $200
    (B) credit Supplies Expense for $200, debit Supplies for $200
    (C) debit Supplies Expense for $400, credit Supplies for $400
    (D) credit Supplies Expense for $400, debit Supplies for $400

9. What is the purpose of preparing an Income Statement?
    (A) To report the net income or net loss
    (B) To show the owner's claims against the assets
    (C) To prove that the accounting equation is in balance
    (D) To prove that the total debits equal the total credits

10. Which account does NOT belong on the Income Statement?
    (A) Salaries Payable
    (B) Rental Revenue
    (C) Advertising Expense
    (D) Sales Returns and Allowances

11. The source document for entries made in a Purchases Journal is a purchase
    (A) order
    (B) requisition
    (C) invoice
    (D) register

12. A business check guaranteed for payment by the bank is called a
    (A) bank draft
    (B) certified check
    (C) cashier's check
    (D) personal check

13. The entry that closes the Purchases Account contains
    (A) a debit to Purchases
    (B) a debit to Purchases Returns and Allowances
    (C) a credit to Purchases
    (D) a credit to Income and Expense Summary

14. Which account would NOT appear on a Balance Sheet?
    (A) Office Equipment
    (B) Transportation In
    (C) Mortgage Payable
    (D) Supplies on Hand

15. Which entry is made at the end of the fiscal period for the purpose of updating the Prepaid Insurance Account?
    (A) Correcting entry
    (B) Closing entry
    (C) Adjusting entry
    (D) Reversing entry

16. Which deduction from gross pay is NOT
    (A) Hospitalization insurance
    (B) FICA tax
    (C) Federal income tax
    (D) New York State income tax

17. What is the last date on which a 2 percent cash discount can be taken for an invoice dated October 15 with terms of 2/10, n/30?
    (A) October 15
    (B) October 17
    (C) October 25
    (D) November 14

18. Which item on the bank reconciliation statement would require the business to record a journal entry?

    (A) A deposit in transit
    (B) An outstanding check
    (C) A canceled check
    (D) A bank service charge

19. Which is NOT an essential component of a computer?
    (A) An input device
    (B) A central processor
    (C) An output device
    (D) A telecommunicator

20. Which group of accounts could appear on a post-closing trial balance?
    (A) Petty Cash; Accounts Receivable; FICA Taxes Payable
    (B) Office Furniture; Office Expense; Supplies on Hand
    (C) Supplies Expense; Sales; Advertising Expense
    (D) Sales Discount; Rent Expense; J. Smith, Drawing

21. The withdrawals of cash by the owner are recorded in the owner's drawing account as
    (A) an adjusting entry
    (B) a closing entry
    (C) a credit
    (D) a debit

22. An account in the General Ledger which shows a total of a related Subsidiary Ledger is referred to as
    (A) a revenue account
    (B) a controlling account
    (C) a temporary account
    (D) an owner's equity account

23 Which type of endorsement is shown below?
    (A) Restrictive
    (B) Blank
    (C) Full
    (D) Qualified

For Deposit Only
Loretta Gonzalez

24. Which is a chronological record of all the transactions of a business?
    (A) Worksheet
    (B) Income statement
    (C) Journal
    (D) Trial balance

25. Which error would NOT be revealed by the preparation of a trial balance?
    (A) Posting of an entire transaction more than once
    (B) Incorrectly pencil footing the balance of a general ledger account
    (C) Posting a debit of $320 as $230
    (D) Omitting an account with a balance

26. The Cash Receipts Journal is used to record the
    (A) purchase of merchandise for cash
    (B) purchase of merchandise on credit
    (C) sale of merchandise for cash
    (D) sale of merchandise on credit

27. On a Systems flowchart, which symbol is commonly used to indicate the direction of the flow of work?
    (A) An arrow
    (B) A circle
    (C) A diamond
    (D) A rectangle

28. Which account balance would be eliminated by a closing entry at the end of the fiscal period?
    (A) Office Equipment
    (B) Owner's Drawing
    (C) Owner's Capital
    (D) Mortgage Payable

29. In a data processing system, the handling and manipulation of data according to precise procedures is called
    (A) input
    (B) processing
    (C) storage
    (D) output

30. Which financial statement reflects the cumulative financial position of the business?
    (A) Bank statement
    (B) Income statement
    (C) Trial balance
    (D) Balance sheet

31. Which account should be credited when recording a cash proof showing an overage?
    (A) Sales
    (B) Cash
    (C) Cash Short and Over
    (D) Sales Returns and Allowances

32. In which section of the income statement would the purchases account be shown?
    (A) Cost of Goods Sold
    (B) Income from Sales
    (C) Operating Expenses
    (D) Other Expenses

33. What is an invoice?
    (A) An order for the shipment of goods
    (B) An order for the purchase of goods
    (C) A receipt for goods purchased
    (D) A statement listing goods purchased

34. A business uses a Sales Journal, a Purchases journal, a Cash Receipts Journal, a Cash Payments journal, and a General Journal. In which journal would a credit memorandum received from a creditor be recorded?
    (A) Sales Journal
    (B) Purchases Journal
    (C) General Journal
    (D) Cash Receipts Journal

35. Which account is debited to record a weekly payroll?
    (A) Employees Income Tax Payable
    (B) FICA Taxes Payable
    (C) General Expense
    (D) Salaries Expense

DIRECTIONS (36—42): Answer any 5 of the 7 questions in this part. For EACH statement or question, write in the LETTER preceding the word or expression that, of those given, best completes the statement or answers the question. [5]

Base your answers to questions 36 through 38 on the classified ads shown below and on your knowledge of accounting-book-keeping.

36. A high school student who has successfully completed an accounting-bookkeeping course in high school would be most qualified for which position?
(A) Accounting clerk
(B) Junior accountant
(C) Accountant
(D) Auditor

ACCOUNTING CLERK
Area business needs an efficient general accounting clerk. Experience maintaining all journals and posting General Ledger through Trial Balance. Must be loyal, conscientious, and dedicated.

ACCOUNTANT
Growing Westchester County company seeks CPA with 1-3 years public accounting experience. Position will involve preparation, review, and research of Federal and State tax matters.

JUNIOR ACCOUNTANT
Junior accountant with bookkeeping experience. Prefer some college accounting. Full benefits including company-paid vacation, pension plan, and profit sharing.

AUDITOR
Highly visible opportunity for ambitious person. Immediate opportunity for advancement. Degree required. Prefer 2 to 3 years audit experience.

---

37. What does the abbreviation CPA represent?
(A) Certified Professional Accountant
(B) Certified Public Accountant
(C) Certified Professional Auditor
(D) Certified Public Auditor

38. Which duty would the accounting clerk NOT be expected to perform?
(A) Journalizing transactions
(B) Posting to the ledger
(C) Preparing a Trial Balance
(D) Preparing an Income Statement

39. Who is responsible for hiring workers in a business firm?
(A) A union
(B) An employment agency
(C) The board of directors
(D) The personnel department

40. What should a person do at a job interview?
(A) Take a friend along for moral support
(B) Use appropriate body language
(C) Tell the interviewer about his or her personal problems
(D) Arrive a few minutes late

41 Which information should NOT be included in a resume?
(A) Prior work experience
(B) Job position sought
(C) Pending job applications
(D) Education

42. Which is NOT considered a fringe benefit offered by the employer to the employee?
(A) Group life insurance
(B) Medical insurance
(C) Union dues
(D) Profit sharing

ANSWERS!

(1–5)   Allow a total of 5 points, 1 point for each of the following:
(1) Bramar Industries
(2) $1,250
(3) $700
(4) Accounts Payable
(5) $533.50

Allow a total of 25 points, 1 point for each of 25 of the following. If more than 25 questions are answered, rate only the first 25.

(6)4	(11)3	(16)1	(21)4	(26)3	(31)3
(7)2	(12)2	(17)3	(22)2	(27)1	(32)1
(8)3	(13)3	(18)4	(23)1	(28)2	(33)4
(9)1	(14)2	(19)4	(24)3	(29)2	(34)3
(10)1	(15)3	(20)1	(25)1	(30)4	(35)4

Allow a total of 5 points, 1 point for each of 5 of the following. If more than 5 questions are answered, rate only the first 5.

(36)1	(38)4	(40)2	(42)3
(37)2	(39)4	(41)3	

BROADCASTING

Columbia School of Broadcasting

Let's imagine that you're applying for an education or a job (or both) in that segment of the entertainment industry that calls itself Broadcasting. You are short, speak with a lateral lisp, and you have a mild facial tic. You make your pitch. You hear, in response, "The field is terribly crowded at the moment. Thanks for coming in. Don't call us. Goodbye." At that you do your best gravelly voiced imitation: "Whatever you sshay, Baby. If you need me, just whishtle." Then watch 'em bogey the whole. Be warned though, broadcasting has little patience for slow-fuse humor and, reasonably enough, can't cope with bad puns whose meager justification derives from the written word.

I f you project your personality well, and you fall within the normal range in reading and writing ability, and your speech is free of stuttering, stammering, and lisping, you might be able to work in what many consider to be a dream field—being paid for playing records, talking about sports, and the like. You don't need to have a voice that can light a gasoline-soaked rag at fifty paces. It would probably help, though, to have something more than your native charm to rely on when trying to get into the broadcasting business. You have to learn about FCC regulations, broadcast signal frequencies, and V.U. meters, not to mention spots, tags, music beds, jingles, doughnuts, segues, and voiceovers. Various schools offer courses that will teach you the requisite skills (assuming, in the case of the responsible ones, that you meet the above prerequisites—you'll have to take the reading and writing test and submit a voice recording before enrolling). In general, they offer courses not only in radio announcing, but for those of us with stammers, stutters, lisps, or other inclinations, radio/television advertising sales and commercial copywriting.

A typical Radio Announcing course consists of several sections. First, you'll polish your breathing techniques, pronunciation, and articulation. Next, you'll learn commercial delivery technique and instruction in types of commercials, timing, marking, jingles, inserts, and tags. Then, there's news gathering, interviewing, and news writing and delivery. A section on music will teach you station formats and music reports, programming, and DJ show content and delivery. A specialty report section will cover sports reports, farm reports, business and financial reports, weather reports, and traffic reports. Finally, you'll have to produce an audition tape, for which you'll need to polish your intros and outros, avoid straight segues, and generally keep your board tight and free of dead air. After passing the final review and the final written exam, you can start sending out your resume and audition tape, and hopefully, before too long, land that dream major-market broadcasting job.

Realistically, you can expect to work a midnight-to-six A.M. shift in Salt Lick, Utah, maybe performing double duty as the night janitor, before you work up to that job in a larger market—and we're still not talking morning DJ with NBC radio in New York City. However, given ambition, perseverance, and an unwavering faith in the American Dream, who knows? Maybe you could become the next generation's Larry King or Casey Kasem.

The questions that follow are from a typical broadcasting school's radio announcer final exam; 70 percent correct is considered passing.

Multiple Choice

1. A "remote" is a broadcast that
   (A) is broadcast too faintly to be easily received far away
   (B) originates from a location other than the studio
   (C) is announced early and taped in order to broadcast at a later time

2. Amplitude Modulation Stations transmit their signals by
   (A) varying the frequency of the broadcast signal
   (B) varying the strength of the broadcast signal
   (C) neither of the above methods

3. A "V.U." meter shows the operator
   (A) the line voltage at the control board
   (B) the volume of the sound being produced by the equipment
   (C) the wattage of the transmitter

4. Which of the following is NOT a good practice to follow in planning a popular music show?
   (A) Every other selection should be a current hit tune
   (B) For every slow tune played, two bright, cheery tunes should be played
   (C) Mix classical and rock-and-roll music

5. A Copy Book primarily contains
   (A) news broadcasts
   (B) the weather reports
   (C) commercials

6. When you are planning a question for a Man-on-the-Street Program, you should phrase it so that it will
   (A) express your own opinion on the subject
   (B) excite varied response from many people
   (C) do neither of these things

7. A "promo" is
   (A) a political announcement
   (B) an announcement about a new feature or about a station's program
   (C) a prerecorded program

8. Which of the following sentences offers you, as the broadcaster, the most protection from a libel suit?
   (A) John Smith, the bank robber, was caught by police as he fled from the scene of the crime
   (B) John Smith, the suspect, was caught by police as he fled from the scene of his crime
   (C) John Smith, the suspect, was caught by police as he fled from the scene of his alleged crime

9. When you place your hand on your chest to see if you can feel it vibrate, you are testing
   (A) the resonance of your delivery
   (B) the pitch of your voice
   (C) the loudness of your voice

10. "Availability" is a broadcasting term which means
    (A) that an announcer is available for work at a certain time
    (B) radio time that can be sponsored by a prospective advertiser
    (C) time that a station has available for a national network broadcast

11. On a telephone call-in program you should not
    (A) clarify a topic for a listener
    (B) place a time limit on the calls, as this inhibits those persons who wish to express their opinions
    (C) express your own opinions on the topics

12. Which of the following is NOT an advantage of Frequency Modulation stations?
    (A) They are not affected by interference noise
    (B) They can broadcast good high-fidelity sound
    (C) They are limited to line-of-sight transmission, just as television stations are

13. A "daytimer" is
    (A) a listener who listens only during the day, usually a housewife
    (B) an announcer who refuses to work the night shift
    (C) a station that is allowed to broadcast only from local sunrise to local sunset

14. "Cold Copy" is a broadcasting term used to indicate
    (A) copy which is unpracticed by an announcer and is read for the first time
    (B) copy which hasn't been used by a station in a long time
    (C) the station's log

15. It is always best, when ad-libbing,
    (A) to stick to one subject
    (B) to speak at your normal announcing speed
    (C) to do both of these things

16. Every three years the FCC requires all radio stations to renew their licenses and to
    (A) submit a complete analysis of all programs and commercials
    (B) promise to do a better job of broadcasting in the next three years
    (C) submit a complete program guide for the next three years

17. The log's most important function is to
    (A) list the announcers who are on duty for the day
    (B) list the commercials that are to be announced during each program
    (C) give the station manager an idea of what an announcer plans to do on his program

18. In order to handle a remote program interruption well, you should
    (A) always have a brief announcement explaining that there is a technical difficulty
    (B) be prepared with a substitute program that will fill what would otherwise be dead air
    (C) do both of these things

19. A tag is
    (A) a label on a record that tells how long each song is
    (B) a live announcement that follows a commercial
    (C) the closing three lines of a DJ show

20. Radio stations make money by
    (A) belonging to a national network
    (B) broadcasting local commercials
    (C) either or both of these methods

21. Which of the following types of musical programs is the rarest in the United States?
    (A) Country and western
    (B) Jazz
    (C) Rock and roll

True or False

1. _____Always announce the manufacturer of a record you play.

2. _____Beginning announcers should try to be as humorous as possible; it relaxes them.

3. _____All radio stations east of the Rockies have call letters beginning with W.

4. _____All radio stations broadcast with at least 10,000 watts of power.

ANSWERS!

78   BROADCASTING

Multiple Choice

1. B
2. B
3. B
4. C
5. C
6. B
7. B
8. C
9. A
10. B
11. C
12. C
13. C
14. A
15. C
16. A
17. B
18. C
19. B
20. C
21. B

True or False

1. F
2. F
3. F
4. F

BUILDING CONTRACTOR

American Schools

Who hasn't observed, often critically, the apparent confusion and waste that surrounds a building site while one is watching, often with apprehension, the fascinating process by which all the pieces come together at each stage of construction? If it happens to be your own house going up, those feelings are hardly trivial.

M ost states have contractor licensing boards, which administer examinations requiring a demonstration of an adequate understanding of state laws, codes, and regulations and of practical knowledge in about twenty "knowledge areas" (in the case of General Contractor) or in one of more than three dozen special fields (in the case of the specific-classification contractors licenses). These special fields range from the mundane (concrete, plumbing, painting) to the relatively arcane (mill work, acoustical, ornamental metal).

From the contractor's point of view, the advantage to having the license is that it allows one to charge more than a given amount for a given job—typically, around $300, including materials. In other words, if you don't have a license and you advertise your services as a painter, say, you wouldn't be legally permitted to charge more than $300, in the typical case, for any painting job. Obviously, that makes it hard to make a serious living. If you're a consumer, the main advantage to hiring a licensed contractor is that you're protected from the consequences of bad work by a bond the contractor has to deposit with the Contractors State License Board, so that if a General Contractor you've hired to remodel your bathroom turns your living room into a swimming pool, the cost of damages is covered. You can also arrange to have a licensed contractor obtain a payment and completion bond so that, if the contractor is unable to complete the work or the job goes sour, bonding company funds will be available to finish the work and pay the bills. Also, of course, the license is intended to be a confirmation of the builder's skill and knowledge, so the chances of bad workmanship are reduced.

The questions that follow are from the American Schools home study courses, which prepare people to pass the General Building Contractor License and about twenty other classification exams in the state of California.

Steel Reinforcing

1. What is the smallest size of rebar used in a single-story residence?
    (A) No. 1
    (B) No. 2
    (C) No. 3
    (D) No. 4

2. What are reinforcing bars primarily used for?
    (A) Absorbing tensile strength
    (B) Absorbing compressive strength
    (C) Supporting underground utility conduits
    (D) None of the above

3. At what depth should anchor bolts be placed in residential concrete footing?
    (A) 3 inches
    (B) 6 inches
    (C) 9 inches
    (D) 12 inches

Concrete

1. The best method of placing concrete under water is
    (A) sacked concrete
    (B) gunite
    (C) tremie pouring
    (D) none of the above

2. The most suitable condition for pouring concrete under water is
    (A) when water temperature is under 45 degrees F
    (B) when water is flowing with a velocity greater than 10 feet per minute
    (C) when water is flowing with a velocity less than 10 feet per minute
    (D) onto a sloped underwater surface

3. A cleat is a
    (A) device for spacing the sides of a form when pouring a concrete footing
    (B) a device used between units of a structure
    (C) a post or column extending into and above the ground and supporting a structural member of a building
    (D) none of the above

4. Honeycombing can occur when
    (A) the forms are not tight
    (B) the concrete separates
    (C) the concrete has not been consolidated
    (D) all of the above

Drywall Construction

1. The vertical and horizontal angles in a steel soffit assembly should be
    (A) horizontal, straight, and level
    (B) level, parallel, and plumb
    (C) straight, level, and plumb
    (D) parallel, vertical, and level

2. The metal screw-on stud wall system has only three major components; studs, track, and
    (A) partition
    (B) soffit
    (C) framing
    (D) gypsum

Electrical

1. What type of thermostat is normally used for controlling the air-conditioning unit in a residence?
    (A) Zero stage
    (B) One stage
    (C) Two stage
    (D) Three stage

2. Proper color codes for identifying conductors in a 220-v circuit are
   (A) white or gray and any other color combination
   (B) black or green and any other color combination
   (C) blue or red and any other color combination
   (D) yellow or red and any other color combination

3. Romex cable that is approved for underground work is classified as
   (A) UF
   (B) HSE
   (C) MTW
   (D) SD

Earthwork and Paving

1. Concrete paving costs are usually expressed in
   (A) square feet
   (B) square yards
   (C) linear feet
   (D) linear yards

2. A sack of cement
   (A) weighs 94 pounds
   (B) weights 376 pounds
   (C) contains 1 cubic foot
   (D) A and C

3. Two-thirds cubic yard of fine aggregate, mixed with 2 cubic yards of coarse aggregate with 33⅓% voids, yields _____ of mixed aggregate.
   (A) 1⅓ cubic yards
   (B) 2 cubic yards
   (C) 2⅓ cubic yards
   (D) 2⅔ cubic yards

4. A _____ is one part cement, two parts sand, and three parts coarse aggregate.
   (A) lean mix
   (B) medium mix
   (C) rich mix
   (D) none of these

5. When the water-cement ratio is high, the strength of the concrete is
   (A) high
   (B) low
   (C) unaffected
   (D) none of the above

Carpet

1. Pile made of wool or synthetic fibers that is machine-stitched into a backing made beforehand is
   (A) tufted
   (B) woven
   (C) punched
   (D) none of the above

2. Which factors must be taken into account when planning the layout of a carpet in a room?
   (A) Pile direction
   (B) Run the longest seam in the room toward the major light source
   (C) Keep seams away from high traffic areas
   (D) All of the above

3. Which of the following should be done prior to beginning a carpet re-installation?
   (A) Remove grilles from heating vents
   (B) Nail uneven boards
   (C) Sweep the floor
   (D) All of the above

Windows and Doors

1. Why should putty be applied with adequate pressure to complete the facing operation on the first pass of the putty knife?
   (A) To prevent the putty from falling from the rabbet
   (B) To conserve on putty
   (C) To ensure a cleaner job
   (D) Because the putty will become increasingly difficult to handle with each subsequent pass

2. If the rubber channel is stretched too far while installing a sliding sash,
   (A) runs may develop in the glass
   (B) the glass may shift in the frame
   (C) water can enter through the rubber channel
   (D) the frame may bow

3. Which of the following is the most important factor to remember regarding glazing sliding windows?
   (A) You must allow for expansion of the glass
   (B) Your measurements must accommodate the pull hardware
   (C) All measurements must be accurate
   (D) The light should be free of distortions

4. Under which conditions will putty not stick to a sash?
   (A) If the sash is too warm
   (B) If the sash is bowed or warped
   (C) If the sash is greasy or dirty
   (D) None of the above

5. Which stop does the glazier apply first when installing glass into a wood sash with stops?
   (A) Top
   (B) Right
   (C) Bottom
   (D) Left

Heating, Ventilating, and Air Conditioning

1. How many fans are required to provide proper airflow through a 240,000-cubic-foot building if building requirements state that the air must be replenished four times an hour? Each fan moves 2,000 cubic feet per minute.
   (A) 6
   (B) 8
   (C) 10
   (D) 12

2. Internal heat can be best maintained during the winter by installing the smallest number of regular single glass windows on which side(s) of a residence?
   (A) North
   (B) South
   (C) East or west
   (D) Northeast or northwest

3. If a metal heating duct is exposed, it should be insulated
   (A) when it is in the attic
   (B) when it is exposed to the exterior
   (C) when it leads into a plenum
   (D) at all times

Landscape Contracting

1. The settling factor when backfilling with loam soil approximates
   (A) 5%
   (B) 12%
   (C) 25%
   (D) 35%

2. Grass-seed labels show all the following
   information except
   (A) purity
   (B) weed seed
   (C) number of seeds per pound
   (D) lot number

3. A benefit of spring-retracted heads is
   (A) a reduction in the amount of damage
       done to sprinklers by mowing equip-
       ment
   (B) greater water coverage per sprinkler
       head
   (C) lower initial cost
   (D) none of the above

Masonry

1. What is a dwarf wall?
   (A) That part of a wall from which an arch
       is suspended
   (B) The lowest part of a wall, pier, monu-
       ment or column
   (C) A wall or partition which does not
       extend to the ceiling
   (D) A projection from the face of a wall
       used to support an ornamental feature

2. What is the minimum thickness of a stone
   masonry wall?
   (A) 6 inches
   (B) 8 inches
   (C) 16 inches
   (D) 20 inches

3. Construction of natural or cast stone laid in
   mortar with all joints thoroughly filled is
   called _____ masonry.
   (A) random rubble stone
   (B) coursed rubble stone
   (C) stone
   (D) all of the above

4. What is a frog and what is another term
   used for it?
   (A) A section of a wall built up and
       racked back on successive courses at
       the corners of a wall, also called a
       lead
   (B) A fragment or chip of stone or brick,
       especially bad or broken brick, also
       called a gallet
   (C) A depression in the bed surface of a
       brick, also called a panel
   (D) None of the above

Painting and Decorating

1. What should be painted first when painting
   a room?
   (A) Walls
   (B) Windowsills
   (C) Trim and mouldings
   (D) Ceilings

2. The best paint for kitchen walls is
   (A) semi-gloss
   (B) flat latex
   (C) oil-base flat
   (D) polyurethane

3. When cleaning a latex brush, it is best to
   use
   (A) alcohol
   (B) gasoline
   (C) water
   (D) turpentine

4. Prior to papering new plaster walls, they
   must be
   (A) coated with wallpaper paste
   (B) sandpapered
   (C) coated with wall sizing
   (D) washed with water and detergent

Plastering

1. Which of the following materials cannot have portland cement plaster applied directly over it?
    (A) Gypsum masonry
    (B) Gypsum plaster
    (C) Gypsum lath
    (D) All of the above

2. What is the minimum number of inches above the grade with which one can place weep screeds?
    (A) 1 inch
    (B) 3 inches
    (C) 6 inches
    (D) 12 inches

Structural Steel

1. Which of the following is a method for binding metal together with heat?
    (A) Fission
    (B) Compression
    (C) Combustion
    (D) None of the above

2. What is the name of a material that will dissolve oxides on a surface, leaving it clean?
    (A) Flux
    (B) Rubbing compound
    (C) Pantothenic acid
    (D) None of the above

3. Which of the following is a type of rivet used in steel framing?
    (A) Buttonheads
    (B) Knuckleheads
    (C) Countersunk
    (D) Both A and C

Solar

1. A solar heating system that depends on mechanical devices to move and distribute the sun's heat from the collector is called a(n)
    (A) active solar system
    (B) passive solar system
    (C) direct solar system
    (D) closed-loop solar system

2. A(n) _____ system utilizes both active and passive solar technology.
    (A) direct
    (B) indirect
    (C) hybrid
    (D) hydronic

3. A differential thermostat regulates the operation of a solar system by responding to differences in
    (A) pressure
    (B) circulation
    (C) temperature
    (D) all of the above

Electrical Signs

1. Which of the following formulas will measure the current flow in a circuit?
    (A) E times R
    (B) R times I
    (C) E divided by R
    (D) I divided by R

2. Which of the following terms is used to designate the positive pole of an electric terminal?
    (A) Cathode
    (B) Geode
    (C) Anode
    (D) None of the above

3. Which of the following terms is used to designate the negative pole of an electric terminal?
   (A) Cathode
   (B) Geode
   (C) Anode
   (D) None of the above

4. How is wattage found?
   (A) Voltage times resistance
   (B) Voltage times amperes
   (C) Resistance times amperes
   (D) Ohms times volts

Roofing

1. A good wood shingle roof is never less than _____ layer(s) thick.
   (A) one
   (B) two
   (C) three
   (D) four

2. Which type of new roof does not require a felt underlay?
   (A) Wood shingle
   (B) Asphalt strip shingle
   (C) Gravel
   (D) Fiberglass shingle

3. When the shingles are woven or laced back and forth, forming the valley, it is a
   (A) closed valley
   (B) full-lace valley
   (C) half-lace valley
   (D) smooth valley

Plumbing

1. A DWV piping system is a
   (A) drain, water, and vent system which empties into a sewer, septic tank, cesspool, or lagoon
   (B) dynamic water, vent system which empties into a septic tank or cesspool
   (C) drain, waste, vent piping system which empties into a sewer, septic tank, cesspool, or lagoon
   (D) water supply piping which is fed by a municipally owned water main

2. Who is responsible for trenching between street connections and a building's foundation?
   (A) The city or town
   (B) The contractor or plumber
   (C) Both A and B
   (D) The owner of the building

3. Who will tap the water main, install the corporation stop, the curb stop, and the "B" box?
   (A) The building owner
   (B) City workers
   (C) The plumber or contractor
   (D) Both B and C

4. Who is responsible for opening up the sewer main and for installing the sleeve connector and the lateral line to the building?
   (A) The sewer department
   (B) The building owner
   (C) The city workers
   (D) The plumber

Safety

1. Which of the following is not a recom-
    mended practice for someone who is han-
    dling epoxies and mastics?
    (A) Do not use in a room with an open
        flame
    (B) Use water to wash off any spills on
        the hands
    (C) Use only in rooms that are tightly
        closed
    (D) Read the label before using

2. Which one of the following is not a recom-
    mended safety measure to be followed
    when electrical equipment is being used?
    (A) Ground all electrical tools
    (B) While they are in use, keep extension
        cords looped over nails
    (C) Use only heavy-duty extension cords
    (D) If the supporting surface is wet, wear
        rubber-soled shoes

3. If someone working nearby should come
    into contact with a live power wire, the
    very first thing that should be done is
    (A) try to shake the person
    (B) turn off the power
    (C) administer first aid
    (D) pull the person off the wire without
        contacting either the person or the
        energized object

4. What must an employer do prior to starting
    work on a job that involves substantial risk
    to employees?
    (A) Rope off the danger area
    (B) Install scaffolding
    (C) Obtain a project permit from the Divi-
        sion of Occupational Safety and
        Health
    (D) Place warning signs around the project

ANSWERS!☞

Steel Reinforcing
1. D
2. A
3. B

Concrete
1. C
2. C
3. A
4. D

Drywall Construction
1. C
2. D

Electrical
1. C
2. A
3. A

Earthwork and Paving
1. A
2. D
3. B
4. C
5. B

Carpet
1. A
2. D
3. D

Glazing
1. A
2. C
3. C
4. C
5. A

Heating, Ventilating and Air Conditioning
1. B
2. A
3. D

Landscape Contractor
1. B
2. C
3. A

Masonry
1. C
2. C
3. D
4. C

Painting and Decorating
1. D
2. A
3. C
4. C

Plastering
1. C
2. C

Structural Steel
1. B
2. A
3. D

Solar
1. A
2. C
3. C

Electrical Signs
1. C
2. C
3. A
4. B

Roofing
1. C
2. A
3. B

Plumbing
1. C
2. B
3. B
4. D

Safety
1. C
2. B
3. D
4. C

BUSINESS ETHICS

MBA Students
vs. Prison Inmates

You're walking behind two young men in business suits on a crowded city sidewalk. You hear this comment pass between them:

"I'm assigned to the boss's son. He's a great business getter, but not a very good accountant. The trouble is, before I learn how to be a crook, I'd like to learn how to do things right."*

Your reaction is to:

(A) Cross quickly to the other side of the street.

(B) Grab the young man by the collar and give him a stern lecture on ethics.

(C) Catch up to the young man and congratulate him on his drive and ambition.

*Paraphrase of actual comment overheard by a *New York Times* reader, as reported in the "Metropolitan Diary" column 3/28/99.

I t seems that the ethics of the business community is always making news for one reason or another, more often bad than good. A study published in 1998 by marketing professors Shaheen Borna of Ball State University and James Stearns of Miami University found the ethical integrity of MBA students to be comparable to that of convicted felons. In fact, the felons showed more concern for consumer safety than the business students, but also tended towards greater loyalty to their own employer. The authors of the study chose to portray their findings as proof that felons should be given a second chance in the business world. None of the MBA students interviewed were from Ball State or Miami's MBA program. (Among the MBA programs whose students *were* included in the interviews are Harvard, Berkeley, Michigan, and Duke.)

Not too long ago, many researchers were hopeful that business ethics would improve as more women rose to positions of responsibility in the work force. Does this reflect a common belief that women are more ethical than men? According to some studies, yes. Several researchers have independently adduced evidence that women show stronger ethics in their evaluations of hypothetical situations of the sort that might arise in a business environment. While other studies have shown no difference between men and women, almost none have shown women to be *less* ethical.

From yet another perspective, some researchers have pointed out that "ethical" men tend to adjudicate situations from the standpoint that ethical rules are abstract concepts that should apply equally to everyone, while "ethical" women are more likely to analyze the details of the particular situation, and to weigh specific potential harm against specific potential benefit to the individuals involved. "Ethical behavior" is a slippery concept.

In the recent study mentioned above, Stearns and Borna presented inmates in three minimum-security prisons in the Midwest with the ethical issues contained in the questions on the pages that follow. Those were the same questions posed ten years earlier by Thomas Jones and Frederick Gautschi as part of a study of students in business programs at a dozen universities. In their answers to the questions posed in Jones and Gautschi's study, women MBA students were slightly less likely than men simply to do as ordered in ethically difficult situations, and more willing to resign in protest; in the Stearns and Borna study, 90% of the respondents were men, so statistically significant comparisons are difficult. The answer section compares the way MBA students and inmates responded.

I. Ranking of ethical priorities

1. The following is a list of ethical issues categories that have been discussed in the popular and/or business press. By checking the appropriate box, indicate how much attention *you* feel that the business community should give to each of the issue categories.

	A Great Deal of Attention	Considerable Attention	Some Attention	Little Attention	No Attention
(A) Product information disclosure to consumers	[ ]	[ ]	[ ]	[ ]	[ ]
(B) Information disclosure regarding operations to stockholders	[ ]	[ ]	[ ]	[ ]	[ ]
(C) Minority hiring and promotions	[ ]	[ ]	[ ]	[ ]	[ ]
(D) Comparable worth for employees	[ ]	[ ]	[ ]	[ ]	[ ]
(E) Arbitrary employee discharges	[ ]	[ ]	[ ]	[ ]	[ ]
(F) Product quality	[ ]	[ ]	[ ]	[ ]	[ ]
(G) Product safety	[ ]	[ ]	[ ]	[ ]	[ ]
(H) Firms' relations with foreign governments	[ ]	[ ]	[ ]	[ ]	[ ]
(I) Community relations	[ ]	[ ]	[ ]	[ ]	[ ]
(J) Rights of employees to disclose company wrongdoing	[ ]	[ ]	[ ]	[ ]	[ ]
(K) Bribery of government officials	[ ]	[ ]	[ ]	[ ]	[ ]
(L) Executive compensation	[ ]	[ ]	[ ]	[ ]	[ ]
(M) Plant closures	[ ]	[ ]	[ ]	[ ]	[ ]

2. Publicly-held firms are required by law to give primacy to the financial interests of their stockholders. Below is a list of various corporate constituencies/stakeholder groups. Putting aside the apparent legal mandate, please indicate by ranking the groups the order in which constituency interests *ought* to be served by the firm. (A rank of 1 indicates first place for the affected group.)

[ ] Stockholders
[ ] Society-at-large
[ ] The local community in which the firm operates
[ ] Neighbors in close proximity to the firm's operations
[ ] Customers
[ ] Employees
[ ] Governmental agencies
[ ] Suppliers

II. Hypothetical situations posing ethical dilemmas

3. Mr. Stern is a long-time, faithful employee of your company. He works in the sales department of the computer test equipment division, where his job is to locate used test equipment that hi-tech companies are willing to part with, negotiate a price, and pass the equipment on to the engineering department for refurbishment and resale.

Mr. Stern used to be one of your company's top sales executives, but lately his productivity has been slipping. For the last two years, his monthly commissions have been lower than those of most of the younger account executives in the sales department, lower even than some of the brand-new sales employees. Part of the problem may be that at his age — 62 — Mr. Stern just might not relate very well to the young computer engineers in the hi-tech companies he's dealing with. His territory also has a fair amount of ethnic diversity, and it might not be a bad idea to add more minority members to the sales department staff. (Mr. Stern is white.) While he is still a faithful and diligent employee, the feeling among upper management is that Mr. Stern is no longer worth his base salary.

What would you do if you were told by your superior to pressure Mr. Stern into early retirement in order to:

i. make room for a younger employee
ii. make room for a member of a minority race, or
iii. save the firm the cost of full benefits?

i. (A) Just do it.
   (B) Object, but still do it.
   (C) Transfer or demote the employee, but don't fire him.
   (D) Suggest early retirement to the employee, but don't pressure him.
   (E) Just don't do it — it's not right.
   (F) Just don't do it — it's not my job, or there might be legal problems.

ii. (A) Just do it.
   (B) Object, but still do it.
   (C) Transfer or demote the employee, but don't fire him.
   (D) Suggest early retirement to the employee, but don't pressure him.
   (E) Just don't do it — it's not right.
   (F) Just don't do it — it's not my job, or there might be legal problems..

iii. (A) Just do it.
   (B) Object, but still do it.
   (C) Transfer or demote the employee, but don't fire him.
   (D) Suggest early retirement to the employee, but don't pressure him.
   (E) Just don't do it — it's not right.
   (F) Just don't do it — it's not my job, or there might be legal problems..

4. Imagine that you are the president of Eubotics, a firm in the highly competitive biotechnology industry. One of your most profitable products is an easily-grown weed that has been genetically engineered to produce a plastic polymer usable for products like beverage containers, egg cartons, and candy packages. While you don't sell the plastic product cheaply, many companies have been buying it because of its environmental advantages — it is renewable, "natural," and even decomposes within about five years.

You have just learned, however, that another company has made an important scientific discovery that will substantially reduce your profit, in the short run at least. NeoBio, one of your main competitors, has developed a technique for altering the chemical structure of ordinary, easily-grown plant products, like wood, leaves, and grasses, into a plastic polymer virtually identical to the one produced by your plastic-producing weed.

You have also learned of the possibility of hiring one of the competitor's employees who knows the details of the discovery. With her help, you think you might be able to adapt NeoBio's conversion technique and help you reduce the threat of market share loss and loss of profit. What would you choose to do?
(A) Hire her.
(B) Hire her, if legal.
(C) Hire, if profitable.
(D) Don't hire; increase R&D instead.
(E) Wait and monitor the competition.
(F) Depends on industry practice.

5. What would you do if, in the previous situation, the employee, an engineer with five years of experience, was asking a guaranteed annual salary of $100,000?
(A) Hire her.
(B) Hire her, if profitable.

(C) Hire her, if the salary is competitive.
(D) Don't hire — her loyalty is questionable.
(E) Just don't hire her.

6. Suppose that you, a middle-level executive, discovered that one of your company's executives had given false testimony before a governmental agency, and that there appeared to be no action forthcoming by top management to deal with the situation. What action, if any, would you take?
(A) Do nothing.
(B) Discuss the issue confidentially with a superior.
(C) Pressure the executive to come clean and expose him if necessary, or disclose the information to an outside party.
(D) Resign.

7. Suppose that you, (i) as president of the company, (ii) as a middle manager, (iii) as an entry-level manager, discovered an unexpected flaw in one of your company's products. The product is a mechanical tree-trimming device with a safety guard that can jiggle loose with the vibration of the motor. While any such tool has inherent dangers, you have determined that if the product were to be marketed, a higher-than-expected incidence of injuries to consumers would result. What action would you take?

i. (A) Do as ordered, or stop production only if profitable.
(B) Inform your superiors or lobby for production halt.
(C) Try indirectly to halt production, perhaps by publicizing the issue.
(D) Stop production.
(E) Resign.

ii. (A) Do as ordered, or stop production only if profitable.
(B) Inform your superiors or lobby for production halt.

(C) Try indirectly to halt production, perhaps by publicizing the issue.

(D) Stop production.

(E) Resign.

iii. (A) Do as ordered, or stop production only
if profitable.

(B) Inform your superiors or lobby for
production halt.

(C) Try indirectly to halt production, perhaps by publicizing the issue.

(D) Stop production.

(E) Resign.

8. The furniture-manufacturing company you
work for specializes in collapsible beds
and tables that are very popular among
apartment-dwellers, since the furniture can
be folded up when not being used, thus
conserving space. The collapsible furniture
line is also popular, of course, among other
people who live in crowded conditions,
such as young families living in small,
affordable "starter" homes.

Suppose that a governmental agency
ordered your company to withdraw a
highly profitable product from the U.S.
market because of safety concerns. Stealth-
Dozer, one of your strongest-selling collapsible beds, has been reported have fold-
ing parts that might close unexpectedly on
a sleeper's fingers, causing injury. You, as
a middle-level manager, learn that top
management has decided to sell the product to the government of an African nation
for use in crowded state-run hospitals,
shelters, dormitories, and military barracks. What action would you take?

(A) Do nothing.

(B) Voice opposition through internal
channels, for example by discussing it
with top management.

(C) Inform the government, or leak it to an
outsider, or question the sale publicly.

(D) Resign in protest.

9. Suppose that you as an entry-level manager
were given access to confidential information that, if disclosed, would show your
company to be engaging in what would
obviously be judged by the public as
unethical behavior. Specifically, through
some highly creative accounting, your
company has been lowering its overhead
by availing itself of certain utilities subsi-
dies that were intended to benefit low-
income families. What action would you
take?

(A) Do nothing.

(B) Talk to a superior, and try to correct
the problem in-house.

(C) Leak the information to an outsider or
disclose it publicly.

(D) Resign.

10. Suppose that as a member of a board of
directors you learned that the chairman of
the board and the CEO had made an illegal contribution of company money to a
recent presidential candidate. The contribution appears to have been given in
exchange for future government contracts.
What would you do?

(A) Do nothing.

(B) Confront the issue internally, either
directly with him or in a closed meeting.

(C) Expose him publicly, by leaking or
publicizing the information.

(D) Resign.

ANSWERS!

I. Ranking of ethical priorities

1. (Importance of ethical issues categories.)

This answer table presents the responses of MBA students and inmates, respectively. Responses are given as a mean and a rank. The "mean response" is calculated by assigning a value of 1 point to a response of "A Great Deal of Attention," 2 points to "Considerable Attention," and so on, down to 5 points for "No Attention." So a mean response of 2 would indicate that the average response for that group was that the issue deserved "Considerable Attention." A rank of 1 indicates that that issue was considered most worthy of attention by that group, while a rank of 13 indicates that that issue was deemed of least importance, and so on.

	MBA Students Mean Response	Rank	Inmates Mean Response	Rank
(A) Product information disclosure to consumers	1.75	3	1.55	2
(B) Information disclosure regarding operations to stockholders	2.148	6	2.63	10
(C) Minority hiring and promotions	2.51	11	2.57	9
(D) Comparable worth for employees	2.97	13	2.55	8
(E) Arbitrary employee discharges	2.48	9	2.37	7
(F) Product quality	1.52	2	1.64	3
(G) Product safety	1.32	1	1.27	1
(H) Firms' relations with foreign governments	2.48	10	2.64	11
(I) Community relations	2.23	7	2.23	6
(J) Rights of employees to disclose company wrongdoing	2.145	5	2.76	12
(K) Bribery of government officials	2.05	4	2.14	4
(L) Executive compensation	2.70	12	2.86	13
(M) Plant closures	2.36	8	2.18	5

2. (Importance of corporate constituencies/stakeholder groups.)

	MBA Students Mean Response	Rank	Inmates Mean Response	Rank
Stockholders	2.44	1	3.12	3
Customers	2.56	2	1.98	1
Employees	2.75	3	2.30	2
Society-at-large	4.82	4	4.12	5
Local community	4.83	5	3.89	4
Neighbors	5.53	6	4.51	6
Suppliers	6.05	7	6.71	7
Governmental agencies	6.81	8	7.82	8

II. Hypothetical situations posing ethical dilemmas

All answers in this subsection are expressed as a percent response by MBA students and inmates respectively. Where the numbers don't add up to 100, other options such as "don't know" were chosen.

3. (Firing a 62-year-old employee.)

MBA Students	Inmates
i. (A) 22.5	(A) 46.3
(B) 3.0	(B) 9.1
(C) 18.6	(C) 10.6
(D) 26.4	(D) 20.3
(E) 15.4	(E) 4.5
(F) 7.6	(F) 4.5

MBA Students	Inmates
ii. (A) 19.1	(A) 23.2
(B) 2.8	(B) 11.7
(C) 17.5	(C) 11.1
(D) 25	(D) 31.1
(E) 19.8	(E) 13.6
(F) 8.7	(F) 4.6

MBA Students	Inmates
iii. (A) 14.9	(A) 13.6
(B) 3.4	(B) 4.5
(C) 17.0	(C) 9.1
(D) 20.5	(D) 31.8
(E) 25.5	(E) 25.2
(F) 9.2	(F) 11.1

Comments: Inmates were more likely to do what was asked of them, a loyalty-oriented response pattern that showed itself throughout most of the questionnaire. Both students and inmates were more likely to agree to fire the employee if the reason was to make room for a younger employee, rather than to make room for a minority employee or just to save money.

4. (Hiring a competitor's employee.)

MBA Students	Inmates
(A) 55.0	(A) 40.9
(B) 17.5	(B) 18.2
(C) 4.0	(C) 0
(D) 7.5	(D) 0
(E) 2.0	(E) 13.6
(F) 0.4	(F) 13.6

5. (Hiring the competitor's employee with a five year/$500,00 guarantee.)

MBA Students	Inmates
(A) 7.9	(A) 18.2
(B) 42.9	(B) 36.4
(C) 11.3	(C) 22.1
(D) 3.6	(D) 14.1
(E) 26.6	(E) 9.1

Comments: The inmates' overall greater loyalty than the MBA students' showed itself as a much greater reluctance to hire the employee, since the employee's willingness to sell his services to the highest bidder would indicate disloyalty to her own prior employer (option D).

6. (False testimony given by a company executive to a government agency.)

MBA Students	Inmates
(A) 28.3	(A) 75.8
(B) 22.9	(B) 20.8
(C) 21.1	(C) 1.6
(D) 6.6	(D) 2.1

Comments: More dramatically than in any of the other situations, the inmates' sense of loyalty held sway here. Authors Stearns and Borna speculate that the incarcerated felons may have harbored "significant animosity" toward the government: "Inmates evidently found it difficult to help the government while giving up loyalty to an employer."

7. (Product flaw causes injuries.)

	MBA Students	Inmates
i.	(A) 3.1	(A) 3.5
	(B) 5.9	(B) 27.3
	(C) 0.7	(C) 31.8
	(D) 88.1	(D) 36.4
	(E) 0.5	(E) 0.0
ii.	(A) 2.5	(A) 4.5
	(B) 57.3	(B) 59.1
	(C) 3.8	(C) 18.2
	(D) 32.6	(D) 18.2
	(E) 2.7	(E) 0.0
iii.	(A) 3.0	(A) 6.6
	(B) 58.3	(B) 63.6
	(C) 4.1	(C) 13.6
	(D) 29.9	(D) 13.6
	(E) 3.4	(E) 0.0

8. (Unsafe product sold to African nation.)

MBA Students	Inmates
(A) 23.2	(A) 59.8
(B) 22.5	(B) 10.7
(C) 19.6	(C) 9.7
(D) 11.5	(D) 0.0

9. (Discover confidential information showing your company in a bad light.)

MBA Students	Inmates
(A) 22.0	(A) 53.5
(B) 25.7	(B) 15.4
(C) 22.0	(C) 5.4
(D) 28.1	(D) 5.2

Comments: Again, the inmates' loyalty showed itself clearly.

10. (Chairman and CEO made illegal political contribution.)

MBA Students	Inmates
(A) 26.2	(A) 39.3
(B) 38.6	(B) 20.7
(C) 16.6	(C) 16.0
(D) 6.7	(D) 12.0

Comments: One thing that's noteworthy here is the percent of inmates who said they would respond to the situation by resigning (option D). Stearns and Borna speculate that this response once again "raises the possibility that government involvement somehow changes inmate perceptions of the ethics of situations."

CITIZEN OF THE UNITED STATES

U. S. Department of Immigration & Naturalization

*Had you not been born a citizen of the United States,
could you have become one if that privilege depended
on your answering these fifteen questions accurately?*

The law states that all those who seek naturalization as U.S. citizens must have "knowledge and understanding of the fundamentals of the history, and of the principles and form of government, of the United States." Thus, all applicants for citizenship are questioned orally on their knowledge of U.S. history and government. Usually, the questions are fairly simple, like the first few below. However, since the theoretical purpose of the citizenship test is to ensure that applicants will have the knowledge necessary to become responsible citizens and voters, and since one can never be sure exactly what the naturalization examiner will ask, applicants are urged to prepare themselves in greater depth than the questions on the citizenship test will probably require. Most of the questions below are therefore more difficult than those usually asked on the test. It is generally assumed, though, that questions of this level of difficulty require knowledge that anyone who understands the fundamentals of U.S. history and government—that is, any good citizen—should have.

1. When was the Constitution adopted?

2. What are the first ten amendments to the Constitution called?

3. What are some of the things that the Bill of Rights guarantees?

4. The national government is empowered to provide for the national defense. What are some of its other powers?

5. The President is voted for by the people of the United States, but directly elected by the electors. Who are the electors?

6. In a presidential election, what happens if no candidate receives a majority of the electoral vote?

7. What are some of the President's powers and duties?

8. What are the twelve Executive Departments whose heads are members of the Cabinet?

9. What wars has the United States fought since the Civil War?

10. Can a communist become a U.S. citizen?

11. How many U. S. Presidents have been killed in office, and who were they?

12. Two Presidents have been elected by the House of Representatives. Who were they?

13. Only one U.S. President has ever been impeached. Who was he?

14. The Senate has some powers that the House of Representatives does not have. What are they?

15. What powers does the House of Representatives have that the Senate does not have?

ANSWERS!

(See pages 108 - 109)

VOTER LITERACY

Before passage of the Voting Rights Act in 1965, the constitutions of seven Southern states had "educational" requirements which were specifically designed to prevent black citizens from exercising their right to vote. These requirements sanctioned the use of various kinds of literacy and constitutional interpretation tests to determine whether or not to enter an individual's name in the voter registration lists.

In 1898 the Louisiana legislature held a constitutional convention whose primary concern was, in the words of one of the delegates, to alter the state constitution in such a way as to "disfranchise as many Negroes and as few whites as possible." Because of these changes in the state constitution, the number of blacks registered to vote in Louisiana between the years of 1910 and 1944 never exceeded one percent of those potentially qualified to vote. After World War II, heightened determination on the part of black servicemen to exercise their voting rights and an increase in black literacy, among other factors, led to a dramatic increase in black registration. By 1954, the proportion of the voting-age black population registered had risen to 27 percent.

In response to this trend, the Louisiana legislature established the Joint Legislative Committee in 1954 "to provide ways and means whereby our existing social order shall be preserved and our institutions and way of life ... maintained"—in other words, to preserve a racially segregated society.

Thus began a period of revitalized discrimination against blacks in the voting process. The arbitrariness of the methods used during this period was unprecedented by anything in post-Reconstruction times. Precinct registrars used two kinds of test as instruments for justifying denial of registration to blacks. A registration form, called an "LR–1"—an "Application for Registration" form requiring information on birth, occupation, residence, and so on—was used as a kind of test to exclude black applicants who filled it out, and a constitutional interpretation test was used to show that black applicants had inadequate knowledge of the state constitution. Registrars who failed to use these tests to exclude blacks from the voting process changed their ways or were removed from office.

From testimony given at U. S. Commission on Civil Rights hearings in the early 1960s, it is clear that the registrars had complete freedom to reject any black's answer as "incorrect." Often, black applicants were given no grounds for rejection of their registration application; at most, they were simply informed that they had made an unspecified error in filling out the LR–1 form, or that their constitutional interpretations were not acceptable. The LR–1 form and the constitutional interpretation test gave an illusion of fairness and objectivity to whites' racially motivated discrimination.

Below we have included sample constitutional interpretation questions and sample questions asked by the precinct registrar in Franklin County, North Carolina, another state with discriminatory voting laws. For those, our research has unearthed no sample answers, but it is plain to see that they are classic examples of questions that elicit answers that the questioner an always claim are "wrong."

Test of Constitutional Interpretation

The following are examples of the kind of passages applicants were required to interpret:

"Nor shall any state deprive a person of life, liberty, or property, without due process of law." "Any person may speak, write, and publish his sentiments on all subjects, being responsible for the abuse of that liberty."

"No person shall be compelled to give evidence against himself in a criminal case."

"No law shall be passed to curtail or restrain the liberty of speech or of the press."

In practice, registrars usually allowed white applicants to skip this stage of the registration process. When black applicants were told that their interpretation was not acceptable, they were rarely told why. Conversely, it seems that any interpretation by a white applicant, in those cases when whites were asked to interpret a passage, would be deemed acceptable by the registrar. For example, one accepted white applicant interpreted the passage about liberty of speech by scrawling "I Agree" on the card the passage was printed on. Another interpreted the other passage on freedom of speech to mean, "Spoken in Right, and Public."

Finally, here are the questions that the registrar in Franklin County, North Carolina, decided black applicants did not answer to her satisfaction:

"What does 'create' mean?"

"Who was the Creator?"

"Do you know how you were born?"

"Are all people born alike?"

"Was I born like Queen Elizabeth?"

"When God made you and Eisenhower, did He make both of you the same?"

The Notorious LR-1 Form

One black applicant testified that a registrar had rejected his form because he had underlined "Mr." when, according to the registrar, he should have circled it. His testimony was contradicted by the registrar, who claimed that the grounds for rejection of the application were misspellings of two words, "October" and "Democratic." She declined, however, to produce the form as evidence that the applicant had indeed made those errors.

Another commonly cited reason for refusal of an application was incorrect computation of age. Note that the form requires the applicant to state his or her exact age in years, months, and days. (There seemed to be disagreement among registrars as to whether the day on which the application was filed was to be included in the computation.) The definition of an "error" in the computation was left completely up to the registrar. But all the registrars who gave testimony at the Commission on Civil Rights hearings agreed that any "error" (however it be defined) in the computation of age would require denial of registration. Thus, it is interesting that one registrar who was called before the commission to give a step-by-step demonstration of how to fill out an LR–1 erred in her age computation by almost a month. Even if all the information was correctly supplied on the form, a registrar could reject the applicant if certain entries were transposed: for example, if the county name was put in the "state" space, and the state in the "county" space, or if the day and month were similarly transposed.

APPLICATION FOR REGISTRATION FORM
OFFICE OF REGISTRAR OF VOTERS

Ward No._____

Prect. No._____

Parish of_____State of Louisiana   Cert. No._____

I am a citizen of the United States and of the State of Louisiana.

My name is Mr.—Mrs.—Miss_____I was born in the

State (or country) of_____, Parish (or county) of_____, on the_____day of

_____, in the year_____ I am now_____years,_____months and_____days of age. I have resided in

this State since_____, in this Parish since_____, and in Precinct No._____,

in Ward No._____of this Parish continuously since_____ I am not disfranchised by any provisions of the

Constitution of this State. The name of the householder at my present address is_____

My occupation is_____My color is_____My sex is_____I am not now registered as a voter

in any other Ward or Precinct of this State, except_____ My last registration was in Ward_____

Precinct_____Parish_____ I am now affiliated with the_____Party.

In each of the following items the applicant shall mark through the word "have" or the words "have not" so that each item will show a true statement about the applicant:

I have (have not) been convicted of a felony without receiving a full pardon and restoration of franchise.

I have (have not) been convicted of more than one misdemeanor and sentenced to a term of ninety (90) days or more in jail for each such conviction, other than traffic and/or game law violations, within five years before the date of making this application for registration as an elector.

I have (have not) been convicted of any misdemeanor and sentenced to a term of six (6) months or more in jail, other than traffic and/or game law violations, within one year before the date of making this application for registration as an elector.

I have (have not) lived with another in "common law" marriage within five years before the date of making this application for registration as an elector.

TURN CARD OVER

I have (have not) given birth to an illegitimate child within five years before the date of making this application for registration as an elector. (The provisions hereof shall not apply to the birth of any illegitimate child conceived as a consequence of rape or forced carnal knowledge.)

I have (have not) acknowledged myself to be the father of an illegitimate child within five years before the date of making this application for registration as an elector.

Signature_____

Sworn to and subscribed before me:_____

(Deputy) Registrar

CHANGE OF ADDRESS

Date_____Address_____Ward No._____Prect. No._____Cert. No._____

Date_____Address_____Ward No._____Prect. No._____Cert. No._____

CHANGE OF NAME

I am now Mr.—Mrs.—Miss_____Date of change_____

Nature of change_____

REMARKS

_____

_____

The following information forms no part of the application but is for use of the registration records:

Parish of_____, State of Louisiana.   Date_____, 19_____

Address_____ Color of eyes_____

Mother's first or maiden name_____ Name of employer_____

Property owner_____ Tenant_____ Boarder_____

1. It was drafted and signed September 17, 1787, by the Continental Congress, and then submitted to the thirteen states for ratification. Rhode Island was the last state to sign it, in 1790.

2. The Bill of Rights. These amendments were proposed by Congress in 1789 and adopted in 1791.

3. The right to a fair trial freedom of speech and, of the press, religious freedom, and the right to peaceable assembly.

4. To make treaties with other countries, to regulate immigration, to regulate commerce abroad and between states, to coin money, to establish post offices, and to provide for the general welfare.

5. 'They are people appointed by each political party in each state who have pledged to vote for their party's candidate for President. Now, it is a strictly honorary position, but it used to be that the electors were supposed to exercise their own judgment in deciding whom to vote for as President.

6. The House of Representatives elects the President from among the three candidates receiving the most votes.

7. To see that the laws are faithfully executed, to approve or veto bills passed by Congress, to appoint federal judges, ambassadors, and Department heads. to make treaties with foreign governments, and to be Commander in Chief of the armed forces.

8. Department of State, Department of the Treasury, Department of Defense Department of Justice, U. S. Postal Service, Department of the Interior, Department of Agriculture, Department of Commerce, Department of Labor, Department of Health, Education and Welfare, Department of Housing and Urban Development, Department of Transportation

9. The Spanish American War, World War I, World War ll, the Korean War, and, unofficially. the Vietnam War.

10. No. There is a law specifically preventing anyone who is a member of a communist party from being naturalized as a citizen of the United States.

11. Four. Abraham Lincoln, James A. Garfield, William McKinley, and John F. Kennedy.

12. Thomas Jefferson and John Quincy Adams.

13. Andrew Johnson. However, he was later acquitted.

14. The Senate elects a Vice-President of the United States in case the electors fail to elect one the Senate tries cases of impeachment, the Senate must give its consent to treaties, and the Senate must approve the President's appointment of Cabinet members, federal judges, and ambassadors.

15. To impeach (but not try) Federal Government officials, to elect the President of the United States if no candidate receives a majority of the vote, and to originate revenue bills.

COLLECTOR, DEALER, DECORATOR

The American Folk Art Institute

Bang! The gavel goes down on Lot #38, a silver snuff box, circa 1726, just sold for $120. A steal. Experts had estimated that this early Georgian piece would bring $300 to $500.

L ot #45. "Portrait of a Girl in a Red Dress" by Ammi Phillips. "Six hundred eighty-two thousand. Once. Twice. Sold, for six hundred eighty-two thousand dollars." Whack! The largest auction price ever paid for an American folk art painting.

The offering and sale of pieces such as these at Christie's in New York, country auctions, antique shops and fairs, church bazaars, and even yard sale.-, are becoming a major recreational and financial attraction for decorators, collectors, and investors.

The Folk Art Institute, a division of the Museum of American Folk Art, now offers a concentration of study in the field of American folk art and related disciplines. The curriculum is designed to provide the recipient of a certificate from the Folk Art Institute with the credentials to pursue a wide range of careers in the folk art field. The student must compile a total of 36 credits (about 12 courses' worth) for certification.

We have reproduced questions from two of the institute's courses, "Collectors, Dealers, and the Market," and "Decorative Folk Arts and the Home." The former is designed to provide specific expertise for future collectors, dealers, and curators. The latter focuses on the social and historical aspects of the decorative arts as they relate to American history, design, and architecture. The questions below were provided by Henry P. Niemann, who teaches these two courses at the institute, and are published in this collection courtesy of the American Folk Art Institute, Dept. BOX, 444 Park Avenue South, New York, NY. 10016.

Multiple Choice (35 pts)

1. The wood most often used for drawer interiors is
   (A) maple
   (B) pine
   (C) oak
   (D) walnut

2. The scrolled foot with curving vertical ribs used on turned legs in the William and Mary period is called a
   (A) snake foot
   (B) slipper foot
   (C) Spanish foot
   (D) spade foot

3. In which period was mahogany furniture introduced?
   (A) Chippendale
   (B) Federal
   (C) Queen Anne
   (D) William and Mary

4. Which wood was never used as a secondary wood?
   (A) Walnut
   (B) Ash
   (C) Maple
   (D) Cherry

5. The name given to the top of eighteenth-century highboys with a broken pediment is
   (A) bellflower
   (B) bonnet
   (C) cartouche
   (D) bowfront

6. The cabriole leg is found on which chair?
   (A) Sheridan
   (B) Queen Ann
   (C) Hitchcock
   (D) Hepplewhite

7. A sideboard foot possessing a triangular notch is called a(n)
   (A) bootjack

(B) bun
(C) arrow
(D) beveled

8. Lacquered decoration was introduced to the West in what century?
   (A) Seventeenth
   (B) Eighteenth
   (C) Nineteenth
   (D) Twentieth

9. Another term for the DUTCH foot is
   (A) bun
   (B) pad
   (C) paw
   (D) claw and ball

10. Which is NOT found on country furniture?
    (A) Veneer
    (B) Paint
    (C) Laminated wood
    (D) Ormolu

11. Kaolin fires to what color?
    (A) Blue
    (B) Yellow
    (C) Red
    (D) White

12. Which medium was NOT used in glazing redware?
    (A) Manganese oxide
    (B) Salt
    (C) Lead
    (D) Alkaline

13. The only ceramic partially vitrified is
    (A) redware
    (B) mudware
    (C) stoneware
    (D) Rockinghamware

14. A rundlet is a type of
    (A) bowl
    (B) platter
    (C) keg
    (D) pitcher

15. Brown "Mudware" was only produced in
    (A) Georgia
    (B) Virginia
    (C) Pennsylvania
    (D) New England

16. Nantucket is well known for which object being produced there?
    (A) Stoneware
    (B) Baskets
    (C) Blanket chests
    (D) Redware

17. Stoneware from which area was rarely marked?
    (A) New England
    (B) Pennsylvania
    (C) Midwest
    (D) South

18. Who did NOT produce stoneware in the eighteenth century?
    (A) Adam Staats
    (B) David Spinner
    (C) John Bell
    (D) Fredrick Carpenter

19. Much of Moravian pottery was produced in
    (A) Massachusetts
    (B) New York
    (C) Ohio
    (D) North Carolina

20. Shakers are known for producing all of the following except
    (A) rugs
    (B) baskets
    (C) "built in.-,"
    (D) stoneware

21. The Amish never employed
    (A) printed fabric in their quilts
    (B) designs in their quilting
    (C) borders on their quilts
    (D) brightly colored fabrics in their quilts

22. Grenfell is known for making
    (A) braided rugs
    (B) hooked rugs
    (C) "Penny" rugs
    (D) all of the above

23. Stuffing patchwork is known as
    (A) calico
    (B) batten
    (C) trapunto
    (D) calimanco

24. The traditional Hawaiian quilts differ from New England examples because
    (A) they use one center template
    (B) their quilting patterns contain cryptic symbolism
    (C) only one woman works a quilt
    (D) all of the above

25. Which is NOT a quilting design?
    (A) Log cabin
    (B) Palampore
    (C) Turkey tracks
    (D) Sunshine and shadow

26. A city in which noted "album" quilts were produced in the 1850s is
    (A) Richmond
    (B) Philadelphia
    (C) Charleston
    (D) Baltimore

27. The Jacquard coverlet was first produced in America in the
    (A) 1800s
    (B) 1810s
    (C) 1820s
    (D) 1830s

28. The "honeycomb" pattern is found on
    (A) overshot coverlets
    (B) summer and winter coverlets
    (C) jacquard coverlets
    (D) double-weave coverlets

29. Candlewick spreads are sometimes referred to as
    (A) whitework
    (B) Berlin work
    (C) counterpanes
    (D) Copperplate cloths

30. Rugs were
    (A) hooked
    (B) yarn-sewn
    (C) braided
    (D) all of the above

31. A plain-weave cotton fabric, usually floral printed and glazed, is
    (A) palampore
    (B) challis
    (C) chintz
    (D) gingham

32. Which textile is woven?
    (A) sampler
    (B) braided rug
    (C) linsey-woolsey
    (D) memorial picture

33. A well-circulated periodical of the nineteenth century from which design sources were taken was
    (A) Godey's Lady's Book
    (B) Miss Petersen's Magazine
    (C) Miss Leslie's Magazine
    (D) all of the above

34. A reversible coverlet consisting of two layers woven simultaneously is known as a
    (A) summer and winter
    (B) linsey-woolsey
    (C) double-weave
    (D) overshot

35. Needlework using two-ply, loosely twisted wool yam usually worked on linen is called
    (A) basting
    (B) crewelwork
    (C) appliqué
    (D) patchwork

Matching Questions (35 pts)

36. Insert the correct letter of each date in column B to a style in column A

COLUMN A	COLUMN B
Chippendale	A. 1725–1750
Mission Furniture	B. 1600–1700
Windsor Chair	C. 1750–1780
Country Furniture	D. 1690–1725
Empire	E. 1780–1820
Federal	F. 1815–1840
William and Mary	G. 1690–1850
Pilgrim	H. 1790–1900
Queen Anne	I. 1730–1830
Shaker Furniture	J. 1900–1925
	K. 1850–1890

37. Insert the correct letter of each object in column B to a name in column A

COLUMN A	COLUMN B
William Hogarth	A. Glazed redware
Starker and Parker	B. Painted samples
Daniel Mauraux	C. Murals
Samuel F. B. Morse	D. Daguerreotypes
John Smibert	E. Samplers
John Bell	F. *Analysis of beauty*
John Dunlap	G. Curvilinear back
Moses Eaton	H. Treatise on "Japanning"
Polly Balsh	I. Mezzotints
Rufus Porter	J. "Gaudy Dutch"
	K. Portsmouth furniture

38. Insert the correct letter of each artist in column B to his location in column A

COLUMN A	COLUMN B
Ammi Phillips	A. Maine, Vermont or New Hampshire
Jacob Maentel	
William Mathew Prior	B. Massachusetts, Connecticut, N. Y. or N. J.
Joseph H. Davis	
Antonio Jacobsen	
Edward Hicks	C. Pennsylvania, Ohio, Indiana or Illinois
Hannah Cohoon	
Henrietta Johnston	
Feliz Lopez	D. Maryland, Virginia, Carolinas or Georgia
Olaf Krans	
James Bard	
Winthrop Chandler	E. Kentucky, Tennessee, Alabama or Mississippi
Gerardus Duyckinck	
Clementine Hunter	
"Grandma" Moses	
	F. Texas, New Mexico, Arizona or California

Fill-in (30 pts)

39. The name of the chair distinguished for its wide crest rail, square seat, rectangular back, and often decorated horizontal slat(s) was the _____

40. One design motif commonly found on Pennsylvania German painted and decorated furniture was the _____

41. Shaker boxes are noted for what distinctive feature? _____

42. Incised decoration found on some redware pottery is known as _____

43. One decorative symbol which was not found on country furniture until after the American Revolution was the _____

44. _____ was one painted technique intended to imitate the finely grained wood used in high-style city furniture of the nineteenth century.

45. Trinkets and decorative objects carved aboard whaling ships are collectively known as _____

46. Highly stylized motifs painted on furniture similar to traditional fraktur motifs used in illuminated manuscripts appear in the Pennsylvania region known as the

_____

47. _____ is the name for pottery possessing a salt glaze.

48. _____ was the name given to a small side table frequently possessing a tilt top which stood on three feet.

Essay Questions

49. Restoration affects the market value of a work of art. Explain this statement. Include in your answer responses to the following questions:
(A) What considerations are involved in the decision-making process to restore an object?
(B) How does restoration affect the value of an object with respect to
    (1) public auctions
    (2) museum gifts

50. Because of different situations and circumstances, there are several types of appraisals which can be made regarding private collections. Compare and contrast any TWO of them.

51. There are many factors which influence the market value of any work of art. Detail any THREE of them and explain.

ANSWERS!

Multiple Choice

1. (B)
2. (C)
3. (C)
4. (A)
5. (B)
6. (B)
7. (A)
8. (A)
9. (B)
10. (D)
11. (D)
12. (B)
13. (C)
14. (C)
15. (A)
16. (B)
17. (D)
18. (C)
19. (D)
20. (D)
21. (A)
22. (B)
23. (C)
24. (D)
25. (B)
26. (D)
27. (C)
28. (B)
29. (A)
30. (D)
31. (C)
32. (C)
33. (D)
34. (C)
35. (b)

Matching Questions

36. (C) Chippendale
    (J) Mission Furniture
    (I) Windsor Chair
    (G) Country Furniture
    (F) Empire
    (E) Federal
    (D) William and Mary
    (B) Pilgrim
    (A) Queen Anne
    (H) Shaker

37. (F) William Hogarth
    (H) Starker and Parker
    (G) Daniel F. B. Morse
    (L) John Smibert
    (A) John Bell
    (K) John Dunlap
    (B) Moses Eaton
    (E) Polly Balsh
    (C) Rufus Porter

38. (B) Ammi Phillips
    (C) Jacob Maentel
    (B) William Mathew Prior
    (A) Joseph H. Davis
    (B) Antonio Jacobsen
    (C) Edward Hicks
    (B) Hannah Cohoon
    (D) Henrietta Johnston
    (F) Feliz Lopez
    (C) Olaf Krans
    (B) James Bard
    (B) Winthrop Chandler
    (B) Gerardus Duyckinck
    (E) Clementine Hunter
    (B) "Grandma" Moses

39. Hitchcock chair
40. tulip
41. finger laps
42. graffito
43. eagle
44. Sponge and feather decoration
45. scrimshaw
46. Mahantango Valley
47. Stoneware
48. Candlestand

Essay Questions

49. The effects of Restoration on marketable value.
    (A) Considerations to restore should involve addressing the following questions: Is the damage part of the object functional or descriptive? Functional parts of an object are worth restoring—that is, movable parts of weathervanes or whirligigs.

    Do the aesthetics demand restoration? Is the viewer's eye able to "fill in" the missing or damaged part without his "eye-flow" being obstructed? For example, the central portion of a quilt is more important than its edges.

    How rare is the specific object? That is, the natural state of an object is more desired the rarer the article—particularly if the form of the missing section is unknown,
    (B) 1   Public auction
    A restored object is never worth as much as a similar item in its original state. However, restoration always increases the value of a piece if the object is intended to be sold at public auction and its cost effective to do so. The public determines value based upon decorative appeal.

2. Museum gift
   Restoring an article intended for a tax deduction to a museum will substantially reduce its chances for acquisition by the museum since the museum's primary objective is to display pieces for historical and social value—the authenticity of the object in its natural state.

50 Abstract of answer for appraisals.
   (A) Insurance appraisal. How much would it cost in today's market to replace the object? (based upon Madison Avenue prices)
   (B) Resale value appraisal. What would a dealer pay for an object? (considerations involve markups to cover overhead as well as clients' interests)
   (C) Estate sale appraisal. What will a willing buyer give a willing seller today? (of primary concern is the region—objects bring different prices in different areas)
   (D) Fair market value appraisal. What would the item bring at public auction? (the retail market)

51. References to three of the following
    factors listed on the financial analysis
    sheet should appear:

OBJECT: _____
General Market Value at Auction: ESTIMATE: Low: $_____ High: _____

		PRICE (A)	PRICE (B)
1	Aesthetics	$ _____	
2.	Uniqueness	$ _____	
3.	Condition		$ _____
4.	Documentation	$ _____	
5.	Restoration		$ _____
6.	Provenance	$ _____	
7.	Public interest	$ _____	
8.	Sub-Total	$ _____	
9.	Total	(A) $ _____ -	(B) $ _____ = (C) $ _____

Analysis:

AESTHETICS: Market value may exceed high/low estimates of similar pieces sold.
   Considerations. Overall design elements.
       PRICE $ _____

UNIQUENESS: Market value according to availability or scarcity of the item.
   Considerations. Specifics as to: maker, craftsmanship, form, color, materials, size.
   %   1   2   3   4   5   6   7   8   9   10*   PRICE   (+) $ _____

CONDITION: Market value according to circumstance of object.
   Considerations. Specifics as to: durability (how "solid" is the piece), wear (deterioration), coloration (how faded is the coloring), restoration (is it in need of repair)
   %   1   2   3   4   5   6   7   8   9   10   PRICE   (–) $ _____

DOCUMENTATION:Market value according to research data.
   Considerations. Unknown: Some: Complete.
   %   1   2   3   4   5   6   7   8   9   10   PRICE   (+) $ _____

RESTORATION: Based upon your assessments so far you may decide the restoration if any is of great importance to the value of the piece or of lesser importance.
   Considerations. Is previous restoration external/internal? If visible, does the restoration detract from the price.
   %   1   2   3   4   5   6   7   8   9   10   PRICE   (–) $ _____

PROVENANCE: Market value according to background history of the piece.
   Considerations. Collections, exhibitions, publications.
   %   1   2   3   4   5   6   7   8   9   10   PRICE   (+) $ _____

PUBLIC INTEREST: Market value according to the amount of auction activity relative to the general category.
   Considerations. Historical/Social significance expressed by the work of art as well as dealers.
   %   1   2   3   4   5   6   7   8   9   10   PRICE   (+) $ _____

*NOTE: +/– $ am't of item according to specifics should be considered in reassessing the value of an object which is initially a subjective one that falls within the range of the estimated valued determined by the auction house based upon previous sales of similar items. Precentages are flexible since specific situations and circumstances will warrant more or less emphasis on any one or more of the factorsk

COMPUTER COMPETENCY

Microsoft Certification/
The Digital University

At press time, Microsoft Chairman Bill Gates' net worth is estimated to be equivalent to:
(A) over ten times the annual military defense budget of France
(B) the annual income of a typical American town of 20,000 inhabitants
(C) the cost of 20,000,000 good haircuts, including a generous tip
(D) all of the above

I n a nutshell, Microsoft certification is a way of showing that you have expertise not just with the operating system that has a virtual monopoly in the business market — Windows — and with other Microsoft products such as Windows NT Server and BackOffice, but also with setting up, running, and trouble-shooting the hardware that uses that software in an office environment. Even for those of you who are reasonably computer literate — you know how to get around the Internet, and can toss around terms like *ISP*, *operating system*, and *network connection* with the best of them — this is hard stuff. You have to learn about LANs and WANs, T1s, the layers of OSI models, routers, NetBIOS Naming Schemes, and other things most people can't even pronounce.

Microsoft has lots of certifications, including Systems Engineer, Database Administrator, Solution Developer, Professional and Site Building, Professional and Internet, and Trainer. Work through a few of these, and you can call yourself, "Joe Doe, MCP, MCSE, MCT, MCDBA." Even *one* of those acronyms after your name will come in a lot handier when trying to get a well-paying job (and perhaps get some tiny portion of those Bill Gates billions to trickle down to you) than BA, MA, or PhD. Take it as a sign of the times.

But be forewarned: every time you pass one exam, Microsoft will be likely to have come out with a new product rendering your prior certification in another area obsolete. Such is the fast-paced nature of the world of high tech. You can get up-to-date information about all the certifications and current Microsoft products at Microsoft's web site, but you will need to be using the Windows operation system to take a brief interactive on-line practice test. Go figure.

The questions and answers in this section were provided by Warren D. Stallings, MSCE, CDP. You get to start out gently with general-knowledge computer questions before moving on to the really tough stuff: questions that test the technical knowledge you need to have in order to get MCSE certification. Warren Stallings is Director of Educational Services at The Digital University in San Francisco, which specializes in the MCP/MCSE Career Training Program, as well as professional education in Microsoft NT Networking, Novell NetWare, Internet connectivity, and business web site development and management. You can contact Operations Director Jennifer S. Terry (who also worked on this section) at The Digital University at (415) 616-9559, or visit their web site at "www.thedigitaluniversity.com."

1. What are the two most widely used hard-
   ware platforms being used at home today?
   (Select two.)
   (A) Sun Microsystems
   (B) Apple Macintosh
   (C) Atari systems
   (D) Intel-based systems

2. Which of the following keys on a computer
   keyboard are also usually found on a type-
   writer?
   (A) shift key
   (B) control key
   (C) caps lock key
   (D) alternate key

3. Personal computers are normally equipped
   with a pointing device to allow the user to
   interact with the system. Which of these
   pointing devices is the most widely used
   today for general-purpose activity?
   (A) track ball
   (B) touch pad
   (C) mouse
   (D) joy stick

4. Which of these pointing devices is normally
   used with games?
   (A) track ball
   (B) touch pad
   (C) mouse
   (D) joy stick

5. In today's modern personal computer systems the mouse normally plugs into the
   serial port or possibly another smaller type
   of connector. What is the proper designa-
   tion for the other connector type?
   (A) high resolution mouse connector
   (B) parallel mouse connector
   (C) PS/2 mouse connector
   (D) IBM mouse connector

6. How can you identify a floppy drive cable
   from any other type of cable?
   (A) It is wider than the other types.
   (B) It has a twist in it.

(C) It is the same as the CD-ROM cable.
(D) By looking at the connector.

7. What Interrupt Request Number does the
   floppy drive use by default?
   (A) 2
   (B) 5
   (C) 6
   (D) 8

8. What Interrupt Request Number does the
   printer parallel port use by default?
   (A) 2
   (B) 4
   (C) 7
   (D) 8

9. What are the two most popular types of
   printer available?
   (A) dot matrix
   (B) ink jet
   (C) line
   (D) laser

10. How is the image clarity of a printer usu-
    ally rated for performance purposes?
    (A) characters per inch
    (B) lines per square inch
    (C) dots per square inch
    (D) pixels per square inch

11. How is the size of a monitor specified?
    (A) width of screen in inches
    (B) height of screen in inches
    (C) width and height of screen in inches
    (D) diagonal length in inches

12. Which two items listed below can directly
    affect the image clarity of your monitor?
    (A) size
    (B) dot pitch
    (C) number of colors
    (D) lines of resolution

13. In terms of the storage capacity of a hard
    disk, which of these units of measure is
    the largest?
    (A) K (kilobyte)

(B) GB (gigabyte)
(C) MB (megabyte)
(D) B (byte)

14. Which of the hard disk controller technologies is most frequently in high-performance systems for use at home?
(A) IDE
(B) EIDE
(C) Ultra DMA
(D) SCSI

15. Identify the two components most likely to provide enhanced processing capabilities in a high-performance computer. (Select two.)
(A) storage capacity
(B) RAM
(C) sound card
(D) CPU (microprocessor)

16. How is the clock speed of a microprocessor rated?
(A) CPS (cycles per second)
(B) MIPS (millions of instructions per second)
(C) MHZ (megahertz)
(D) CCS (clock cycles per second)

17. What is the most widely used unit of measure today for RAM in high-performance systems?
(A) byte
(B) kilobyte
(C) megabyte
(D) gigabyte

18. The data in your computer travels around on an electronic highway often referred to as a bus. Of the four types of buses listed below, which is considered to be the highest speed?
(A) EISA
(B) ISA
(C) PCI
(D) MCA

19. What are the three Local Area Network topologies most frequently used in business today?
(A) bus
(B) star
(C) ring
(D) mesh
(E) dual recirculating rings
(F) tree

20. Which of the Local Area Network topologies listed below provides equal access to all PCs participating in the network and functions the most reliably under a heavy traffic load?
(A) star
(B) mesh
(C) ring
(D) bus

21. In a Local Area Network, the length of a specific cable is too long for the signal to travel reliably. As a result, the signal loses strength and degrades into an unreliable form. What is this process called?
(A) signal strength loss
(B) signal attenuation
(C) signal degradation
(D) unreliable signal

22. In the design of a Local Area network, you need to hook two types of cable together, 10BaseT and 10Base2. What is the simplest device that can accomplish this and increase (regenerate) the signal strength at the same time?
(A) gateway
(B) router
(C) brouter
(D) repeater
(E) passive hub
(F) bridge

23. If you need to establish communications between a network in New York using Novell NetWare and the IPX/SPX protocol, and a network in San Francisco using Microsoft NT and the NetBEUI protocol, which of the following devices would you need?
    (A) router
    (B) brouter
    (C) bridge
    (D) gateway

24. If your Microsoft NT-based LAN is using the NetBEUI protocol and network traffic has increased to the point where the system is slowing down, which device would you use to segment the network into logical areas and localize traffic flow as much as possible?
    (A) brouter
    (B) router
    (C) bridge
    (D) gateway

25. In a bus network, if a single workstation is having difficulty communicating, but all other workstations and servers are working fine, what is the most likely problem?
    (A) bad terminator
    (B) missing terminator
    (C) broken or disconnected cable
    (D) bad NIC or improperly installed NIC

26. In an Ethernet-based network designed to operate at 10 MBs speed, what are the four types of standard media that can be used? (Select four.)
    (A) 10BaseT
    (B) 10BaseUTP
    (C) 10Base2
    (D) 10BaseSTP
    (E) 10Base5
    (F) 10BaseCOAX
    (G) 10BaseFL

27. In configuring 100 MBs Ethernet, three specific types of medium can be used. Which ones? (Select three.)
    (A) 100BaseT
    (B) 100BaseT4
    (C) 100BaseTX
    (D) 100BaseFX
    (E) 100BaseX
    (F) 100BaseFL

28. In setting up controls over individual access to the company's LAN, which of the following parameters cannot be tailored for a specific user whose account is first set up as a part of Account Policies?
    (A) time of day user can log on
    (B) day of week user can log on
    (C) whether or not the user can dial into the system using RAS
    (D) the date the user's account expires
    (E) how often the user can change his or her password
    (F) whether or not the user can change the password over and over again
    (G) which specific PCs a user can log into the network from
    (H) what kinds of software the user can operate on a local PC
    (I) where the user can store information on a local PC
    (J) whether or not the user can create folders on a local PC

29. What is the main function of the Primary Domain Controller (PDC) in a Microsoft NT server-based network?
    (A) to store all company data
    (B) to provide e-mail capabilities to all users
    (C) to authenticate user logon and manage access to all network resources
    (D) to monitor the status of all other servers and workstations on the network

30. In providing access to a server-based network resource (such as a folder containing data) to a specific user in a network, access level controls are implemented in two areas; identify them. (Select two.)
    (A) sharing
    (B) user access controls
    (C) security/permissions
    (D) resource access controls

31. Mary is a member of a Sales and Marketing group. She needs to have access to the folder named Projects. What level of access will Mary have remotely and locally given the following?

Group Name	Share Permission	NTFS Permission
Sales	Change	Add & Read
Marketing	Full Control	Change

    (A) full control remotely, change locally
    (B) change remotely, full control remotely
    (C) change remotely, add & read locally
    (D) change remotely, change locally

32. What is the purpose of a DHCP server in a Microsoft TCP/IP-based network?
    (A) to set up a Remote Access Service for user working at home
    (B) to automate the process of configuring TCP/IP network activity in the network
    (C) to monitor the TCP/IP network activity in the network
    (D) to manage the security and access control in a TCP/IP network

33. What is the difference between an Incremental Backup procedure and a Differential Backup procedure when archiving important company data?
    (A) The Incremental Backup procedure backs up all the files created that day and does not mark them, while the Differential Backup procedure just backs up the files that changed that day.
    (B) The Incremental Backup procedure backs up all the files created since the last full backup and does not mark them, while the Differential Backup procedure backs up the files added and changed since the prior day and marks the files as having been backed up.
    (C) The Differential Backup procedure backs up all the files created that day and does not mark them, while the Incremental Backup procedure just backs up the files changed that day.
    (D) The Differential Backup procedure backs up all the files created since the last full backup, while the Incremental Backup procedure just backs up the files changed that day.

34. Where is all of the critical operating system management and configuration data kept in a Windows NT-based computer?
    (A) the control panel
    (B) the system applet
    (C) the registry
    (D) the services configuration panel

35. In a bus network, which problems are likely to affect only the ability of a single computer to function in the network?
    (A) improper termination of a segment
    (B) a bad or improperly configured NIC card
    (C) a broken or loose cable in a segment
    (D) the use of several different cable types in the same segment

36. In a star network, what is the effect if a cable is cut between a hub and a workstation?
   (A) All network activity stops immediately.
   (B) A beacon packet is sent out by the downstream neighbor to begin network diagnostics.
   (C) The workstation loses its ability to function as do all other workstations connected to the same hub.
   (D) The one workstation loses its ability to function in the network but can still be used locally.

37. In a ring network, what is the effect if the NIC in a specific PC malfunctions?
   (A) All network activity stops immediately.
   (B) A beacon packet is sent out by the downstream neighbor after seven seconds, the packet forces each NIC to do a self-diagnostic, and when the bad NIC is identified, it is dropped from the ring.
   (C) A beacon packet is sent out by the PC with the bad NIC to alert all other PCs in the ring that it is having a problem.
   (D) It has no effect on the network.

38. How do you use an NT Emergency Repair Disk, when you are having a problem with an NT workstation?
   (A) Boot the computer with the Emergency Repair Disk and follow the instructions.
   (B) Boot the computer with a DOS disk and then use the Emergency Repair Disk and follow the instructions.
   (C) Go to the \WINNT folder on the computer, type WINNT and then use the Emergency Repair Disk when prompted.
   (D) Use the three NT Workstation install disks to start the computer and select the Repair Options when it is presented. Insert the Emergency Repair Disk and follow the instructions.

39. A user has been playing with the Video Display Driver setting on the computer and is now unable to get the computer to boot up properly. What corrective action should you begin?
   (A) Boot the computer with the NT Emergency Repair Disk.
   (B) Boot the computer with the three NT Workstation install disks.
   (C) Select the "Last Known Good Configuration" option from the boot menu.
   (D) Select the [VGA Mode] boot option and then fix the problem.

40. A user has been playing with the installation of a new sound card and making registry setting changes. When the NT workstation is rebooted, neither boot menu option works. What should the user do?
   (A) Select the [VGA Mode] boot option and then fix the problem.
   (B) Boot the computer with the NT Emergency Repair Disk.
   (C) Select the "Last Known Good Configuration" option from the boot menu.
   (D) Boot the computer with the three NT Workstation install disks.

41. Assuming they are different partitions, what files are typically found in the NT "Boot" partition rather than in the NT "System" partition?
   (A) The Boot partition contains the IO.SYS file as well as the MS-DOS.COM file.
   (B) The Boot Partition contains the NTLDR, NTDETECT and BOOT.INI files.
   (C) The Boot Partition contains the main portion of the functional NT operating system in a folder normally labeled \WINNT.
   (D) The Boot Partition contains the Master Boot Record for your hard drive.

ANSWERS!☞

1. (B) and (D)
2. (A)
3. (C)
4. (D)
5. (C)
6. (B)
7. (C)
8. (C)
9. (B) and (D)
10. (C)
11. (D)
12. (B) and (D)
13. (B)
14. (C)
15. (B) and (D)
16. (C)
17. (C)
18. (C)
19. (A), (B), and (C)
20. (C)
21. (B)
22. (D)
23. (C)
24. (C)
25. (D)
26. (A), (C), (E), and (G)
27. (B), (C), and (D)
28. (I)
29. (C)
30. (A) and (C)
31. (D)
32. (B)
33. (D)
34. (C)
35. (B)
36. (D)
37. (A)
38. (D)
39. (D)
40. (C)
41. (C)

COPYEDITING

Professional Freelancer's Test

I know of no freelance editor who doesn't own a

~~I don't know a single solitary free-pen who~~
~~doesn't own, yea worship, her~~ copy of "the
little book," as Strunk and White has come
to be known. It cautions writers to "omit
needless words," especially polysyllabic
pomposities the writer ~~sticks in~~ uses to get attention, not to get her meaning across clearly.

The content of those two sentences has no
bearing on these tests. I just wanted to see
if our copyeditor would let me get away with
~~some of this stuff.~~

A.U.: Redundant?

Au: Many other sources more
common: Chicago manual of style,
words into type.

✓Au: Pompous?

h his or
)Au: If so, delete?

irrelevancies and colloquialisms ⊙ *Au: Is your meaning retained?*

These sample tests, created by a working freelancer, are used by several publishers to evaluate freelancers' skills ~~before hiring them~~. The typewritten manuscripts ⊙/⅄/ for copyediting and the typeset galley proofs reproduced here look just like the actual manuscripts and proofs professionals slog through day after day. However, the ~~number of~~ errors on these examples ~~is~~ greater and somewhat more egregious than *are*/ most authors and typesetters inflict on their publishers.

There are two sets of tests: copyediting from manuscript and proofreading from typeset copy. The first set contains two tests, one in fiction and one in nonfiction. Answers to the tests are by no means absolute. Every copyeditor and proofreader has a different slant on his or her work, and every publishing house has a slightly different attitude toward style. These pages present tests ~~such as are~~ regularly employed by the publisher of this book and other major publishers to determine the qualifications of free-pens applying /r for work cleaning up messy manuscripts so the authors won't blow their credibility.

COPYEDITING

July 25, 1870

Ive has some narrow ecsapes in my life,but this tops them all.
I had been a normal day with bathing at Steve and Sydneys' next door.
<u>They</u> have hot water! I had came back and started to fix dinner for
my self. I decided to take down the garbage. I saw a Porto Rican
going up the stairs when I was going down. I did'nt think about it.
I had left the door open as usually do when I empty the garage.
When I returned to the pad I found, this same cat in the bath room,
holding a rather large knife.

He told me to be quiet, that he just wanted to hideout for awhile.
He said the man was after him, I told him to sit down and offered him
a drink.

He drank some orange juice. I was cool, I was trying my damndest
to keep it together. I felt the adrenaline pumping away into my
every vain. He said that the police were after him, cause he had
just beaten somebody up. He said, and I am using his terminology--
some 'nigger' had burnt him and that some oldl lady had called the
cops when she hard the fight.

We agreed that the man was a drag, I didn't tell him that I
didn't share his rascist attitude towards black people. He asked me
if I had any money, I said No, and told him about the hard times we
were having. He said that he was a dope friend showed me his tracks
and said that he'll do anything for money while waving the gun in my
face.

I asked him how long he's been on junk. He said, on and off for
7 years, not including the time that he's spent in jail. I asked
him how much he spends a day on junk. He said $36 dollars a day.

He asked about room-mates. I told him about Andrea and Leicaand showed him pictures of them then I told him that they are on welfare and showed him the Welfare food that they gave you. He asked me about boy-freinds and I told him about Jose. (He was Puerta Rican too)

He told me thet he was into stealing things, and began walking around pad, sort of apraising my paltry and few posessions. He made reference to sevral items of mine, e.g. my giutar, and my radio, and my ring. He found a ten dollar bill in one of the bureau. I told him that it was Andra's to pay the kids doctor bill. He plocketted it. He found my pot stash and offered to roll him a joint. He did'nt want any. He asked if I had any smack. I didn't. He said that he was sick and started to bending over at the waste, kind of cluching at his stomach. I asked him if he had ever tired the drug, rehabi-litaion programs. He said that they didn't work.

He asked me if I ever heard of Sharen Tate. Sure, who hasn't? Wierd thoughts ran though my mind. Knivings, rape, torture. I tired to keep it together. He asked me if I was virgin. I said of course not, what does that have to do with anything.?" I figured that a junkie in as bad a shape as this guy probably wouldn't be able to get it up anyway. But he was getting freaky, and I didn't like that at all. He had been in the apartment to long. He heard some-thing outside, and asked me to go out and look out the window to see if it was the pigs.

"O.K.I'll go look if you let me hold the knife. "He handed me the knife. I went to the window and I turned around he said, "You think, I'm stupid", and clicked out another knive. I gave him back the one that I was holding. There was no sense in fighting him with the knive. I would be torn to shreads in seconds. He kept

COPYEDITING

Mao's Contribution to Marxist-Leninist Ideology

<u>INTRODUCTION</u>

Any attempt to devaluate the extent of Mao Tse-tung's contribution to the development of Marxism Lenism must at the out-set
come to terms with the nettlesome problen of interperting Maos
writings: determining not simply the content but the intent of Mao's
often-ambiguious and ocasionally conterdictory statement.

The root of the difficulty lays in the fact that " the degree
of allegance Mao has displayed to the doctrines of Marx and Lennon
have varied at different times . . .He either has insisted on a
rigourous fidelity to the original context of a paticular tenent or
has deliberately distorted or ignored the context his primary
guideline having been his need of the moment."[1] This tenency to
altar theory in accord with the exigiencies of a particular situation is certainly unique to Mao, but in combination with his
decided emphases on practice rather than theory makes the task of
evaluating the real signifigance of his statements unsually difficult.

Unlike Marx and Lennin, Mao Tse Tung has made no attempt to
systematise his teachings.

"'Marxism-Leninsim,' he reminded the partys' intellect
uals in 1942, 'has no beauty, no mystical value; it is
simply very useful. . . . those who regard Marxism-Leninism
as a religious dogma: Your dogma is less useful than
excrement.'"[2]

1. Arthur Cohen, <u>The Communism of Mao Tse-tung</u>. Chicago & London:
        The University of Chicago Press, 1964).

2. Bianco, Lucien, <u>Origins of the Chinese Revolution</u> 1914-1945,
        (London,University of Oxford Press), p. 79

A man who avows such beleifs will understandably be little concerned with the over all cohesiveness of his 'theory'.

To obfuscate matters, further there is no distingtion between Mao, the theoretician, and Mao, the political strategist, in his writings. Quite often his pronouncments have been shrewdly calculated to achieve an affect completely outside the realm of political philosophy. For example in order to molify the Soviet Union during the last few years of his struggle agianst Chang Kai-Shek, Mao was careful to preserve appearences, and not to challenge the recieved doctrine. Thus he represented his movement as proletarian even when it was not . . ."[2]

In view of these hermenutical problems, it seems that an attempt to deprive a cosistent political theory from Mao's writings alone would be to use a Chinese adage "Climbing a tree to look for fish." Therefore, I will not attempt a detailed analysis of Maos works but rather have tried to interpert Mao's thought in the context of actual events in the course of the Revolution, and the early period of re-socialization that followed it.

The first task in evaluating Mao's contribution of Marist-Leninist theory is to debunk the popular misconceptions: that Mao's pheasant rebellion was an original and unique element in the history of socialist thought.

The demise of the Capitalist Order, and its replacement by the classless society, was envisioned by Marx as an inevitable result of economic contradictions inherent in the nature of Capitalism. There

[3]R.N. Carew-Hunt, The Theory and Practice of Communism. (Pengiun Books: 1950) p. 261

PROOFREADING

You know I can still remember my frist job in a restarant—or maybe it was my second, I don't know but I could hardly play at all: strictly the key of C.

Anyway, it was only my second night and the knots and my stomach were just beginning to unravel. Nobody had thrown any ash trays my way yet; I'd even gotten a tip or two. But then, on my break the owner—a lean, flinty eyed young man, who seemed very serious about everything, but especially money—called me over. He said that he liked what I was doing but "couldn't I shoot the music out a little more?" He went on like that for a few minutes, but I wasn't listening to anything except the veins pounding out a funreal march in my inner ear I got the idea tough.

"Shot the music out a little more,"—and there I was nearly paralysed trying to keep all the bad nots *sotto* voce. I stood their alone at the bar for the rest fo my break, feeling the sweat dampen my stiff, new shirt, cluching my glass of icewater, hopping that maybe, if I squeezed hard enough, my fingers would get frozen to the sides.

"And then I remembered a peice I'd been working on at home. It was rag time—very fast and flashy, with big handfuls of arpegios—I intended to play it just yet; it was'nt ready, think it was called Catastrophe Rag." I hadn't there were a few rough spots that still needed work, and I wasn't even sure if I'd remember it from beginning tò end. But it seemed like my only chance.

So at the end of the break, I marched bravely back to the piano, blew my hands to warn them up and wham–I struck the opening chords. As soon as I started, I knew something strange was hapening without taking my eye's off the key board I could feel everyone's head turning in my direction, and just as surelv as if I could see them, I knew a few people were smiling, pleased at the cock-eyed rythms coming out of the piano.

It felt like electricity was running through my veins that night—the notes seem to pop up and glow on the keyboard; like they were magne-tized, drawing myfingers to the right places at just the right times. I may have played better since, but I can't ever remember playing quite as perfectly. I was more like listening than play-ing.

I was so excited after that rag I wanted to play for ever—and I nearly did. By closing time the only people still around to listen are the bart-ender and the bus boys. I fiinally quite when they were turning off the lights, and the hostess, a slim blond not much older than me, said the owner wanted to see me in the back. I don't know what those old cooks must have thought was wrong with me as I strod through the streaming kitchen, grinning like a tipsey politi-cain.

The owner was sitting in his office, a tiny room, all cluttered up with old menus and ad-vertisments, hunched over a pile of account books. When I knocked he looks up quizziclly at first—like he had just forgotten something.

Then I saw the light in his eyes turn a cool blue. "You're fired." He said it simply and finally, almost like "good night."

"Thanks," I said softly. I took the cheek he handed me and left.

ANSWERS!

COPYEDITING

July 25, 1970

Designer note dateline

Au: 1970 OK?

I've had some narrow escapes in my life, but this tops them all. I had been a normal day with bathing at Steve and Sydneys next door. They have hot water! I had came back and started to fix dinner for myself. I decided to take down the garbage. I saw a Porto Rican going up the stairs when I was going down. I didn't think about it. I had left the door open, as usually do when I empty the garage. When I returned to the pad, I found this same cat in the bath room holding a rather large knife.

He told me to be quiet, that he just wanted to hideout for awhile. He said the man was after him. I told him to sit down and offered him a drink.

He drank some orange juice. I was cool, I was trying my damndest to keep it together. I felt the adrenaline pumping away into my every vain. He said that the police were after him, cause he had just beaten somebody up. He said, and I am using his terminology, some "nigger" had burnt him and that some old lady had called the cops when she hard the fight.

Au: "but" OK?

We agreed that the man was a drag, but I didn't tell him that I didn't share his racist attitude towards black people. He asked me if I had any money. I said no, and told him about the hard times we were having. He said that he was a dope fiend, showed me his tracks, and said that he'd do anything for money, while waving the knife in my face.

Au: "knife" OK, as above?

I asked him how long he'd been on junk. He said on and off for seven years, not including the time that he'd spent in jail. I asked him how much he spends a day on junk. He said thirty-six dollars a day.

Au: deletion OK?

He asked about room-mates. I told him about Andrea and Leica and showed him pictures of them, then I told him that they were on welfare and showed him the welfare food that they gave you. He asked me about boyfriends and I told him about José, who was Puerto Rican too.

He told me that he was into stealing things, and began walking around the pad, sort of appraising my paltry and few possessions. He made reference to several items of mine, my guitar, my radio, and my ring. He found a ten-dollar bill in one of the bureaus. I told him that it was Andrea's to pay the kids doctor bill. He pocketed it. He found my pot stash, and offered to roll him a joint. He didn't want any. He asked if I had any smack. I didn't. He said that he was sick and started bending over at the waist, kind of clutching at his stomach. I asked him if he had ever tried the drug-rehabilitation programs. He said that they didn't work.

He asked me if I had ever heard of Sharon Tate. Sure, who hadn't? Weird thoughts ran through my mind. Knifings, rape, torture. I tried to keep it together. He asked me if I was a virgin. I said, of course not, what does that have to do with anything?" I figured that a junkie in as bad shape as this guy probably wouldn't be able to get it up anyway. But he was getting freaky, and I didn't like that at all. He had been in the apartment too long. He heard something outside, and asked me to go and look out the window to see if it was the pigs.

"O.K. I'll go look if you let me hold the knife." He handed me the knife. I went to the window, and as I turned around he said, "You think I'm stupid," and clicked out another knife. I gave him back the one I was holding. There was no sense fighting him with the knife. I would be torn to shreds in seconds. He kept

Au: changes ok?

Au: Andrea ok, as above?

Au: change comma to question mark?

COPYEDITING

Ⓐ Mao's Contribution to Marxist-Leninist Ideology

Ⓑ INTRODUCTION

Any attempt to evaluate the extent of Mao Tse-tung's contribution to the development of Marxism-Leninism must at the outset come to terms with the nettlesome problem of interpreting Mao's writings, determining not simply the content but the intent of Mao's often ambiguous and ocasionally contradictory statement.

The root of the difficulty lies in the fact that " the degree of allegance Mao has displayed to the doctrines of Marx and Lenin have varied at different times. . . . He either has insisted on a rigorous fidelity to the original context of a paticular tenent or has deliberately distorted or ignored the context, his primary guideline having been his need of the moment."[1] This tenency to alter theory in accord with the exigencies of a particular situation is certainly not unique to Mao, but, in combination with his decided emphasis on practice rather than theory, makes the task of evaluating the real significance of his statements unusually difficult.

Unlike Marx and Lenin, Mao Tse-tung made no attempt to systematize his teachings. In 1942 "Marxism-Leninism," he reminded the party's intellectuals, "has no beauty, no mystical value; it is simply very useful. . . . those who regard Marxism-Leninism as a religious dogma: Your dogma is less useful than excrement."[2]

1. Arthur Conen, The Communism of Mao Tse-tung (Chicago and London: University of Chicago Press, 1964).

2. Bianco, Lucien, Origins of the Chinese Revolution 1914-1945 (London: University of Oxford Press, 1971) p. 79.

A man who avows such beliefs will understandably be little concerned with the over all cohesiveness of his "theory."

To obfuscate matters further, there is no distinction between Mao the theoretician and Mao the political strategist in his writings. Quite often his pronouncements are shrewdly calculated to achieve an effect completely outside the realm of political philosophy. For example, in order to molify the Soviet Union during the last few years of his struggle against Chang Kai-shek, Mao was careful to preserve appearances, and not to challenge the recieved doctrine. Thus he represented his movement as proletarian even when it was not."[3]

In view of these hermenutical problems, it seems that an attempt to deprive a cosistent political theory from Mao's writings alone would be, to use a Chinese adage, "climbing a tree to look for fish." More illuminating than is the interpretation of Mao's thought in the context of actual events in the course of the revolution and the early period of re socialization that followed it.

The first task in evaluating Mao's contribution to Marist-Leninist theory is to debunk the popular misconceptions that Mao's peasant rebellion was an original and unique element in the history of socialist thought.

The demise of the capitalist order and its replacement by the classless society were envisioned by Marx as inevitable results of economic contradictions inherent in the nature of capitalism. There

---

[3] R. N. Carew-Hunt, *The Theory and Practice of Communism* (Baltimore, Maryland: Penguin Books, 1950), p. 261.

PROOFREADING

You know, I can still remember my first job in a restarant—or maybe it was my second, I don't know, but I could hardly play at all, strictly the key of C.

Anyway, it was only my second night, and the knots and my stomach were just beginning to unravel. Nobody had thrown any ash trays my way yet; I'd even gotten a tip or two. But then, on my break, the owner—a lean, flinty, eyed young man, who seemed very serious about everything, but especially money—called me over. He said that he liked what I was doing but couldn't I shoot the music out a little more?" He went on like that for a few minutes, but I wasn't listening to anything except the veins pounding out a funreal march in my inner ear, I got the idea tough.

"Shot the music out a little more,"—and there I was nearly paralysed trying to keep all the bad nots *sotto* voce. I stood their alone at the bar for the rest fo my break, feeling the sweat dampen my stiff, new shirt, cluching my glass of icewater, hopping that maybe, if I squeezed hard enough, my fingers would get frozen to the sides.

And then I remembered a peice I'd been working on at home. It was rag time—very fast and flashy, with big handfuls of arpegios—I intended to play it just yet; it wasn't ready think it was called Catastrophe Rag." I hadn't there were a few rough spots that still needed work, and I wasn't even sure if I'd remember it from beginning to end. But it seemed like my only chance.

So at the end of the break, I marched bravely

back to the piano, blew my hands to warm them up and wham I struck the opening chords. As soon as I started, I knew something strange was happening, without taking my eyes off the keyboard, I could feel everyone's head turning in my direction, and just as surely as if I could see them, I knew a few people were smiling, pleased at the cock-eyed rythms coming out of the piano.

It felt like electricity was running through my veins that night the notes seem to pop up and glow on the keyboard like they were magnetized, drawing my fingers to the right places at just the right times. I may have played better since, but I can't ever remember playing quite as perfectly. I was more like listening than playing.

I was so excited after that rag I wanted to play for ever—and I nearly did. By closing time the only people still around to listen are the bartender and the bus boys. I finally quite when they were turning off the lights, and the hostess, a slim blond not much older than me, said the owner wanted to see me in the back. I don't know what those old cooks must have thought was wrong with me as I strod through the streaming kitchen grinning like a tipsey politician.

The owner was sitting in his office, a tiny room, all cluttered up with old menus and advertisments, hunched over a pile of account books. When I knocked he looks up quizziclly at first like he had just forgotten something.

Then I saw the light in his eyes turn a cool blue. "You're fired." He said it simply and finally, almost like "good night."

"Thanks," I said softly. I took the check he handed me and left.

WRITING COMPETENCY

M.I.T. Freshman

In 1982, the observation that "engineers or humanists who cannot write well may not do well" inspired MIT to institute a writing requirement for its incoming freshmen. Each of the two phases of the requirement may be satisfied in any of a number of ways. To satisfy Phase One, an incoming student may present a score of 750 or higher in the College Board Achievement Test in English Composition With Essay, or receive a passing grade in one of four writing classes, or submit a 5-page paper of expository prose written for an MIT class. Most graduates choose a fourth option of passing a Freshman Writing Evaluation Exam, which is given at the beginning of each academic year. About 65% of the students who take the exam pass it, most with a rating of "marginal pass." The second phase of the requirement is designed to engage upperclass students in the more specialized forms of writing used within their professional disciplines.

Freshman Writing Evaluation

Write a clear, coherent expository essay for a general reader. Good organization and structure are essential in maintaining a flow within the essay. Support generalizations with appropriate details and examples; pay special attention to grammar, punctuation, and spelling.

Below are three topics. Choose ONE and write an essay of about 500 words. You have 90 minutes to complete the exercise. Use the first 20 to 30 minutes to plan, organize, and develop your essay on scratch paper. Take the remaining time to write the essay.

1. An unidentified defense physicist recently explained his participation in Strategic Defense Initiative (S.D.I., or, popularly, "Star Wars") research with this statement:

"Some say we've made Faustian deals with the Devil, and there's an element of truth in it, if you happen to look at national defense as the Devil, which I do not. I'm being paid to work in a lab that's more exciting than a toy store. I'm given all the fancy hardware I need for my work, which has to do with very short-wave-length lasers. Do you realize what magnificent scientific tools such lasers will one day give us? We could use them to make holographic movies of the interaction of molecules in living cells, catalyzing the whole field of cancer research. X-ray or gamma-ray lasers will help us understand the nature of life at its most basic level.

Sure, we're working on weapons, and we hope they'll be very good weapons. But the biggest payoff for many of us is the thrill of personal scientific achievement—achievement that in many cases would be impossible without Star Wars tools."

This quotation embodies many of the ambiguities inherent in participating in S.D.I. research. Pick one or two ideas within the quotation and defend or reject them as bases for participating in S.D.I. work. Buttress your argument with at least three ideas and reach a conclusion.

2. Last year a young American student named Matthew Fraser received a three-day suspension from high school for using an extended sexual metaphor in a school assembly speech nominating a friend for a position in student government. Matthew and his family objected to the suspension and took their case all the way to the U.S. Supreme Court. Writing for the majority in *Bethel School District No. 403 versus Fraser,* Chief Justice Warren Burger held that "The First Amendment does not prevent school officials from determining that to permit a vulgar and lewd speech . . . would undermine the school's basic educational mission."

While agreeing with the majority opinion, Justice William J. Brennan, Jr., stressed the importance of defining "vulgar," "lewd," and "obscene." Justice Brennan found Matthew's speech "no more 'obscene,' 'lewd,' or 'sexually explicit' than the bulk of programs currently appearing on prime-time television or in the local cinema."

Justice John Paul Stevens, dissenting from the majority opinion, stated that "Vulgar language, like vulgar animals, may be acceptable in some context and intolerable in others." He emphasized the importance of context, suggesting that language such as that found in Matthew's speech might be "regarded as rather routine" along many school corridors.

With which of these opinions do you agree? Argue one issue of this case and use at least three supporting statements as you develop your discussion and conclusion.

3. The recent television miniseries about the life of Peter the Great omitted certain truths—Peter's epilepsy, for one—while including certain untruths—Peter's meeting with William the Second and Isaac Newton. In defending the script, Producer Marvin Chomsky said, "I think the miniseries should be concerned with the spirit and flavor of the times rather than a historic chronology which may tend to get dull and boring." When a reporter asked scriptwriter Edward Anhalt whether he thought it was better to learn something *wrong* than not to learn anything at all, Anhalt replied, "I'm afraid I am saying that."

Do you agree or disagree with Anhalt and Chomsky's position? State your own in an essay buttressed by at least three supporting arguments and reach a conclusion.

CPA

American Institute of Certified Public Accountants

If you aren't born with the understanding of how a Balance Sheet behaves and why it makes practical sense for it to do so, no amount of training will ever liberate you from accepting that esoterica as an act of faith.

The Uniform CPA Examination prepared by the Board of Examiners of the American Institute of Certified Public Accountants is the most widely used exam in the licensing process of the various state boards of accountancy to ensure the technical and professional competence of CPA candidates. (If you managed to work your way through that introductory sentence, maybe you won't find the questions so terribly difficult.)

The exam consists of four sections: Accounting Practice, Auditing, Business Law, and Accounting Theory. Each section tests candidates' knowledge by the use of multiple-choice (60 percent of each section), essay, or problem-type questions. Scoring 75 percent correct is considered passing for each section. Multiple-choice questions are graded by an optical scanning machine, and essay and problem-type questions are graded by a professional staff specifically engaged for this purpose, with the roles reversed on leap years to provide a mutual check and to make sure everyone is awake and free of malfunctions.

Accounting Practice

1. On January 1, 1986, Carr Company pur-
    chased Fay Corporation 9% bonds with a
    face amount of $400,000 for $375,600, to
    yield 10%. The bonds are dated January 1,
    1986, mature on December 31, 1995, and
    pay interest annually on December 31.
    Carr uses the interest method of amortizing
    bond discount. In its income statement for
    the year ended December 31, 1986, what
    total amount should Carr report as interest
    revenue from the long-term bond invest-
    ment?
    (A) $40,000
    (B) $37,560
    (C) $36,000
    (D) $34,440

2. On July 1, 1986, Hart signed an agreement
    to operate as a franchisee of Ace Printers
    for an initial franchise fee of $120,000. The
    same date, Hart paid $40,000 and agreed to
    pay the balance in four equal annual pay-
    ments of $20,000 beginning July 1, 1987.
    The down payment is not refundable and
    no future services are required of the fran-
    chisor. Hart can borrow at 14% for a loan
    of this type. Present and future value fac-
    tors are as follows:

    Present value of 1 at 14% for 4 periods:
      0.59
    Future amount of 1 at 14% for 4 periods:
      1.69
    Present value of an ordinary annuity of
      1 at 14% for 4 periods: 2.91

    Hart should record the acquisition cost of
    the franchise on July 1, 1986, at
    (A) $135,200
    (B) $120,000
    (C) $98,200
    (D) $87,200

3. Kew Company leased equipment for its
    entire nine-year useful life, agreeing to pay
    $100,000 at the start of the lease term on
    December 31, 1985, and $100,000 annu-
    ally on December 31 of the next eight
    years. The present value on December 31,
    1985, of the nine lease payments over the
    lease term, discounted at the lessor's
    implicit rate known by Dew to be 10%,
    was $633,000. The December 31, 1985
    present value of the lease payments dis-
    counted at Kew's incremental borrowing
    rate of 12% was $597,000. Kew made a
    timely second lease payment. The total
    lease liability at December 31, 1986, was
    (A) $0
    (B) $100,000
    (C) $694,000
    (D) $750,000

4. On January 17, 1987, an explosion
    occurred at a Cord Company plant causing
    extensive property damage to area build-
    ings. Although no claims had yet been
    asserted against Cord by March 10, 1987,
    Cord's management and counsel concluded
    that it is reasonably possible Cord will be
    responsible for damages, and that
    $2,500,000 would be a reasonable estimate
    of its liability. Cord's $10,000,000 compre-
    hensive public liability policy has a
    $500,000 deductible clause. In Cord's
    December 31, 1986 financial statements,
    which were issued on March 25, 1987,
    how should this item be reported?
    (A) No footnote disclosure or accrual is
        necessary
    (B) As a footnote disclosure indicating the
        possible loss of $500,000
    (C) As an accrued liability of $500,000
    (D) As a footnote disclosure indicating the
        possible loss of $2,500,000

5. The Tone Company is the defendant in a lawsuit filed by Witt in 1985 disputing the validity of a copyright held by Tone. At December 31, 1985, Tone determined that Witt would probably be successful against Tone for an estimated amount of $400,000. Appropriately, a $400,000 loss was accrued by a charge to income for the year ended December 31, 1985. On December 15, 1986, Tone and Witt agreed to a settlement providing for cash payment of $250,000 by Tone to Witt, and transfer of Tone's copyright to Witt. The carrying amount of the copyright on Tone's accounting records was $60,000 at December 15, 1986. What would be the effect of the settlement on Tone's income before income tax in 1986?
   (A) No effect
   (B) $60,000 decrease
   (C) $90,000 increase
   (D) $150,000 increase

6. On January 1, 1984, Bray Company purchased for $240,000 a machine with a useful life of ten years and no salvage value. The machine was depreciated by the double declining balance method and the carrying amount of the machine was $153,600 on December 31, 1985. Bray changed retroactively to the straight-line method on January 1, 1986. Bray can justify the change. What should be the depreciation expense on this machine for the year ended December 31, 1986?
   (A) $15,360
   (B) $19,200
   (C) $24,000
   (D) $30,720

7. Joe Neil, CPA, has among his clientele a charitable organization that has a legal permit to conduct games of chance for fund-raising purposes. Neil's client derives its profit from admission fees and the sale of refreshments, and therefore wants to "break even" on the games of chance. In one of these games, the player draws one card from a standard deck of 52 cards. A player drawing any one of four "queens" wins $5, and a player drawing any one of 13 "hearts" wins $2. Neil is asked to compute the price that should be charged per draw, so that the total amount paid out for winning draws can be expected to equal the total amount received from all draws. Which one of the following equations should Neil use to compute the price (P)?
   (A) $5 - 2 = \dfrac{35\,P}{52}$

   (B) $\dfrac{4}{52}\,(5) + \dfrac{13}{52}\,(2) = \dfrac{35\,P}{52}$

   (C) $\dfrac{4}{52}\,(5 - P) + \dfrac{13}{52}\,(2 - P) = P$

   (D) $\dfrac{4}{52}\,(5) + \dfrac{13}{52}\,(2) = P$

Auditing

1. Which of the following statements best describes the auditor's responsibility regarding the detection of material errors and irregularities?
   (A) The auditor is responsible for the failure to detect material errors and irregularities only when such failure results from the nonapplication of generally accepted accounting principles
   (B) Extended auditing procedures are required to detect material errors and

irregularities if the auditor's examination indicates that they may exist

(C) The auditor is responsible for the failure to detect material errors and irregularities only when the auditor fails to confirm receivables or observe inventories

(D) Extended auditing procedures are required to detect unrecorded transactions even if there is no evidence that material errors and irregularities may exist

2. When unable to obtain sufficient competent evidential matter to determine whether certain client acts are illegal, the auditor would most likely issue

(A) an unqualified opinion with a separate explanatory paragraph

(B) either a qualified opinion or an adverse opinion

(C) either a disclaimer of opinion or a qualified opinion

(D) either an adverse opinion or a disclaimer of opinion

3. When there are few property and equipment transactions during the year, the continuing auditor usually makes a

(A) complete review of the related internal accounting controls and performs compliance tests of those controls being relied upon

(B) complete review of the related internal accounting controls and performs analytical review tests to verify current year additions to property and equipment

(C) preliminary review of the related internal accounting controls and performs a thorough examination of the balances at the beginning of the year

(D) preliminary review of the related internal accounting controls and performs extensive tests of current year property and equipment transactions

4. Without the consent of the client, a CPA should *not* disclose confidential client information contained in working papers to a

(A) voluntary quality control review board

(B) CPA firm that has purchased the CPA's accounting practice

(C) federal court that has issued a valid subpoena

(D) disciplinary body created under state statute

5. Prior to commencing the compilation of financial statements of a nonpublic entity, the accountant should

(A) perform analytical review procedures sufficient to determine whether fluctuations among account balances appear reasonable

(B) complete the preliminary phase of the study and evaluation of the entity's internal accounting control

(C) verify that the financial information supplied by the entity agrees with the books of original entry

(D) acquire a knowledge of any specialized accounting principles and practices used in the entity's industry

6. When an independent accountant's report based on a review of interim financial information is incorporated by reference in a registration statement, the Securities and Exchange Commission requires that the prospectus clarify that the accountant's report is not

(A) a part of the registration statement within the meaning of the Securities Act of 1933

(B) subject to the Statements on Standards for Accounting and Review Services

(C) to be relied upon due to the limited nature of the procedures applied

(D) included in the company's quarterly report on Form 10-Q

7. Which of the following best describes the auditor's reporting responsibility concerning information accompanying the basic financial statements in an auditor-submitted document?
   (A) The auditor should report on all the information included in the document
   (B) The auditor should report on the basic financial statements but may not issue a report covering the accompanying information
   (C) The auditor should report on the information accompanying the basic financial statements only if the auditor participated in the preparation of the accompanying information
   (D) The auditor should report on the information accompanying the basic financial statements only if the document is to be distributed to public sharehold-ers

8. Parker is the in-charge auditor with administrative responsibilities for the upcoming annual audit of FGH Company, a continuing audit client. Parker will supervise two assistants on the engagement and will visit the client before the field work begins.

   Parker has started the planning process by preparing a list of procedures to be performed prior to the beginning of field work. The list includes:
   (1) Review correspondence and permanent files
   (2) Review prior year's audit working papers, financial statements, and auditor's reports
   (3) Discuss with CPA firm personnel responsible for audit and nonaudit services to the client, matters that may affect the examination
   (4) Discuss with management current business developments affecting the client

   Required: Complete Parker's list of procedures to be performed prior to the beginning of field work.

Business Law

Questions 1–3 are based on the following information:

White, Grey, and Fox formed a limited partnership. White is the general partner and Frey and Fox are the limited partners. Each agreed to contribute $200,000. Grey and Fox each contributed $200,000 in cash while White contributed $150,000 in cash and $50,000 worth of services already rendered. After two years, the partnership is insolvent. The fair market value of the assets of the partnership is $150,000 and the liabilities total $275,000. The partners have made no withdrawals.

1. If Fox is insolvent and White and Grey each have a net worth in excess of $300,000, what is White's maximum potential liability in the event of a dissolution of the partnership?
   (A) $62,500
   (B) $112,500
   (C) $125,000
   (D) $175,000

2. Unless otherwise provided in the certificate of limited partnership, which of the following is correct if Fox assigns her interest in the partnership to Barr and only White consents to Barr's admission as a limited partner?
   (A) Barr will not become a substituted limited partner unless Grey also consents
   (B) Barr will have the right to inspect the partnership's books
   (C) The partnership will be dissolved
   (D) Barr will become a substituted limited partner because White, as general partner, consented

3. Unless otherwise provided in the certificate of limited partnership, which of the following is correct if Grey dies?
   (A) Grey's executor will automatically become a substituted limited partner
   (B) Grey's executor will have all the rights of a limited partner for the purpose of settling the estate
   (C) The partnership will automatically be dissolved
   (D) Grey's estate will be free from any liabilities which may have been incurred by Grey as a limited partner

Questions 4 and 5 are based on the following information:

On March 1, Mirk Corp. wrote to Carr offering to sell Carr its office building for $280,000. The offer stated that it would remain open until July 1. It further stated that acceptance must be by telegram and would be effective only upon receipt.

4. For this question only, assume that Carr telegrammed its acceptance on June 28 and that it was received by Mirk on July 2. Which of the following statements is correct?
   (A) A contract was formed when Carr telegrammed its acceptance
   (B) A contract was formed when Mirk received Carr's acceptance
   (C) No contract was formed because three months had elapsed since the offer was made
   (D) No contract was formed since the acceptance was received after July 1

5. For this question only, assume that on May 10, Mirk mailed a letter to Carr revoking its offer of March 1. Carr did not learn of Mirk's revocation until Carr received the letter on May 17. Carr had already sent a telegram of acceptance to Mirk on May 14, which was received by Mirk on May 16. Which of the following statements is correct?
   (A) Carr's telegram of acceptance was effective on May 16
   (B) Mirk's offer of March 1 was irrevocable and therefore could not be withdrawn prior to July 1
   (C) Mirk's letter of revocation effectively terminated its offer of March 1 when mailed
   (D) Carr's telegram of acceptance was effective on May 14

6. Baker fraudulently induced Able to sell Baker a painting for $200. Subsequently, Baker sold the painting for $10,000 to Gold, a good faith purchaser. Able is entitled to
   (A) Rescind the contract with Baker
   (B) Recover the painting from Gold
   (C) Recover damages from Baker
   (D) Rescind Baker's contract with Gold

Questions 7 and 8 are based on the following information:

On April 5, 1987, Anker, Inc. furnished Bold Corp. with Anker's financial statements dated March 31, 1987. The financial statements contained misrepresentations which indicated that Anker was solvent when in fact it was insolvent. Based on Anker's financial statements, Bold agreed to sell Anker 90 computers, "F.O.B.—Bold's loading dock." On April 14, Anker received 60 of the computers. The remaining 30 computers are in the possession of the common carrier and in transit to Anker.

7. If, on April 28, Bold discovered that Anker was insolvent, then with respect to the computers delivered to Anker on April 14, Bold may
   (A) reclaim the computers upon making a demand
   (B) reclaim the computers irrespective of the rights of any subsequent third party
   (C) not reclaim the computers since ten days have elapsed from its delivery
   (D) not reclaim the computers since it is entitled to recover the price of the computers

8. With respect to the remaining 30 computers in transit, which of the following statements is correct if Anker refuses to pay Bold in cash and Anker is not in possession of a negotiable document of title covering the computers?
   (A) Bold may stop delivery of the computers to Anker since their contract is void due to Anker's furnishing of the false financial statements
   (B) Bold may stop delivery of the computers to Anker despite the fact that title had passed to Anker
   (C) Bold must deliver the computers to Anker on credit since Anker has not breached the contract
   (D) Bold must deliver the computers to Anker since the risk of loss had passed to Anker

9. On March 1, Dun purchased $50,000 of equipment from Lux Corp. for use in Dun's manufacturing process. Dun paid for the equipment with funds borrowed from Best Bank that same day. Dun executed a security agreement and financing statement covering Dun's existing and after-acquired equipment. On March 7, Dun was involuntarily petitioned into bankruptcy under the liquidation provisions of the Bankruptcy Code and a trustee in bankruptcy was appointed. On March 9, Best properly filed the financing statement. Which of the parties will have a superior security interest in the equipment?
   (A) Best, because it perfected its security interest within the permissible time limits
   (B) Best, because it had a perfected purchase money security interest without having to file a financing statement
   (C) The trustee in bankruptcy because the trustee became a lien creditor prior to the time Best perfected its security interest
   (D) The trustee in bankruptcy because the filing of the financing statement after the commencement of the bankruptcy case would be deemed a preferential transfer

10. John Reed, a wealthy businessman, established an inter vivos trust on January 1, 1986 to provide for the financial needs of his son and wife. The written trust agreement signed by Reed provided for income to his wife, Myrna, for her life with the remainder to his son, Rodney. Reed named Mini Bank as the sole trustee and transferred stocks, bonds, and two commercial buildings to the trust. The accounting period selected for the trust was the calendar year.

During the first year of the trust's existence, Mini made the following allocations to principal and income arising out of transactions involving the trust property:
• With regard to the sale of $25,000 of stock, $20,000 to income representing the gain on the sale of stock and $5,000 to principal representing the cost basis of the stock
• $95,000 to income from rental receipts earned and received after the trust was created
• $60,000 to income and $2,000 to principal as a result of a stock dividend of 400m shares of $5 par value common stock at a time when the stock was selling for $20 per share
• $10,000 to income for bond interest received and which is payable semiannually on April 1 and October 1
• $35,000 to principal as a result of mortgage payments made by the trust on the commercial buildings

The instrument creating the trust is silent as to the allocation of the trust receipts and disbursements to principal and income.

Required: Answer the following, setting forth reasons for any conclusions stated.
(A) Have the requirements been met for the creation of a valid inter vivos trust?
(B) Indicate the proper allocation to principal and income of the trust receipts and disbursements described above under the majority rules, ignoring the tax effect of each transaction.

Accounting Theory

1. A company borrowed cash from a bank and issued to the bank a short-term noninterest-bearing note payable. The bank discounted the note at 10% and remitted the proceeds to the company. The effective interest rate paid by the company in this transaction would be
   (A) equal to the stated discount rate of 10%
   (B) More than the stated discount rate of 10%
   (C) Less than the stated discount rate of 10%
   (D) Independent of the stated discount rate of 10%

2. A December 15, 1986, purchase of goods was denominated in a currency other than the entity's functional currency. The transaction resulted in a payable that was fixed in terms of the amount of foreign currency and was paid on the settlement date, January 20, 1987. The exchange rates between the functional currency and the currency in which the transaction was denominated changed at December 31, 1986, resulting in a loss that should
   (A) not be reported until January 20, 1987, the settlement date
   (B) be included as a separate component of stockholders' equity at December 31, 1986
   (C) be included as a deferred charge at December 31, 1986
   (D) be included as a component of income from continuing operations for 1986

3. Five thousand (5,000) shares of common stock with a par value of $10 per share were issued initially at $12 per share. Subsequently, one thousand (1,000) of these shares were acquired as treasury stock at $15 per share. Assuming that the par value method of accounting for treasury stock transactions is used, what is the effect of the acquisition of the treasury stock on each of the following?

	Additional Paid-in Capital	Retained Earnings
(A)	Increase	No effect
(B)	Increase	Decrease
(C)	Decrease	Increase
(D)	Decrease	Decrease

4. An inventory loss from a market price decline occurred in the first quarter. The loss was not expected to be restored in the fiscal year. However, in the third quarter the inventory had a market price recovery that exceeded the market decline that occurred in the first quarter. For interim financial reporting, the dollar amount of net inventory should
   (A) decrease in the first quarter by the amount of the market price decline and increase in the third quarter by the amount of the market price recovery
   (B) decrease in the first quarter by the amount of the market price decline and increase in the third quarter by the amount of decrease in the first quarter
   (C) not be affected in the first quarter and increase in the third quarter by the amount of the market price recovery that exceeded the amount of the market price decline
   (D) not be affected in either the first quarter or the third quarter

5. An investment in marketable securities was accounted for by the cost method. These securities were distributed to stockholders as a property dividend in a nonreciprocal transfer. The dividend should be reported at the
   (A) fair value of the asset transferred
   (B) fair value of the asset transferred or the recorded amount of the asset transferred, whichever is higher
   (C) fair value of the asset transferred or the recorded amount of the asset transferred, whichever is lower
   (D) Recorded amount of the asset transferred

6. A proposed project has an expected economic life of eight years. In the calculation of the net present value of the proposed project, salvage value would be
   (A) excluded from the calculation of the net present value
   (B) included as a cash inflow at the estimated salvage value
   (C) included as a cash inflow at the future amount of the estimated salvage value
   (D) included as a cash inflow at the present value of the estimated salvage value

ANSWERS!

Accounting Practice
1. B
2. C
3. C
4. B
5. C
6. C
7. D

Auditing
1. B
2. C
3. D
4. B
5. D
6. A
7. A
8. Additional procedures to be performed prior to the beginning of field work are:
   (5) Read the current year's interim financial statements
   (6) Discuss the scope of the examination with management of the client
   (7) Establish the timing of the audit work
   (8) Arrange with the client for adequate working space
   (9) Coordinate the assistance of client personnel in data preparation
   (10) Establish and coordinate staffing requirements including time budget
   (11) Hold a planning conference with assistants assigned to the engagement
   (12) Determine the extent of involvement, if any, of consultants, specialists, and internal auditors
   (13) Consider the effects of applicable accounting and auditing pronouncements, particularly recent ones
   (14) Consider the need for an appropriate engagement letter
   (15) Prepare documentation setting forth the preliminary audit plan
   (16) Make preliminary judgment about materiality levels
   (17) Make preliminary judgment about reliance to be placed on internal accounting controls
   (18) Update the prior year's written audit program

Business Law
1. C
2. A
3. B
4. D
5. A
6. C
7. A
8. B
9. A
10. (A) Yes. The elements necessary to set up a valid inter vivos trust have been met. John Reed as the creator (grantor or settlor) transferred stocks, bonds, and buildings which constituted the trust res (corpus or principal) to the trust with a present intent to create a trust. The trust instrument which designated Mini as trustee was set up for a lawful purpose and named Myrna as the income beneficiary and Rodney as the remainderman.

(B) Where the trust instrument is silent as to the allocation of the trust receipts and disbursements to principal and income, the following rules apply:

With respect to the $25,000 proceeds on the sale of the stock, most states require that the entire $25,000 be allocated to principal. Therefore, the allocation of $20,000 to income and $5,000 to principal is incorrect.

The allocation of $95,000 in rental receipts to income is correct since the entire amount was earned and received after the creation of the trust.

The allocation of stock dividend to principal and income is incorrect in the vast majority of states. Even under the minority rule, an allocation of a stock dividend to principal based on the par value of the shares distributed is incorrect, i.e., 400 shares x $5 par value = $2,000. Under the majority rule, the entire stock dividend is allocated to principal.

The allocation of the full $10,000 bond interest to income is incorrect since one-half ($2,500) of the semiannual payment received on April 1, 1986, had already accrued when the trust was created on January 1, 1986. Therefore, the proper allocation should be $2,500 to principal and $7,500 to income.

The $35,000 of mortgage payments allocated to principal is correct to the extent such payments represent a repayment of the mortgage debt. Any portion of such payments which are deemed to be interest on the mortgage should be allocated to income.

Accounting Theory
1. B
2. D
3. D
4. B
5. A
6. D

ELEMENTARY SCHOOL TEACHER

Texas State Board of Education

In the late 1970s the Lone Star State discovered, as many other states have also, that an embarrassing number of the people it hired to teach the three R's to children in grades 1 through 5 had not learned the three R's adequately themselves. Before nodding knowingly in patronizing superiority, it might be revealing to take a shot oneself at these representative questions selected from the examination an applicant must now pass before being allowed to teach in Texas elementary schools.

About the Testing Program. In 1981, the Texas legislature passed Senate Bill 50, which requires that persons seeking educator certification in Texas perform satisfactorily on comprehensive examinations. The State Board of Education mandated the development of a testing program as part of the state's educator certification requirements. The purpose of these examinations is to ensure that each educator has the necessary content and professional knowledge to teach in Texas public schools. The first half of the test which follows consists of questions selected from the Elementary Comprehensive exam (Language Arts, Mathematics, Science, Social Science, Fine Arts, and Health and Physical Education). The second half consists of "Professional Development Elementary" questions representing the subareas of Instructional Planning and Curriculum Development, Assessment and Evaluation, Instructional Methodology and Classroom Management, and Principles of Education. The answer section identifies the objective to which each question relates.

Elementary Comprehensive

1. Which of the following basic listening skills is prerequisite to the others?
   (A) Identifying stated main ideas
   (B) Making generalizations
   (C) Drawing conclusions
   (D) Comparing different points of view

2. Which of the following factors is the most important indication of a child's readiness for reading?
   (A) Motor development
   (B) Maturational age
   (C) Physical development
   (D) Chronological age

Read the passage below from Mythology, by Edith Hamilton; then answer the questions that follow.

The first written record of Greece is the Iliad. Greek mythology begins with Homer, generally believed to be not earlier than a thousand years before Christ. The Iliad is, or contains, the oldest Greek literature; and it is written in a rich and subtle and beautiful language which must have had behind it centuries when men were striving to express themselves with clarity and beauty, an indisputable proof of civilization. The tales of Greek mythology do not throw any clear light upon what early mankind was like—a matter, it would seem, of more importance to us, who are their descendants intellectually, artistically, and politically, too. Nothing we learn about them is alien to ourselves.

3. Which line from the passage is a statement of fact?
   (A) The tales of Greek mythology do not throw any clear light upon what early mankind was like.
   (B) Nothing we learn about them is alien to ourselves.
   (C) It is written in a rich and subtle and beautiful language which must have

   had behind it centuries when men were striving to express themselves with clarity and beauty.
   (D) The *Iliad* is, or contains, the oldest Greek literature.

4. The author's point of view toward the subject of this passage is one of
   (A) humorous indulgence
   (B) respect and admiration
   (C) tongue-in-cheek flattery
   (D) longing and nostalgia

5. Which of the following sentences is capitalized correctly?
   (A) My aunt told Uncle Leon about the documentary she saw at the Biograph Theater.
   (B) In the Southern Hemisphere, the first day of winter is in june.
   (C) The Riveras plan to spend their vacation in California at Yosemite national Park.
   (D) Gloria's room had an Eastern exposure, and the sun woke her up at dawn.

6. Which sentence demonstrates proper pronoun-antecedent agreement?
   (A) The council of officials has announced his decision.
   (B) All public parks will close its gates at 5:00 P. M.
   (C) All wardens must report to her stations by 5:15 P. M.
   (D) Workers in public parks must display their identification cards.

7. Which of the following is a compound sentence?
   (A) Sonya painted the sign, and 1 did the lettering.
   (B) Without a dictionary, 1 couldn't check my spelling.
   (C) No one noticed the mistakes until this morning.
   (D) Of twelve words on the sign, three wore misspelled.

8. What number is represented below?

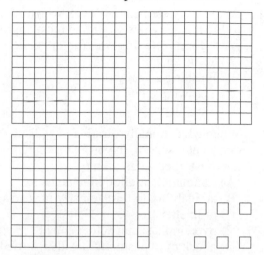

(A) 136
(B) 316
(C) 361
(D) 631

9. Marcy is practicing for a track meet. Each day she runs around a quarter-mile track two and one-half times. How many miles does she run in five days?
(A) ⅝ miles
(B) 1¼ miles
(C) 3⅝ miles
(D) 12½ miles

10. Everything in a hardware store is being sold at 20 percent off the regular price. Mark bought a garden hose regularly priced at $12.95 and a wheelbarrow regularly priced at $23.95. What operations are needed to calculate how much Mark had to pay?
(A) Divide 0.20 by $23.95 and add $12.95.
(B) Add $12.95 and $23.95 and multiply the sum by 0.8.
(C) Multiply $23.95 by 0.20 and add $12.95.
(D) Subtract $12.95 from $23.95 and multiply by 0.2.

11. How many lines of symmetry does an equilateral triangle have?
(A) One
(B) Two
(C) Three
(D) Four

12. Humans are responsible for the extinction of other species primarily through
(A) environmental pollution
(B) experimental hybridization
(C) hunting and poaching
(D) habitat destruction

13. Replacement of a cold air mass by a warm air mass is usually first indicated by the formation of which cloud type?
(A) Cirrus
(B) Cumulonimbus
(C) Cumulus
(D) Stratus

14. Edward is writing a brief report on specific examples of extreme weather conditions in the United States. Which of the following pieces of information would be most relevant to his report?
(A) A hurricane is defined as a storm in which winds blow at greater than 74 miles per hour near the storm center.
(B) The highest temperature ever recorded was in Libya in 1922; it was 136 degrees Fahrenheit.
(C) In the Texas panhandle snowfall averages about 2 feet each year.
(D) The greatest rainfall ever recorded in 1 minute was 1.23 inches; it occurred in Unionville, Maryland.

15. In the United States, all citizens have the responsibility to
(A) petition the government
(B) exercise freedom of religion
(C) serve on juries
(D) determine the rate of income tax

16. Use the map below to answer the question that follows.

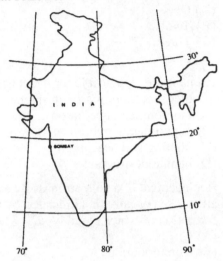

According to the map, Bombay, India, is located at approximately which longitude and latitude?
(A) longitude 73°E., latitude 19°N
(B) longitude 21°N; latitude 73°E
(C) longitude 73°E; latitude 21°N
(D) longitude 19°N; latitude 73°E

17. The Monroe Doctrine was intended to
(A) promote commercial relations with the Concert of Europe
(B) protect American sailors from involuntary service
(C) prevent European expansion in Latin America
(D) open the southeastern United States to settlement

18. Which of the following activities would be most helpful for a sixth grader in developing his or her individual response to art?
(A) Matching artistic techniques to artworks
(B) Participating in a critique of various artworks
(C) Matching artists to their works
(D) Learning terminology associated with art criticism

Professional Development

1. At the early elementary level, which of the following activities would be most appropriate for developing fine-motor skills?
(A) Tying shoelaces
(B) Flushing a swing
(C) Throwing a ball
(D) Skipping rope

2. When educationally disadvantaged students enter school, the problems they face are most often a function of
(A) traumatic childhood incidents
(B) an inability to think clearly in solving problems
(C) overemphasis on achievement
(D) a lack of exposure to positive, varied experiences

3. Which of the following criteria is most important in determining whether a given learning opportunity is appropriate for an elementary class?
(A) Levels of cognitive and psychomotor development among students
(B) Content of available textbooks
(C) Usefulness of the subject matter in life outside the classroom
(D) Testing programs in use at the school

4. Which of the following is most important for a teacher to consider when selecting materials for a specific lesson?
(A) Relationship to learner objectives
(B) Popularity of the material
(C) Relationship to the teacher's personal interests
(D) Publisher of the material

5. Recent data from nationwide standardized tests show that students in the Everett school district scored below average in mathematics skills. Based on these data, which is the most appropriate short-term goal for this school district?
   (A) Emphasize higher-level skills in mathematics
   (B) Assess students' strengths and weaknesses in reading
   (C) Improve Everett's curriculum in reading and mathematics
   (D) Compare the Everett curriculum with those of other districts

6. A class has just read "Jack and the Beanstalk." Which of the following questions would be most appropriate for a teacher to ask if the objective of the lesson is to teach interpretive reading skills?
   (A) How many times did Jack climb the beanstalk?
   (B) Who planted the beanstalk?
   (C) What did Jack do before he climbed the beanstalk?
   (D) Why did Jack climb the beanstalk the third time

7. In the scope and sequence of social studies skills, the emphasis of objectives in the elementary grades tends to follow a progression from
   (A) history to politics
   (B) self to family to community
   (C) culture to economics
   (D) world to nation to neighborhood

8. A teacher notes that on a particular multiple-choice test item, about the same number of students chose each of the four responses. This most likely means that the
   (A) item was too easy for the students
   (B) students did not follow the directions
   (C) item had two correct responses
   (D) students were guessing at the answer

9. One advantage of essay tests as compared with multiple-choice tests is that essay tests
   (A) are more easily standardized
   (B) allow for more creative responses
   (C) can be completed in a shorter period of time
   (D) are easier to score

10. When using a criterion-referenced test, student test scores should be compared with
    (A) average statewide scores
    (B) scores of other students
    (C) a preset standard of mastery
    (D) national norms

11. Which of the following should be the first step in teaching material related to a new learning objective?
    (A) Assign related readings
    (B) Give a preview of new vocabulary
    (C) Present the necessary information
    (D) Explain the purpose of the lesson

12. A teacher plans to teach students how to locate resources in the school library. How could the teacher approach this objective using didactic methodology?
    (A) Encourage independent exploration to discover how library materials are organized
    (B) Have students find materials through a process of trial and error
    (C) Teach one skill at a time and provide frequent practice
    (D) Give students a self-directed guide to using the library

13. A teacher has passed out reading material with a brief glossary of new words. The best way to ensure that students understand the new words is to assign the students to
    (A) circle the new words where they occur in the text
    (B) read the material aloud to each other
    (C) write sentences using the new words
    (D) arrange the new words in alphabetical order

14. Good rapport between students and teachers is most likely to occur in classrooms in which
    (A) rules are permissive
    (B) students determine the pace of instruction
    (C) decisions are made democratically
    (D) teacher expectations are clear and reasonable

15. Which of the following is the most effective way to manage instruction for an elementary class involving students with a wide range of ability?
    (A) Divide the class into small groups according to level
    (B) Use the same materials for all students to challenge the weaker ones
    (C) Assign extra work to those students who are furthest behind
    (D) Work directly with the weakest students and ask others to work on their own

16. When applying discipline in an elementary school classroom, it is most important for the teacher to be
    (A) compassionate
    (B) firm and strong
    (C) consistent
    (D) broad-minded

17. In the school system, a major function of setting long-range educational goals is to
    (A) provide overall direction for the curriculum
    (B) make sure parents know what their children are learning
    (C) find out what students need to learn
    (D) eliminate repetition from one grade to another

18. According to the Family Educational Rights and Privacy Act, also known as the Buckley Amendment, parents have the right to
    (A) select the public schools their children will attend
    (B) inspect and review their children's educational records
    (C) withhold information about their children from school officials
    (D) attend classes with their children to monitor progress

ANSWERS! ☛

(See pages 166 - 170)

SUNDAY SCHOOL TEACHER

Presbyterian Educator Certification Council
The questions in this section are selections from the Presbyterian Associate Christian Educator Certification exam, which, along with a combination of study and teaching experience, is part of a process of obtaining teaching certification in the Presbyterian Church.

The exam as a whole tests examinees on their knowledge of biblical interpretation, reformed theology, Presbyterian polity, human development, educational theory and practice, and program/mission development. Answers are evaluated according to what they reveal about the examinee's sensitivity to others, thoroughness of approach to each subject, consistency of theology and educational philosophy, and clarity of expression. For more information, contact the Presbyterian Church Vocation Agency, 475 Riverside Drive, New York, NY 10115-0094.

Situational Questions (answer any 3)

Describe the words and actions you would use to respond to each situation and your reasoning for responding in such ways and any steps you would take to follow up. You should fill in the details to establish the context as you imagine it in each situation. Please limit each response to 300 words or less.

1. You have a husband and wife team of first grade Church School teachers with whom you have become very well acquainted. One Sunday they stop you and say, "Our son, Dan, has never been baptized and now he's almost seven. Is that something we should do before he gets any older? And if we decide to go ahead, we'd like you to baptize him."

2. The sixth grade Church School teacher has told you that he does not intend to use class time for "Mickey Mouse arts and craft activities." "We have too much to cover to mess with mobiles and silly plays. If they have their Bibles and their workbooks and I have a blackboard and a piece of chalk, I'm in business."

How do you respond?

3. A member of your congregation corners you in the hall and says, "What would it take to make a switch in the Bible that we give our third graders? I'd like to see us go to the *Living Bible* instead of the Revised Standard Version. I really like the way it puts things. I'm sure it would be easy enough for the kids to read. I'd be willing to cover the cost."

4. You receive a phone call from a member of the Naomi Circle saying she is not going to go any longer. "Our study leader is just out to upset us," the caller says. "Yesterday she brought in her paraplegic neighbor to help her lead our study of Psalm 8. Now you've got to admit that makes no sense. Why, it almost contradicts the idea of the Psalmist."

5. A member of your confirmation class says in the midst of a class discussion, "Do you have to believe everything you say in the creeds? I don't like that part of the Apostles' Creed about the 'holy catholic church' because there's lots of stuff Catholics believe that I can't buy!"

6. Your congregation is moving from simultaneous worship and church school to a "two separate hours" format. The session worship committee asks you to "find something constructive for the elementary kids to do during the second hour so they won't have to sit through worship."

Elementary Comprehensive

1. Objective: Identify listening skills Correct Response: (A) Identifying stated main ideas is a literal comprehension skill that would be a prerequisite to more advanced cognitive skills such as making generalizations, drawing conclusions, and comparing different points of view.

2. Objective, Analyze reading readiness concepts
Correct Response: (B) Reading readiness is, most dependent on cognitive development and the development of characteristics such as attention span. These are most highly correlated with maturational age. Motor development and physical development are less important in reading readiness. Chronological age is not a reliable indicator of reading readiness.

3. Objective: Apply evaluative comprehension skills in reading
Correct Response: (D) Response D is an objective, factual statement. The other responses are the author's subjective impressions,

4. Objective: Apply evaluative comprehension skills in reading
Correct Response: (B) The sentence "The *Iliad* is, or contains, the oldest Greek literature, and it is written in a rich and subtle and beautiful language clearly expresses the author's respect and admiration for the subject of the passage.

5. Objective: Use correct spelling, punctuation, and capitalization
Correct Response. (A) Sentence A is capitalized correctly: "Uncle Leon" and "Biograph Theater" are both proper nouns, but "(My) aunt" is not. In sentence B, "june" should be capitalized; the names of the months are always capitalized. In sentence C, all three words in the proper name

should be, capitalized: "Yosemite National Park." In sentence D, "Eastern" should not be capitalized. Names of points of the compass and adjectives derived from them (e.g.? north, northern) are not capitalized when they simply refer to direction; when they refer to specific geographical regions (e.g., the West) or to specific geographical names (e.g., the Southern Hemisphere), they are capitalized.

6. Objective: Use proper agreement in English composition
Correct Response: (D) Only in sentence D does the pronoun ("their") agree in number with its antecedent ("Workers").

7. Objective: Identify sentence structures
Correct Response: (A) Response A is a compound sentence because it is composed of two independent clauses, but no subordinate clauses. Responses B, C, and D are simple sentences.

8. Objective: Apply knowledge of numeration (e.g., place value, counting)
Correct Response: (B) The diagram represents the number 316: three groups of 100, plus one group of 10, plus six 1's (300 + 10 + 6).

9. Objective: Use multiplication
Correct Response: (C) If Marcy runs around a quarter-mile track two and one-half times each day, she runs five-eighths of a mile daily.

$$(1/4 + 1/4 + 1/8, \text{ or } 2 \ 1/2 \times 1/4 = 5/8)$$

In five days she runs $5 \times 5/8 = 25/8 = 3 \ 1/8$ miles.

10. Objective: Apply problem-solving strategies
Correct Response: (B) Everything in the store is being sold at 20 percent off, or 80 percent of, the regular price. To calculate how much Mark had to pay requires

adding the two regular prices ($12.95 and $23.95), then finding 80 percent of the sum (multiply by 0.8).

11. Objective: Recognize plane and solid geometric figures and transformations (e.g., translations, reflections, rotations)
Correct Response: (C) Three lines of symmetry can be drawn in an equilateral triangle, as in the diagram below. A line of symmetry bisects a figure, resulting in two mirror-images, with the line of symmetry representing the mirror. Three such lines can be drawn in an equilateral triangle.

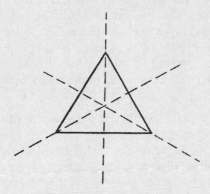

12. Objective: Understand the principles of ecological interactions
Correct Response: (D) Humans have brought about the extinction of other species primarily by destroying their habitats, which are the physical and biological environments in which they live. Examples of this destruction include logging and burning forests, building dams, and paving large areas with asphalt and concrete. Environmental pollution, hybridization, hunting, and poaching have caused extinction of some species, but far fewer than has destruction of habitat.

13. Objective: Understand weather and climate
Correct Response. (A) High, thin cirrus clouds characteristically indicate the, replacement of a cold air moss by a warm air mass. The lighter, warmer air slides up over the denser, colder air. As the warm air rises and cools, cirrus clouds form at high altitudes.

14. Objective: Apply critical thinking skills in social studies
Correct Response: (D) Of the four choices response D is the only example of an extreme weather condition in the United States. Response A defines what a hurricane is but does not note any example of a hurricane's occurrence, Response B specifies an example that occurred in Libya, not in the United States. Response C notes an annual average, which is neither a specific example nor an extreme weather condition.

15. Objective: Analyze rights and responsibilities of U.S. citizenship
Correct Response: (C) The U. S. Constitution guarantees the right to a fair trial in a court of law, by a jury of one's peers. In order to ensure that this right will be provided, citizens have the responsibility to serve on a jury when called. Petitioning the government and exercising freedom of religion rights, not responsibilities. Determining the rate of income tax is the responsibility of government, not of individual citizens. balance-beam exercises will help develop balance and coordination.

16. Objective: Understand geography concepts
Correct Response: (A) Lines of longitude run north-south, indicating distance east or west of the prime meridian. Lines of latitude run east-west, indicating distance north or south of the equator. Bombay lies

about 73 degrees east of the prime meridian and 19 degrees north of the equator.

17. Objective: Apply knowledge, of United States history
Correct Response: (C) The Monroe Doctrine, issued by President Monroe in 1823, was intended to prevent any further European expansion in Latin America. The United States supported the independence movements of Latin American countries during this period and did not want to tolerate any further colonization in the Western Hemisphere that might threaten its own existence.

18. Objective: Develop understanding and appreciation of art
Correct Response: (B) Participating in a critique of various artworks would be most helpful in developing a sixth grader's individual response to art because it is an affective exercise that requires the student to make comments and express personal opinions. Matching techniques to artworks, matching artists to their works, and learning the terminology of art criticism all require cognitive knowledge but do not necessarily elicit any kind of personal response.

Professional Development

1. Objective: Apply knowledge of stages and characteristics of development at the elementary level
Correct Response: (A) Tying shoelaces is an appropriate activity for developing fine-motor skills at the early elementary level. Pushing a swing, throwing a ball, and skipping rope are more related to gross-motor skills.

2. Objective: Recognize characteristics and needs of educationally disadvantaged students

Correct Response: (D) Educationally disadvantaged students often lack exposure to a variety of positive, stimulating experiences. They are no more likely than their nondisadvantaged classmates to have experienced early trauma or to suffer from intellectual disabilities, nor are they likely to be from an environment that placed too much emphasis on achievement.

3. Objective: Design instruction to enable elementary students to achieve educational goals and objectives
Correct Response. (A) Of the four criteria listed, students' levels of cognitive and psychomotor development are most important in determining whether a given learning opportunity is appropriate. If students' levels of development are inappropriate, the content of available textbooks, applications of the subject matter, and testing programs become less consequential.

4. Objective: Apply procedures for planning instructional lessons
Correct Response: (A) The most important of the factors to consider when selecting instructional materials is their relationship to what students are expected to learn, The, popularity of the materials, a teacher's personal interests, and the publisher may be secondary concerns

5. Objective: Derive goals and objectives appropriate to learner needs
Correct Response: (B) Since scores for reading skills were below average, assessing students' strengths and weaknesses in reading is the most appropriate short-term goal, Weaknesses that are identified could then be addressed.

6. Objective: Understand the reading curriculum
Correct Response: (D) Answering the question, "Why did Jack climb the

beanstalk the third time?" requires students to apply interpretive reading skills. The other questions listed involve literal reading skills.

7. Objective: Understand the social studies curriculum
   Correct Response: (B) The scope and sequence of social studies objectives at the elementary level commonly progresses from the individual to larger social units such as the family and community. History to politics, culture to economics, and world to nation to neighborhood are not typical progressions in the elementary social studies scope and sequence of objectives.

8. Objective: Understand principles of testing and measurement
   Correct Response: (D) An approximately equal distribution among the responses to a multiple-choice item is most likely an indication that students were guessing.

9. Objective: Apply principles for developing assessment instruments
   Correct Response: (B) One advantage of essay tests as compared with multiple-choice tests is that essay tests allow students to be more creative in their responses. On essay tests, students design their own responses, whereas on. multiple-choice tests, students choose responses from among several that are offered. In general, essay tests are more difficult to standardize, require more time to complete, and are more difficult to score than multiple-choice tests of comparable length.

10. Objective: Apply principles of evaluation to monitor student progress and evaluate student achievement
    Correct Response: (C) Criterion-referenced tests are designed to allow student

performance to be assessed in relation to a preset standard of mastery. In general, criterion-referenced tests, are not assigned to assess the performance of students in relation to other students.

11. Objective: Apply knowledge of principles of instruction
    Correct Response: (D) In order to orient students and increase the benefits of instruction, the purpose of new lessons should be explained to students before instruction begins. New vocabulary may be taught either before or at the same time as the presentation of the lesson. Related readings are best assigned after students have a context provided by instruction.

12. Objective: Analyze teaching strategies for delivering basic instruction
    Correct Response: (C) Didactic methodology is based upon instructional; presentation and teacher-student interaction. Only response C is typical of this methodology.

13. Objective: Apply knowledge of reading skills to instruction in the content areas
    Correct Response. (C) Writing sentences using the new words would require understanding these words. Therefore, this assignment would best ensure that students understand the words. Circling the words in the text, reading the material aloud, and alphabetizing the words would not require understanding the words.

14. Objective: Identify principles and technique of classroom organization
    Correct Response: (D) When a teacher's expectations are clear and reasonable. students are more likely to respect and meet them, and a good teacher-student rapport Is established. A good rapport is less likely to develop in environments where rules are permissive and/or students determine the rules and pace for instruction.

15. Objective: Analyze principles of instructional management at the elementary level

Correct Response: (A) An effective way to manage instruction in a class whose members have a wide ran of ability is to divide the class into small groups composed of students of similar ability. As an overall strategy, it is less appropriate to work with only one segment of a class, or to use materials poorly suited to students' levels.

16. Objective: Apply principles of discipline management at the elementary level

Correct Response: (C) According to research on classroom management, the most important factor in classroom discipline is for the teacher to be consistent. Being compassionate, firm and strong, or broad-minded is less important and does not necessarily reflect consistency.

17. Objective: Understand the process of educational goal setting

Correct Response: (A) A major function of setting. long-range educational goals is to provide a framework and direction for the curriculum. Long-range, goals are not typically designed to inform parents about what students are learning, assess needs, or fine tune the curriculum

18. Objective: Identify rights and responsibilities in education

Correct Response: (B) The Family Educational Rights and Privacy Act (Buckley Amendment), passed by Congress in 1974, addresses issues related to personal information contained in school records. Provisions of this act allow parents to gain access to their children's educational records.

ENGINEER

Engineer-in-Training & Professional Engineer

When we learned that the most popular engineering specially was civil, we decided to include portions of that exam in this collection if only to set an example to other specialties and professions. If the people who build our roads and bridges can be civil, why can't the rest of us who drive on them?

T his section contains typical questions from two exams used in the process of professionally registering engineers: the Engineer-in-Training (or E-I-T) exam, a broad-based exam reviewing the fundamentals of engineering; and the Professional Engineering (or P. E.) exam, a specialized exam usually taken in an individual's specific branch of engineering. We have selected questions from the civil, chemical, electrical, and mechanical branches of the Professional Engineering exams. Both exams are administered by state boards of engineering registration. Requirements vary somewhat from state to state, but the usual procedure to obtain a professional engineering license is a four-step process: completing a four-year degree in engineering, passing the E-I-T exam, accumulating professional experience, and passing the P. E. exam in one's field.

Engineers need a P. E. license to open their own consulting firms, and may not advertise their services without a license. In addition, many engineers have found that a P. E. license can lead to promotions and higher salaries.

Both the E-I-T and P. E. exams are given in all states twice a year, in mid-April and late October. The E-I-T exam consists of 240 multiple-choice questions; the examinee must answer 210. The questions cover a wide range of basic engineering subjects, including mathematics and physical science. In recent years, one needed to answer approximately half the questions correctly to pass the exam; about two-thirds of those taking the E-I-T exam have passed.

The P. E. exam consists of problem sets requiring deeper knowledge of fewer, more highly specialized subjects than the E-I-T exam. The P. E. exam is an open-book, free-response exam, in which credit may be given for work shown, even if the final answer is incorrect. Approximately half of those taking this exam pass it each year.

For more information about these exams, contact your state board of engineering registration, or the National Council of Engineering Examiners in Clemson, SC, or Professional Publications, Inc., at the following address: Professional Publications, Inc., P.O. Box 199, Dept. 280, San Carlos, CA 94070 (415-593-9119).

Engineer-In-Training

1. What is the determinant of the following matrix?

$$\begin{bmatrix} 6 & -4 & 2 \\ 9 & 6 & 1 \\ 3 & -1 & -2 \end{bmatrix}$$

(A) +20
(B) -36
(C) -204
(D) +73
(E) -120

2. The equation $x^2 + y^2 - 4x + 2y - 20 = 0$ describes
(A) a sphere centered at the origin
(B) a circle of radius 5 centered at the origin
(C) an ellipse centered at (2, -1)
(D) a circle of radius 5 centered at (2, -1)
(E) a parabola with vertex at (2, -1)

3. A $15,000 drill press will be depreciated over 10 years by the fixed percentage method. If the salvage value is $2800, what percentage of the initial book value is the annual depreciation?
(A) 8%
(B) 10%
(C) 12%
(D) 14%
(E) 16%

4. A submerged body will be stable if the center of buoyancy
(A) is located at the body's centroid
(B) and center of gravity are in the same horizontal plane
(C) coincides with the center of gravity
(D) is directly below the center of gravity
(E) is directly above the center of gravity

5. A horizontal pipe section 1000 feet long has a total energy loss of 26.2 feet. If the inside pipe diameter is 12 inches and the flow velocity is 10 ft/sec, what is the Darey-Weisbach friction coefficient?
(A) 0.0170
(B) 0.0080
(C) 0.0017
(D) 0.0002
(E) 0.0008

6. An office coffee percolator requires 1 gallon of water each day to replace evaporation losses. The percolator is acting as
(A) a dehumidifier
(B) both a latent and sensible heat source
(C) a sensible heat source only
(D) a latent heat source only
(E) a hygroscopic device

7. An ideal gas of molecular weight 24 is contained in a 30-ft^3 tank. If the temperature is 90°F and the pressure is 250 psia inside the tank, what is the weight of the gas in the tank?
(A) 3 pounds
(B) 31
(C) 73
(D) 1213
(E) 573

8. What is the efficiency of an ideal Carnot cycle operating between IOO°F and 900°F?
(A) 90%
(B) 89%
(C) 59%
(D) 16%
(E) 11%

9. Why is less current required to deposit 1 mole of Ag from $AgNO_3$ than 1 mole of Cu from $CuCl_2$ in the same amount of time?
(A) Ag has a higher susceptibility.
(B) $CuCl_2$ is insoluble.

(C) Ag has a lower relaxation constant.
(D) Ag has a smaller oxidation number.
(E) Ag has a lower ionization energy.

10. How is the equilibrium constant defined for the following reaction?

$$H_2 + I_2 \rightarrow 2HI$$

(A) $\dfrac{[HI]^2}{[H_2][I_2]}$ (B) $\dfrac{[H][I]}{[H^+][I^-]}$

(C) $\dfrac{[H^+][I^-]}{[HI]^2}$ (D) $\dfrac{[HI]}{[H_2][I_2]}$

(E) $\dfrac{[H_2][I_2]}{[HI]^2}$

11. What is the magnitude of the couple shown below?

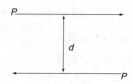

(A) 0 (C) Pd (E) 1.0
(B) ½Pd (D) 2Pd

12. The post in the figure below has a weight of 86 pounds. All surfaces are smooth. What is the tension in cable AB which will keep the post (BC) from sliding?

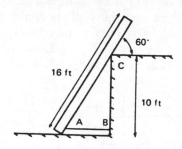

(A) 26.3 lb (D) 44.7 lb
(B) 29.8 lb (E) 25.8 lb
(C) 27.9 lb

13. The coefficient of friction between a 100-pound block of ice and the surface on which it moves is .20. What acceleration is experienced by the block due to the 100-pound force shown below?

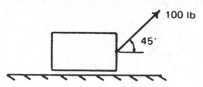

(A) .68 ft/sec² (D) 20.9 ft/sec²
(B) 13.6 ft/sec² (E) 25.3 ft/sec²
(C) 17.1 ft/sec²

14. The first derivative of kinetic energy with respect to velocity is
(A) force
(B) power
(C) kinetic energy squared
(D) momentum
(E) acceleration

15. El (d³ y/dx³) can be solved without integration for
(A) shear (C) deflection (E) stress
(B) moment (D) beam slope

16. The force necessary to punch a ½"-diameter hole through ½" plate steel (ultimate strength 43,000 psi) is approximately
(A) 68 pounds
(B) 4220 pounds
(C) 34,000 pounds
(D) 56,000 pounds
(E) 68,000 pounds

17. What is the current in the resistor R3?

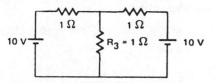

(A) 3.33 amps (D) 13.33 amps
(B) 6.67 amps (E) 30.0 amps
(C) 10.0 amps

18. A wye-connected, 3-phase, 440-volt alternator has a limit of 40 amps per coil. If the alternator supplies a line current of 25 amps at a power factor of .60, what is the power per phase?
(A) 6600 W
(B) 6350 W
(C) 5080 W
(D) 10,560 W
(E) 3810 W

19. The hardness of steel may be increased by heating to approximately 1500°F and quenching in oil or water if
(A) the carbon content is between 0.2% and 2.0%
(B) the carbon content is above 3%
(C) the carbon content is less than 0.2%
(D) all carbon is removed and the steel only contains chromium, nickel, or manganese
(E) the steel has been rolled, not cast

20. A finned heat exchanger surrounded by air carries high-temperature steam. Why should fins be placed on the outside instead of the inside?
(A) High-temperature steam is too corrosive for thin metal fins.
(B) The fins serve as a dust filter.
(C) The fins increase the heat transfer coefficient of the air.
(D) The primary resistance to heat flow is on the outside, and the fins reduce this resistance.
(E) Placement of the fins is not critical. However, external fins are easier to manufacture.

21. Which of the values below comes closest to a pole of

$$F(s) = \frac{2(s+4)}{s(s-3)}$$

(A) −4   (C) 3   (E) ⅔
(B) 2   (D) 6

22. How would variable X be printed out as a result of the following sequence of FORTRAN statements?
X = 59432.79
J = FIX(X)
WRITE J(5,10)
10 FORMAT (14)
(A) 9432
(B) 5943
(C) 59433
(D) 59432
(E) ****

23. The density of $_{26}Fe^{56}$ is 7.86 g/cc. What is the approximate volume of an iron atom?
(A) .8 EE-23 cubic centimeter
(B) 1.2 EE-23 cubic centimeter
(C) 7.3 EE-23 cubic centimeter
(D) 9.3 EE-23 cubic centimeter
(E) 43.0 EE-23 cubic centimeter

Chemical Engineering

1. Water is supplied at 50 gpm to a pressure vessel operating at 20 psig and 80°F. A surge tank, vented to the atmosphere, is provided as shown. During normal operations, the check valve is open. The equivalent length of the stand pipe to the pressure vessel is 100 ft. and includes all elbows, fittings, and expansion.
(A) Under normal flow conditions, what is the level of water in the surge tank?
(B) If the pump shuts off suddenly and the cheek valve closes immediately, how long will it take for the flow to the pressure vessel to decrease by 5%?

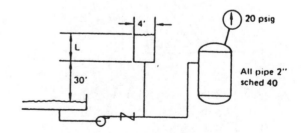

Civil Engineering

1   You have been hired as a consultant to a client affected by an OSHA ruling. The client's factory has been inspected and has been found to have substandard illumination. Your client has told you that, if the new illumination system required is too expensive, he will shut down the plant. Such a shutdown will reduce the client's before-tax profit by $30,000 per year. You propose three types of lighting (see table), but you are unable to determine which is best because your client does not know which interest rate should be used. What is the minimum attractive rate of return (MARR) associated with each lighting system? Which system should be chosen?

type	initial cost	annual cost	gradient cost	salvage after 20 years
mercury	$30,000	$13,000	$2000	$3000
fluorescent	45,000	12,000	1900	13,000
metal-halide	54,000	10,000	1800	3000

2   For the beam cross section shown, determine the maximum resisting moment based on (a) working strength design and (b) ultimate strength design.

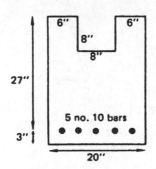

$f'c = 3000$ psi
$fc = 1350$ psi
$fy = 50,000$ psi
$fs = 20,000$ psi
$n = 9$

Electrical Engineering

1. Given the power system shown, find the output and power factor of generator G_1.

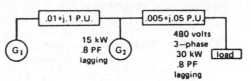

2. Use an 8:1 multiplexer with permissible inputs of A, $\bar{A}$, 0, and 1 to design the function

$$f = \bar{A}BD + AC + \bar{A}B\bar{C}D + \overline{ABCD}$$

Mechanical Engineering

1. An orbiting spacecraft has an argon gas manipulator for deployment of a solar panel. The arm of the manipulator is connected to a 3"-diameter piston with an 8"-stroke requiring a 36-pound thrust in one direction only. The argon gas is compressed to 1500 psig in a 0.1-ft' bottle. The bottle temperature is maintained at 380°R. There is a pressure regulator in the gas line. How many cycles will the bottle of argon gas provide? What will be the pressure in the gas bottle at the time of launch if the ambient conditions are 14.7 psia and 540°R?

2. A 2"-diameter solid 1020 cold-drawn steel shaft on simple supports carries two pulleys at a noncritical speed. The shaft ultimate strength is 69,000 psi. Yield stress is 48,000 psi. The endurance limit in complete reversal is 35,000 psi. Poisson's ratio is .283. It is required that the deflection not exceed .04 inches at any point and that the maximum angle of twist not exceed .3°. Does the shaft meet the specifications?

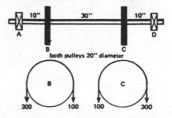

ANSWERS!

ENGINEER-IN-TRAINING

1. C   EXPAND BY THE FIRST COLUMN

$$6\begin{vmatrix} 6 & 1 \\ -1 & -2 \end{vmatrix} - 9\begin{vmatrix} -4 & 2 \\ -1 & -2 \end{vmatrix} + 3\begin{vmatrix} -4 & 2 \\ 6 & 1 \end{vmatrix}$$

$$= 6(-12+1) - 9(8+2) + 3(-4-12)$$
$$= 6(-11) - 9(10) + 3(-16) = -66 -90 -48$$
$$= -204$$

2. D THIS IS NOT A CUBIC, SO IT CANNOT BE A 3-D SPHERE BECAUSE OF THE −4X AND +2Y TERMS IT CANNOT BE CENTERED AT THE ORIGIN. FACTORING,

$$(x-2)^2 + (y+1)^2 = 20 + 4 + 1 = 25$$

THIS IS A CIRCLE OF RADIUS 5 CENTERED AT $(2, -1)$.

3. A THE INITIAL BOOK VALUE IS 15,000

EACH YEAR, DEPRECIATION $= \frac{1}{10}(15,000 - 2800)$
$$= 1220$$

$$\frac{1220}{15,000} = .081$$

4. E FOR A TOTALLY SUBMERGED OBJECT, THE CENTER OF MASS (C.G.) MUST BE BELOW THE CENTER OF BUOYANCY.

5. A $h_6 = \frac{6Lv^2}{2Dg}$ or $f = \frac{2Dg\,h_6}{Lv^2}$

$$f = \frac{(2)(\frac{8}{12})(32.2)(26.2)}{(1000)(10)^2} = .01687$$

6. B THE PERCOLATOR GIVES OFF BOTH STEAM AND HEAT.

7. B $M = \frac{PV}{RT} = \frac{(250)(144)(30)}{\left(\frac{1545}{24}\right)\left(\frac{460+90}{B}\right)} = 30.5$

8. C $\eta = \frac{(900+460) - (100+460)}{900+460} = .588$

9. D

10. A

11. C $M = Pd$

12. E LENGTH AB $= \frac{10}{TAN 60°} = 5.77$

$$\sum M_B \; \circlearrowright : (86)(8)\cos 60° - B\cos 30°(10)$$
$$- B\sin 30°(5.77) = 0$$
$$B = 29.78$$
$$|AB| = B_x = (29.78)(\cos 30°) = 25.8$$

13. D

$$F_y = F_x = 70.7$$
$$F_{friction} = .20(100 - 70.7) = 5.86$$
$$a_x = F/m = \frac{(70.7 - 5.86)}{\frac{100}{32.2}} = 20.88 \; ft/sec^2$$

14. D $\frac{d}{dV}\left(\frac{1}{2}mV^2\right) = mV$

15.

16. C $A_{SHEAR} = \frac{1}{2}(\pi)\left(\frac{1}{2}\right) = .7854$

$F = (43,000)(.7854) = 33,772$ LB

17. B USE SUPERPOSITION AND SYMMETRY, DUE TO THE LEFT HAND SOURCE ALONE

$I_t = \dfrac{10\ V}{1 + \dfrac{(1)(1)}{1+1}} = 6.67$

$I_{R_3} = \frac{1}{2}(6.67) = 3.33$

DUE TO SYMMETRY, $2(3.33) = 6.67$

18. E $V_{phase} = \dfrac{440}{\sqrt{3}} = 254$

$P = (254)(25)(.60) = 3810$ WATTS

19. A

20. D
BOTH C AND D COULD BE ARGUED. PROBABLY, D IS BEST

21. C
S=0 AND S=3 MAKE THE DENOMINATOR ZERO.

22. E
J = 59432 (INTEGER)
SINCE J HAS MORE THAN 4 DIGITS, IT WILL OVERFLOW THE AVAILABLE SPACE AND APPEAR AS ****

23. B
THE ATOMIC WEIGHT OF IRON IS 56. THE VOLUME OF 1 gMOLE (56 g) IS

$\dfrac{56}{7.86} = 7.12$ CC

$\dfrac{7.12}{6.023\ EE23} = 1.18\ EE-23$

Chemical Engineering

1. A

ASSUME FIGURE AT LEFT   SINCE PROBLEM UNCLEAR

BERNOULLI BETWEEN POINTS 1 & 2

$$Z_1 + \frac{V_1^2}{2g} + P_1 = Z_2 + \frac{V_2^2}{2g} + P_2 + h_f$$

$$\Delta z + \frac{\Delta V^2}{2g} + \frac{\Delta P}{\rho} + h_f = 0$$

$$30 + 0 + \frac{(20 - P_1)144}{62.19} + h_f = 0$$

$$h_f = \frac{L}{D} \frac{V^2}{2g} f$$

L = 100 ft

D = 2.067 inches

E = .0002

f = .0229

$\rho = 62.19 \, lb/ft^3 \, @ \, 80°F$

$\mu = .85 \, cp \, @ \, 80°F$

$$N_{Re} = 50.6 \frac{Q\rho}{d\mu} = \frac{(50.6)(50)(62.19)}{(2.067)(.85)}$$

$$N_{Re} = 89553.3$$

$$V = .408 \frac{Q}{d^2} = .408(50)/2.067^2 = 4.774 \, ft/sec$$

$$h_f = \left(\frac{100}{2.067/12}\right) \frac{4.774^2}{2(32.2)} (.0229) = 4.70 \, ft$$

$$30 + 0 + (20 - P_1)(2.3159) + 4.70 = 0 \quad \Rightarrow P_1 = 34.985 \, psig$$

velocity in stand pipe = 0

$$\frac{34.985 \times 144}{62.19} = 81 \, ft \, of \, H_2O \quad \Rightarrow L = 81 - 30 = 51 \, ft$$

B   find P_1 at $(.95)(50) = 47.5$ gpm.

assume f constant $= .0229$

from 3→2 $\Delta z + \dfrac{\Delta v^2}{2g}^{\!\!0} + \Delta P + h_f = 0$ $h_f = (h_f)_{OLD} \dfrac{130}{100} (.95)^2 = 5.51$ ft

from 1→2 $\Delta z^{\,30} + \dfrac{\Delta v^2}{2g} + \Delta P + h_f = 0$ $h_f = (h_f)_{OLD} \,.95^2 = 4.241$ ft

         $\dfrac{\Delta P}{\rho} = 34.241 \Rightarrow P_1 = 34.78$ psig

from 4→1 $\Delta z + \dfrac{\Delta v^2}{2g} + \Delta P + h_f = 0$ $h_f = (h_f)_{OLD} \dfrac{30}{100} (.95)^2 = 1.27$ ft

$L + 30 + \left[\left(\dfrac{2.067}{48} \right)^2 - 1 \right] \dfrac{4.774^2}{2(32.2)} + (0 - 34.78) \dfrac{144}{62.19} + 1.27 = 0 \Rightarrow L = 49.6$ ft

$v_{average \ in \ 4" \ pipe} = \left[(1.00 + .95)/2 \right] 4.774 \dfrac{2.067^2}{48^2} = .0086$ ft/sec

$t = d/v = 4/.0086 = 465$ seconds

Civil Engineering

1. WORK IN THOUSANDS OF DOLLARS

MERCURY LIGHTING

$$PW = -30 -13(P/A, i\%, 20) -2(P/G, i\%, 20)$$
$$+30(P/A, i\%, 20) +3(P/F, i\%, 20)$$

$$= -30 +17(P/A, i\%, 20) - 2(P/G, i\%, 20)$$
$$+ 3(P/F, i\%, 20)$$

TRY 10%:

$$= -30 + 17(8.5136) - 2(55.4069) + 3(.1486)$$
$$= 4.36$$

TRY 5%:

$$= -30 + 17(12.4622) - 2(98.4884) + 3(.3769)$$
$$= -13.99$$

INTERPOLATE:

$$ROR = 5 + (10-5)\frac{13.99}{13.99 + 4.36} = \boxed{8.8\%}$$

REPEAT FOR BETTER ACCURACY

FLUORESCENT

$$PW = -45 +18(P/A) - 1.9(P/G) + 13(P/F)$$

TRY 10%:

$$= -45 +18(8.5136) -1.9(55.4069) +13(.1486)$$
$$= 4.9$$

TRY 5%:

$$= -45 + 18(12.4622) -1.9(98.4884) +13(.3769)$$
$$= -2.91$$

INTERPOLATE:

$$ROR = 5 + (10-5)\frac{2.91}{2.91 + 4.9} = \boxed{6.9\%}$$

METAL HALIDE

$$PW = -54 +20(P/A) -1.8(P/G) +3(P/F)$$

TRY 20%:

$$= -54 +20(4.8698) -1.8(21.7395) +3(.026)$$
$$= 4.3$$

TRY 25%:

$$= -54 +20(3.9539) -1.8(14.8932) +3(.0115)$$
$$= -1.7$$

INTERPOLATE:

$$ROR = 20 + (25-20)\frac{4.3}{4.3 + 1.7} = \boxed{23.6\%}$$

DETERMINE THE MINIMUM MARR NECESSARY TO SELECT EACH ALTERNATIVE.

FLUORESCENT: THE MARR NOT TO CHOOSE THIS ALTERNATIVE WOULD HAVE TO BE GREATER THAN 6.9%.

MERCURY LIGHTING: DO AN INCREMENTAL ANALYSIS, COMPARING TO FLUORESCENT.

INCREMENTS:

INITIAL COST: 45 -30 = 15 (MORE)

ANNUAL COST: 12 -13 = -1 (SAVINGS)

GRADIENT: 1.9 - 2.0 = -.1 (SAVINGS)

SALVAGE: 13 - 3 = 10

TRY 10%:

$$PW = -15 + 1(8.5136) + .1(55.4069) + 10(.1486)$$
$$= 0.54$$

TRY 15%:

$$PW = -15 + 1(6.2593) + .1(33.5822) + 10(.061)$$
$$= -4.77$$

$$ROR = 10 + (15-10)\left(\frac{.54}{.54-(-4.77)}\right) = 10.5\%$$

WE CONCLUDE THAT, IF MERCURY IS CHOSEN, THE INCREMENT EARNS 10.5% AND THE AVERAGE ROR IS 8.8%. SINCE 10.5 > 8.8, THE MARR NOT TO CHOOSE MERCURY WOULD HAVE TO BE GREATER THAN 8.8%

METAL HALIDE: COMPARE WITH MERCURY.

INCREMENTS:

INITIAL COST: 54 - 45 = 9

ANNUAL COST: 10 - 12 = -2

GRADIENT: 1.8 - 1.9 = -.1

SALVAGE: 3 - 13 = -10

TRY 25%:

$$PW = -9 + 2(3.9539) + .1(14.8932) - 10(.0115)$$
$$= .28$$

SINCE PW > 0, ROR > 25% ON INCREMENT.

SINCE THE INCREMENTAL ROR OF 25% EXCEEDS 23.6% THE MARR NOT TO CHOOSE METAL HALIDE WOULD HAVE TO BE GREATER THAN 23.6%

2.A

AREA OF NO. 10 BARS IS
$$5(1.27) = 6.35 \text{ IN}^2$$
THE EQUIVALENT CONCRETE AREA OF
THE STEEL IS $9(6.35) = 57.15 \text{ IN}^2$

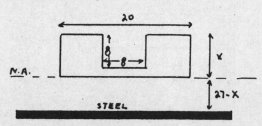

LOCATE THE NEUTRAL AXIS:
$$(20)(x)\left(\frac{x}{2}\right) - (8)(8)(x-4) = (27-x)(57.15)$$
$$x^2 - .685x - 128.7 = 0$$
$$x = 11.69 \quad (\text{OKAY})$$

THE CENTROIDAL MOMENT OF INERTIA IS
$$I_c = \frac{(20)(11.69)^3}{3} - \left[\frac{(8)(8)^3}{12} + (64)\left(11.69 - \frac{8}{2}\right)^2\right]$$
$$+ 57.15(27-11.69)^2$$
$$= 19920 \text{ IN}^4$$

SINCE $\sigma = \frac{Mc}{I}$, $M = \frac{\sigma_{max} I}{c}$

TO KEEP $\sigma_c < 1350$, (GIVEN)
$$M_c = \frac{(1350)(19920)}{11.69} = \boxed{\begin{array}{l}2.3 \text{ EE6 IN-LBF} \\ 1.92 \text{ EE5 FT-LBF}\end{array}}$$

TO KEEP $\sigma_s < 20,000$ (GIVEN)
$$M_s = \frac{(20,000)(19920)}{(9)(27-11.69)} = 2.89 \text{ EE6 IN-LBF}$$

SO M_c GOVERNS

2.B

AT ULTIMATE STRENGTH, THE STEEL IS AT 50,000
PSI, AND THE COMPRESSIVE BLOCK IS AT
$$.85 f_c' = (.85)(3000) = 2550 \text{ PSI}$$
FIND THE HEIGHT OF THE STRESS BLOCK FOR
BALANCED DESIGN AT ULTIMATE LOADING. ASSUME
THE STRESS BLOCK IS MORE THAN 8" FROM THE
TOP OF THE BEAM. FROM EQN. 14.18,
$$A_s f_y = (.85) f_c' A_{comp}$$
$$(6.35)(50,000) = (2550)\left[a(6+6) + 8(a-8)\right]$$

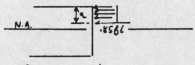

$$A_{comp} = 124.51$$
$$a = 9.43$$

FROM EQN 14.24, THE NOMINAL STRENGTH IS
$$M_N = A_s f_y (\text{MOMENT ARM})$$
$$= (6.35)(50,000)\left(27 - \frac{9.43}{2}\right) = \boxed{7.08 \text{ EE6 IN-LBF}}$$

(THE FACTOR ϕ IS AN ACI CODE PROVISION
AND IS NOT PART OF ULTIMATE STRENGTH
THEORY.)

Electrical Engineering

1. $Assumptions:$ $P_L = P_{base} \times pf$

$$P_{base} = \frac{30 KW}{.8} = 37,500$$

$$|I_L| = I_{base}$$

$$|V_L| = V_{base}$$

take V_L = reference = $1 \angle 0°$

$$I_L = 1 \angle -\cos^{-1} .8$$

$$V_2 = I_L (.005 + j.05) + V_L$$

$$= 1.034 + j.037 = 1.035 \angle 2.05°$$

then

$$I_2 = \frac{.5}{V_2} \angle \tan^{-1} .8 + 2.05 = .483 \angle -34.82°$$

$$I_1 = I_L - I_2 = .403 - j.324 = .517 \angle -38.78°$$

$$V_1 = (.01 + j.1) I_1 + V_2 = 1.07 + j.074$$

$$S_1 = V_1 I_1^* = .555 \angle 42.7°$$

$$= .407 + j.377$$

then

$$P_1 = .407 \times 37.5 K = 15.26 \ KW$$

$$Pf = \frac{.407}{.555} = .734 \ lagging$$

$$V_1 = |1.07 + j.074| \times 480 = 515 \ V_{\ell-\ell}$$

2. Use A as the least-significant variable in Veitch diagram

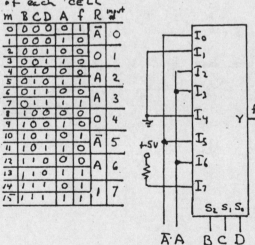

All other entries are zero

Construct truth table with A as the RESIDUE VARIABLE, using the minterm numbers from the Veitch diagram (in lower right-hand corner of each CELL

m	B	C	D	A	f	R	input #
0	0	0	0	0	1	$\bar{A}$	0
1	0	0	0	1	0		
2	0	0	1	0	0	0	1
3	0	0	1	1	0		
4	0	1	0	0	0	A	2
5	0	1	0	1	1		
6	0	1	1	0	0	A	3
7	0	1	1	1	1		
8	1	0	0	0	0	0	4
9	1	0	0	1	0		
10	1	0	1	0	1	$\bar{A}$	5
11	1	0	1	1	0		
12	1	1	0	0	0	A	6
13	1	1	0	1	1		
14	1	1	1	0	1	1	7
15	1	1	1	1	1		

Mechanical Engineering

1. THE SWEPT PISTON VOLUME IS

$$V = AL = \left(\frac{\pi}{4}\right)(3)^2(8) = 56.55 \text{ IN}^3$$

THE REQUIRED PRESSURE AT THE PISTON FACE IS

$$P = \frac{F}{A} = \frac{36}{\left(\frac{\pi}{4}\right)(3)^2} = 5.09 \text{ PSIG}$$

ASSUME THE PRESSURE GIVEN IS WITH RESPECT TO A VACUUM. THEREFORE, PSIG = PSIA.

FOR ARGON (FROM PAGE 6-15) THE REDUCED PRESSURE AND TEMPERATURE ARE

$$\frac{P}{P_c} = \frac{1500}{705.0} = 2.13$$

$$\frac{T}{T_c} = \frac{380}{272.2} = 1.4$$

THE CORRESPONDING COMPRESSIBILITY FACTOR IS .77. THE MASS OF THE BOTTLED ARGON IS

$$M = \frac{PV}{ZRT} = \frac{(1500)^{LB/IN^2}(144)^{IN^2/FT^2}(.1)^{FT^3}}{(.77)(38.70)^{FT/^\circ R}(380)^\circ R}$$

$$= 1.908 \text{ LB}$$

SIMILARLY, THE MASS OF ARGON WHEN THE PRESSURE HAS BEEN REDUCED TO 5.09 PSIG IS

$$M = \frac{PV}{RT} = \frac{(5.09)(144)(.1)}{(38.70)(380)}$$

$$= .005$$

THE MASS OF ARGON USED PER CYCLE IS

$$M = \frac{(5.09)(144)(56.55)}{(12)^3(38.70)(380)} = 1.63 \text{ EE-3 LB}$$

THE MAXIMUM # OF CYCLES BEFORE THE TANK CONTENTS DROP BELOW PSIG IS

$$N = \frac{1.908 - .005}{1.63 \text{ EE-3}} = \boxed{1167.5 \text{ CYCLES}}$$

A FIRST ESTIMATE OF THE PRESSURE ON THE GROUND IS

$$P = \frac{mRT}{V} = \frac{(1.908)(38.70)(540)}{(.1)(144)} = 2769 \text{ PSIA}$$

THE REDUCED PROPERTIES ARE

$$\frac{P}{P_c} = \frac{2769}{705.0} = 3.93 \qquad \frac{T}{T_c} = \frac{540}{272.2} = 1.98$$

FROM FIGURE 6.11, Z = .96 SO

$$P_{GROUND} = (.96)(2769) = 2658 \text{ PSIA}$$

2.

$$I = \frac{1}{4}\pi r^4 = \frac{1}{4}(\pi)(1)^4 = .7854 \text{ IN}^4$$

ASSUME E = 3 EE7 PSI

$$Y_{max} = \frac{(400)(10)}{(3\text{EE}7)(.7854)}\left[\frac{(50)^2}{8} - \frac{(10)^2}{6}\right]$$

$$= .05''$$

$$\boxed{\text{DOES NOT MEET DEFLECTION SPECS}}$$

THE TWIST IS

$$\Theta = \frac{TL}{GJ} \quad (\text{IN RADIANS})$$

$$T = (300 - 100)\left(\frac{20}{2}\right) = 2000 \text{ IN-LBF}$$

$$L = 30$$

FROM EQUATION 14.77

$$G = \frac{E}{2(1+\mu)} = \frac{3\text{EE}7}{2(1+.283)} = 1.17 \text{ EE7 PSI}$$

$$J = \frac{\pi d^4}{32} = \frac{\pi (2)^4}{32} = 1.571 \text{ IN}^4$$

$$\Theta = \frac{(2000) \text{ IN-LB } (30) \text{ IN}}{(1.17 \text{ EE7}) \text{ PSI } (1.571) \text{ IN}^4} = 3.26 \text{ EE-3 RAD}$$

$$\phi = \frac{\Theta (360)}{2\pi} = \frac{(3.26 \text{ EE-3})(360)}{2\pi} = .187^\circ$$

$$\boxed{\text{DOES MEET TWIST SPECS}}$$

EXECUTIVE ASSISTANT

Katharine Gibbs School

"Take a letter, George."
"Yes, Ma'am."

Your assistant may well know more than you do about Hotel and Restaurant Management, Business Administration, and Microcomputing/Accounting if she acquired her skills at the Katharine Gibbs School. And in case you think that Gibbs is attended mostly by young ladies from good Boston families, it may be news to you that there are now seven Katharine Gibbs campuses (five of which are outside of New England), that those campuses are attended by men as well as women, and that financial aid is available.

Most of the Katharine Gibbs programs feature vocational courses in such areas as business math, computer software applications, and keyboarding. Gibbs straddles the line between academics and vocational training with its Associate in Applied Science in Secretarial Arts program, a two-year degree program that not only involves courses in such skills as office management, keyboarding, and computer software applications, but also requires students to take more traditional academic courses in the humanities and social sciences, such as literature, macro- and microeconomics, and psychology.

The questions that follow are from the Executive Assistant and several Gibbs programs designed to prepare students for a career in the "Office of the 21st Century." Students will develop skills to make decisions, to communicate effectively, to use business applications software and to solve information management problems.

For more information about all the programs that Gibbs offers, contact the campus nearest you. (See the Credits section in the back for addresses of the campuses.)

Business Communications

1. Which of the following cannot be modified by an adverb?
   (A) Adjective
   (B) Adverb
   (C) Verb
   (D) Noun

2. Which sentence is expressed correctly?
   (A) It is she whom we believe will be promoted.
   (B) It is she who we believe will be promoted.
   (C) It is her whom we believe will be promoted.
   (D) It is her who we believe will be promoted.

3. Which of the following is acceptable in modern business writing?
   (A) As per your instructions
   (B) In accordance with your instructions
   (C) Following your instructions
   (D) Pursuant to your instructions

4. Indicate which sentence is expressed correctly.
   (A) All the assistant's received a three week's vacation.
   (B) All the assistants' received a three week's vacation.
   (C) All the assistance received a three weeks' vacation.
   (D) All the assistants received a three weeks' vacation.

5. Which of the following words is spelled correctly?
   (A) Accommodate
   (B) Subpeona
   (C) Procede
   (D) Questionaire

Speedwriting

1. The primary rule in any shorthand system is
   (A) write what you hear
   (B) write all vowels
   (C) write the first three letters of each word
   (D) write out all numerals

2. In Speedwriting shorthand the capital letter "N" stands for
   (A) in, not
   (B) "ence"—"end"—"ent"
   (C) number
   (D) "ing" or necessary

3. This speedwriting brief form symbol / represents
   (A) per month
   (B) it is, its, it's
   (C) it, at
   (D) to, too

4. In Speedwriting the capital, printed, and disjoined "T" represents
   (A) subway
   (B) transportation
   (C) travel/trip
   (D) "trans"

5. In Speedwriting the symbol for the period (.) is
   (A))
   (B) @
   (C) x
   (D) \

Business Math

1. Pat Alves bought a new refrigerator for $695.75. Pat gave the salesperson seven $100 bills. What change did Pat receive?
   (A) $433.05
   (B) $217.90
   (C) $27.05
   (D) $4.25

2. Harry Morton traveled 9,880 miles. His car averaged 19 miles per gallon. Assuming a gallon of gas costs $1.45, what was Harry's gasoline cost for the trip?
   (A) $547
   (B) $754
   (C) $574
   (D) $457

3. A note dated July 15 and due on September 18 runs for exactly
   (A) 71 days
   (B) 54 days
   (C) 65 days
   (D) 15 days

4. What number increased by 2,000 equals 4,768?
   (A) 1,768
   (B) 4,012
   (C) 2,768
   (D) 768

5. To convert a percent to a decimal,
   (A) move the decimal point two places to the left
   (B) add a second % symbol
   (C) move the decimal point four places to the right
   (D) multiply by 90 and delete the % symbol

Accounting

1. The record used to record the original transactions in their entirety is called a
   (A) journal
   (B) ledger
   (C) capital statement
   (D) personal withdrawal

2. The process of transferring the amounts from the journal to the ledger is called
   (A) journalizing
   (B) recording
   (C) ledgerizing
   (D) posting

3. The general journal has two amount columns; the *left* column is the
   (A) debit column
   (B) credit column
   (C) total column
   (D) items column

4. The form used for detailed listing of items being deposited in the bank is the
   (A) signature card
   (B) check record
   (C) deposit slip
   (D) bank statement

5. The entry to record the sale of merchandise on account requires a debit to
   (A) accounts payable
   (B) accounts receivable
   (C) sales
   (D) cash

Keyboarding

1. Page numbering of all pages after page 1 of unbound and leftbound reports appears
   (A) on line 7 at the top right margin
   (B) on line 4 at the top right margin
   (C) centered on line 4

2. The most common method of citing references within a report is by
   (A) using a reference list at the end of the report
   (B) using internal referencing within the report (author, date, page number)
   (C) typing footnotes at the bottom of the page on which they are cited

3. How many horizontal spaces are available on paper that is 8 /2 by 11 inches, using elite pitch?
   (A) 102
   (B) 85
   (C) 66

4. The most commonly used letter style in offices today is
   (A) block style
   (B) Administrative Management Society style
   (C) modified block style

5. When an attention line is used in a letter it appears as
   (A) a double space above the salutation
   (B) the second line in the address
   (C) a double space below the salutation

Machine Transcription

1. The best way to transcribe machine dictation is to
   (A) type as you listen   (B)   listen to the whole tape before you type from it
   (C) listen to as much as you can memorize, then type it

2. The most important transcription skill is
   (A) fast typing
   (B) good listening skills
   (C) formatting documents
   (D) English skills

3. One advantage of machine transcription as compared with shorthand is
   (A) the assistant is with the executive who is dictating
   (B) the transcriptionist works from the actual voice of the dictating person, so work can often be more accurate
   (C) machine transcription requires that the executive be in his or her office

4. When you receive a tape to be transcribed, you should preview the work before you begin typing. One of the things you do in this preview is
   (A) listen to any correction messages or special instructions
   (B) set your margins
   (C) enter the date at the top of the stationery

5. After a letter is typed, it should be
   (A) sent immediately to the originator
   (B) signed and mailed by the transcriptionist
   (C) inspected and proofread for quality
   (D) checked and mailed by the proofreader without being returned to the originator

Office Systems and Procedures

1. The professional organization for secretaries is known as
   (A) American Secretaries Association
   (B) Professional Secretaries International
   (C) Administrative Secretaries International
   (D) Society of Professional Secretaries

2. Which of the following is NOT an acceptable time management principle?
   (A) Assign priorities to work
   (B) Set deadlines for work
   (C) Follow a daily work plan
   (D) Do routine items during the most productive time of day

3. The following class of mail may be insured:
   (A) first class
   (B) second class
   (C) third and fourth classes
   (D) all of the above

4. A letter containing valuable legal papers should be sent
   (A) certified
   (B) insured
   (C) registered
   (D) special handling

5. Which of the following travel duties may be performed for the employer by the executive assistant?
   (A) Preparing an itinerary
   (B) Obtaining a passport
   (C) Purchasing traveler's checks
   (D) All of the above

6. If an error is found in the minutes at subsequent meetings of an organization, the secretary should
   (A) recopy the minutes to incorporate the changes
   (B) attach a separate sheet at the end of the original minutes to show the changes
   (C) have the chairperson make the corrections on the original copy
   (D) make the corrections and additions on the original copy

ANSWERS!

Business Communications

1. D
2. B
3. C
4. D
5. A

Speedwriting Shorthand

1. A
2. B
3. C
4. D
5. D

Business Math

1. D
2. B
3. C
4. C
5. A

Accounting

1. A
2. D
3. A
4. C
5. B

Keyboarding

1. B
2. B
3. A
4. C
5. B

Machine Transcription

1. C
2. D
3. B
4. A
5. C

Office Procedures

1. B
2. D
3. D
4. C
5. A
6. D

FIREFIGHTING

Mental and Physical Ability Requirements

*Q: Which nationally known fire-fighting institution is
best known to the general public?*

A: Smoke Enders.

Pretty much every kid (male kid, at least) has dreamed about rescuing fair maidens from burning buildings and riding lickety-split down Main Street in a gleaming red fire engine, sirens blaring. See if the following description squares with your childhood image.

A firefighter must fight fires while wearing work apparel and equipment weighing 45 to 55 pounds. While in full gear the firefighter may be required to carry 50 pounds of hose or rescue a citizen inside a burning building. (So far, squares pretty well, doesn't it?) A firefighter's duties may include fire prevention, emergency calls, and postfire salvage and cleanup. (Hmm, don't know about this part, sounds too much like cleaning your room.) A firefighter must be a team player and must be able to get along with a variety of people. A firefighter must have good judgment, good communication skills, mechanical aptitude, the ability to perform arithmetic computations, and the ability to comprehend and learn firefighting material. (Hmm, sounds too much like school.)

A firefighter must be able to work in a paramilitary organization; that is, a firefighter must be able to follow orders. In addition, a firefighter must be able to live at close quarters and work nontraditional hours. A firefighter usually works a 24-hour shift, with 48 or 72 hours off between shifts, depending on the department.

In case the forgoing has revived your childhood dreams, you might want to know about salary and qualifications. Starting salaries for firefighters these days run from about $24,000 to $30,000. In most departments, a firefighter must be at least 18, have a valid driver's license, be a high-school graduate, pass a medical exam, have normal night vision, color vision, depth perception, and hearing, and have a good driving record and a background free of felony convictions.

If you're still interested, you might want to know that you have to pass an examination to be eligible for hiring. Most departments have a three-stage examination: a written test, a physical agility test (see the sidebar following this section), and an oral interview. The written test is sometimes the only component of the exam that determines your rank on an eligibility list. Usually, though, the written test has a weight equal to 35-60 percent of the final grade. Most physical ability tests are simply pass/fail, but some are given a small weighting. The oral interview is usually given a weight of 40-60 percent of the final grade.

The written test usually measures verbal reasoning, table interpretation, reading comprehension, mechanical aptitude, map reading, and mathematics. Occasionally, the ability to comprehend and learn firefighting material, fire chemistry, and building construction is measured by the written test, in which case the selecting agency usually provides a study guide containing material the candidate is expected to learn before the test.

The oral interview usually measures interpersonal relations, oral communication, judgment, and motivation to become a firefighter. Open-ended questions are usually asked during the interview. For example, in order to evaluate the candidate's motivation to be a firefighter, the candidate may be asked, "Why do you want to be a firefighter?" (To which a favorable response might involve a discussion of what you would like to contribute to the community, reference to the respect you have for someone who is a firefighter, or the like).

The exam that follows is typical of those administered by city fire departments. It was provided by Deborah P. Ashton, Ph.D., Office of Personnel Resource Management, City of Oakland, CA.

Multiple Choice

Before answering the multiple choice questions make sure you have a watch. It is important to bring a watch to the written test as written tests are normally timed.

Verbal Reasoning

1. If A is bigger than B but smaller than C; and D is smaller than A but bigger than B then
    (A) A is the biggest
    (B) B is the smallest
    (C) C is smaller than B
    (D) D is bigger than C

2. If a person falls through thin ice while walking across the ice, the best way for you to try to rescue the person is to:
    (A) run across the ice to the person and pull the person out of the icy water as quickly as possible
    (B) tie one end of a rope to your car and the other end to your waist and walk across the ice
    (C) tie one end of a rope to your car and the other end to your waist and crawl across the ice on your stomach
    (D) walk across the ice very carefully on the tip of your toes then pull the person to safety

3. Energy in a gaseous state is fuel for a fire. Energy in a solid or liquid state is a fuel source. If the previous statements are true, which of the following statements is the best answer?
    (A) If oil gas is energy in a liquid state; oil gas is fuel for a fire
    (B) If dichlorosilane is energy in a gaseous state; dichlorosilane is fuel for a fire

    (C) If hay is energy in a solid state; hay is a fuel source
    (D) Both statements A and B are correct
    (E) Both statements B and C are correct

4. All oxidizers are inflammable gases. All inflammable gases are combustible. Some inflammable gases are poisonous. Therefore:
    (A) all oxidizers are poisonous
    (B) all poisonous gases are oxidizers
    (C) all combustible gases are oxidizers
    (D) all oxidizers are combustible

5. 37.94 X .65
    (A) 2.4661
    (B) 24.161
    (C) 24.661
    (D) 241.61

6. 243 is 27% of
    (A) 9.0
    (B) 65.61
    (C) 656.1
    (D) 900.0

7. 5 feet, 8 inches
    $\underline{-2\ feet,\ 10\ inches}$

    (A) 2 feet, 8 inches
    (B) 2 feet, 10 inches
    (C) 3 feet, 2 inches
    (D) none of the above

8. If fire helmets were 10 for $80.00 and are now 12 for $111.00, what is the percent of increase?
    (A) 1.25%
    (B) 15.625%
    (C) 27.93%
    (D) 72.072%

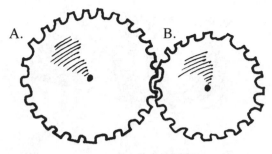 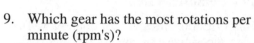 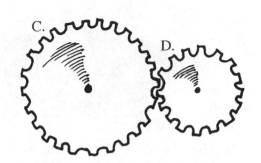

9. Which gear has the most rotations per
   minute (rpm's)?
   (A) Gear A
   (B) Gear B
   (C) Gear C
   (D) Gear D
   (E) Both Gears A and C

10. Which drawing is the best way to move the
    boulder?
    (A) Drawing A
    (B) Drawing B
    (C) Drawing C
    (D) Drawing D
    (E) Drawing E

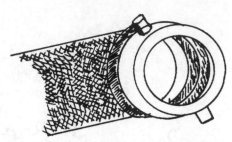

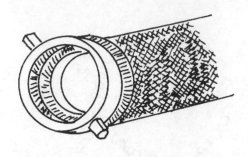

11. Above are the ends of two hoses. Which device below would you use to connect these two ends?
    (A) Device A
    (B) Device B
    (C) Device C
    (D) Device D

A.

B.

C.

D.

Reading Comprehension

The City of Lobos hires approximately 30 firefighter trainees every two years. The individuals selected must pass the written test, the physical agility, and the oral interview. The candidates selected usually are within the top 10% of the list established from the firefighter test. Once hired as trainees, they attend the City's Fire Academy for 12 weeks. Trainees must pass the academy in order to become firefighters. Of the 30 candidates selected as trainees, only 25 complete the training at the academy.

The academy focuses on the home fire safety program, fire behavior, and fire fighting. The academy emphasizes that the most important aspect of the home fire safety program is the proper installation of smoke detectors. The second most important aspect is a family escape plan. The third most important aspect is minimizing fire hazards by not smoking in bed or when intoxicated, by not leaving children alone at home, and by not cleaning with inflammable liquid, like kerosene.

The academy instructors teach the basic facts about the behavior of fire. The most important element to fire is heat. Even if fuel for a fire exists, it cannot ignite without heat and oxygen. Heat travels in three ways:

1. Conduction, which is from solids to solids which are in contact with each other;
2. Convection, which is through the circulation of heated liquids and gases; and
3. Radiation, which is when a hot body transmits heat to a cold body, for example, light transmitted through a magnifying glass

Fire is most likely to spread if heat is traveling through convection. Air has enough oxygen to keep a fire burning. That is why it is important to either eliminate the heat or to reduce the amount of oxygen (smother the fire).

According to the academy lectures, fire can be fought by one or a combination of the following:

1. By removing fuel from the fire area
2. By removing oxygen from the fire area
3. By cooling the involved or exposed combustible materials to a temperature lower than their ignition temperature

Please answer questions 12–14 using the previous text.

12. How many firefighter trainees are successful in completing the training at the academy?
(A) 10
(B) 12
(C) 25
(D) 30

13. According to the Fire Academy for the City of Lobos, the second most important aspect to the home fire safety program is
(A) not smoking in bed or when intoxicated
(B) the proper installation of smoke detectors
(C) not leaving children alone
(D) a family escape plan

14. According to the text, fire is most likely to travel if heat is traveling through
(A) conduction.
(B) convection.
(C) radiation.
(D) air.

Table Interpretation

15. According to Table 1 (on the following page), which shift is on duty at 2:00 A.M. on November 17th?
(A) Shift A
(B) Shift B
(C) Shift C

Answer Questions 16 and 17 using Table 2 on the following page.

16. How much pump pressure is needed to pump 600 gpm through two 200-foot leads of 2¾-inch hose at 80 NP?
(A) 90
(B) 95
(C) 100
(D) 105

Table 1: Fire Department Work Schedule for November*

*Each shift is 24 hours. Each shift begins at 0800/8:00 A.M. of the date listed.

△ "A" Shift Working

○ "B" Shift Working

▽ "C" Shift Working

NOVEMBER

SUN	MON	TUE	WED	THU	FRI	SAT
DECEMBER	DECEMBER	1 △	2 ○	3 ▽	4 △	5 ○
6 ▽	7 △	8 ○	9 ▽	10 △	11 ○	12 ▽
13 △	14 ○	15 ▽	16 △	17 ○	18 ▽	19 △
20 ○	21 ▽	22 △	23 ○	24 ▽	25 △	26 ○
27 ▽	28 △	29 ○	30 ▽			

Table 2: Hydraulics Chart

GPM	NO LEADS	HOSE SIZE	NP PSI	FL/100´	PUMP PRESSURE NEEDED FOR 200´	300´	400´
250	1	2 3/4"	80	10 PSI	100	110	120
600	2	2 3/4"	80	12 PSI	105	115	130
700	2	2 3/4"	100	16 PSI	130	150	165
800	2	2 3/4"	80	20 PSI	120	140	160
600	3	2 3/4"	80	6 PSI	90	100	105
700	3	2 3/4"	100	8 PSI	115	125	130
800	3	2 3/4"	80	10 PSI	100	110	120
250	1	3"	80	5 PSI	90	95	100
600	2	3"	80	8 PSI	95	105	110
700	2	3"	100	12 PSI	125	135	150
800	2	3"	80	16 PSI	110	130	145
600	3	3"	80	4 PSI	85	90	95
700	3	3"	100	6 PSI	110	120	125
800	3	3"	80	8 PSI	95	105	110

GPM = gallons per minute; waterflow

No. Leads = number of hoses

NP = nozzle pressure = amount of pressure created by water being discharged from a nozzle

PSI = pressure in pounds per square inch

FL/100' = friction loss per 100 feet of hose

200', 300', and 400' = length of hose

17. How much FL/100 feet is there for 800 gpm being pumped through three leads of 3-inch hose at 80 NP?
(A) 8 PSI
(B) 10 PSI
(C) 16 PSI
(D) 20 PSI

Answer Questions 18-20 using the map given on the following page.

18. If there is a fire located in section C7, the most likely location of the fire dwelling is
(A) the Community Shopping Center on the corner of D Street and Machado Court
(B) the library on Stevens Street
(C) the corner of Hardeman Street and Maude Avenue
(D) the corner of D Street and Stratton Court

19. If there is a fire located in section B3, the most likely location of the fire dwelling is
(A) the corner of East Castro Valley Blvd. and Old Dublin Road
(B) the Palomares School on Palomares Road
(C) the corner of Crow Canyon Road and Beacon Hill Drive
(D) Fairview Elementary School on Maude Avenue

20. If you are located at the fire station on Cull Canyon Road in section B2 and there is a fire at the corner of Elm Street and Pine Street in section A4, the best route to take to the fire scene is to go south on Cull Canyon Road to Crow Canyon Road:
(A) take a left on Crow Canyon Road and proceed north to Cold Water Drive; take a right on Cold Water Drive and proceed northeast to Jensen Road; take a right on Jensen Road and proceed southeast to East Castro Valley Blvd.; take a right on East Castro Valley Blvd.

and proceed southwest to Grove Way; continue southwest on Grove Way to Redwood Road; take a right on Redwood Road and proceed north to Pine Street; take a right on Pine and proceed east to the corner of Elm Street and Pine Street
(B) continue south on Crow Canyon Road to Castro Valley Blvd.; take a right on Castro Valley Blvd. and proceed west to Aspen Avenue; take a left on Aspen and proceed south to Pine Street; take a right on Pine Street and proceed west to the corner of Elm Street and Pine Street
(C) continue south on Crow Canyon Road to East Castro Valley Blvd.; take a left onto East Castro Valley Blvd. and proceed east to the 580 Freeway; take I-580 West to the Greenview Drive exit. At Greenview Drive, make a right onto Elm Street; proceed north to the corner of Elm Street and Pine Street
(D) continue south on Crow Cayon Road to the 580 Freeway; take the I-580 West to Grove Way and proceed southwest to Redwood Road; take a right on Redwood and proceed north to Pine Street; take a right on Pine Street and proceed to the corner of Elm Street and Pine Street

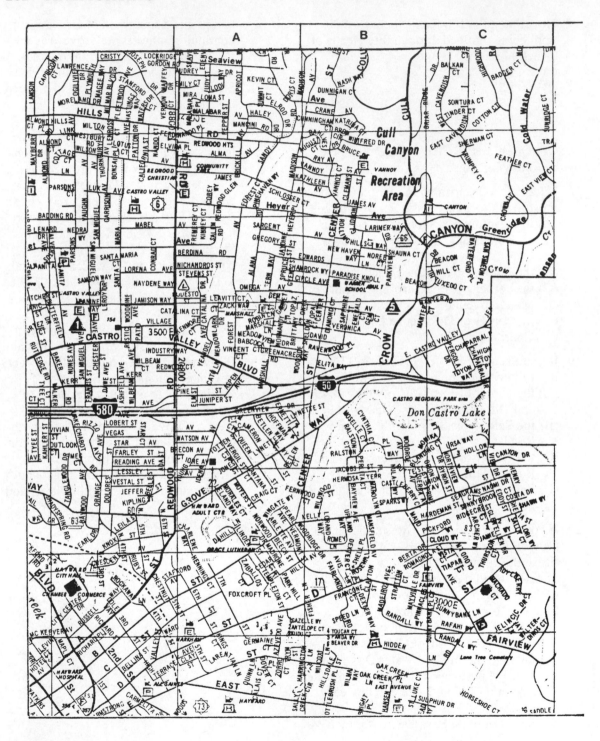

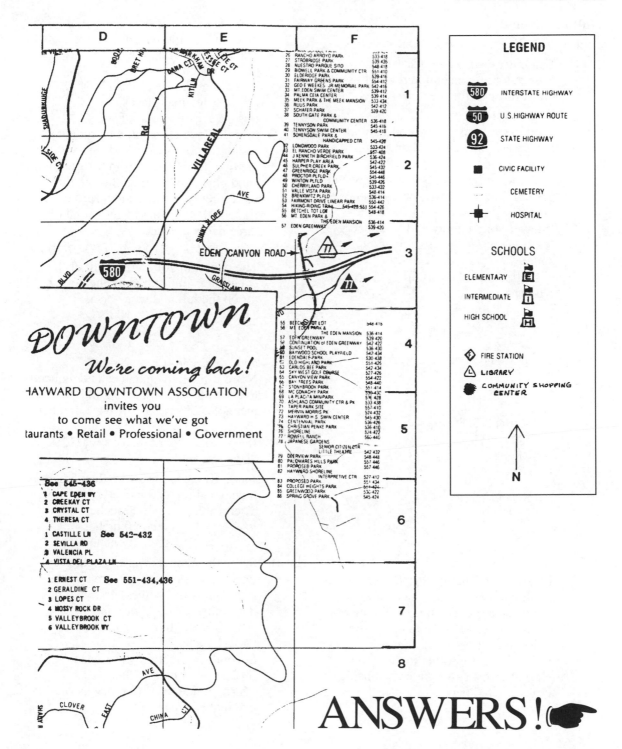

ANSWERS!

Multiple Choice

1. B   Visualize the relationship:

2. C   You must distribute your weight evenly, since concentrated weight will break through the ice

3. E   Equations:
If oil gas = liquid energy and liquid energy = a fuel source then oil gas = a fuel source
If dichlorosilane = gaseous energy and gaseous energy = fuel for fire then dichlorosilane = fuel for fire
If hay = solid energy and solid energy = a fuel source then hay = a fuel source

4. D   Visualize the relationship:
Known:

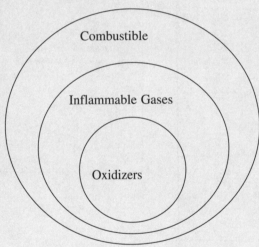

Please note: There is insufficient information to determine if any, all, or some oxidizers are poisonous. While there is sufficient information to know some poisonous gases are inflammable, there is insufficient information to know if all poisonous gases are inflammable or if any are oxidizers.

5. C   Note: Count your decimal places when multiplying. The multiplicand, 37.94, has two decimal places plus the multiplier, .65, has two decimal places; this gives you a total of four decimal places in the product. Similarly, .01 X .3 = .003. Since there are two decimal places in the multiplicand plus one decimal place in the multiplier, you must add a zero to the right of the decimal to get a total of three decimal places.

$$
\begin{array}{r}
37.94 \\
\times\ .65 \\
\hline
18970 \\
22764 \\
\hline
246610 = \\
24.661
\end{array}
$$

6. D   Since 27% = 27/100, 243/x = 27/100. The denominator on the right of the equation is multiplied by the numerator on the left and vice versa.
Thus,   27x = 243 X 100
          27x = 24,300
          27x/27 = 24,300/27;
and   x = 900
Note: If the percentage can be reduced to a smaller fraction, it should. For example, 243 is 25% of what number?
          25% = 25/100 =¼
If   ¼ = 243/x then 1x = (243 X 4)
and   x = 972

7. B   Since 12 inches = 1 foot then 5 feet, 8 inches = 4 feet, 20 inches
Therefore,   4 feet, 20 inches
             − 2 feet, 10 inches
             ─────────────────
              2 feet, 10 inches

8. B   Since the helmets were bought previously in lots of tens and are bought now in lots of twelves, first you must determine the cost per unit:
$80/10 = $8.00
$111/12 = $9.25
Second, subtract the difference
$9.25 − $8.00 = $1.25
Third, divide the difference by the original cost per unit:

$1.25/$8 = .15625 which equals 15.625%

Note: The difference is divided by the original cost whether you are calculating percent of increase or decrease.

9. D The smaller gear must rotate more times per minute in relation to the larger gear. Just as a shorter person must take more steps to cover the same distance as a taller person.

10. A It is easier to move the boulder with leverage.

11. B Both ends of hose need to be able to screw onto the device.

Reading Comprehension Hints

12. C First, if only two or three ques-
13. D tions are asked about the reading pas-
14. B sage, read the questions and answers before reading the passage. Second, if several questions are asked about the passage, read the passage then answer the questions you are sure you know, then, as time allows, skim the passage for the remaining answers. Third, if time is limited, and there is no penalty for guessing, make an educated guess to the questions about which you are uncertain.

15. A You know that a shift starts at 8:00 A.M., so the shift from the previous day is on duty at 2:00 A.M. Check the symbol for the previous day to determine the correct answer.

16. D Since the 2⅔" hose is at the top of the table, you need only look at the top half. Now find 600 under GPM. There are only two 600 GPMs listed for 2⅔" hose. Select the one for two leads. It has 80 NP. Now follow the row across to the column for which pump pressure

is needed for a 200' lead. The correct answer is the cell where the correct row and the correct column intersect.

17. A Since 3" hose is at the bottom of the chart, you need only look at the bottom half. Now find 800 under GPM. It is listed only twice with 3" hose. Select the one for three leads. It has 80 NP. Now follow the row across to the column for FL/100'; 8 PSI is in the cell.

18. A For questions 18 and 19 find the correct cell by using the letter column and number row of the section given, then see which location listed as a possible answer is in the cell where the letter column and number row intersect.

19.   C

20.   B Find the intersecting cell for each coordinate given, B2 and A4, then find the most direct route.

PHYSICAL AGILITY EVENTS

It is important that you are in good health before taking the agility test: The test is strenuous and so is the necessary preparation. It is recommended that you check with your doctor before beginning to prepare for the agility test. Running and weight lifting may be good preparation. Women should work especially on upper body strength because this is the area in which women have most difficulty. For best results, begin preparing at least 12 weeks before the test.

The physical agility events may vary from department to department. Two physical agility (ability) tests are listed here. One is the test used by the City of Oakland, California; the other is used by the City of Seattle, Washington.

Physical Agility Test
City of Oakland

Applicants perform the tasks wearing a fire helmet, turnout coat, gloves and breathing apparatus, and regulator (weighing approximately 45 pounds). This equipment is provided for you in the various sizes offered by the manufacturer, and you will be assisted in donning it properly. If you have your own pair of work gloves, you may wear them to take the test.

1. **Hose Drag**: Candidate picks up two sections of a 150-foot length of dry, 2 /2 inch hose, loops them over each shoulder, and pulls it until it is straight, 150 feet out. Candidate then pulls the entire length of straightened hose 15 feet further.

2. **Hose Carry/Stair Climb**: Candidate runs to drill tower where he/she picks up a high rise bundle of hose (approximately 50 pounds) and carries it up the stairs to the fourth floor and places it on the floor.

3. **Hose Hoist**: On the fourth floor of the drill tower, candidate goes to the landing and pulls up a coil of 50 feet of 1 /2-inch hose, uncharged, from the ground to the fourth floor landing, using a hand-over-hand pull sequence. Candidate brings the coil up to the landing and rests it on the edge and then lowers the coil back to the ground using the same hand-over-hand technique.

4. **Smoke Ejector**: On the fourth floor, candidate goes to the hose bundle he/she carried upstairs in Event Number 2, picks it up and carries it down the stairs and places it on the ground where he/she found it. Candidate runs to the smoke ejector (on the ground), picks it up, carries it to a simulated door frame (6 feet 8 inches tall), and hangs it from the top of the frame.

5. **Citizen Rescue**: Candidate runs to the next event where he/she grasps a lifelike dummy weighing approximately 160 pounds and pulls him from a chair onto the floor, leaving the chair in an upright position. In a low position (under 3 feet in height) candidate drags the dummy 20 feet across a carpeted surface.

6. **Dry Hose Load**: Candidate proceeds to a stack of four dry hose rolls, picks up each roll one at a time and places them on a fire engine tailboard, one atop another, until all four are stacked on the tailboard. Candidate then replaces all four hose rolls in their original place, in a straight stack, and runs to the finish line thus completing the exam.

PHYSICAL ABILITY TEST
CITY OF SEATTLE

These tests are VERY strenuous. If you have had a recent illness, surgery, or are under medication, ask your doctor if it is safe for you to take the tests. If you are unable to take the tests, you may be rescheduled within a reasonable period of time.

This includes five events designed to determine your overall physical ability to enter the Fire Fighter Pre-Recruit Program. The events in this test are as follows:

1.   **Fan Lift**: In 30 seconds, lift a 53-pound fan off the floor and place the hooks on the top of the fan on a door jamb that is 82 inches high, then lift the fan off the door jamb and set it on the floor.

2.   **Weight Hoisting Event**: While standing on the seventh floor of the drill tower, candidates must hoist, from ground level, an 80-pound sandbag that is tied to the end of a rope. This is a timed event—40 seconds maximum.

3.   **Hose Carry, Climb, and Run**: The candidate must remove an 85-pound pack of hose from a storage rack on the side of a truck and place it over the shoulder. The task is to run 100 feet to a building and up stairs to the fourth floor level. The hose pack is unloaded and a second one, just like the first, is picked up; the candidate then returns down the stairs to ground level and runs back to the finish line. This is a timed event—2 minutes maximum.

4.   **Seated Steep Incline Press**: Candidate must fully press 95 pounds overhead one time while positioned on an incline board which is angled so as to be nearly vertical. To ensure correct form, the candidate will be secured to the incline board with a wide strap.

5.   **Barbell Curls**: The candidate must fully curl 85 pounds one time while positioned so that the back is firmly braced against a vertical board. To ensure correct form, the candidate will be secured to the vertical board with a wide strap.

GRAPHOLOGY

Handwriting Analysis

Can you pick out which of the handwriting specimens on the following pages was written by an individual with an I.Q. under 65 and which by an individual with an I.Q. over 120?

Graphology—the study of personality through handwriting—is currently gaining popularity in the U.S. A painstaking science with numerous practical applications, graphology has been widely used in Europe for many years, especially by employers to screen job applicants. It is in the area of employee evaluation that the field's greatest growth is likely to occur in this country during the next decade or so.

The modern science of graphology was pioneered in the early nineteenth century by the French Abbé Jean-Hippolyte Michon, who developed a system of "fixed signs" or letter-forms which corresponded to personality traits. Although considered somewhat simplistic and one-dimensional by today's standards, Michon's work nevertheless represents the first detailed, systematic analysis in a hitherto haphazard and impressionistic field. In the late nineteenth century, Wilhelm Preyer and other German psychologists increased the sophistication and accuracy of graphological analysis by integrating into it the study of other aspects of handwriting, such as speed, pressure, and rhythm. Preyer developed a theory of what he called "brain writing," so called because he held that aspects of an individual's psyche found expression in the idiosyncrasies of his or her script, whether written with the use of the hand, the mouth, or the foot.

Present-day applications of graphology include the detection of physical and psychic illness, evaluation of I.Q., and the determination of dishonesty or criminality in writing. In an employee evaluation, the graphologist looks for similarities or discrepancies between a job description provided by the employer and characteristics of the applicant as revealed in a handwriting sample.

Some of the elements a graphologist takes into consideration when performing an analysis are slant, pressure, speed, rhythm, size, spacing, and the nature of the "connectives" used to join letters in script. Since handwriting must be viewed holistically, graphologists caution against a simplistic, atomistic analysis of individual elements as necessarily corresponding to particular personality traits. However, for the sake of illustration, we can generalize that, for example, rightward slant may indicate future or outward orientation, leftward slant roughly the opposite; heavy pressure may indicate energy and depth of feeling and emotion, light pressure sensitivity, adaptability, or passivity; a dominant lower zone (found in the descending parts of such letters as "g" and "y") may indicate strong sexual energy or athletic interest, and a dominant upper zone (in such letters as "l" and "k") may relate to mental activity, imagination, or spirituality.

One reaction graphologists often encounter from the uninitiated is skepticism that any aspect such as slant could really indicate anything about an individual's personality. After all, we are taught in school to write with a rightward slant. Also, we are all familiar with overall national differences in handwriting styles. If Germans are taught to write with a more vertical slant than Americans, does that mean that they are less outgoing or future-oriented?

The graphologist would respond that national styles are indeed taken into account in any responsible handwriting analysis. And it is undeniable that, though two people may be taught the Palmer Method in the third grade, their handwriting styles twenty years later will in all likelihood differ considerably, even to the untrained eye. It is in these deviations from Palmer that the graphologist finds significance. Even if an individual never departs from the style he or she is taught in school, such lack of originality would itself be highly revealing of his or her personality.

Those on the West Coast who are interested in pursuing a study of graphology would do well to contact Ted Widmer of the Graphological Society of San Francisco (he demystified the subject for the editors of this book). In New York City, the New School for Social Research offers good courses in graphology. Other graphologists, many of whom offer instruction, may be found in your local yellow pages under "Handwriting Analysts." You should take with a grain of salt any instructor's claim to make you a "certified graphologist," since there is as yet no meaningful process of licensing or certification.

The questions that follow represent three uses of graphology: employee evaluation, personality compatibility evaluation, and I.Q. evaluation. The analyses are abridged from *Handwriting Analysis: A Guide to Personality* by David Battan (International Resources, 1984). One of the foremost authorities in the field of graphology, Mr. Battan emphasizes the need to include all aspects of the writing sample in the analysis and utilizes worksheets to ensure a systematic approach. The worksheets, the book, and other titles in the field of graphology are available from International Resources, P.O. Box 3113, Pismo Beach CA 93449. The sections which highlight graphology methods and use Mr. Battan's examples are necessarily condensed. A thorough study of the methods, along with hundreds of examples of celebrity writing, are available in *Handwriting Analysis*.

1. Of the following eight handwriting samples, two demonstrate average intelligence (90-109 I.Q.), two would be classified as slightly above average or bright (110-119 I.Q.), two exhibit high intelligence (120-139 I.Q.) and two are indicative of genius (I.Q. of 140 or above). Analyze the eight samples and rank them in order of intelligence, from average to genius.

A. *Jack came in this took Mother to work*

B. *[handwriting sample in German script]*

C. *You arrive at Victoria Station go to St. Pancras Station*

D. *I would suggest checking the before mailing anything as a of them are no longer in opera*

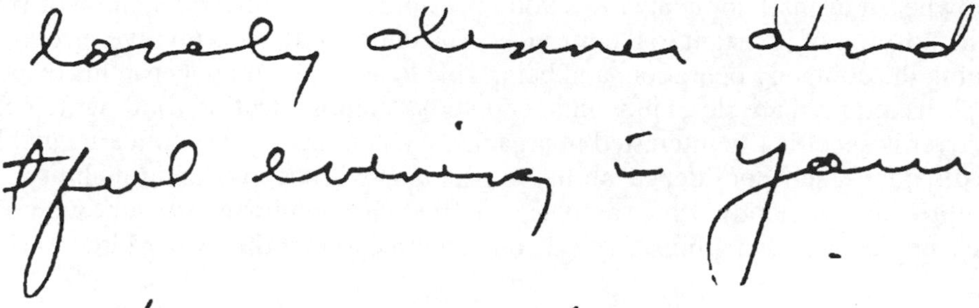

lovely dinner and

E.

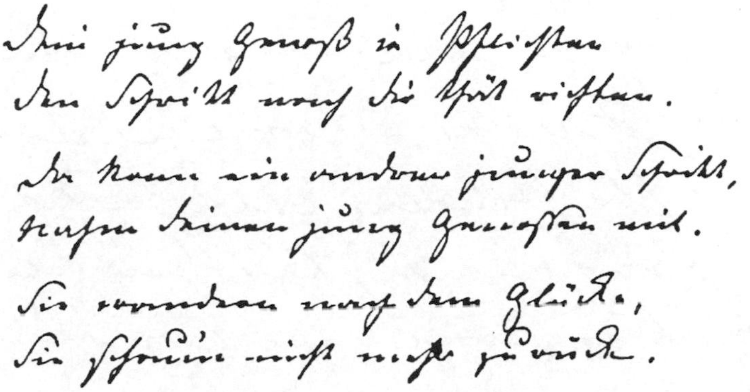

#ful evening in your

F.

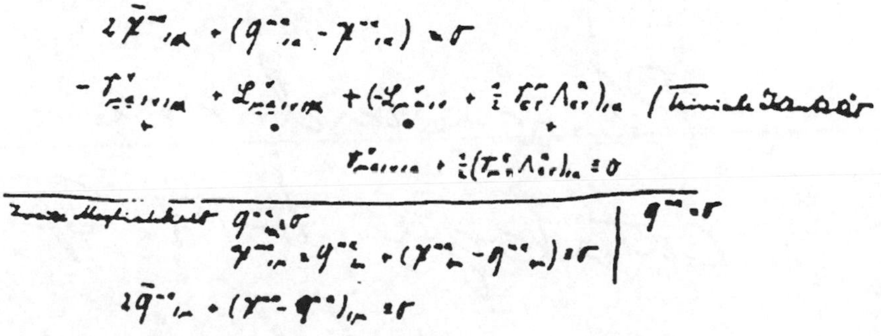

G.

H.

ions. As for the specific myth work, lets [see]
primitive. Just as primitive artifacts are
to us lies in their direct expression of
nature. You simply cannot make this

2. The owner of a small company hires you to perform a personnel evaluation of two applicants for the position of assistant to the manager. The duties of the job involve meeting the public, learning the company operation, and being able to assist the manager in his responsibilities. The skills required are flexibility and good verbal communication (both written and oral). The employer is specifically interested in organizational ability, ability to learn quickly, ability to take directions, self-confidence, ability to get along with people, and reliability. You are given the following two handwriting samples, one from each applicant, to work with. Based on these samples, which applicant would you recommend that the owner hire?

A.

B.

3. Three couples hire your services to analyze their chances of handling long-term commitments to each other. They submit to you the three pairs of handwriting samples below. Based on your analysis of characteristics displayed in their handwriting, which couple(s) would most likely be compatible, and which would not?

A.

Judy, I need a stateme

physician saying "its" "OK" fo

working and how long —

B.

Denmark to Oslo, Norw
was very beautiful. I ha
first Class Cabin; but I
got up at 4 in the morn
to see the magnificent
sailing on the Fjos to C
P.S. 90% of the guests a
Orion are American —. b

country. It is extremely rare. It is a list of ships s
for his last command, HMS Director, 9 years after
the Bounty mutiny. It was sold several years
through Hamilton's auction at just less than 80
could be sold for much more than that.

Finished her basic t
that now she's state
an air base? When she
me, she hadn't bee
her work yet, but I

ANSWERS! ☞

1. Average intelligence (90-109 I.Q.): A and D
   Bright (110-119 I.Q.): C and E
   High Intelligence (120-139 I.Q.): F and H
   Genius (140+ I.Q.): B and G

Analysis by category:

Average (A and D): 48% of the population ranges from 90 to 109 I.Q. Handwriting in this range usually looks childlike or at least very conventional. The middle zone tends to be larger than the upper or lower zone. Letters are connected and often well-formed. The connecting strokes and letters are rounded. There is a general appearance that the writing is drawn rather than written. The two examples lack originality, imagination, and rhythm.

Bright (C and E): Examples in this class show angles in the writing and signs of rhythm. The writing is still conventional but has lost the childlike quality. The middle zone is less dominant.

High intelligence (F and H): In the 120-139 I.Q. range, the writing often becomes less conventional. The basic characteristics present are a reduction in the size of the writing, good rhythm, and many angles in the script. The writing takes on an individual character. Strokes may be used between words but with consistency and rhythm.

Genius (B and G): I.Q. of 140 or above is seldom encountered, since this class represents only 1.5% of the population. The writing styles of two people in this range may appear to have few characteristics in common—they are highly individualized. The writing will be small, the rhythm superior, and breaks frequent between letters but in a well-defined and consistent pattern. If words are connected by strokes, the pattern will be consistent with a highly developed form. The samples here are of Ludwig van Beethoven (B) and Albert Einstein (G).

2. Recommendation: Hire A rather than B.

Details of analysis and recommendation*:

A: The slant is rightward with very good to superior rhythm but lacks originality. The pressure is light. The light pressure indicates sensitivity and combined with the slant indicates a responsiveness to others.

The small middle zone and small writing indicate an ability to concentrate and a modest self-concept; confidence and persistence are shown in the firmly ending downstrokes and the fluidity of the writing. The spacing between the letters confirms interest in other people but the narrow letters indicate that he is cautious about expressing things about himself.

There are many garlands in the writing. Considering the rightward slant and the degree of connectiveness, he is not only able to communicate with others, but he is also consistent in his thinking process. He carries through on projects logically. Some of the letters are pointed and some are rounded, showing that he grasps ideas quickly but considers the facts before taking action.

The t-bars are of medium length and some display the conventional form typically found in the handwriting of schoolteachers. This shows a certain amount of moderation, discipline, and self-respect. I-dots are absent in the writing, but this does not show a lack of attention to detail or a lack of memory; he does not interrupt his flow of writing to go back to make the i-dots. This indicates a desire to get on with business without unnecessary interruptions. The loops are narrow and in some strokes they are absent. This demonstrates his practical nature and realistic approach.

Thus, the applicant for the position has many of the characteristics specified by the employer. He has good organizational ability and the ability to learn quickly. He is careful in checking out facts before taking action but accomplishes this with a consistent pattern. He follows through on assignments and shows both persistence and self-confidence. He has the ability to take direction from others and does not overemphasize his own importance. In this sense, he is flexible; he respects the ideas and feelings of others. He works fast and does not like to get bogged down with unnecessary detail. There is a positive tendency to respond to other people with genuine feeling, concern, and sensitivity. He can get along well with others and has the ability to communicate.

B: The slant of the writing is slightly to the right and the pressure is heavy with an uneven shading. The general rhythm of the writing is poor. A negative interpretation is given to the character traits because of the poor rhythm. He shows an emotional unevenness that allows his feelings to interfere with his judgement.

The upper zone letters dominate, but they are tall and stiff. He is bothered by conscience, and there is a suggestion that there may be conflict here. The writing is of medium size and the spacing between the letters and the width of the letters are normal. These writing characteristics indicate a struggle between what he wants to do and what he thinks he should do. The heavy, shaded, uneven pressure indicates his strong self-indulgence.

The form of connectiveness is primarily arcades, but these are moderate with some breaks in the writing. The tendency indicated by this combination is a lack of respect for others and a tendency to impose his own ideas on others. This may also show some indecision. There are some angles, but they are poorly executed, indicating tension.

The t-bar crossings are moderate in length, and there are two variations in these crossings: the first is a downward slant, indicating temper and aggressiveness, and the second is a tent-shaped t-bar crossing, indicating that he is stubborn and resents authority. The i-dots are rounded and placed high and slightly to the right. This shows good memory, but the placement of the dot over the i suggests some impatience with detail. The loops are narrow in both the upper and lower zones and have a muddy quality which shows two characteristics: a lack of imagination and a strong appetite for pleasure.

In sum, applicant B does not possess characteristics required by the employer. There are deficiencies in his organizational ability and a tendency to be indecisive and to overlook detail. At times, he would be influenced by the way he thinks things should be done rather than trying more original but consistent approaches. He can learn quickly but is indecisive in action and purpose. There may be conflict in putting into action what he has learned. The inability to take direction would present problems. He resents authority and has a strong tendency to be stubborn. He demonstrates a strong interest in himself and is concerned with satisfying his own desires. He does not demonstrate any real warmth toward people and would have a tendency to ignore others' feelings and interests.

*Although it is not usually possible to determine the sex of an individual from his or her handwriting, we may assume here that you have been given the names of the applicants for identification purposes, and that the names indicate that both applicants are male.

3.   (A) Both write with light pressure and similar slant. Both have very small handwriting with tall strokes in the upper zone.These two individuals have similar temperaments; they are both reserved in emotional expression and would be able to talk over any problems or differences that may arise. Each enjoys time alone and can respect the other's desire to have time alone to pursue individual interests. The small writing shows an ability to concentrate, patience, and inner strengths. The tall upper strokes reveal similar values and similar degrees of intellectual interest. The lower zone loops are also similar. In sum, these two individuals are a very good match. They are both sensitive people who use logic rather than emotion to solve problems; they share the need for individual creativity and in general have shared values.

(B) This couple display similar personality traits, but the similarity of these traits suggests potential problems. Both react emotionally, which you can determine from the rightward slant. The large, rather showy capital letters indicate a tendency to be in the limelight and to exaggerate.

The lower letters extend into the next line of writing below; this is a sign of getting involved in too many things at the same time. The fact that they both react impulsively makes this trait even more significant; usually the combination of these two traits results in poor financial management and impulse buying. In sum, there would be difficulty in this relationship because they are both impulsive and react emotionally, and because each wants to be the center of attention. A lasting relationship between these two would probably fail. You can be sure it would be eventful and full of fireworks!

(C) In one sample, the slant is vertical, the writing is small, and the spacing is narrow. Arcades are used in the connective form. From this we can infer strong control of emotions and a retiring personality; his or her approach is conservative and analytical. The other sample displays large writing with a large middle zone. The slant is to the right and we find initial strokes at the beginning of letters. He or she is clearly an extrovert with a strong interest in social activities. There would be a tendency to be demanding and possessive. In sum, their interests and temperaments are too far apart for a successful relationship. After a while one would probably withdraw and the other would probably feel unloved and neglected.

HISTORY STUDENT, U. S.

The New York Times

The Korean and Vietnam wars were similar in all of the following respects EXCEPT

   (A) warnings were voiced by some respected military leaders against the United States becoming bogged down in a land war in Asia

   (B) domestic support of the war declined, as the possibility of a quick and decisive United States military victory grew remote

   (C) United States troops were engaged against an essentially guerilla enemy

   (D) the war remained limited rather than leading to war directly between, or among, the major powers

This question, no. 38, was answered incorrectly by more college students than any of the others in this exam. Only 16 percent answered it correctly. Question no. 16 was the one the most students answered correctly.

I n 1975 *The New York Times* solicited the expertise of some of the country's most respected historians to select a list of topics that are basic to an understanding of American history. The Educational Testing Service was commissioned to write a test that could be used to measure the level of historical knowledge of an important segment of the population: the college freshmen who might be the future national leaders.

In 1976, year of the U.S. Bicentennial, a carefully selected statistical cross section of 1,856 college freshmen on 194 American campuses were given the test. When the results were in, it turned out that the students had scored an average of only 50 percent -56 percent on the group of basic questions and 42 percent on the more detailed group.

The results showed that, while the students generally knew the high points of U.S. history, they had limited knowledge of details and of the, context surrounding major events. Most of the students knew the contents of the Bill of Rights (question 5) and recognized the Louisiana Purchase (question 8), for example, but few had an accurate conception of the origins of religious tolerance (question 2) and the nature of Reconstruction (question 13).

In 1943 college freshmen took a similar test that demanded much more detailed factual knowledge. They scored about the same, from which one might infer that today's yuppies know less than their parents about U.S. history. In the 1976 survey, incidentally, the characteristic of our heritage selected by the most students from a variety including "democracy" and "immorality" was the word "materialism." Ninety-two percent thought that quality was either "very" or "somewhat" characteristic of our past.

The *Times* also gave the first 24 questions from the test to 20 prominent citizens, including Supreme Court Justice Potter Stewart and Secretary of State Cyrus Vance. They scored an average of 81 percent—versus the 56 percent the college freshmen scored on those particular questions. Only one, Mt. Holyoke College President David B. Truman, got all 24 correct.

Forty of the forty-two questions in the original test appear on the following pages. Two had to be dropped from the collection for technical reasons of reproduction. The answers to all the questions include figures representing the percentage of students who selected each of the possible answers, along with interpretations of the significance of the way the students responded to each question.

1. English colonization differed from Spanish and French colonization in that the English
    (A) were the first to understand and act upon the economic potential of New World colonies
    (B) came to the New World mainly as settlers rather than soldiers, missionaries, and trappers
    (C) controlled vaster lands and larger populations
    (D) established better relations with the Indians and blacks

2. Which of the following contributed most to the development of religious toleration in the British colonies?
    (A) The stand of Roger Williams in defense of liberty of conscience
    (B) The Puritan guarantee of religious freedom to settlers in the Massachusetts Bay colony
    (C) The common interest of each of the numerous sects in preventing domination of any of the others
    (D) The attitude of religious indifference that permeated the colonial aristocracy

3. The preamble (introductory section) of the Declaration of Independence appeals to which of the following principles?
    (A) Governments founded in popular consent
    (B) Strict majoritarian rule
    (C) The right of all men to protection of their property
    (D) The right of all citizens to vote

4. The federal Constitution explicitly authorized the
    (A) creation of presidential nominating conventions
    (B) power of federal courts to declare acts of Congress unconstitutional
    (C) creation of the cabinet
    (D) power of Congress to regulate interstate commerce

5. The Bill of Rights explicitly provides for all of the following EXCEPT
    (A) freedom of speech and of the press
    (B) freedom of enterprise
    (C) freedom of assembly and of petition
    (D) the right of trial by jury

6. The aim of the Monroe Doctrine, as it was proclaimed in 1823, was to
    (A) prevent the outbreak of democratic revolutions in Latin America
    (B) guarantee preferential trading rights to the United States in Latin America
    (C) secure a territorial outlet for American slavery in Latin America
    (D) ensure that the United States rather than Europe would be the dominant power in the Western Hemisphere

7. All of the following characterized the Jacksonian Democrats EXCEPT
    (A) hostility toward the institution of slavery
    (B) support for freedom of economic opportunity
    (C) opposition to special privilege and large business corporations
    (D) opposition to internal improvements at federal expense

Questions 8–11 refer to the shaded areas shown on the maps below.

Territorial Growth of the United States

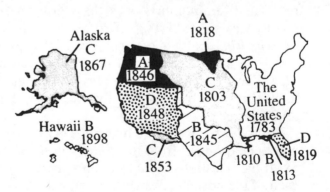

8. Which areas did the United States acquire by purchase?
   (A)
   (B)
   (C)
   (D)

9. Which areas did the United States acquire by annexation?
   (A)
   (B)
   (C)
   (D)

10. Which areas did the United States acquire by war or the threat of seizure?
    (A)
    (B)
    (C)
    (D)

11. Which areas did the United States acquire by negotiated settlement of boundary disputes?
    (A)
    (B)
    (C)
    (D)

12. In the politics of the decade before the Civil War the issue of slavery focused on whether
    (A) racial equality should be the foremost national priority
    (B) slavery should be permitted to exist in the territories
    (C) slavery should be eliminated where it already existed in the states
    (D) the foreign slave trade should be reopened

13. Republican policies toward the South during the post-Civil War Reconstruction can be described most accurately as
    (A) aiming consistently to protect the interests of postwar big business at the expense of the newly freed slaves
    (B) leading to unparalleled corruption among the entrenched carpetbagger governors and their allies in the black dominated legislatures of the defeated states
    (C) leading to significant but only partially implemented constitutional changes on the state level in the South and also on the national level
    (D) leading to an effective program of land redistribution that gave to large numbers of newly freed slaves "forty acres and a mule"

Questions 14–16 refer to the following business leaders.
   (A) John D. Rockefeller
   (B) Andrew Carnegie
   (C) J. Pierpont Morgan
   (D) Henry Ford

14. Which business leader adapted the trust as a device for large-scale industrial organization?
    (A)
    (B)
    (C)
    (D)

15. Which business leader mobilized the power of the banks to curb industrial competition and to facilitate corporate mergers and reorganizations?
    (A)
    (B)
    (C)
    (D)

16. Which business leader pioneered the mass-production assembly line?
    (A)
    (B)
    (C)
    (D)

Questions 17–20 refer to the following groups,

    (A) Northern and Western Europeans (e.g., Germans and Irish)
    (B) Southern and Eastern Europeans (e.g., Italians and Russians)
    (C) African slaves
    (D) Mexicans

17. For which group were the peak years of entry into the United States 1700–1800?
    (A)
    (B)
    (C)
    (D)

18. For which group were the peak years of entry into the United States 1840–1880?
    (A)
    (B)
    C)
    (D)

19. For which group were the peak years of entry into the United States 1885–1915?
    (A)
    (B)
    (C)
    (D)

20. For which group were the peak years of entry into the United States 1910–1930?
    (A)
    (B)
    (C)
    (D)

21. The defeat of the Versailles Treaty in the Senate after the First World War was due to the
    (A) growing conviction in the United States that the Kellogg-Briand Pact outlawing war posed a better alternative for the future conduct of foreign affairs
    (B) widespread view in the United States that proposed neutrality legislation to prohibit citizens from traveling on belligerent ships except at their own risk would suffice to keep the United States out of future European wars
    (C) inability of President Wilson and his political opponents to reach a compromise on the issue of United States participation in the collective security arrangements of the League of Nations
    (D) widespread view in the United States that the League of Nations had been tainted by its admission of the Soviet Union to membership

22. Which of the following best describes the domestic changes brought about by the New Deal?
    (A) The enactment of a number of new economic regulations, joined with new relief and welfare measures
    (B) A vast increase in governmental ownership of business
    (C) A major redistribution of income and wealth in favor of the poorest segment of the population
    (D) The restoration of a free market as a result of effective antitrust action

23. In the years immediately after the Second World War, the United States assumed
    (A) the dominant role in an alliance of Western nations for the purpose of containing Soviet power
    (B) its traditional policy of noninvolvement in world affairs
    (C) the burden of arming friendly democratic nations with atomic weapons
    (D) the leadership of Third World countries seeking independence from their colonial rulers

24. Before the Supreme Court's decision in 1954 that racial segregation in the public schools was unconstitutional, the Court had
    (A) refused to consider cases about racial segregation

(B) justified racial segregation in public facilities by the "separate-but-equal" doctrine

(C) been prevented from considering cases about racial segregation by Southern filibusters in Congress

(D) required desegregation of public facilities "with all deliberate speed," but stopped short of ordering the President to enforce the decision

25. Even in areas where the right to vote was widespread, voters in the British colonies consistently returned a relatively small number of wealthy and prominent men to office. This indicates that

(A) the British government suppressed the idea of democracy in the colonies until just before the American Revolution

(B) the colonists generally did not regard deference to one's "betters" as being incompatible with political liberty

(C) the wealthy and prominent controlled the colonial electorate

(D) apathy was the prevailing characteristic of colonial politics

26. From 1763 to 1776, the chief aim of colonial resistance to British policies was to

(A) bring about a long-suppressed social revolution against the colonial aristocracy

(B) achieve in America the ideals proclaimed in the French Revolution

(C) ensure that the colonists were represented in Parliament

(D) restore what the colonists perceived to be the rights of Englishmen

27. All of the following contributed to Great Britain's defeat in the American Revolution EXCEPT

(A) an initial tendency to underestimate the scope and intensity of the rebellion

(B) the rapid defection of loyalists to the patriot cause after the battle of Bunker Hill

(C) the indecisiveness of General Howe in exploiting colonial military weaknesses

(D) the French decisions to provide money, supplies, and military and diplomatic support to the colonists

28. The Articles of Confederation were most severely criticized in the 1780s for their lack of

(A) a plan for the admission of new states

(B) equal representation of the states in Congress

(C) a bill of rights

(D) a national taxing power

29. In the decade after the ratification of the Constitution, the American political party system developed from all of the following EXCEPT

(A) the belief of the founding fathers that a two-party system was crucial to the maintenance of a stable political order

(B) the conflict engendered by Secretary of the Treasury Alexander Hamilton's proposed economic policies

(C) the conflict engendered by the foreign policies of George Washington's administration in relation to Great Britain and France

(D) ideological differences between Hamilton and Thomas Jefferson over the nature of republican government

30. The feminist movement, which. originated in the second quarter of the nineteenth century, succeeded in accomplishing all of the following before the Civil War EXCEPT

(A) broadening the right of married women to hold property in their own names

(B) gaining the right of women to vote in national elections

(C) expanding the opportunity for women to receive a college education

(D) improving the job opportunities for women in the teaching profession at the elementary level

31. The strategy of the Confederacy at the start of the Civil War was based on all of the following assumptions EXCEPT
    (A) cutting the North in two by seizing Washington and thrusting northward into Maryland and Pennsylvania would force the North to sue for peace
    (B) the dependence of Great Britain and France on Southern cotton would lead them to grant diplomatic recognition and give military aid to the Confederacy
    (C) arming the slaves would help the South to offset superior Northern manpower
    (D) Southern control of the port of New Orleans would induce the states in the upper Mississippi Valley to join the Confederacy

32. Federal policy toward Indians between the 1880s and the 1930s was based mainly on the assumption that
    (A) the Indians should be assimilated into white society
    (B) Indian culture and tribal organization should be nurtured
    (C) interference with Indian culture and tribal organization should not be permitted
    (D) the Indians should be removed from their homeland areas and relocated in Indian Territory

33. The aim of the Open Door policy of 1900 was to
    (A) guarantee American industry a supply of cheap labor from China
    (B) protect American commercial interests against discrimination in China
    (C) establish China as a buffer against Russian and Japanese expansion
    (D) encourage the forces of liberalism in China to throw off the yoke of European domination

34. In the first decade of the twentieth century, black leaders debated the issues of direct political action to obtain civil rights and the type of training or education blacks should seek. The chief figures in these debates were
    (A) Benjamin Banneker and Frederick Douglass
    (B) Booker T. Washington and W.E.B. DuBois
    (C) Marcus Garvey and Father Divine
    (D) A. Philip Randolph and the Rev. Martin Luther King, Jr.

35. A major issue debated among progressives during the first two decades of the twentieth century was whether
    (A) labor unions should be organized by craft or by industry
    (B) the federal government should establish a social security system
    (C) the federal government should permit the free coinage of silver
    (D) the federal government should abolish economic monopolies or permit them to exist under regulation

36. Collective bargaining between labor and management became widespread in American industry after
    (A) the voluntary acquiescence of large industries that had suffered major strikes in the late nineteenth century
    (B) a Supreme Court decision written by Justice Holmes in the early twentieth century
    (C) legislation enacted during the administration of President Wilson before the First World War
    (D) legislation enacted during the administration of President Franklin D. Roosevelt in the 1930s

37. President Harry S. Truman's decision to have the atomic bomb dropped on Japan was influenced by all of the following considerations EXCEPT the

(A) desire to counter Republican charges that the Democrats were the party of appeasement and defeat

(B) desire to avoid the large number of casualties that would occur in a United States invasion of Japan

(C) desire to prod the Soviet Union to be more cooperative as it began to formulate its postwar plans

(D) difficulty of devising a test demonstration of the atomic bomb that would unfailingly impress the Japanese government

38. The Korean and Vietnam wars were similar in all of the following respects EXCEPT

(A) warnings were voiced by some respected military leaders against the United States becoming bogged down in a land war in Asia

(B) Domestic support of the war declined, as the possibility of a quick and decisive United States military victory grew remote

(C) United States troops were engaged against an essentially guerilla enemy force

(D) the war remained limited rather than leading to war directly between, or among, the major powers
    . . . 3 saddlers, 3 hatters, 4 blacksmiths, 4 weavers, 6 boot and shoemakers, 8 carpenters, 3 tailors, 3 cabinet makers, 1 baker, 1 apothecary, and 2 wagon makers' shops —2 tanneries, 1 shop for making wool carding machines, 1 with a machine for spinning wool. 1 manufactory for spinning thread from flax, 1 nail factory, 2 wool carding machines . . . Within the distance of six miles from the town were—9 merchant mills, 2 grist mills, 12 saw mills, 1 paper mill with 2 vats, 1 woolen factory with 4 looms and 2 fulling mills

39. The diversity of local manufacturing shown in the census above for a small town in Ohio in the early nineteenth century was characteristic of an area that had yet to

(A) adopt the system of rectangular land surveys and establish credit facilities for persons buying land at public auction

(B) make the transition from a barter to a cash economy

(C) accumulate an adequate supply of skilled labor to facilitate industrial growth

(D) be made accessible as a market for Eastern manufacturers by the construction of canals and railroads through the Appalachian barrier

40. In the first half of the twentieth century, the best evidence of social mobility in the United States as a whole is found in the increase in the

(A) number of new millionaires from decade to decade

(B) average per capita income from decade to decade

(C) percentage of white-collar workers whose fathers worked at blue-collar industrial jobs

(D) percentage of agricultural workers who migrated to the cities

ANSWERS! ☛

1. (A) 15
    (B) 78
    (C) 5
    (D) 2
    Answer A is wrong because the French and Spanish were as aware as the Brutish of the economic potential and, in fact, acted earlier to exploit it. Only students who scored low generally missed this question.

2. (A) 16
    (B) 38
    (C) 35
    (D) 11
    Students choosing B did realize that Puritans insisted on religious conformity. Some very good students chose A, correctly identifying Roger Williams with religious liberty but overestimating his impact.

3. (A) 56
    (B) 7
    (C) 31
    (D) 6
    Protection of property, C, the most popular wrong answer, was commonly cited, with life and liberty, as an eighteenth-century right, but Jefferson used "pursuit of happiness" because would he thought Europeans would be more likely to sympathize with it.

4. (A) 9
    (B) 48
    (C) 16
    (D) 28
    The power to declare Congressional acts unconstitutional, B, was never given to the courts directly. The Supreme Court first asserted this authority in its 1803 decision in Marbury v. Madison.

5. (A) 2
    (B) 73
    (C) 11
    (D) 14
    A "peak" topic most students knew. Above average scores were achieved by Western students (78 percent) and by students identifying themselves as politically left or right (76. percent).

6. (A) 10
    (B) 24
    (C) 7
    (D) 59
    As in most questions on diplomacy, male students did better than females (66 to 51 percent). Commercial treaties negotiated shortly after the Monroe Doctrine provided that the United States be put on a per with Latin America's other trading partners.

7. (A) 41
    (B) 11
    (C) 22
    (D) 25
    Black students, who generally did not perform as well as whites in this test, did about as well as whites (39 to 42 percent) in knowing that Jacksonian Democrats were not characteristically hostel to slavery. Students in the political middle outscored students on the left.

8. (A) 2
    (B) 5
    (C) 84
    (D) 4

9. (A) 16
    (B) 48
    (C) 6
    (D) 26

10. (A) 9
    (B) 37
    (C) 7
    (D) 43

11. (A) 57
    (B) 12
    (C) 10
    (D) 18
    On these four related questions, students overwhelmingly knew the purchase of Louisiana and Alaska, but had difficulty with the other means of territorial expansion. Students tended to confuse territiories added by annexation, such as Texas, with those acquired by war or the threat of seizure, such as the Mexican Cession that included California.

12. (A) 4
    (B) 58
    (C) 31
    (D) 6

Although C, the most popular wrong answer, was what the abolotionists wanted, Lincoln's policy was to contain slavery. The question differentiated sharply between the most able students and the least able. It was answered correctly by 82 percent of the top scoring third of the students compared to 39 percent on the lowest third, a greater than average sperad between the two groups.

13. (A) 17
    (B) 36
    (C) 32
    (D) 15

Wrong answer B, which drew the most responses and attracted a large number of the best students, reflects a common myth. The post Civil War corruption in the North was as bad as the South's; the carpetbaggers were not entrenched but rather were turned out of office in most southern states before the end of Reconstruction; and blacks achieved a short-lived majority in only one state legislature, South Carolina's.

14. (A) 39
    (B) 32
    (C) 23
    (D) 6

15. (A) 32
    (B) 21
    (C) 44
    (D) 3

16. (A) 1
    (B) 3
    (C) 3
    (D) 93

Students made their best score of any question on the test in identifying Henry Ford, the man who said "History is Bunk," but the wrong answers on 15 and 15 suggest a blurring of the images of Carnegie, Morgan and Rockefeller. In 1943, 71% of the students identified Rockefeller correctly as an oil tycoon.

17. (A) 23
    (B) 6
    (C) 65
    (D) 5

18. (A) 43
    (B) 13
    (C) 23
    (D) 20

19. (A) 24
    (B) 50
    (C) 7
    (D) 19

20. (A) 13
    (B) 32
    (C) 4
    (D) 52

Students tended to know when people who populated their region of the country had arrived. Westerners outscored all others, 57 to 49%, on the Mexican immigrants (20); 54% of the Easterners were right on Southern and Eastern Europeans (19) compared to 43% of Southerners, and Midwestern students scored 49% to 41% for others on the Germans and Irish (18). Blacks did essentially as well as whites on when the slaves were brought in (17). One major misconception was that large numbers of Southern and Eastern Europeans continued to arrive after World War I.

21. (A) 13
    (B) 45
    (C) 60
    (D) 13

More than the usual number of students (17%0 simply skipped this question which required fairly detailed knowledge as well as a sense of chronology. A refers to an issue in the 1920s, B and D to issues in the 1930s. Eastern students did better (66%0 than those in other regions.

22. (A) 64
    (B) 9
    (C) 13
    (D) 14

The most popular wrong answers, C and D, did not happen, although there was an antitrust campaign late in the New Deal. Students on the political left were more apt (67%0 to get this right, as were students who said their high school courses had emphasized conceptual approaches to history (69%).

23. (A) 68
    (B) 11
    (C) 8
    (D) 13
    As in other diplomatic questions, men outscored women, 73% to 62%; whites outscored blacks 70% to 47% and students on the political right or left outscored those in the middle 70% to 66%.

24. (A) 10
    (B) 69
    (C) 9
    (D) 11
    The phrase "all deliberate speed" did not even occur in the 1954 Brown v. Board of Education decision but in 1955 Supreme Court decision. Southern students did worst on this, 66% while Westerners did best 74%.

25. (A) 12
    (B) 27
    (C) 50
    (D) 12
    In choosing C over B, the students may have been imposing on the past a later, concept of democracy. Generally, better students chose B, and students whose high school courses stressed analysis outscored those whose courses did not 29% to 23%.

26 (A) 15
    (B) 8
    (C) 34
    (D) 42
    Students who chose (C) the most popular wrong answer, may have been recalling the slogan of "No Taxation without Representation," which as, plea by the colonists for self-taxation rather than for seats in Parliament. The 42% correct on this compares to 73% correct on a question about the Bill of Rights and 56% on the preamble to the Declaration of Independence.

27. (A) 12
    (B) 52
    (C) 22
    (D) 14
    As on other military questions, male students outscored females, 59%,to 45 %. Loyalists did not interpret that British defeat as a crucial setback.

28. (A) 12
    (B) 28
    (C) 24
    (D) 35
    The Articles of Confederation did provide for equal representation of the state in Congress and it was the Constitution, rather than the Articles, that was criticized for its lack of a bill of rights. Student performance paralleled their handling of an earlier question on which only 28% knew that the Constitution authorized Congress to regulate interstate commerce.

29. (A) 30
    (B) 17
    (C) 36
    (D) 18
    The historians preparing the test had thought this an easy question because the founding fathers regarded political parties as harmful and destructive and made no provision for nominating candidates. Washington's al farewell address in 1796 specifically and emphatically warns the country against the dangers of parties.

30. (A) 19
    (B) 67
    (C) 6
    (D) 17
    The suffragists did not succeed until 1920 with the passage of the 19th Amendment. Men outscored women on this 71% to 62%, a gap of nine percentage points that was double the gap between the sexes for

the test as a whole. Students on the political left outscored those on the right 71% to 64%

31. (A) 14
    (B) 12
    (C) 67
    (D) 7
The idea of arming the slaves was considered only toward the very end of the war and although a few black troops were recruited, none actually served in battle. Southern students scored just as much below other students on this item as they lagged on the test as a whole.

32. (A) 19
    (B) 6
    (C) 6
    (D) 69
In choosing D on this, the second toughest question on the test, the students apparently were not familiar with the chronology of Indian history. The Dawes Severalty Act of 1887, the major attempt at Indian reform legislation of the nineteenth century, was based on the assumption that the reservation system had been a failure. Western students dud better, 22%, than other students. In their later comments, the freshman often complained that the test had slighted Indian history.

33. (A) 28
    (B) 38
    (C) 19
    (D) 15
The most popular wrong; answer, A, is incorrect because America was, to the contary, trying to keep the Chinese out. In 1882 Congress passed the Chinese Exclusion Act, following the influx of workers for the railroad development.

34. (A) 21
    (B) 50
    (C) 11
    (D) 18

Banneker was an eighteenth-century figure and Douglas essentially a Pre Civil War, figure. Garvey was most prominent in the 1920s, Divine in the 1930s; Randolph from the 1930s through the 1960s and King until his assassination in 1968. Whites outscored blacks 51% to 42%, but that margin was smaller than the 11 percentage points by which whites outscored blacks on the total test.

35. (A) 21
    (B) 18
    (C) 14
    (D) 48
Both A and B are New Deal issues that did not come to the fore until the mid-1930s, while C had faded as an issue after William Jennings Bryan's defeat in 1896. Eastern students outscored those in other regions 53% to 45%.

36. (A) 29
    (B) 17
    (C) 17
    (D) 37
Students may have chosen A in the belief; that the formation of the American Federation of Labor, an event they often cite as Characteristic of the nation's past, had assured the recognition of unions for bargaining. Students over 20 years old outscored their younger counterparts 42% to 35%. One student in five simply skipped the question.

37. (A) 45
    (B) 10
    (C) 12
    (D) 33
D was the: most popular wrong choice, apparently reflecting a continued disbelief in the Truman Administration's rationale for not making a test drop. C has gained increasing acceptance among historians after first being propounded by the New

Left historians. 51 % of male students, knew A.

38 (A) 25
    (B) 31
    (C) 17
    (D) 27

This was the hardest question for students, whose interest in Korea may be waning with the passage of time. Older students were better informed, 20% correct, than those under 20 years old, 16%. In wrongly choosing B, students overlooked, for instance, Republican calls for ending the war. Blacks did as well as whites on this and on a question about, when African slaves came to America, the only two questions on which they did as well as whites.

39. (A) 7
    (B) 18
    (C) 41
    (D) 33

This and the following question measure students' ability to deal with raw historical data, their "inquiry" skill. Those choosing C did not recognize that the manufacturing represented in the census required skilled handicrafts.

40. (A) 5
    (B) 29
    (C) 32
    (D) 34

Changes in per capita income, B, do not measure how much people were able to advance their relative social or economic standing. D measures an urban influx without telling whether the workers got better jobs. In any event, C is the most direct yardstick because the nation was predominantly industrial by 1920.

U.S. HISTORY AT HARVARD

The Archives of Harvard University

We searched the university's archives for history exams given to students in historically pivotal years. The trick is to answer these questions as if you had just celebrated your own twenty-second birthday the year each exam was given to Harvard seniors.

For example: the first U.S. troops landed in Europe in July. The Russian armies collapsed on Germany's eastern front in December. The next year the war in Europe was over. Harvard seniors who sat down to their final exam in U. S. history in May of 1917 were aware of the World War (not World War I but "the World War" they didn't know about the second one yet). The answers they gave to the exam reproduced here from Harvard's archives may have been influenced by the fact that universal conscription, known now as "the draft," had just been instituted in the United States and it was out there after graduation, waiting for them with open trenches.

We almost titled this section "History Then and Now." Seniors studying for the 1946 exam had celebrated the end of "The War" just before they started their school year. VJ Day came very quickly after atomic bombs exploded on two Japanese cities whose names were probably less known then than they are now, forty years later. The class of 1964 may or may not have thought that the signing of a limited nuclear test ban treaty with the Soviet Union was a crucial step in our history. They certainly were deeply affected by the assassination of the President only two months into their senior year.

There are no answers recorded in the university archives because, as you see, all questions require interpretive and expository "essay"-type responses for which a single complete or correct answer cannot exist. It may also he

interesting to note that, though Harvard has been teaching for 300 years, it has been teaching what we now think of as U. S. history subjects for only the last 130. (For about the first 100 years there wasn't any "U. S." to have a history; for a while after that, there was hardly enough "history" to coagulate into a course of study.) In lieu of answers we have supplied reminders of some events that were exploding around these students or were crouching around the corner.

1858:

Questions 8 and 9 in this exam given to the senior class of 1858 by Professor Henry Warren Torrey are the first ones found in Harvard University's archives that might also be posed in the 1980s in an exam dealing with the academic subject we now call U. S. History.

The seniors taking this exam may well have listened to Congressman Lincoln debate with Douglas that year; have read Uncle Tom's Cabin, published in what today would have been their junior year in high school; heard their fathers' strong opinions on whether those who voted James Buchanan into the presidency a year and a half earlier got what they deserved; or perhaps remembered their mothers' horror at the news of John Brown's Pottawatomie Massacre. It is not likely, but is possible, that the mother of one of these students attended Oberlin College, which started in 1833 with a (gulp!) coeducational charter; or to Mt. Holyoke College, founded the year Hawthorne's Twice Told Tales was published. Melville's Moby Dick and Whitman's Leaves of Grass would have been best sellers in these students' childhood memory.

1. Trace the territorial growth and decline of the *Austro-Spanish power*, from the end of the fifteenth century to the middle of the seventeenth.

2. Name *six dates* in the political or constitutional history of England, with the events to which they belong.

3. Supposing the *rule succession* to the throne to have been always the same in England, in what cases has it been *departed from* since the Norman Conquest?

4. Name the different *assemblies in Europe* which resulted from "the attempt at mixed organization"; and account for the success of *the experiment in England.*

5. What *four elements* made up the *free institutions of England* at the end of the sixteenth century?

6. Describe the political and the religious character of *the three reforming parties in the time of Charles I.*

7. What did the people of England gain by the Glorious Revolution and the Act of Settlement?

8. Describe *the three forms of government in the Anglo-American Colonies* prior to the American Revolution.

9. Give the amended mode of electing the President and Vice-President of the United States.

10. What great enterprises, discoveries, *and inventions* distinguish the *fifteenth* century?

1863:

In the midst of the news of Grant's Vicksburg victory during the War Between the States (now commonly called the Civil War), Harvard University seniors in the final exam administered on June 12, 1863, may have answered questions VI (2), (4), (5) and VII (4), (5), (6) differently from the way a student at Harvard today might fill the pages of his or her blue-book—even supposing that contemporary student to be Southern White or Northern Conservative. More students in 1863 might have shown interest in question VIII had they known then that this author of a scandalous essay on women would share his first and middle names with the actor Booth who would assassinate their president two years from then.

[N. B.—Omit one;—either III., V., or VIII. Adopt, for convenience of examination, the Roman and Arabic numeration used in this paper.]

I.   Account for the fall (1) of the Coalition Ministry in 1783. (2) of Pitt in 1801; (3) of the Ministry of "All the Talents" in 1807; (4) of Peel's Short Administration of 1834–5.

II.   State the Defects in the Representative System in England, and show how far and in what way they were remedied by the Reform Act of 1832.

III. Dissolution of Parliament;—when resorted to, and how brought about? Its operation as a *constitutional check.*

IV.   Impeachment, in England and in the United States:—as to (1) the agency of the Houses; (2) the mode of proceeding; (3) the purpose and the present real efficacy of the power; and (4) the penalty on conviction.

V.   The Confederation (1781–9):—as to legislative and executive organization and power; and as to the chief *defects* in the plan and the working of it.

VI.   Give the provisions of the Constitution as to (1) the Obligation of Contracts; (2) the reckoning of the Representative Population; (3) the Election of a President in failure of an Electoral choice; (4) the admission of New States; (5) the suppressing of Insurrection; (6) Habeas

Corpus; (7) the declaring of War and making of Peace (N. B. unlike the English Constitution); (8) Treason (*i.e.*, its Definition).

VII. (1) How does the Constitution limit the right of Eminent Domain? (2) What power has Congress in regard to Piracy? (3) By what vote is a Treaty confirmed? a Nomonation? (4) Who may vote for a Representative in Congress? (5) "No State shall enter into any Compact with another State":—which is *absolute?* which is *qualified* by other words, and how? (6) In what places does the Constitution *allude* to Slavery? (Answer generally, or quote the words.) (7) What is the exposition of the words, "ex post facto Law"? (8) By whom is to be taken the Oath to "support," and by whom the Oath to "preserve, protect, and defend," the Constitution?

VIII. Give a brief account of John Wilkes's difficulties with the House of Commons.

IX. The Public Lands of the United States:—as to *Geography,* and the *time* and *manner* of acquisition.

1865:

The class of 1865 lived in tumultuous times. Students took this exam nine weeks after General Lee surrendered at Appomattox; 62 days after the President of the United States had been shot during a performance of *Our American Cousin* at Ford's Theatre. A student of the 1860s might understand the killer's motives; many people thought that John Wilkes Booth shot Lincoln more from a deranged need for personal publicity than for any ideological motive.

By December, their Constitution would be amended for the thirteenth time. The new addition said: "Neither slavery nor involuntary servitude . . . shall exist within the United States, or any place subject to their jurisdiction." Congress was getting ready to pass the Civil Rights Act, over President Johnson's veto, prohibiting the states from enforcing "Black Codes" legislation that restricted the way blacks could exercise their legal rights as citizens. The XIVth Amendment passed a year later in Congress despite the opposition of all Southern states. It recognized the citizenship of blacks and punished states that did not enforce those rights. A year after that, the President's struggle for the power of his Executive Office over Congress resulted in his impeachment and brought him within one vote of conviction while loyalty votes were administered to public officials and accusations of treason against the federal Constitution rang out in the houses of Congress.

Sound familiar? It was as if all the most dramatic events of the 1960s and 1970s were crammed into these students' senior year and the two years after they graduated: a bloody war ended; a historically powerful president was killed by a shot from nowhere; violent efforts to restrict and to enfranchise blacks collided in law and in fact; an often grotesque struggle for power between the White House and Congress ended in impeachment; the effectiveness of the Constitution to guide its enforcers came into question.

Have you learned enough to lean into these questions with compassion for the time in which they were asked?

Constitution: write *two*

I. (1) Habeas Corpus; (2) Calling forth the Militia; (3) Declaring War; (4) Making Peace; (5) Definition of Treason; (6) President's Oath; (7) Direct Taxes, how apportioned? (8) Domestic Violence in a State

II. (1) Tenure of Judicial Office; (2) Electors of Representatives; (3) Number of Presidential Electors; (4) Impeachable Offences; (5) Reprieve and Pardon; (6) Salaries of Judges; (7) Salary of President; (8)Punishment of Treason

III. (1) Trial by Jury, and the Exceptions; (2) Mode of Amendment; (3) Appointments to Office; (4) Explain "Bill of Attainder" and "Ex post facto Law"

1870:

In their junior year, the graduating seniors in the Harvard class of 1870 who worked on Section II of this Elective History exam probably knew firsthand of these events that could have affected their answers:

1. The Sioux Indians wiped out Captain Fetterman's cavalry at Oglala when these students were freshmen.

2. The federal government decided to move the Plains Indians off their hunting lands onto small farming communities in the Black Hills and in Oklahoma. That same year—their freshman year—Custer's horse cavalry was wiped out at Little Big Horn.

3. The Union Pacific and Central Pacific drove a golden spike to join their transcontinental railroad across public land the year before these boys took this test.

4. In 1870 the buffalo-hunting Plains Indians were already running out of buffalo because the railroads shot them to feed the laborers who laid the track; the hides were popular with city folk, and "buffalo hunts" became a white man's fad. "Public" lands that traditionally sustained Indian tribes and 14 million buffalo were "acquired" by the government, By the time these young Harvard students were 30 years old, the buffalo were extinct, the Indian lands were "under control" at a cost of $1 million per dead Indian, and the Gold Rush was on.

Elective History [Take *four* of six.]

VII. "What capacity to legislate on the subject of *commerce* resides in the Nation, and in the States respectively?"

VIII. The Public Lands of the United States. Early and later acquisitions. The right to make new acquisitions.

IX.   The Dartmouth College case. The difference between private and municipal Corporations. The application (as to Corporations) of the clause relating to the Obligation of Contracts.

X.   "Cases arising under the Constitution" may be brought under four heads. Name them, and give instances or illustrations.

XI.   Take four important Constitutional Cases. State the question at issue in each, and the decision.

XII. It has been said that "the Bill of Rights of 1689 is reproduced in the Constitution of 1787." Show by a careful analysis and comparison how far this statement is true in the letter and in spirit.

1917:

Students took this exam a matter of weeks after the United States entered World War I.

Government 4

1. Explain the following: (a) due diligence, (b) *force majeure*, (c) *infra praesidia*, (d) *uti possidetis*, (e) continuous voyage, (f) internment.

2. States X and Y are parties to the Hague Conventions.,The *Dolphin*, flying the flag of neutral state M, and belonging to a citizen of state M, has made four trips carrying coal from a port of state M to the fleet

of X. On the fifth trip, while returning from the fleet, the *Dolphin* is captured by a cruiser of Y and brought to a prize court. What disposition should be made of the ship; how should the captain, a citizen of state X, be treated; and how should five able seamen, citizens of state M, be treated?

3. (a) "Resistance either real or constructive by a neutral carrier is, with a view to the law of nations, unlawful." (b) "A trade by a neutral in articles contraband of war is, therefore, a lawful trade, though a trade from necessity subject to inconvenience and loss." Discuss the above.

1928:

Students took this exam during a period of economic boom and of a dramatic concentration of wealth into the hands of a few corporations.

History

1. What were the principal issues involved in the struggle for Irish Home Rule?

2. Discuss the historical significance either of the Rhine or the Strait of Gibraltar.

3. Compare Metternich's policy of intervention with the policy pursued by the United States in the region of the Caribbean.

4. In what sense was the discovery of America a "natural product of the times"?

5. What were the economic consequences of the founding of Alexander's empire?

Government

1. What is the political significance of the growth of government by administrative boards and commissions in the United States?

2. It is sometimes said that the British House of Commons has completely surrendered control over the budget to the Cabinet. Is this true? Contrast the practice of Fascist Italy.

3. What changes have taken place in the laws regulating suffrage in the greater world powers since the last War? Discuss the political significance of these changes.

4. What have been the effects of the doctrine of Checks and Balances in American State Government?

5. What is the present status of the so-called "outlawry of war"? What are the difficulties in the way of the realization of this ideal?

Economics

1. How do you think advertising tends to affect the value of advertised products? Does it promote the general economic welfare?

2. Which of the following characterizations of profits seems to you most satisfactory and which least satisfactory: wages of supervision; reward for risk-bearing; gain from exploitation of labor; producer's surplus?

3. Discuss the following statement: "It now takes much less time to produce the goods we need than it did before modern improvements were introduced. A great deal of this extra time is wasted in unemployment and seasonal slack periods. The five-day week would remedy this situation."

4. Discuss the significance of the change which has taken place in the amount of this country's gold holdings since the World War,

5. Discuss the following statement: "As banking in this country grows more and more complex it is more and more diffi-

cult clearly to define the actual purposes and economic functions of our commercial banks."

1930 and 1931:

Students took these exams shortly after the great stock market crash of October 1929 that ushered in the Great Depression. The Eighteenth Amendment (Prohibition), ratified in 1920, had not yet been repealed.

1930

Government 1

1. The following statement was made before the Senate lobby investigating committee by Mr. Joseph Grundy, representative of the Pennsylvania Manufacturers' Association:

   "Such states as Arizona, South Dakota, Idaho, Mississippi, Montana, Arkansas, Georgia, and South Carolina do not pay enough toward the upkeep of the government to cover the costs of collection, and states like Pennsylvania, hamstrung as they are by adverse legislation, support these backward commonwealths and provide post offices, river improvements and other federal aid, figuratively on a gold platter. *It was a great mistake each State was given two Senators.*"

2. On December 2, 1929, it was announced that the United States State Department had forwarded, through the French Foreign Office, a note to the Government of Russia urging the latter to observe the provisions of the Kellogg-Briand Pact, "to refrain or desist from measures of hostility," and "to come to an agreement . . . upon a method for resolving by peaceful means the issues over which they [Russia and China] are at present in controversy." In replying through the same channel the Soviet Acting Commissar of Foreign Affairs termed the note an unjustified attempt to intervene in Chinese-Russian negotiations and consequently it could not be considered as a friendly act; surprise was expressed that the United States, which, by its own desire, does not have any official relations with the Soviet Union, should find it possible to give the Soviet Government advice and directions. *(a)* Was the action of the United States "intervention"? *(b)* Was the action of the United States "an unfriendly act"? *(c)* Might the action of the United States and reference in the United States note to the Soviet Government as the "Government of Russia" be legally interpreted as constructive recognition? Of what? *(d)* Does the absence of recognition preclude all "official relations" between states?

3. Prior to 1922 a certain organization raised in the United States two loans, amounting to $6,000,000, through subscription by individuals. The avowed purpose was "to set up by force in Ireland a republic of Ireland, which would be free and independent of any allegiance whatsoever to the Government of Great Britain and Ireland." Subscribers received a certificate, signed by "Eamonn de Lorean, president," saying that it "is exchangeable if presented at the treasury of the republic of Ireland one month after the international recognition of the said republic for one $ . . . gold bond of the republic of Ireland." In 1927 a balance of some $2,000,000 remained on deposit in a New York City bank. No such republic was established and the Irish Free State in 1927 sought a judgment of its title as legal successor.
   Decision.

1930

Government 19

Give your own opinions and the reasons on which you base them. You may restrict your citation of authorities to the cases discussed in the classroom.

1. An international conference on the treatment of foreigners was recently convened to conclude a treaty for the elimination of "certain disabilities and inequalities which still exist in respect to travel, residence, property rights and business activities." The government of the United States sent a technical expert in a consultative capacity, who announced to the conference that under the federal constitution the above matters were within the exclusive jurisdiction of the several States.

   Do you agree with this view of the extent of the treaty-making power?

2. Defendants were convicted of conspiracy to violate the National Prohibition Act. The government discovered the conspiracy and collected evidence subsequently admitted at the trial by employing a lineman to tap the telephone wires of the defendants. The tapping was made without trespass upon any property of the defendants, but was nevertheless admittedly criminal.

   Should the conviction thus obtained be affirmed? 277 U.S. 438.

3. "There can be no connection between the fact that Mr. Cummings entered or left the State of Missouri to avoid enrollment or draft in the military service of the United States and his fitness to teach the doctrines or administer the sacraments of his church; nor can a fact of this kind or the expression of words of sympathy with some of the persons drawn into the Rebellion constitute any evidence of the unfit-ness of the attorney to practice his profession or of the professor to teach the ordinary branches of education." Justice Field

   "Men or women who are Marxian Socialists have no right to be in the school system because such teachers believe in the overturn by force of those elements on which our civilization is based." The Associate Supt. of Schools in New York City.

   Comment.

1931

Division of History, Government, and Economics/Government Regulation of Industry

1. Discuss the nature, purpose and results of vertical combination. Does it need regulation as much as other types?

2. Discuss the forms and significance of discriminations in railway rate-making. Which of the discriminations, if any, tend to persist under government ownership?

3. With reference to what phase of banking activity do you think public regulation most desirable? least desirable?

4. To what degree do the policies of either the Federal Trade Commission or the Tariff Commission support the charge that "government in the United States, no matter what party is in power in Washington, has become paternalistic in its attitude toward business?"

5. "The Federal Reserve System exercises quasi-govemmental powers over banking as a whole and through it over the entire business organism." Comment.

6. "Mr. Hoover is one of our outstanding exponents of the principle of quasi-governmental organization in business, with government acting in a supervisory capac-

ity but not in that of a dictator. He has so far drawn the line at the extension of price-fixing into the realm of business." Comment.

7. "The only serious attempts at enforcement of the Sherman law have been in the assaults on organized labor, to which the law was never intended to apply."
   Comment.

1946:

Students took this exam seven months after the drafting of the U. N. charter, and five months after the United States hastened the end of World War II by dropping atomic bombs on the Japanese cities of Hiroshima and Nagasaki.

Government 4a

1. *(a)* "In the age of the atomic bomb, no questions can be considered 'domestic.' If international courts are to be limited by traditional concepts as to the extent of their authority, then schemes for the pacific settlement of disputes are indeed futile,"
   Discuss, citing the case of "The Tunis-Morocco Decrees" and the traditional techniques for adjudicating international disputes.

   OR

   (b) Do you believe it true that "international law favors the status quo"? In what ways does the doctrine "Pacta Sunt Servanda" affect the problem of peaceful change?

2. "The question of organizing measures of coercion in support of international law is insoluble as long as whole states are the units to be coerced." Discuss, with reference to (a) the so-called system of "self-help," (b) the experience of the League of Nations, and (c) the provisions in the Charter of the United Nations Organization, citing the material contained in the reading period selection.

1964:

Students took this exam during a period when Congress, the Supreme Court, and presidential administrations had shown their readiness to initiate and enforce desegregation in the South. The Civil Rights Act, which outlawed racial discrimination and segregation in public accommodations, schools, and other areas, had been proposed by the time students took this test; it was upheld by the Supreme Court later that year.

American Government

1. The public accommodations section of the proposed Civil Rights Act of 1964 has generated much discussion. Its supporters have been divided as to whether federal action might best be based on the "commerce clause" or on the 14th Amendment. Discuss the constitutional and political advantages either of relying on the "commerce clause" or of relying on the 14th Amendment.

2. "The authority of the Supreme Court rests on the sense of legitimacy it holds with the American people in general and with the legal community in particular. This legitimacy is being rapidly and dangerously eroded by the Court's involvement in such highly political areas as reapportionment and desegregation and by the effects of a generation of 'legal realism' within the legal community."

3. "The case for judicial self-restraint in primarily economic issues but for judicial activism in regard to political and civil liberties boils down to an acceptance or rejection of the 'preferred position' doctrine."

4. One of the most striking developments in American constitutional history has been the gradual application of the standards set by the federal Bill of Rights to the activities of state governments. Discuss the extent to which this has been done and the rationales by which it has been justified.

International Law and Relations

1. Do the multiple restraints on American foreign policy find any parallel in the experience of Soviet foreign policy? Analyze the similarities and/or differences with specific reference to such factors as the nature of the international system, the obligations of alliance, the role of domestic politics, institutions, and values.

2. Write an essay on the principle of nonintervention, analyzing its practicality as a matter of international law.

1986

History

1. What patterns do you see in this table on what children aged 12–20 were doing in Detroit in 1900? Can you suggest some explanation for the group differences here?

Percent	Sons Working	In School	At Home
Native Am White	40	55	5
Black	50	50	0
Irish	49	43	8
Polish	64	26	10
Jewish	30	53	17

Percent	Daughters Working	In School	At Home
Native Am White	17	56	27
Black	41	46	13
Irish	40	43	17
Polish	56	26	15
Jewish	61	17	22

HISTORY OF THE U.S. IN THE U.S.S.R

Private School of the Soviet Mission to the U.N.

Diplomats from the Soviet Union assigned to the United Nations in New York want their children to be educated as they would be in their own homeland, of course. To answer that need, the Soviet Mission runs a school for the elementary and intermediate grades staffed by Soviet teachers. The history teachers there prepared the following outline to reveal what aspects of U.S. history a child in the Soviet school system would be expected to learn.

Like Harvard's exams, Soviet exams seldom use multiple-choice or fill-in test formats requiring brief single-fact answers, so no answers are provided here. Unlike the Harvard exams, however, the trick here is to compare your own knowledge of this subject by projecting yourself into another cultural and political dimension, rather than projecting your knowledge of your own culture and politics into different periods of time in their evolution.

The elementary and secondary education system in the U. S. S. R. is similar to our own in its grade/age level divisions: Elementary (grades 1–4, ages 6–10); Pre-secondary (grades 5–9, ages 11–15); Secondary (grades 10–11, ages 16–17).

The curriculum is based first upon general fields of study, and then split into separate disciplines within each field. The goals of elementary and secondary schooling are the preparation for work and the well-rounded and harmonious development of each student's capacities as an individual to think independently and energetically.

Soviet schools accord a special place to the study of history. The curriculum provides students with a knowledge of the evolution of society from ancient times to our day, both in the Soviet Union and in foreign countries. They examine primary-source documents from which they are encouraged to form a scientific understanding of the natural laws of progression of society, and chronologically to trace the role of the popular masses as makers of history and the significance of the individual personality in history.

Their study of World History outside Russia runs parallel to the history of their own country in each chronological period starting with the 5th grade.

5th grade/The History of the Ancient World

An 11-year-old is expected to answer oral and written questions that require a knowledge of, for example:

- The culture of ancient India and China: The written language, scientific knowledge, art.
- The Greek language, its meaning in our times. School in Greece. The Olympic Games.
- Theater in Greece. The significance of the theater in the lives of the Greeks. Greek architecture and sculpture.
- Science. The development of the study of the natural sciences and of history.
- The contribution of the ancient Greeks to the progress of world culture.
- Roman culture from the end of the Republic to the beginning of the Empire including literature, architecture, sculpture, the calendar, the art of oratory, and the influence of Greek on Roman culture.

6th grade/The History of the Middle Ages

- The Byzantine Empire: Education, monuments, architecture, representational art (mosaics, frescoes, icon painting).
- The culture of the countries of the Caliphate: The development of the sciences (astronomy, mathematics,

medicine, geography) and arts (architecture, decorative handicrafts).

7th grade/Russian History

The entire school year is devoted to the study of mother Russia from ancient times to the mid-seventeenth century. In later grades students continue to study Soviet history parallel to their study of the history of the outside world.

8th–10th grades/Modern History

The Modern History of foreign countries is taught in the 8th and 9th grades, and covers the period from the middle of the seventeenth century to the beginning of the twentieth.

A 13-year-old Soviet student approaches the world outside the Soviet Union from a cultural as well as a political viewpoint. The study of Western European culture includes the Renaissance (the works of Leonardo da Vinci, Michelangelo, and Raphael, Rabelais, Thomas Moore, and William Shakespeare).

European history also includes the principal writers of the Romantic period (Goethe, Schiller, Byron), and of Realism (Balzac, Dickens), the study of music (Bach, Mozart, Beethoven, Chopin), and the fundamental schools of painting (Classicism, Romanticism, Realism).

One of the primary educational aims of this course is to develop in the students, in accordance with their level of maturity, a knowledge of the formation and development of capitalist structures and of their most essential features and contradictions.

In the model of the histories of various foreign countries, one can trace the transition of society from feudalism to capitalism.

Capitalism, as a social structure, became most firmly established in England, France, and the United States; thus the study of these countries occupies a significant place in the Modern History course. The historical preconditions for the development of capitalism in these countries and the characteristic peculiarities and content of this process in each of them are examined separately.

The course material substantially deepens and expands the students' knowledge of the historical peculiarities of the development of these countries; it allows them to draw conclusions about the natural laws governing social processes.

Familiarity with the history of other countries allows the students to be brought to an understanding of the general natural laws of the historical transition to capitalism and at the same time to see the inevitable variety of forms of this progression in various countries.

An 8th-grade student of United States history is expected to be able to describe the following developments, including explanation of their causes and effects from the colonization of America by the British through the effects of the Civil War.

1. English colonies in North America in the eighteenth century.
2. The War for Independence of England's colonies in America (the first bourgeois revolution in North America) including its basic causes and immediate reasons for the first violence.
3. Black slavery.
4. The annihilation of the Indians.
5. The "Declaration of Independence."
6. The defeat of England.
7. The formation of the United States of America.
8. The role played by George Washington.
9t The Constitution of the United States, its progressive features and bourgeois narrow-mindedness.
10. The meaning of the revolutionary War for Independence in the context of world struggle against imperialist domination, and class privilege, and economic forces.
11. The United States in the first half of the nineteenth century.

12. The growth of capitalism in the United States.
13. The expansion and aggression of the United States, and its territorial boundaries.
14. The Civil War (the second bourgeois revolution in the United States).
15. The causes of the outbreak of the Civil War.
16. The formation of the Republican Party.
17. The election of Abraham Lincoln to the Presidency.
18. The revolt of the Southern slaveholders.
19. The major battles in the course of the Civil War that led to the victory of the North.
20. The Homestead Act and the abolition of slavery.
21. The meaning of the Civil War to the US.

If asked to summarize the material covered in the first half of the school year, an 8th grader would be expected to describe the character of the American people's war for freedom from English rule, and the content of the most important documents of the American Revolution—the Declaration of Independence and the Constitution. A 14-year-old Soviet student must be familiar with the names of Jefferson, Franklin, Paine, Washington, and the other bearers of the revolutionary traditions of the American people.

The second half of that 8th-grade year would prepare him or her to answer oral examination questions documenting the following positions. The character and particular features of the Civil War that finally transferred power from the hands of the plantation and slaveowners to those of the powerful bourgeoisie; the slavery of the blacks, which had been hindering the development of capitalism, was abolished; the Homestead Act had precipitated the settlement and assimilation of the West; why, near the end of the nineteenth century, did the United States move to first place in the world with respect to the volume of industrial production, significantly ahead of England and Germany.

Specific questions asked of a 15-year-old Soviet student would probably include:

(A) Why was English colonization, in contrast to that of the French, carried out by the masses?

(B) From your study of the Declaration of Independence, establish and prove this position: "The principles voiced in the Declaration of Independence were directed against the feudal orders and against the colonial yoke."

(C) Analyze and substantiate the historical developments of American imperialistic policies exemplified by the announcement by U.S. President McKinley concerning the Philippines.

A 9th grader is examined on U. S. History from the 1880s through the 1930s. Students are expected knowledgeably to discuss the following topics and show understanding of their causes and effects:

1. The principal capitalist countries at the end of the nineteenth and beginning of the twentieth century.
2. The rapid industrial and agrarian development and the concentration of manufacture and of monopoly in the United States.
3. The imperialism of the United States.
4. Bourgeois democracy as the instrument of the rule of big industrial capital.
5. The oppression of blacks.
6. The labor and socialist movements in the United States including the founding of the American Federation of Labor (AFL).
7. The intensification of class antagonisms in the beginning of the twentieth century.
8. The aggression of the United States in Central America (Cuba and other countries).
9. The policies of the United States in China.

10. The transformation of the United States into the most prominent imperialist world power from 1924–1939.
11. Foreign and domestic policies that reflected imperialist and capitalist ambition.
12. The magnitude of industrial production.
13. The worldwide economic crisis.
14. The intensification of class antagonism.
15. Franklin Roosevelt's "New Deal."
16. Domestic policies on the eve of World War II.

In the 10th grade, students focus on the background of contemporary world affairs. They are expected to demonstrate their command of the following facts and developments:

1. The principal capitalist countries after World War II.
2. The role of the United States as the chief imperialist power.
3. The economy after World War II.
4. Anticommunism in the United States.
5. Foreign and domestic policies under Eisenhower and Truman.
6. The creation of the military blocs, the wars in Korea and Indochina.
7. Soviet-American negotiations in the 1970s.
8. The policies of the United States in its current stage.
9. The U.S. Communist Party in the United States.

INTERIOR DECORATING

Academy of Art College

Decorator: "But, darling, are you sure you want me to install track shelving over the walnut paneling in the dining room so you can display Andy's cookie jars?"

Client: "Just because you didn't buy them for me, darling, doesn't mean they aren't worth looking at."

An interior decorator or designer, according to the National Council for Interior Design Qualification, is someone who: "identifies, researches, and creatively solves problems pertaining to the function of the interior environment; performs services relative to interior spaces, including programming, design analysis, space planning, and esthetics, using specialized knowledge of interior construction, building codes, equipment, materials, and furnishings; and prepares drawings and documents relative to the design of interior spaces in order to enhance and protect the health, safety, and welfare of the public." The interior designer thus requires much more than an esthetic sensibility and familiarity with fabrics; he or she must have acquired much of the technical knowledge commonly associated with the field of architectural design.

In several states, it is illegal to call yourself an interior designer without first acquiring a license, for which the primary requirement is passing the NCIDQ examination; the exam is also a prerequisite to joining one of the professional organizations in the field, such as the American Society of Interior Designers and the Institute of Business Designers. To qualify for taking the exam, you have to have had several years of relevant professional experience, some of which may be substituted by schooling in a university-level interior design program. The exam itself consists of two parts: a 3½-hour multiple-choice section, testing knowledge of such areas as interior design theory, building construction, materials, and history of the field; and a 10-hour design section consisting of a jury-scored realistic design problem involving a design concept statement, space planning, and furniture selection and arrangement.

The questions that follow should give you a fairly clear picture of the sort of knowledge required in the field and on the exam. We've left out questions pertaining to drier, more technical aspects such as drawing up contracts and knowledge of building codes. The questions were provided by Nancy Brown, ASID, a faculty member of the Academy of Art College in San Francisco, which has one of the most highly ranked interior design programs in the country; for information about the courses and degrees they offer, contact the Interior Design Department, Academy of Art College, 2300 Stockton Street, Suite 300, San Francisco CA 94133, tel. (415) 274-2200 or (800) 544-ARTS.

Multiple Choice

1. The science that seeks to adapt the environment to its users is called
    (A) metamerism
    (B) ergonomics
    (C) anthropometrics

2. What one element helps to give balance to a room?
    (A) A window on every wall
    (B) A fireplace
    (C) Matching wallpaper and draperies
    (D) Furniture of varied heights

3. In a formal living room, which two are out of place?
    (A) Damask sofa
    (B) A lambrequin
    (C) Windsor chair
    (D) Bergere chair
    (E) Pewter wall sconces

4. Which two elements are typical of Queen Anne style?
    (A) Cabriole leg
    (B) Straight tapered legs
    (C) Bee motif
    (D) Shell carving

5. Which two elements are typical of Thomas Chippendale's furniture?
    (A) Extensive use of oak
    (B) Chinese fretwork
    (C) Gothic design motifs
    (D) Shield-shaped motifs

6. Which two could be found in a Victorian living room?
    (A) Antimacassers
    (B) Marquetry table
    (C) Eames chair
    (D) Belter chair

7. Where was hard-paste porcelain first successfully produced in Europe?
    (A) England
    (B) France
    (C) Saxony
    (D) Holland

8. What two contributions has India made to Western design?
    (A) Batik fabric
    (B) Copper pots
    (C) Dhurrie rugs
    (D) Paisley prints

9. Three leaders of the Bauhaus School were
    (A) William Morris
    (B) Walter Gropius
    (C) John Goddard
    (D) Le Corbusier
    (E) Mies van der Rohe
    (F) Frank Lloyd Wright

10. Which two would not be seen in a Roman villa?
    (A) Ceramic tile
    (B) Trompe l'oeil
    (C) A triptych
    (D) A vitrine
    (E) Hot water pipes

11. Two items that could be found in an informal living room include
    (A) a pine armoire
    (B) an Aubusson carpet
    (C) a plaid loveseat
    (D) a torchier

12. Which architectural element would best divide a wall?
    (A) Cornice
    (B) Dado
    (C) Soffit
    (D) Corbel

13. What is the best lighting for a dining room?
    (A) Chandelier
    (B) Recessed ceiling lights
    (C) Spots and uplights
    (D) All of the above

14. Which two materials conduct most heat and cold?
    (A) Brick
    (B) Glass
    (C) Metal
    (D) Wood
    (E) Cork

15. Which two design elements can add drama to a room?
    (A) Deep wall color
    (B) A lot of accessories
    (C) One well-lighted piece of art
    (D) A variety of patterns

16. Which three are natural fibers?
    (A) Silk
    (B) Rayon
    (C) Cotton
    (D) Ramie
    (E) Acetate

17. Choose three ways to make a room seem larger.
    (A) Paint walls a cool color
    (B) Use a lot of pattern
    (C) Use several large upholstered pieces
    (D) Upholster main pieces in light, solid-colored fabric
    (E) Use some mirror

18. What two events influenced 17th-century European furniture styles and decorative arts?
    (A) Versailles became a royal residence
    (B) Edict of Nantes revoked
    (C) Dutch East India Company founded
    (D) England established a colony in Virginia

19. What two events influenced 18th-century European furniture styles and decorative arts?
    (A) Formula for hard-paste porcelain perfected
    (B) Louis XVI and Marie Antoinette beheaded
    (C) Industrial Revolution
    (D) American Revolution

20. What two events influenced 19th-century furniture styles and decorative arts?
    (A) Napoleon's conquest of Egypt
    (B) Source of Ganges River discovered
    (C) Excavations at Pompeii
    (D) Italian Republic established

21. What one invention has had the greatest influence on 20th-century furniture and decorative arts?
    (A) Invention of atomic power
    (B) Invention of plastics
    (C) Invention of frequency modulation

22. One way to identify a Persian rug is
    (A) shag pile
    (B) lack of human form as a design element
    (C) pastel coloring

23. The best light to read by is
    (A) ambient lighting
    (B) shielded task lighting
    (C) track lighting

24. Which two color combinations stimulate us to be active?
    (A) Pastel pink and white
    (B) Lemon chiffon and celadon green
    (C) Candy apple red and forest green
    (D) Orange and mustard yellow

25. Which two statements are *not* true?
    (A) Warm hues are restful
    (B) The only true neutral colors are black, white, and gray
    (C) Complementary hues are directly opposite on the color wheel
    (D) Objects appear smaller against a dark wall

26. What three factors are important to discuss with a client during the first interview?
    (A) Client's lifestyle
    (B) Client's education
    (C) Client's budget restrictions
    (D) Site restrictions
    (E) City codes

27. What three factors would be considered when laying out a furniture plan for a living room?
    (A) Which existing pieces of furniture will be used
    (B) What color does client prefer
    (C) What is circulation pattern
    (D) Where will television be placed
    (E) What window treatment will be used

28. What one factor is most important when mixing patterns?
    (A) You must like them all
    (B) Patterns must vary in size
    (C) All patterns should be made of the same fabric

29. New laws require contract designers to consider what three areas?
    (A) Energy efficiency
    (B) Color codes
    (C) The handicapped
    (D) Hazardous materials
    (E) Maintenance standards

30. What two pieces of furniture are uniquely American?
    (A) Handkerchief table
    (B) Hitchcock chair
    (C) Hunt table
    (D) Pembroke table

31. The two best qualities of wool carpet are its
    (A) resistance to soil
    (B) resistance to insects
    (C) resistance to static
    (D) durability

32. Since the 1950s most carpet has been manufactured on
    (A) a tufting loom
    (B) a Jacquard loom
    (C) an Axminster loom

33. Japanning is
    (A) furniture made in the Japanese style
    (B) a technique of applying a lacquer finish to furniture
    (C) Japanese calligraphy

34. Two important factors when planning a new kitchen include
    (A) task and ambient lighting
    (B) traffic patterns
    (C) wine storage
    (D) display space

35. Three 20th-century furniture designers are
    (A) Eero Saarinen
    (B) Henry Belter
    (C) Michael Thonet
    (D) Duncan Phyfe
    (E) Marcel Breuer
    (F) John Goddard

36. Three 20th-century architects are
    (A) Frank Lloyd Wright
    (B) Andrea Palladio
    (C) Philip Johnson
    (D) Michael Graves
    (E) Christopher Wren
    (F) James Hoban

37. Who was the first American interior decorator?
    (A) Nancy McClelland
    (B) Elsie de Wolfe
    (C) Letitia Baldrige
    (D) Diana Vreeland

38. Two factors that determine the successful design of a room are
    (A) using all of the client's furniture
    (B) the color scheme
    (C) the furniture arrangement
    (D) the placement of windows and doors

39. What three factors are important in the furniture arrangement of a room?
    (A) Balance
    (B) Style
    (C) Scale
    (D) Budget
    (E) Proportion

40. Balance in furniture arrangement is defined as
    (A) good distribution of weight, height, and size
    (B) good distribution of colored objects
    (C) good distribution of client's own furniture

41. Which is not a good utilization of space in a dead corner?
    (A) A decorative screen
    (B) An important object of art
    (C) Conversation grouping
    (D) A specimen plant

42. What one factor must be considered when laying out the plan for a living room?
    (A) Book storage
    (B) Conversation grouping
    (C) Display of art collection
    (D) Entertainment center

43. Three ways to achieve color harmony include
    (A) use equal areas of contrasting colors
    (B) contrast light against dark
    (C) use equal amounts of warm and cool colors
    (D) contrast bright against dull
    (E) use bits of white, no matter what the scheme
    (F) use equal amounts of shades

44. Which two medical environments should be painted in a cool color?
    (A) Pediatric area
    (B) Orthopedic ward
    (C) Physiotherapy room
    (D) Psychiatric ward

45. To practice interior design in most states one needs
    (A) a contractor's license
    (B) an architect's license
    (C) a resale or sales tax number
    (D) a college degree

46. Which two are not part of the styling of a sofa?
    (A) Knife edge
    (B) Kick pleat
    (C) Jabot
    (D) Dovetail
    (E) Welting

47. Which three are not part of detailing of a breakfront?
    (A) Gallery
    (B) Escutcheon
    (C) Dado
    (D) Chevel glass
    (E) Broken pediment
    (F) Gimp

48. The National Trust for Historic Preservation was founded by
    (A) the Daughters of the American Revolution (the DAR)
    (B) the American Institute of Architects (AIA)
    (C) the Congress of the United States

49. In textile weaving, which two statements are *incorrect?*
    (A) Warp threads run lengthwise on the loom
    (B) A damask pattern is woven on a Jacquard loom
    (C) Jacquard weaves produce a smooth, glossy fabric
    (D) Twill weaves show definite horizontal lines
    (E) Pile weaves make a three-dimensional fabric

50. Three decorative objects unique to France are
    (A) a Chinese export porcelain
    (B) a Sevres figurine
    (C) a Gobelin tapestry
    (D) a silver epergne
    (E) a trumeau
    (F) a Capo di Monte bowl

51. Three decorative objects unique to America are
    (A) scrimshaw
    (B) a banjo clock
    (C) salt-glazed stoneware
    (D) Moravian fancywork
    (E) painted tinware

Matching

1. Match best use of following types of lighting:
   (A) halogen
   (B) fluorescent
   (C) incandescent

   (1) warm, soft, low light level
   (2) special effects
   (3) energy efficient, high light level

2. Match material with typical style:
   (A) marble
   (B) gold leaf
   (C) chrome
   (D) wrought iron

   (1) Louis XV
   (2) Jacobean
   (3) Victorian
   (4) Art deco

3. Match what is ideal distance between
   (A) sofa and coffee table
   (B) occupied dining chair
   (C) occupied desk chair

   (1) 3 feet
   (2) 1 foot
   (3) 1 /2 to 2 feet

4. Match style/period with typical wood used in furniture making:
   (A) black walnut
   (B) mahogany
   (C) pine
   (D) teak
   (E) satinwood
   (F) oak

   (1) Louis XVI
   (2) Queen Anne
   (3) Colonial American
   (4) Victorian
   (5) Arts and Crafts
   (6) Ming

5. Arrange the following pieces of furniture on the plan below, keeping in mind balance, traffic patterns, conversational groupings, and television viewing. The room is 19 by 15 feet and one square equals one foot. Furniture sizes are given in inches.

(1) sofa (84 wide by 30 deep)
(2) coffee table (60 by 24)
(3) 2 club chairs (30 by 30)
(4) occasional table (18 by 28)
(5) chest (34 by 18 by 28 high)
(6) cabinet with doors (42 by 20 by 72 high)
(7) ottoman (30 by 24)
(8) round occasional table (30 by 30)
(9) wing chair (30 by 34)
(10) floor lamp with tray table (12 by 12)
(11) three table lamps

6. Match decorative object with period or style:

(A) stained-glass lamp
(B) Wedgewood urn
(C) faience bowl
(D) wrought-iron weathervane
(E) lacquer screen

(1) French Provincial
(2) Art Nouveau
(3) Pennsylvania Dutch
(4) Chinese
(5) Georgian

7. Match the following color term with the definition:

(A) tint
(B) hue
(C) chroma
(D) value

(1) degree of intensity of a color
(2) a hue to which white is added
(3) degree of lightness or darkness of a color
(4) a specific tint or shade

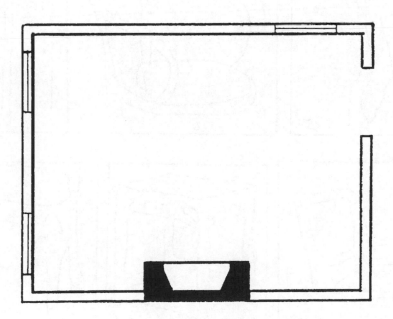

8. From the sketches below, match the chair back and legs to the appropriate period or style.
   (A) Ming
   (B) Hepplewhite
   (C) Chippendale
   (D) French Provincial
   (E) Louis XVI
   (F) Thonet bentwood
   (G) Queen Anne
   (H) Bauhaus/Breuer

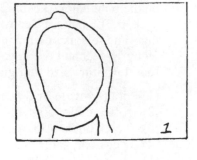

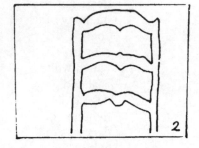

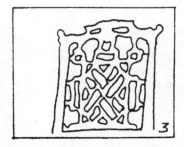

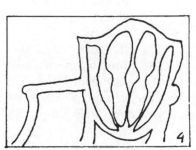

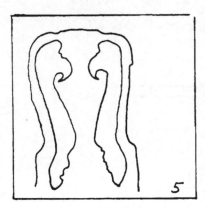

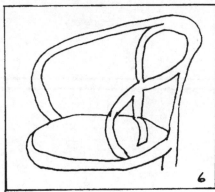

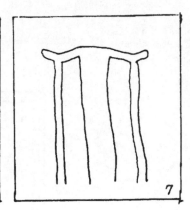

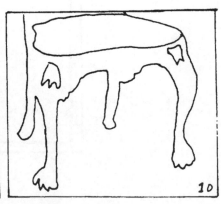

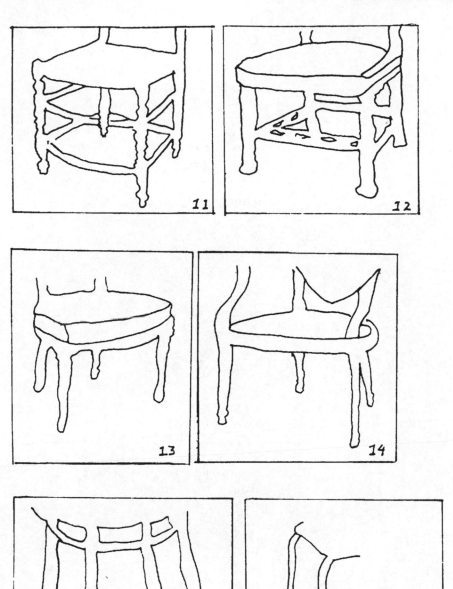

ANSWERS!

Multiple Choice

1. B
2. D
3. C and E
4. A and D
5. B and C
6. A and D
7. C
8. C and D
9. B, D, and E
10. C and D
11. A and C
12. B
13. D
14. B and C
15. A and C
16. A, C, and D
17. A, D, and E
18. B and C
19. A and C
20. A and C
21. B
22. B
23. B
24. C and D
25. A and D
26. A, C, and D
27. A, C, and D
28. B
29. A, C, and D
30. A and B
31. A and D
32. A
33. B
34. A and B
35. A, C, and E
36. A, C, and D
37. B
38. B and C
39. A, C, and E
40. A
41. C
42. B
43. B, D, and E
44. C and D
45. C
46. C and D
47. C, D, and F
48. C
49. C and D
50. B, C, and E
51. A, B, and D

Matching

   A: 2
   B: 3
   C: 1
2. A: 3
   B: 1
   C: 4
   D: 2
3. A: 2
   B: 3
   C: 1
4. A: 4
   B: 2
   C: 3
   D: 6
   E: 1
   F: 5
5. See two answers on next page
6. A: 2
   B: 5
   C: 1
   D: 3
   E: 4
7. A: 2
   B: 4
   C: 1
   D: 3
8. A: 7 and 9
   B: 4 and 14
   C: 3 and 12
   D: 2 and 11

E: 1 and 13
F: 6 and 15
G: 5 and 10
H: 8 and 16

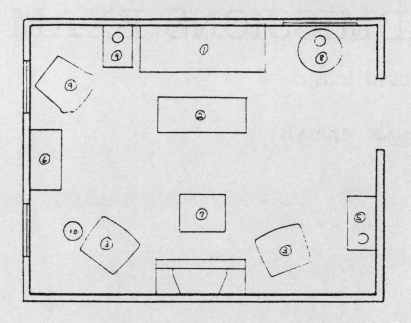

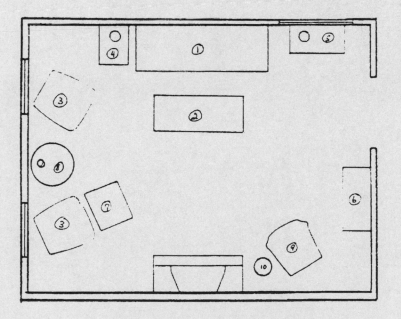

JAPANESE UNIVERSITY ADMISSIONS EXAM

Kyotsu Ichiji

たかが入試、されど入試！

One of the most notorious elements of the Japanese educational system is the *Kyotsu Ichiji*, or national university entrance exam. Unlike the SAT exam, the Japanese university exam is a test not so much of aptitude as of substantive knowledge that one is expected to acquire in high school. Actually, no one is expected to acquire all of the knowledge tested in the exam in the normal course of high school, and realistically no one does. Hence, even the best students may hire tutors, at fees of perhaps $40 an hour at the current exchange rate, for periods of a year or maybe even two, to help them perform well on the exam.

A number of students each year commit suicide because of this test, either worn out from the stress of preparing for it, or because of the loss of face in failure. The one consolation for the student is that, once he or she gains admission to a university, all the hard work is pretty much over. In the U.S., we're used to high school being a typically frivolous affair, with college being somewhat more demanding, and grad school being downright grueling. In Japan, the system is more or less reversed. While high school is stressful and demanding, college is a time to drink copious amounts of beer and *sake* and maybe do a little schoolwork on the side; the job one gets afterward is determined much more by where one goes to school than how one does *in* school.

The exam consists of about a dozen subjects, of which the student is required to take seven. Of those seven, three (Math, English, and Japanese) are obligatory; the remaining four must be chosen from the natural and social science categories.

From the exam, we have chosen 10 from the World History section and 5 from a section that could be translated roughly as Social Relations. These questions are from the most recent *Kyotsu Ichiji*.

World History

As the characteristics of war differ according to place and time, so too peace has had different meanings throughout history.

The so-called "Pax Romana" (Roman Peace) was synonymous with domination by Rome. In medieval Europe, "peace by God" came to be advocated by the Church to prohibit fighting among secular leaders as a means of settling disputes. At the same time, however, the Church did involve Europe in warfare against "heathens" or "heretics." At the time of the Crusades, the Pope _____, who
      1
achieved the Church's greatest power—of which the humiliation of the English King John was one manifestation—instituted severe anti-Semitic policies.

In Asia, too, various conceptions of peace emerged. In China, for example, among the thinkers of the ancient time, _____ proclaimed absolute aversion to
     2
war, appealing to mercy, charity, and love of one's fellow man and to pacifism, while Meng-tsu urged the unification of China under peace by the "Royal (or Divine) Conduct."

1. Of the following statements, select the wrong one.
    (A) The period of "Pax Romana" usually refers to the time between Augustus and the Five Good Emperors
    (B) The territory of the Roman Empire was largest at the time of Trajan
    (C) Roman citizenship was gradually granted to the nearby people under their domination
    (D) Christianity, which called for the liberation of slaves, became the Empire's religion and slavery disappeared

2. Select the name of the Pope who fits (**1**) in the passage above:
    (A) Gregory VII
    (B) Urban II
    (C) Innocent III
    (D) Boniface VIII

3. Select the name of the thinker who fits (**2**) in the passage above:
    (A) Mo-tzu
    (B) Sun-tzu
    (C) Shang Yang
    (D) Hsün-tzu

Due to the Reformation and the rise of absolutist nations, the old orders of medieval Europe collapsed. As a result, numerous wars took place in modern Europe. In the 17th century, as a reaction to the calamities of war, new measures for maintaining peace were formulated, including international laws. As a consequence, "peace" often stood for the maintenance of a balance of power among the major powers. The balance of power during the period of absolutism, however, suffered serious damage from the French Revolution and the Napoleonic Wars at the turn of the 19th century. To repair this balance, the Congress of Vienna was held. From then until the 1870s, peace was maintained by the British hegemony, with the potential oppositions among the major powers unresolved.

4. Of the following statements about Grotius, the "Father of International Law," select the correct one.
    (A) He wrote "On the Law of War and Peace" during the Dutch Republic's revolt against Spain

(B) He advocated the reconstruction of the medieval order with the Pope at its center

(C) He considered rational international relations to be based on the natural laws

(D) He said that the foundation of peace lies in the unity of each nation under a strong monarch

5. The principle of "balance of power" was adopted at the Congress of Vienna. Of the following statements about the balance of power at the time of the Congress, select the wrong one:

(A) England adopted an anti-continental policy to prevent any single nation from becoming a superpower

(B) To achieve a balance of power, it was agreed that small countries like Poland should become independent

(C) Major powers yearned for the expansion of their territories, so the meeting was merely a scrambling for new land by the powers

(D) In order to justify the changing of national borders at the major powers' will, a policy of "substitutionism" was adopted, and Austria renounced the Netherlands to acquire Northern Italy

6. With regard to the British hegemony, the situation of general world peace at this time was designated "Pax Britannica." Of the following statements about Pax Britannica, select the correct one:

(A) Under the peace, England did not have wars overseas, and expanded free international trade

(B) What disturbed the power balance of Europe was Russia's advancement into Balkan territories, taking advantage of the decline of the Ottoman Empire

(C) Bismarck, having unified Germany, attempted the expansion of its power, and consequently international tension increased

(D) Because the United States proclaimed the Monroe Doctrine, the English capitalists were not able to advance into Central and South America

World War I brought overwhelming human and material losses. In view of this, the demand for peace and order was strongly made after the war. In this context, the League of Nations was established as the international organization for maintaining peace by collaboration. Among its activities, international meetings were held on disarmament and international security. However, despite such efforts, another war broke out. After World War II, in October 1945, the United Nations was organized to maintain peace despite differences of political systems and individual beliefs, and various organizations were created to promote international collaboration and communication in such areas as security, economics, social affairs, and culture. At the same time, facing such situations as regional disputes and the Cold War, movements of non-alliance and positive neutralism arose, involving independence from the Soviet Union and the United States and anti-colonialism. Yet there were still many international disputes, and many difficulties for the establishment of real international peace.

7. Select the correct combination of countries that were not affiliated with the League of Nations when it was established:

(A) the United States, the Soviet Union, and Germany

(B) the United States, England, and Japan

(C) China, Vietnam, and India

(D) Germany, France, and England

8. Select the correct statement about the result of the Washington Conference held during 1921-1922:
   (A) the reduction of the annual reparations of Germany was endorsed
   (B) the Japan-England alliance was abrogated
   (C) the maintenance of the Rheinland and mutual security were promised
   (D) warfare as a means for settling international disputes was denounced

9. With regard to the United Nations, select the correct statement from the following:
   (A) the permanent members of the Security Council are the United States, the Soviet Union, England, France, and Japan
   (B) to settle international disputes, the U.N. established NATO
   (C) its headquarters are in Geneva, Switzerland
   (D) UNESCO was established by the U.N. to promote free cultural exchange throughout the world

10. Select the one person who is not an appropriate representative of the movement of non-alliance and neutralism mentioned above:
   (A) Nehru
   (B) Tito
   (C) Franco
   (D) Sukarno

Social Relations

Questions 1–5 refer to the following dialogue:

Student A: The *Kyotsu Ichiji* will be over today. How are you doing so far?

Student B: Not too bad, but I hate to take exams. With all this pressure, I feel like the "right to receive education" that our Constitution assures is the "duty to receive education."

A: You really shouldn't say things like that. There are many people who cannot afford to go to university even though they want to.

B: Right, the right to receive education is one of the fundamental human rights, and sure I know it's important...

A: And also, the right to receive education is a kind of social right, so it has a positive aspect, that is, we are entitled to petition the government for an improvement in the education provided to us.

B: I think it's true, yes. However, take, for example, the problem of textbook authorization. People are arguing that it is virtually a censorship on education by the government. Isn't there another level of consideration which is distinct from the issue of social rights?

A: Yeah, you may be right. After all, there are two kinds of relation between the government and education, one being, say, the right to have freedom, and the other being social rights. And I think this duality makes the issues associated with education especially complicated.

B: Besides, the present system of college entrance, you know, these awful exams, is badly influencing education in general. Of course, we don't have time to argue about it right now.

A: But see, we shouldn't be indifferent to the real social issues by being too preoccupied with our entrance exam.

B: Well, maybe. Anyway, let's do our best on the rest of the subjects today.

1. Select the statement which is inappropriate as a reason for respecting fundamental human rights:
    (A) the fundamental human rights have been obtained through the struggle against injustice done by the national government
    (B) all individuals live within society, and thus must always act by giving priority to the public welfare of society as a whole
    (C) in order to achieve administration for the people based on the principle of democracy, the assurance of the fundamental human rights is an indispensible prerequisite
    (D) people have rights given by nature, and must be treated equally and assured freedom in terms of them

2. Select the one statement which is inappropriate as an explanation of social rights:
    (A) they were proposed to solve social and economic problems that came about as a result of the development of capitalism
    (B) they were first formulated in the Weimar Constitution, where it also was stated that the right to own property is accompanied by duties
    (C) people suffering from poverty are entitled to request living expenses from the government by making an appeal to the court, directly on the basis of the social rights defined in Article 25 of the Constitution

(D) to respond to the social rights, the government must promote the social welfare, social security, and public health

3. It has been debated whether the system of textbook authorization, whereby only those books that are authorized by the Ministry of Education can actually be used as textbooks in elementary and high schools, might be in violation of the Constitution, and certain Articles of the Constitution are typically cited. Of the following three Articles of the Constitution, mark the invariably-cited one(s) with (1), and mark the one(s) that has (have) no relevance to the issue with (2).
    (A) Prohibition of censorship (Article 21, Section 2)
    (B) Rectification (Article 29, Section 3)
    (C) Freedom of learning (Article 23)

4. Select the government's proper educational policy with regard to the right to liberty:
    (A) the government provides textbooks used in elementary and junior high schools (i.e. at the level of mandatory education) free of charge
    (B) in order to establish rich and varied opportunities for education, the government establishes vocational high schools as well as ordinary ones
    (C) the government enlarges school libraries and enhances accessibility to them
    (D) the government defines the curriculum and demands that teachers follow it
    (E) the government provides scholarships for those who are unable to go to school for financial reasons

5. Select the statement which best describes
   the social problems representing violations
   of fundamental human rights:
   (A) the system of public access to informa-
       tion, which is at work at various levels
       of local government, is not provided
       for by any national law
   (B) the Supreme Court has passed judg-
       ment several times on the issue of the
       ratio of representatives to the Diet.
       However, the government hasn't yet
       made any changes in the ratio
   (C) even though bodies like Japan National
       Railways, the Telecommunications
       Agency, and the Tobacco Agency have
       become private, the workers in these
       companies, like public servants, are
       denied the right to strike due to the
       highly public nature of their
       occupation
   (D) the government takes the position that
       giving prayers in an official capacity at
       the Yasukuni Shrine* might violate the
       Constitution, which stipulates the sep-
       aration of church and state; thus, no
       Prime Ministers have ever given
       prayers at the shrine

   *The Yasukuni Shrine is a highly sacred
   monument where all those killed in war are
   symbolically buried. (In Japanese society,
   dying in war also qualifies one for
   deification.)

ANSWERS!☛

World History

1. A
2. C
3. A
4. C
5. B
6. B
7. A
8. B
9. D
10. C

Social Relations

1. B
2. C
3. A: 1
    B: 2
    C: 1
4. D
5. A

KITCHEN MASTER

California Culinary Academy

*With the Bureau of Labor Statistics projecting a 50%
increase through 1995 in the demand for restaurant
chefs, the culinary arts look like a good field to enter.
It seems that no matter how uncertain the economic
present may be, people will always want to go out to
dinner. In fact, as economic conditions deteriorate,
people's need for entertainment seems to increase.
And don't forget for a moment that success in commercial food service has at least as much to do with entertainment skills—including set design, makeup, and
timing – as it does with culinary inventiveness. Still,
chefs get to name the dishes they invent, which gives
them a shot at immortal fame. Hint: The wisest chefs
seem to choose shellfish for their inventions and name
them for others who command considerably more
power and notoriety than they. Witness Napoleons,
Oysters Rockefeller, Crab Louis, and Shrimp Scampi.
(If you cannot identify what is wrong with the foregoing Hint you might want to reconsider choosing this
field as a career goal. See facing page*.)*

There's a stereotype of the *Chef de Cuisine* that places him beyond the heights that we mere mortals can attain. He's a great artist, with a temperament to match—unreasonable, unpredictable, jealous, and arrogant by turns, but able to create works of culinary art so sublime they send even jaded palates into rapture.

As you might suspect, though, this stereotype of the chef as tempestuous *artiste* is not a good representation of most chefs, or even the ideal chef. The ideal chef is a problem-solver and diplomat, both in the kitchen and in the dining room. And while it may be true that to be a great culinary artist requires at least a touch of divine inspiration, it also requires systematic training and a lot of hard work. Given the predictions of growth in the food service industry, you might reasonably have purely pragmatic motives for deciding to work for the privilege of wearing the *toque blanche* (incidentally, it rhymes with the "bloke's paunch").

One way to make the transition from, say, waitressing, homemaking, Sybaritic idleness or an unpromising career in housing construction to one in the culinary arts is to attend a culinary school to learn the requisite skills. Don't think it'll be easy—professional food preparation involves a lot of hard work over the burner lines and stock pots. If you can take it, though, you can be pretty sure you won't be out of a job unless you want to be. For example, a survey of the graduates of the California Culinary Academy, where we obtained the test questions that follow, indicates that 96% of them are successfully employed in the culinary profession, as chefs, caterers, and food writers.

The Academy puts its students through an intensive 16-month program that includes instruction in the disciplines related to the operation of a food service organization. Their program emphasizes classical culinary methods and techniques and lots of practical kitchen work, but also includes training in other areas related to running a restaurant, such as purchasing and sanitation. The test questions on the following pages give you a taste of the kind of knowledge a professional chef must command. For more information about their program, write: California Culinary Academy, Admissions—BK, 625 Polk Street, San Francisco, California 94102.

*A Napoleon, though crusty as both Emperor and dessert, is not otherwise a shellfish. (See gray Answer page **)

Pastry

1. *Creme Patissiere* is made from
   (A) Milk, sugar, vanilla, eggs, and cream
   (B) Milk, sugar, vanilla, egg yolks, and corn starch
   (C) Cream, sugar vanilla, and egg whites
   (D) Milk, sugar, vanilla, and egg yolks

2. Frangipan is
   (A) A lemon-based filling
   (B) A hazelnut meringue cake filling
   (C) A bittersweet chocolate mix
   (D) An almond-based filling

3. A dough without salt
   (A) Rises only if there is enough gluten
   (B) Does not rise at all
   (C) Rises very fast
   (D) Rises very slowly

4. What is the maximum butter addition for a sponge made with the cold method?
   (A) 4/5 of the sugar weight
   (B) 2/3 of the sugar weight
   (C) 1/2 of the sugar weight
   (D) 1/2 of the flour weight
   (E) 2/3 of the flour weight
   (F) 4/5 of the flour weight

5. How many turns should a puff paste be given?
   (A) 4 single
   (B) 2 double and 1 single
   (C) 4 double

6. Which of the following desserts is not churned during freezing?
   (A) Granite
   (B) Parfait
   (C) Spoom
   (D) Sorbet

7. Which flour has the highest gluten strength?
   (A) Whole wheat
   (B) White
   (C) Rye
   (D) Bread

Garde Manger

1. Salad greens with a distinct flavor require a
   (A) Piquant dressing
   (B) Emulsified dressing
   (C) Mild dressing
   (D) Hot dressing

2. The most important part of salad presentation and service is
   (A) The amount served
   (B) The choice of platter
   (C) The salad's eye appeal
   (D) The salad's dressing

3. *Hors d'oeuvre chaud* serving equipment and food should always be
   (A) Polished and chilled
   (B) Polished and refrigerated
   (C) Polished and hot
   (D) Polished and cooled

4. Savouries are served
   (A) Before the soup
   (B) After the sweets
   (C) Before the roast
   (D) After the soup

5. The most suitable method of cookery for noisettes of lamb is
   (A) Braising
   (B) Sautéing
   (C) Broiling
   (D) Roasting

Production

1. *Pommes Nature* are
   (A) Cut in egg shape and boiled
   (B) Cut in egg shape, blanched, browned, and roasted
   (C) Sliced and sauteed in butter and thyme

2. Sauce Bordelaise is from what group of sauces in a demi glaze base?
   (A) White wine reduction
   (B) Red wine reduction
   (C) Fortified wine

3. What is the name of the base sauce used when making Mornay Sauce?
   (A) Chicken *Veloute.*
   (B) *Bechamel*
   (C) Cream Sauce

4. What goes into Polonaise garniture?
   (A) Bread crumbs and cheese
   (B) Bread crumbs, hard boiled eggs and parsley
   (C) Flour, eggs, and bread crumbs

5. If you were asked to bring a *"chinois,"* which piece of equipment would you get?
   (A) A fine drumsieve
   (B) A small colander
   (C) A ricer
   (D) A conical strainer

6. What is the correct name for the coarsely cut root vegetables used in the preparation of stocks, stews, and braises?
   (A) *Brunoise*
   (B) *Jardiniere*
   (C) *Paysanne*
   (D) *Mirepoix*

7. When braising vegetables, we often blanche the vegetables to remove
   (A) The excess acidity
   (B) The natural starches
   (C) The natural sugars

8. The most suitable cut from which to make *Escalopes de Porc* is
   (A) Topside
   (B) Silverside
   (C) Loin
   (D) Shin

9. The best marrow bones in a beef carcass are to be found in the
   (A) Full forequarter
   (B) Shoulder
   (C) Rump and loin
   (D) Butt

10. Serve which sauce with roast pork loin?
    (A) *Sauce Robert*
    (B) *Sauce Velouté Ordinaire*
    (C) *Sauce Choron*
    (D) Mornay

11. *Poeler* is a method of stewing.
    [ ] True   [ ] False

12. Cream cannot be added to boiling liquids and sauces.
    [ ] True   [ ] False

13. *Remouillage* is a culinary term for the reheating of a stock.
    [ ] True   [ ] False

14. A raft is used to remove impurities from the stock, when preparing a *consommé.*
    [ ] True   [ ] False

15. Oxidation of fresh fruit for salad preparations may be prevented by placing the fruit in a water and salt solution.
    [ ] True   [ ] False

ANSWERS!

Pastry

1. B
2. D
3. C
4. C
5. C
6. A
7. D

Garde Manger

1. A
2. C
3. C
4. A
5. B

Production

1. A
2. B
3. B
4. B
5. D
6. D
7. A
8. C
9. D
10. A
11. False
12. True
13. False
14. True
15. True

**Furthermore, though the excess of garlic usually inflicted on *Shrimp Scampi* is notoriously powerful, *Scampi* is not the name of a notorious Tuscan doge. It is the Italian word for "shrimp," which redundancy marks a low point of invention in the naming of dishes.

LAWYER

New York Bar

*The "bar" before which a student is admitted to prac-
tice law is which of the following?*

*(1) The railing in a courtroom which encloses the
area where court business is transacted in a civil
court or*

*(2) the barrier in the English Inns of Court that
once separated the seats of the "benchers" who
expound cases of law to the students seated on the
other side of the barrier.*

*The answer is neither known beyond reasonable
doubt nor is it relevant to the practice of law in the
state of New York. What is relevant to those aspiring
to end up on the business side of that bar examination
in this: The investment of time and money, the necessary talent for retaining relevant trivia, and the
monastic pall it casts over one's social life are all considerably greater when one studies for the New York
Bar Exam at full throat than when one harkens to the
few but representative echoes presented here.*

S ubject to a few limited exceptions, every applicant for admission to the practice as an attorney and counselor at law in the state of New York must meet certain requirements relating to legal education and must also pass the New York State bar examination, of which the following questions are a representative sampling. Applicants must also pass the Multistate Professional Responsibility Examination (MPRE). The exceptions relate to attorneys from other jurisdictions who are eligible for admission without examination if they meet certain educational requirements and have actually practiced or engaged in law school teaching for at least five of the immediately preceding seven years.

The bar examination is prepared, administered, and graded by the New York State Board of Law Examiners ("the Board"). The Board consists of members of the New York Bar appointed by the Court of Appeals. The Board members have a staff of legal assistants, and the Board also has administrative and clerical employees who work under the direction of its Executive Secretary.

Applicants who pass the bar examination and the MPRE are certified by the Board to the respective Appellate Divisions of the Supreme Court for inquiry by Committees on Character and Fitness into their moral character and general fitness to be members of the Bar.

Applicants should address their inquiries to the State Board of Law Examiners, 90 State Street, Albany, New York 12207, or communicate with the Board by telephone (518-463-2841; in New York State 800-342-3335).

Multiple Choice Questions

Each of the following questions poses four suggested alternative answers. Only one of those alternatives is the correct answer, and you are to choose the answer which you believe to be the correct one.

1. New York State has a statute which grants an exemption from liability for rent to any welfare tenant residing in a multiple dwelling having building violations that endanger the health and safety of the residential tenants. Since 1984, T, a welfare recipient, and his family, have rented an apartment in a building owned by L. The remaining tenants in L's building include two other families receiving welfare and a fourth family not on welfare. L has not installed fire doors and fire escapes required by law for this type of building. T has refused to pay the agreed rent to L, and L has commenced eviction proceedings against T. T pleaded the rent exemption statute as an affirmative defense. L has moved to dismiss T's defense on the ground that the statute is unconstitutional because it (1) impairs L's contractual rights against T and (2) denies L equal protection of the law by providing sanctions only against landlords of welfare tenants. L's motion should be granted on
   (A) ground (1) only
   (B) ground (2) only
   (C) both grounds (1) and (2)
   (D) L's motion should be denied

2. X Inc. wished to induce A, a self-employed engineer, to supervise its research laboratory. In a letter to A, dated February 1, 1981, X Inc. offered to employ A under terms outlined in the letter for five years at an annual salary of $75,000. The letter stated that the offer would be kept open until April 1, 1981. The offer is irrevocable

(A) until April 1, 1981, only if supported by consideration
(B) until April 1, 1981, even in the absence of consideration
(C) for a reasonable time only, regardless of consideration
(D) The offer is revocable at any time before acceptance

3. In order to induce P to purchase S's bracelet, S fraudulently represented to P that the bracelet was made of gold. Relying upon S's representation, on October 15, 1979, P paid S the purchase price of $350 and received the bracelet. On October 20, P discovered that, as S knew, the bracelet was not made of gold and was worth only $150. Had it been made of gold, it would then have been worth $650. P immediately tendered the return of the bracelet and demanded the return of his $350. S refused to accept the bracelet or return any money. P continued to wear the bracelet until July 15, 1980, when P commenced an action against S for rescission and damages. P is not entitled to rescind the contract but is entitled to recover damages of
   (A) $200 only
   (B) $300 only
   (C) $500
   (D) P is entitled to rescind the contract but is not entitled to recover damages

4. X, a director and shareholder of Y Corp., a domestic business corporation, has applied to Y Corp. for a loan of corporate funds to be used by X to purchase inventory for his own business, which is solvent and does not compete with Y Corp. Y Corp., which has only one class of shares, is in excellent financial condition. Y Corp. may properly make the loan to X upon approval of
   (A) its board of directors only
   (B) its board of directors and holders of a majority of the shares held by disinterested shareholders

(C) its board of directors and holders of at least two-thirds of the shares held by disinterested shareholders

(D) Y Corp. may not properly make the loan to X

5. The board of directors of C Corp., a corporation recently formed to engage in the advertising business, unanimously adopted resolutions (1) to issue 100 fully paid C Corp. shares to A, an attorney, in consideration for the legal services A rendered in the organization of C Corp. and (2) to issue 100 fully paid C Corp. shares to E, an experienced advertising executive, in consideration for E agreeing to work for C Corp. as an account executive for a five-year term.

(A) Only resolution (1) is valid

(B) Only resolution (2) is valid

(C) Both resolutions (1) and (2) are valid

(D) Neither resolution (1) nor (2) is valid

6. A sold explosives to D knowing that D intended to use the explosives to blow up V's house. A was wholly indifferent to D's purpose. D did in fact so use the explosives and V, who was home at the time, was killed in the explosion. D was arrested and prosecuted for arson and murder, but was acquitted of both crimes on the ground that D was mentally incompetent. A may properly be found guilty of

(A) arson, as an accessory of D, but not murder

(B) arson and murder, as an accessory of D

(C) criminal facilitation, but not arson or murder

(D) A may not properly be found guilty of arson, murder, or criminal facilitation because D was acquitted

7. W commenced an action for divorce against her husband, H, and H served an answer. W has moved for an order of temporary maintenance. H opposed W's motion on the grounds that (1) H and W continue to reside together, (2) W has failed to establish a reasonable probability of success in her action, and (3) W is not in danger of becoming a public charge. The court must deny W's motion if H proves

(A) (1) only

(B) (2) only

(C) (3) only

(D) The court is entitled to order temporary maintenance regardless of proof of (1), (2), or (3)

8. Shortly before his arrest for murder, H told his wife, W, that he had killed V while burglarizing V's home. Their 17-year-old son was present during this conversation. After H's arrest and while he was still in jail, H was treated by P, a physician, for appendicitis. During this treatment, H told P that he had killed V. On the trial of the indictment charging H with murder, over H's objections, the District Attorney offered the testimony of both (1) W and (2) P that H had admitted killing V. The court should permit

(A) (1) but not (2)

(B) (2) but not (1)

(C) both (1) and (2)

(D) neither (1) nor (2)

9. M drew a check for $500 on his account in B Bank payable to the order of N, his nephew, and gave the check to N as a birthday gift. M had sufficient funds in his account to pay the check, but as a result of clerical error, B Bank refused to honor the check on the ground that M's account was overdrawn. M died the next day. N has a cause of action to recover $500 on the check against

(A) both B Bank and M's estate

(B) neither B Bank nor M's estate

(C) B Bank only

(D) M's estate only

10. S was injured when she slipped on the ice in the parking lot of G's grocery store. S commenced an action against G seeking to recover damages for her injuries, alleging negligent maintenance of the parking lot by G. G's answer consisted of a general denial.

Upon demand, G is entitled as a right to a bill of particulars with regard to S's claim and the bill of particulars must be verified
(A) only if S's complaint was verified
(B) only if S demands a verified bill of particulars
(C) in any event
(D) G is not entitled to any bill of particulars without a court order

11. In April 1979, P, while a passenger in a car owned and operated by D, was injured when D's car was involved in a collision with a car owned and operated by B. Q was a passenger in E's car. In July 1979, P commenced an action against both D and B for damages for the serious personal injuries P sustained in the accident. On the trial of P's action against D and E in November 1981, P recovered a judgment against D only. In January 1982, Q commenced an action against both D and B for the serious personal injuries Q sustained in the accident. In Q's action, the judgment in P's prior action
(A) is both a complete defense to E and a determination that D was negligent
(B) is a complete defense to E but not a determination that D was negligent
(C) is not a defense to B but is a determination that D was negligent
(D) is neither a defense to B nor a determination that D was negligent

12. P commenced an action against D to recover for his serious personal injuries suffered when P was struck by a car

owned and operated by D. After trial, the jury returned a $50,000 verdict in favor of P. Upon interviewing J, one of the jurors, after the trial, D's attorney learned that (1) the jurors deliberately disregarded the trial judge's charge regarding the effect of P's culpable conduct because they felt sorry for P, and that (2) the verdict represented a compromise among the jurors because they had been unable to agree upon a verdict. D's lawyer timely moved to set aside the verdict. In support of the motion, J will be competent to testify as to
(A) both(1) and (2)
(B) neither (1) nor (2)
(C) (1) only
(D) (2) only

13. Pursuant to a signed written lease, T leased an office from L for a term of one year commencing January 1, 1982, and expiring December 31, 1982, at the agreed rental of $300 per month. The lease was silent concerning the effect of T's holding over. T, in fact, did not vacate the premises on December 31, and continued to occupy the office. L accepted T's monthly rental payments for January and February 1983, but on January 25, T received a letter from L demanding a monthly rental of $400 commencing March 1,1983. T has not responded to L's letter. As of March 1, T was entitled to remain a tenant
(A) until December 31, 1983, at $300 per month rent
(B) until December 31, 1983, at $400 per month rent
(C) on a month-to-month basis at $300 per month rent
(D) on a month-to-month basis at $400 per month rent

14. R, a real estate broker, orally requested S, a sign manufacturer, to provide R with 200 signs reading "For Sale by R Real Estate."

It was orally agreed that R would pay S $8000 for the signs. S manufactured 100 signs himself and arranged for the manufacture of the other 100 signs by M, another manufacturer. R now refuses to accept the signs, although all 200 are ready for delivery. In an action by S against R for damages for breach of contract, the statute of frauds is a defense
(A) only with respect to the signs manufactured by M
(B) only with respect to the signs manufactured by S
(C) with respect to all of the signs
(D) The statute of frauds is not a defense with respect to any of the signs

15. H and W were divorced in February 1985. Under the terms of a property settlement agreement signed by them on January 2, 1985, W was required to transfer shares worth $50,000 to H. W had paid $30,000 for the shares in 1981. The shares were transferred by W to H last week. For federal income tax purposes, W has realized a gain of $20,000 and
(A) H has a basis of $50,000 in the shares
(B) H has a basis of $30,000 in the shares
    For federal income tax purposes W has realized no gain and
(C) H has a basis of $50,000 in the shares
(D) H has a basis of $30,000 in the shares

16. S, a five-year-old boy, was walking with his father, F, in a public park. S wandered away from F and was seriously injured when he was struck by a car owned and operated by D on a public road in the park. After the accident, F put S in his car and was rushing to a hospital when F lost control of his car and it struck a light pole, causing S's original injuries to be aggravated. Thereafter, S, by his mother, M, commenced an action against D and F, to recover damages against D for S's original and aggravated injuries, and against F for

S's aggravated injuries only. D cross-claimed against F, demanding judgment against F for all or part of any judgment which S might recover against D, on the sole ground that the original accident had been caused by F's carelessness in supervising S. F has moved (1) to dismiss D's cross-claim against him on the ground that it does not state a cause of action. F has also moved (2) to dismiss S's complaint against F on the ground that S, as a matter of law, has no right of action against his father, F, to recover for his injuries. The court should grant
(A) neither motion (1) nor motion (2)
(B) motion (1) only
(C) motion (2) only
(D) both motions (1) and (2)

17. On January 10, 1986, C, a reputable and experienced contractor, agreed with O, pursuant to a written contract, to steam-clean the exterior of an office building owned by O. The contract required C to furnish and install the necessary barricades, scaffolding, and all other tools necessary for the job. On January 15, C began the agreed work. C's employees erected the necessary scaffolding which projected over a portion of the sidewalk below. Later that day, E, one of C's employees, negligently dropped a hose, from which steam was emanating, from the scaffold onto the sidewalk below. P, a pedestrian, was struck by the falling hose and badly burned by the steam. No barricades had been erected on the sidewalk to protect pedestrians or warn them of the work in progress, as required by the contract. P has no cause of action against O because
(A) C was an independent contractor
(B) the contract required C to erect the barricades
(C) E, C's employee, alone was negligent
(D) P has a cause of action against O

18. In 1979, T duly executed his will, part of which read, "I give the Picasso drawing I own, valued at $10,000, to my friend, F." On December 15, 1982, T increased the amount of fire insurance on the drawing from $10,000 to $15,000, its market value at that time. The drawing was totally destroyed in a fire in T's library on December 31, 1982. T died on January 15,1983. F survived T, but F died intestate on February 10, leaving his son, S, as his sole distributee. On February 15, B, the executor of T's estate, received the $15,000 proceeds from the fire insurance on the Picasso drawing. S is entitled to

(A) nothing, because the drawing was destroyed prior to T's death
(B) nothing, because F has died
(C) $10,000 only
(D) $15,000

Essay Question

In January 1983, A was indicted for burglary in connection with the theft of $15,000 worth of securities and jewelry from the home of B, an elderly woman. Pursuant to a warrant, duly issued, for A's arrest, P, a police officer who knew A, arrested A at his home. P immediately advised A of his *Miranda* rights, placed him in handcuffs, and took him to the police station. Once there, P again advised A of his *Miranda* rights. A acknowledged that he understood his rights, but he stated that he wished to waive them. Then, in response to P's questioning, A made a written statement, which he signed, admitting that he had committed the burglary.

A was then permitted to contact his attorney, L, and upon arriving at the police station, L advised P that A was not to be questioned further. All questioning then ceased, and A was thereafter arraigned, pleaded not guilty, and was released on bail.

On February 1, 1983, A and his friend, F, agreed to rob D's drug store. F examined the layout of the store and secured a gun which he gave to A for use in connection with the planned robbery. On February 14, before the commission of the robbery, F had a change of heart, vigorously urged A to abandon the plan, and demanded that A return the gun which F had given him. A refused to do so, and F informed A that he would have nothing further to do with A or with the planned robbery.

On February 15, A entered D's drug store and, using the gun which F had given him, demanded money from the drug store clerk at gun point. The store was equipped with a silent alarm which was activated by the clerk. In response to the alarm, P, who was patrolling the neighborhood in a police car, was dispatched to the drug store. P arrived while A was still in the drug store, and P placed A under arrest and informed A of his *Miranda* rights. A then told P that he wished to waive his rights, and, in answer to P's questions, A orally stated that he and F had carefully planned the robbery of D's drug store for the past two weeks. Before taking A to the police station, P searched A, found securities in A's pocket, and took possession of them. It was thereafter discovered that the securities were those stolen from B's home.

A and F were subsequently indicted for conspiracy to commit robbery of D's drug store.

Prior to the trial of either indictment, A's attorney, L, made the following motions on undisputed proof of the foregoing pertinent facts:

1. L moved in the prosecution against A for burglary, to suppress the use in evidence of (i) A's written statement admitting that he had committed the burglary of B's home, and (ii) the securities which had been taken by P from A's pocket;

2. L moved, on behalf of A in the prosecution against A and F for conspiracy to commit robbery of D's drug store, to suppress the use in evidence of A's oral statement to P regarding the plan to rob that store.

    (A) How should the court decide the numbered motions?

    (B) On the foregoing facts, can F properly be found guilty of conspiracy to commit robbery of D's drug store, and what defenses, if any, does F have?

ANSWERS!

Multiple Choice

1. D
2. B
3. C
4. B
5. A
6. C
7. D
8. C
9. B
10. C
11. C
12. B
13. D
14. D
15. D
16. B
17. D
18. D

Essay Question

(A) (1) In the burglary prosecution against A, L's motion to suppress should be granted as respect A's written statement admitting the burglary but denied as respects the securities taken from A's pocket. (2) In the conspiracy prosecution, L's motion to suppress A's oral statement regarding the plan to rob D's drug store should be granted.

(B) F can properly be found guilty of conspiracy to rob D's drug store. The defense of renunciation is not available to F.

Reasoning

(A) (1) The court should grant L's motion to suppress A's written statement admitting that he had committed the burglary of B's home. A's indictment for burglary marked the formal commencement of a criminal action against him and, at that time, his right to counsel under the New York Constitution indelibly attached (*People v. Settles,* 46 N.Y.2d 154). Consequently, even though A was not then represented by an attorney, A could not waive his right to counsel in the absence of counsel. A's written statement must be suppressed even though it was not coerced and was taken after the *miranda* rights were properly administered.

L's motion to suppress the securities which had been taken by P from A's pocket should be denied. Except in a few narrowly circumscribed instances, the Fourth Amendment condemns warrantless searches and seizures as unreasonable (*Coolidge v. New Hampshire,* 403 U.S. 443, 445; *People v Belton,* 50 N.Y. 2d 447, 450, rev'd 543 U.S. 454). One exception is that a search without a warrant may be made, as an incident to a lawful arrest, of the arrestee's person and the area within his immediate control (*People v. Knapp,* 52 N.Y. 2d 351). The scope of such a search is limited to the area from within which the arrestee might gain possession of a weapon or destructible evidence (*Chimel v. California,* 395 U.S. 752, 763; *People v. Belton, supra,* 50 N.Y. 2d at 450). When officer P entered D's store, he had reasonable and probable cause to place A under arrest, and no arrest warrant was necessary (*CPL Sec.* 140.10). The securities subsequently taken by P from A's pocket were properly seized in a search incident to this lawful arrest.

(A) (2) L's motion to suppress the use in evidence of A's oral statement to P regarding the plan to run D's drug store should be granted. The Court of Appeals has held that the police may not question a suspect whom they know to be represented by counsel, even if counsel has been retained in connection with a separate, unrelated charge, unless that suspect waives his right to counsel in the presence of counsel (*People v. Bartholomeo,* 53 N.Y. 2d 225, 231; *People v. Rogers,* 48 N.Y. 2d 167). In this instance, it is evident that officer P was aware, when he took A's oral statement, that A was represented by counsel in connection with the burglary charge then pending against him. P had spoken with L, A's attorney, several weeks earlier in connection with A's burglary charge. In addition, P knew A, and presumably he would remember that A was actually represented by counsel. Accordingly, A could not waive his right to counsel in the absence of counsel, and L's motion to suppress A's oral statement should be granted.

(B) On the facts presented, F can properly be found guilty of conspiracy to commit robbery of D's drug store, and his defense of renunciation will fail. A person is guilty of conspiracy when, with intent that conduct constituting a crime be performed, he agrees with one or more persons to engage in or cause the performance of such conduct (*Penal Law Sec. 105.20*). However, a person cannot be convicted of conspiracy unless an overt act is alleged and proved to have been committed by one of the conspirators in furtherance of the conspiracy (*Penal Law Sec. 105.20*). A and F agreed on February 1, 1983, to rob D's drug store, and on that date, F formed the requisite intent for the crime of conspiracy. Furthermore, the overt act requirement was satisfied by F's examination of the drug store and securing of the gun to be used in the robbery.

The defense of renunciation will not protect F from a conviction of conspiracy. To assert successfully the defense of renunciation to a charge of conspiracy, a defendant must prove by a preponderance of the evidence (*Penal Law Sec. 25.00, subd. 2*) that, under circumstances manifesting a voluntary and complete renunciation of his criminal purpose, he prevented the commission of the crime (*Penal Law Sec. 40.10, subd. 4*). Here, F was unsuccessful in preventing A from committing the robbery, and the fact that the crime was actually prevented by P will not relieve F of criminal responsibility for the conspiracy.

MARITIME CAPTAIN

U.S. Coast Guard

"Harry, darling, I'm so glad now that we decided on a bare-boat charter for our vacation in the islands. Just look at those colored lights. It's like Christmas in the tropics."

"What colored lights, Marjorie? Oh oh. That is a tug with a 200-meter tow and we are on a collision course. Go get the life vests, baby."

A captain licensed by the U.S. Coast Guard to command a vessel of 70 tons or more 100 miles offshore has more to his or her day than dressing for dinner at the captain's table. The following questions are representative of those used on U.S. Coast Guard Master/Mate and Operator licensing examinations. They cover a wide range of topics found on the exams, from weather to first aid. We excerpted the questions from a Master/Mate & Operator Sample USCG Test/Exam Preparation manual published by Houston Marine Training Services in Kenner, LA. To find out about exam preparation courses, write Houston Marine, Dept. BOT, 1600 20th Street, Kenner, LA 70062.

Seamanship

The following questions on seamanship include material on martin-spike seamanship, ship handling, stability, and vessel equipment.

1. Manila mooring lines in which the strands are right-hand layed
   (A) should be coiled in a clockwise direction (B) should be coiled in a counterclockwise direction (C) may be coiled in either a clockwise or a counterclockwise direction (D) should never be coiled

2. The backstay is a line or wire supporting the mast and leading from the mast to the
   (A) bow (B) beam (C) stern (D) none of the above

3. Where is the upper tween deck located?
   (A) Aft above the main deck (B) Below the second deck (C) Below the main deck and above the lower tween deck (D) Above the lower engine-room deck and below the after fire room

4. The openings in the bulwarks to drain water off the deck are called
   (A) bilges (B) freeing ports or scuppers (C) portholes (D) limber holes

5. What is the term for the area from the water line to the deck?
   (A) Draft (B) Freeboard (C) Deadrise (D) Camber

6. What signal would you use to indicate to someone in distress that "you are seen and assistance will be given as soon as possible"?
   (A) Green star shell (B) Red parachute flare (C) Waving a white flag horizontally (D) Orange smoke

7. "Heave to" means
   (A) turn the bow into the waves (B) turn the stern into the waves (C) put the waves on the stern (D) throw a line

8. All of the following are true of nylon versus manila line EXCEPT
   (A) nylon has a higher initial cost (B) nylon lasts five times longer than manila

(C) a splice in nylon would require one less tuck than in manila (D) nylon will stretch up to 40 percent of its length without danger of parting

9. Which of the following is the most common method of securing a line to a bitt?
   (A) A round turn on a bitt farthest from the pull of the tow and then figure eights (B) A round turn on a bitt closest to the pull of the tow and then figure eights (C) Figure eights and then a round turn at the top of the bollards (D) Only figure eights are necessary on both bitts

10. When making a line fast to a piling or spar, which of the following would you use?
    (A) Clove hitch (B) Square knot (C) Granny knot (D) Carrick bend

11. When hove to in heavy seas with the engines of your motorboat stopped, you may prevent broaching by
    (A) using a sea anchor (B) alternative shifting of the rudder (C) lashing the helm (D) shifting weight to the stern

12. Your vessel is at the dock with only one line, the after bow spring, leading from the bow aft to the dock, and you go ahead on your engines. Which of the following would happen?
    (A) The bow would go out and the stern in (B) The bow would go in and the stern out (C) Both bow and stern would go out (D) Both bow and stern would go in

13. Two vessels are abreast of each other and passing port to port in a confined waterway. What would you expect as you approach the screws of the other vessel?
    (A) Your speed would significantly increase (B) Your draft would decrease (C) Your bow would sheer toward the other vessel (D) Your bow would sheer away from the other vessel

14. On a twin-screw twin-rudder vessel, the most effective way to turn in your own water with no way on is to put

(A) one engine ahead and one engine astern, with full rudder (B) one engine ahead and one engine astern with rudder amidships (C) both engines ahead with full rudder (D) both engines astern with full rudder

15. If you are backing a single-screw vessel with rudder amidships, which of the following is true?
(A) The bow will swing to starboard (B) The bow will swing to port (C) The stern will swing to starboard (D) The vessel will back in a straight line

16. You are under way, running close and parallel to a steep bank. What effect would the bank have on your vessel?
(A) Bank cushion at the bow and bank suction at the stern cause your vessel to sheer away from the bank (B) None; your vessel would continue in a straight line (C) Bank suction at the bow and bank cushion at the stern cause your vessel to sheer toward the bank (D) Bank suction at both bow and stern

17. If you are standing a wheel watch and you hear that a man has fallen overboard on the starboard side, you should prepare to
(A) turn hard to starboard (B) turn hard to port (C) proceed to throw a life ring to mark the spot (D) hold the rudder amidships

18. When anchoring in calm water, it is best to
(A) maintain slight headway while letting go the anchor (B) wait until the boat is dead in the water before letting go the anchor (C) have slight sternway on the boat while letting go the anchor (D) let the anchor go from the stern with the anchor cable leading from the bow

19. You are anchored using a scope of 5:1 and heavy weather is setting in. You should
(A) decrease scope to 2:1 (B) leave scope unchanged (C) increase scope to 9:1 (D) veer cable to bitter end

Sailing Addendum

Applicants who qualify for a license as "operator of auxiliary sailing vessels" must take an extra examination ("addendum") on sailing principles, equipment, and techniques. The following questions pertain to this addendum.

1. To get out of irons
(A) pull in the sheets and drop the centerboard (B) tack immediately (C) remain perfectly still until the wind direction changes (D) release the sheets, back the jib or mainsail, retract the centerboard

2. When going to windward, wind pressure can be divided into three components:
(A) heeling, sideways, and forward (B) heeling, forward, and astern (C) windward, heeling, and leeway (D) sideways, windward, and forward

3. Not only does the jib provide its own lift to windward, it also
(A) helps funnel wind across the windward side of the mainsail (B) decelerates the wind over the mainsail (C) provides blanketing effect for the mizzen (D) helps funnel the wind across the leeward surface of the mainsail

4. The names of the three corners of a triangular sail are
(A) head, tack, and foot (B) head, tack, and clew (C) luff, tack, and clew (D) leach, luff, and foot

5. A catamaran which capsizes will tend to
(A) recover completely and sail upright (B) turn completely upside down (C) lie flat in the water with sails parallel to the water's surface (D) lose initial stability capsized and upside down

General Navigation

The following questions are on "general navigation" principles, including charts, aids to navigation, publications, and plotting techniques.

1. Leeway is
    (A) the difference between the true and compass course (B) the momentum of the vessel after her engines have been stopped (C) the lateral movement of the vessel downwind of her intended course (D) displacement of the vessel multiplied by her speed

2. Your vessel is making way through the water at a speed of 15 knots. Your vessel traveled 30 nautical miles in 2 hours 20 minutes. What current are you experiencing?
    (A) A following current at 2.5 knots (B) A head current of 2.5 knots (C) A following current of 5 knots (D) A head current of 5 knots

3. You are returning to port on a course of 090 deg. T at a speed of 15 knots. An ocean current is setting 135 deg. T at 4 knots. After 2 hours running time, your boat will most likely be
    (A) ahead and to the right of your intended track line (B) ahead and to the left of your intended track line (C) behind and to the right of your intended track line (D) behind and to the left of your intended track line

4. Which of the following describes an ebb current?
    (A) Horizontal movement of the water away from the land following low tide (B) Horizontal movement of the water toward the land following low tide (C) Horizontal movement of the water away from the land following high tide (D) Horizontal movement of the water toward the land following high tide

5   Ocean currents such as the California current are caused mostly by
    (A) winds (B) temperature (C) Coriolis effect (D) diurnal tides

6. What does the chart notation "25 feet APR 1955" which is printed in the harbor entrance channel indicate?
    (A) The channel was 25 feet wide during April 1955 (B) The channel was 25 feet deep during April 1955 (C) The channel width has been maintained to 25 feet since April 1955 (D) The channel depth has been maintained to 25 feet since April 1955

7. In reference to sightings doubling the angle on the bow, what are you trying to determine?
    (A) The distance the object is from you at the time of the second bearing (B) The time between sightings (C) The speed of your vessel (D) The direction of the object

8. One degree of latitude equals
    (A) 1 mile (B) 4 miles (C) 6 miles (D) 60 miles

9. When operating in the Atlantic Ocean off of New York City, a vessel should be in
    (A) north latitude, east longitude (B) north latitude, west longitude (C) south latitude, east longitude (D) south latitude, west longitude

10. After an object is sighted broad on the bow, your vessel continues on a constant course at varying speeds for 20 minutes, covering a distance of 5 miles by the time that the object is abeam. How far are you off the object when abeam?
    (A) 2 miles (B) 5 miles (C) 10 miles (D) It cannot be determined with the information given

11. You leave port and sail to the fishing grounds in a position 30 miles due west. Upon arrival at this position, you shut down the engine. While you have been fishing, your boat has been drifting with an ocean current which is setting 345 deg. T at 2 knots. After 3 hours, heavy fog sets in, and you decide to return to port. What is the approximate course you would expect to steer?
    (A) 070 deg. T (B) 080 deg. T (C) 090 deg. T (D) 100 deg. T

12. You are underway at 5 knots and see on the radar a contact 10 miles directly astern. Twelve minutes later the contact is 8 miles

directly astern. What is the estimated speed of the contact?
(A) Dead in the water (B) 10 knots (C) 13 knots (D) 15 knots

13. A boat is equipped with two 100-gallon fuel tanks. At cruising speed, the boat consumes 17 gallons of fuel per hour. The boat departed port with both tanks full and traveled at cruising speed for 4 hours to the fishing grounds. The boat consumed an additional 28 gallons of fuel while idling and maneuvering about the fishing grounds. What is the maximum number of hours the boat can run at cruising speed with the remaining fuel on board?
(A) 3   (B) 6   (C) 9   (D) 12

14. When you are entering a harbor at night, an interrupted quick flashing light will signify a
(A) mid-channel buoy (B) fairway buoy (C) turn buoy (D) junction buoy

15. When you are steering on a pair of range lights and find the upper light is to the right of the lower light, you should
(A) come left (B) come right (C) stop and wait until they come in line (D) continue ahead as long as you can see both lights

16. When coming in from seaward, which of the following is true concerning the numbers on buoys on the right-hand side of the channel?
(A) Odd, decreasing (B) Even, decreasing (C) Odd, increasing (D) Even, increasing

17. What is a lubber's line?
(A) A line pointing to true north (B) A line on the compass card (C) A line aligned with the ship's keel representing the ship's heading (D) A line parallel to the boat's transom

18. The true course is 080 and variation is 22 degrees East. The deviation is 3 degrees West. The compass course is
(A) 055   (B) 061   (C) 058   (D) 099

19. An occulting light is one in which
(A) the period of darkness exceeds the period of light (B) there is only a partial eclipse of light (C) the period of light exceeds the period of darkness (D) the period of light equals the period of darkness

20. Low water at a particular area occurred at 1750. The number obtained from the tide tables is 3.5, the charted depth is 10 feet. What was the depth of water in this area at low tide?
(A) 6.5   (B) 10.0   (C) 13.5   (D) Slightly less than 10 feet as the charted depth is based on mean low water

21. You would expect to find the least water over a bar at which tide?
(A) Low water neap (B) Low water spring (C) Slack Hood (D) Maximum ebb

22. Mariners are first warned of any serious defect or important changes to aids to navigation by which of the following means?
(A) Marine broadcast "Notice to Mariners" (B) Weekly notices to mariners (C) Corrected edition of charts (D) Light list

23. The course from one point to another may be found by placing parallel rules on the points and then moving the rulers to the midpoint of the nearest
(A) compass rose (B) magnetic compass (C) pelorus (D) course protractor

24. Your boat is equipped with a depth finder of the flashing type. You are receiving multiple flashes, the first flash showing 12 feet of water under the keel and the last flash showing 24 feet of water. You should assume that there is
(A) 12 feet of water under the keel (B) 18 feet of water under the keel (C) 24 feet of water under the keel (D) something is wrong with the depth finder

25. What VHF channel does the Coast Guard use to broadcast routine weather reports?
(A) Channel 13 (B) Channel 16 (C) Channel 21 or 22 (D) Channel 44

26. The true course to a harbor entrance is 270 deg. The variation in the area is S deg. E. The compass deviation on a westerly heading is 7 deg. E. What is the magnetic compass course to steer to make good 270 deg. T?
(A) 258 deg. (B) 268 deg. (C) 272 deg. (D) 282 deg.

Weather

The following questions on weather include material on air masses, fog, weather instruments, clouds, and weather warnings.

1. In what direction do cyclonic storms rotate in both hemispheres? (I) Clockwise in the Southern Hemisphere (II) Counterclockwise in the Northern Hemisphere
(A) I only (B) II only (C) Both I and 11(D) Neither I nor II

2. Relative humidity is the percentage of moisture in the air at a specific
(A) barometric pressure (B) temperature (C) dew point (D) wind condition

3. In order for fog to occur,
(A) the land or water must be colder than the air next to it (B) the temperature of the air must he lowered to or below the dew point (C) the lower layers of air must be colder than the layers above them (D) all of the above

4. After a cold front passes, all the following would be true EXCEPT
(A) the wind would veer (B) the temperature would decrease (C) atmospheric pressure would increase (D) cloud cover would increase

5. As a warm front passes an observer,
(A) the temperature rises and pressure becomes steady (B) the temperature rises and the pressure rises (C) the temperature rises and pressure drops (D) the temperature drops and pressure drops

6. Which statement is true concerning the speed of fronts?

(A) Cold fronts move faster than warm fronts (B) Cold fronts move more slowly than warm fronts (C) Cold fronts and warm fronts move with equal speed (D) Cold fronts move more slowly at the northern end, thus allowing the warm front to overtake the northern section

7. If you were located in a low-pressure area in the Northern Hemisphere with the wind in your face, the center of the low would be located
(A) to the right and in front of you (B) to the right and behind you (C) to the left and behind you (D) to the left and in front of you

8. What is normal atmospheric pressure at sea level?
(A) 28.92 inches of mercury (B) 29.92 inches of mercury (C) 28.00 inches of mercury (D) 30.00 inches of mercury

9. Readings taken from an aneroid barometer should be corrected for which of the following factors? (I) Latitude of the vessel (II) Height above sea level
(A) I only (B) II only (C) Both I and 11(D) Neither I nor II

10. On a calm day you observe a tall cumulus cloud with a well-defined top and rain falling from its dark base. As you approach the cloud, you would expect the wind to
(A) decrease abruptly (B) increase abruptly (C) back, shifting in a counterclockwise direction (D) remain steady

11. On a clear warm day you notice the approach of a tall cumulus cloud. The cloud cover has hard well—defined edges and rain is falling from the dark lower edge. Should this cloud pass directly overhead,
(A) it will be preceded by a sudden increase of wind speed (B) it will be preceded by a sudden decrease of wind speed (C) the wind speed will not change as it passes (D) the wind speed will back

rapidly to the left in a counterclockwise direction as it passes

12. You are in the Northern Hemisphere experiencing generally good weather with winds from the southwest. Which statement is true?
(A) You are under the influence of a low pressure (B) You are under the influence of a low-pressure center located north of you (C) You are under the influence of a high-pressure center located south of you (D) You are under the influence of a high-pressure center located north of you

13. The wind speed and direction observed from a moving vessel is known as
(A) coordinate wind (B) true wind (C) apparent wind (D) anemometer wind

14. A square red flag with a black center displayed at a yacht club would indicate wind speeds in excess of
(A) 38 mph (B) 55 mph (C) 74 mph (D) 100 mph

15. Which of the following lists clouds from the highest in the sky to the lowest?
(A) Altostratus, cirrostratus, and stratus
(B) Cirrostratus' altostratus, and stratus
(C) Stratus, cirrostratus, and altostratus
(D) Altostratus, stratus, and cirrostratus

16. In the eye of a tropical cyclone, which of the following conditions would you expect to encounter?
(A) Wind speed of 64 knots (B) Wind speed of 40 knots (C) Calm seas (D) Calm wind

Unified Rules

The following questions are on the Inland Navigational Rules of the Road. All license applicants are tested on these rules.

1. Vessels under what length need not show lights when at anchor in special anchorage areas?
(A) 7 meters (B) 12 meters (C) 20 meters (D) 50 meters

2. While towing astern in inland waters, what lights would be shown on the towing vessel?
(A) A stemlight (B) Two towing lights in a vertical line (C) One yellow towing light above the stemlight (D) None of the above

3. If you were towing alongside in inland waters, what lights would you display?
(A) Sidelights, sternlight, and masthead light (B) Sidelights, sternlight, and a towing light (C) Sidelights and a sternlight (D) Sidelights, two masthead lights, and two towing lights

4. In lieu of normal running lights, a vessel less than 12 meters in length may show
(A) a sternlight (B) a masthead light (C) sidelights and an all-round white light (D) sidelights and a sternlight

5. While meeting another vessel you sound two blasts on the whistle. The other vessel answers your signal with one blast. You should
(A) sound the two-blast signal again (B) pass on the side you indicated with your two-blast signal (C) answer the one-blast signal (D) sound five or more short and rapid blasts

6. Your vessel is backing from a pier into a narrow channel and no other vessels are in sight. You should sound
(A) three short blasts (B) one long blast (C) one prolonged blast followed by three short blasts (D) one prolonged blast

7. In inland waters, your vessel is meeting another vessel head to head. You should
(A) exchange one short blast, alter course to the left, and pass starboard to starboard (B) exchange one short blast, alter course to the right, and pass port to port (C) exchange two short blasts, alter course to the left, and pass starboard to starboard (D) exchange two short blasts, alter course to the right, and pass port to port

8. On the Mississippi River a power-driven vessel upbound meets a downbound vessel with a tow. Which vessel has the right of way?
(A) The upbound vessel (B) The downbound vessel (C) The vessel sounding the first signal (D) The vessel making the first maneuver

9. In which area do the Inland Rules of the Road not apply?
(A) Puget Sound, Washington (B) The Ohio River (C) Tampa Bay, Florida (D) Long Island Sound

10. A vessel displaying a green light in a vertical line over a white light on the center line above the level of the sidelights would be
(A) under sail (B) towing astern (C) trawling (D) engaged in pilotage duties

11. A rowboat in inland waters at night would exhibit
(A) a white light shown from sunset to sunrise (B) a white light shown in sufficient time to prevent collision (C) a combined lantern showing green to starboard and red to port and shown from sunset to sunrise (D) a combined lantern showing green to starboard and red to port and shown in sufficient time to prevent collision

12. If you sight three white lights in a vertical line on another vessel, it is a
(A) power-driven vessel pushing a barge (B) power-driven vessel towing more than 200 meters of tow (C) power-driven vessel towing less than 200 meters of tow (D) vessel in distress

13. If you are under way in fog and you hear the rapid ringing of a bell followed by a gong, it is a
(A) pilot vessel (B) vessel aground (C) vessel anchored which is less than 100 meters (D) vessel anchored which is 100 meters or more

14. A vessel at anchor in fog would sound which signal to warn an approaching vessel?
(A) A short, a prolonged, and a short blast (B) Five short blasts (C) No signal provided (D) A prolonged blast followed by two short blasts

15. The purpose of the screens required to be fitted on a vessel's sidelights is to
(A) prevent the lights from being seen across the bow (B) prevent the lights from shining in the pilot's eyes (C) protect the lights from being damaged (D) increase the intensity of the lights by reflecting off the screen

16. What is the minimum length of vessels required to show two anchor lights?
(A) 40 meters (B) 50 meters (C) 60 meters (D) 70 meters

17. A vessel engaged in diving operations will exhibit which of the following?
(A) A red pennant (B) A rigid replica of the International Code Flag "A" (C) A red light (D) A diamond shape

18. At night you sight a red light over a white light. What could it be?
(A) A pilot vessel not making way (B) A fishing vessel at anchor (C) A vessel restricted in ability to maneuver (D) A vessel aground

19. You are under way and approaching a bend in the channel where vessels approaching from the opposite direction cannot be seen. You should sound
(A) one blast 4 to 6 seconds in duration (B) three blasts, each 4 to 6 seconds in duration (C) one continuous blast until you can see around the bend (D) one blast 8 to 10 seconds in duration

Regulations

The following questions on regulations cover material appropriate to the operation of vessels under 1000 gross tons. This part of the Coast Guard exam is commonly an "open book" test, with applicants allowed to use the relevant sections of the Code of Federal Regulations to find the answers.

1. If children are carried on board your vessel, you are required to carry how many life preservers suitable for children?
(A) A life preserver for each child on board (B) Life preservers for half the children on board (C) Life preservers equal to one-half the total number of people on board (D) Life preservers equal to 10 percent of the total number of people on board

2. The penalty for a person having been convicted of a first-offense narcotics violation is
(A) suspension of license for three months (B) revocation of license (C) probation for four months (D) a warning

3. If a person flashes a searchlight in the wheelhouse of another vessel under way, he may be penalized by
(A) imprisonment of 6 months (B) suspension or revocation of license (C) a fine of $1000 (D) all of the above

4. The official number and net tonnage of a documented vessel is
(A) not required to be marked anywhere on the vessel (B) required to be marked on the vessel's main beam (C) required to be marked on the vessel's stern (D) required to be marked on the vessel's keel

5. In the machinery of all uninspected motor vessels there must be one type B-II hand-portable fire extinguisher for every horsepower or fraction thereof
(A) 500 (B) 1000 (C) 1500 (D) 2000

6. Where can you find the official number of a vessel?
(A) Vessel certification (B) Certificate of Inspection (C) Official Registry (D) All of the above

7. Where would you pump bilges in a harbor?
(A) Into the harbor (B) Into a barge or holding tank (C) Into the bottoms (D) None of the above

8. What is the name given to the marks on the side of the vessel that show the limits to which she may be loaded?
(A) The draft marks (B) A plimsoll mark (loading) (C) The water line (D) Markings on the main deck

9. A person who operates a vessel in a grossly negligent manner which endangers the life, limb, or property of any person may be Subject to a
(A) fine or imprisonment of not more than one year, or both (B) fine or imprisonment, or both, only if injury or damage results (C) fine up to $100 in addition to the cost of any damage caused (D) fine and/or imprisonment only if there is a loss of life

10. If you look at the station bill aboard ship you see that 10 seconds' ringing of the general alarm followed by continuous sounding of the whistle is
(A) "Man Overboard" (B) "Fire and Emergency" (C) "Abandon Ship" (D) "Dismissal"

11. To prevent sparking when filling tanks, nozzles should be made of
(A) brass or bronze (B) steel (C) iron (D) ferrous metal

Colregs

The following questions are on the International Collision Prevention Regulations, which are commonly known as the "COLREGS." Applicants with licenses restricted to inland waters only are not tested on these rules.

1. You are approaching another vessel at night. You can see both red and green sidelights and, above the level of the sidelights, three white lights in a vertical line Under International Rules the vessel may be
(A) not under command (B) towing a tow more than 200 meters astern (C) trawling (D) underway and dredging

2. A power-driven vessel of less than 7 meters in length where maximum speed does not exceed 7 knots may display
(A) sidelights and a sternlight (B) sidelights and an all-round white light (C) lights of a sailing vessel (D) lights of a fishing vessel

3. On international waters in a dense fog you hear a whistle signal ahead of one prolonged blast followed by three short blasts. This signal indicates a
(A) fishing vessel under way trawling (B) manned vessel being towed (C) pilot vessel under way making a special signal (D) vessel not under command

4. In international waters you are coming up astern of another vessel. You sound one short blast. What does this signal mean?
(A) I intend to overtake you on your starboard side (B) I am changing course to port (C) I intend to overtake you on your portside (D) I am changing course to starboard

5. When two vessels are meeting head to head, in International Rules,
(A) each vessel shall alter her course to starboard and pass on the port side of the other (B) the vessels shall exchange whistle signals (C) the vessels shall pass starboard to starboard (D) vessel A shall sound one short blast and alter course to starboard so as to get out of the way of vessel B

6. You intend to overtake a vessel in a narrow channel, and you intend to pass along the vessel's port side. How should you signal your intention?
(A) One short blast (B) Two prolonged blasts (C) Three short blasts (D) Two prolonged followed by two short blasts

7. You are the stand-on vessel in a crossing situation on the high seas. You have observed the bearing of the approaching vessel and feel that it has not taken sufficient action to avoid collision. You, therefore, sound the danger signal. What is the earliest time at which you may take some additional action?
(A) Immediately upon sounding the danger signal (B) When the other vessel is within half a mile (C) When action by the other vessel alone cannot avoid collision (D) At no time; you must maintain course and speed

8. The term "power-driven vessel" refers to any vessel
(A) with propelling machinery aboard whether it is in use or not (B) making way against the current (C) with propelling machinery in use (D) traveling at a speed greater than that of the current

9. The term "safe speed" is defined as a speed at which a vessel
(A) can take proper and effective action to avoid collision and be stopped within a distance appropriate to the prevailing circumstances and conditions (B) can stop within half the distance of visibility (C) does not exceed 10 knots (D) can be stopped within twice the length of the vessel

10. Risk of collision with another vessel shall be deemed to exist when
(A) the bearing is steady and the range is increasing (B) the bearing is steady and the range is decreasing (C) the bearing is steady and the range is steady (D) All of the above

11. A fishing vessel engaged in fishing in a narrow channel meets a sailboat in the channel. Which vessel has the right of way?
(A) The sailboat because it is sailing (B) The fishing vessel (C) The sailboat if it is going upstream (D) The sailboat because vessels fishing in the channel cannot impede any vessel in the channel

12. Two sailing vessels are approaching each other. Which statement is correct?
(A) The vessel on the port tack gives way to a vessel on the starboard tack (B) The vessel to leeward gives way to the vessel to windward (C) Vessels with wind on different sides, the leeward gives way to the windward vessel (D) In a meeting situation, neither vessel has the right of way

13. Which statement correctly applies to the situation where a sailing vessel is overtaking a power-driven vessel?
(A) The power-driven vessel must keep out of the way of the sailing vessel (B) Special circumstances apply (C) The sailing vessel must keep out of the way of the power-driven vessel (D) The vessel which has the other vessel to the right must keep out of the way

14. An overtaking situation occurs when one vessel approaches another from more than degrees abaft the beam.
(A) 0 (B) 11.25 (C) 22.5 (D) 45

15. When is a sailing vessel not considered the privileged vessel?
(A) In a crossing situation (B) In a meeting situation (C) When overtaking another vessel (D) When being overtaken

16. While under way in fog, you hear a vessel ahead sound two blasts on the whistle. You should

(A) sound two blasts and change course to the left (B) sound whistle signals only if you change course (C) sound only fog signals until the other vessel is sighted (D) not sound any whistle signals until the other vessel is sighted

17. While under way in fog, you hear a whistle signal consisting of one prolonged blast followed immediately by two short blasts. Such a signal is sounded in fog by
(A) vessels at anchor (B) vessels under way and towing (C) vessels in danger (D) pilot vessels

18. A vessel is towing three vessels astern in restricted visibility. What fog signal should the second vessel in the tow give?
(A) One prolonged blast (H) One prolonged and two short blasts (C) One prolonged and three short blasts (D) No signal is sounded

19. As defined in the International Rules of the Road, the masthead light is a white light visible from right ahead to how many degrees abaft the beam?
(A) 0 degrees (B) 22.5 degrees (C) 45 degrees (D) 90 degrees

20. You are overtaking a vessel at night and you observe a yellow light showing above the stern light of the overtaken vessel. The overtaken vessel is
(A) under way and dredging (B) pushing ahead or towing alongside (C) towing astern (D) a pilot vessel

21. In a passing situation in international waters, you should sound
(A) one whistle if you intend to pass to starboard (B) two whistles if you intend to pass to port (C) one whistle if you alter course to starboard (D) two whistles if you intend to alter course to port

22. On international waters you are towing two barges astern. The length of the tow from the stern of the tug to the stern of the last barge is 250 meters. How many forward white masthead lights should be displayed on the towboat at night?
(A) 1 (B) 2 (C) 3 (D) 4

ANSWERS!☞

Seamanship

1. A
2. C
3. C
4. B
5. B
6. D
7. A
8. C
9. B
10. A
11. A
12. B
13. C
14. A
15. A
16. A
17. A
18. C
19. C

Addendum

1. D
2. A
3. D
4. B
5. B

General Navigation

1. C
2. B
3. A
4. C
5. A
6. B
7. A
8. D
9. B
10. B
11. D
12. D
13. B
14. D
15. A
16. D
17. C
18. B
19. C
20. C
21. B
22. A
23. A
24. A
25. C
26. A

Weather

1. C
2. B
3. D
4. D
5. A
6. A
7. B
8. B
9. B
10. B
11. A
12. C
13. C
14. B
15. B
16. D

Unified Rules

1. C
2. C
3. D
4. C
5. D
6. D
7. B
8. B
9. A
10. C
11. B
12. B
13. D
14. A
15. A
16. B
17. B
18. B
19. A

Regulations

1. D
2. B
3. D
4. B
5. B
6. B
7. B
8. B
9. A
10. B
11. A

Colregs

1. B
2. B
3. B
4. D
5. A
6. D
7. A
8. C
9. A
10. B
11. D
12. A
13. C
14. C
15. C
16. C
17. B
18. D
19. B
20. C
21. c
22. C

MASSAGE THERAPY

Atlanta School of Massage

"Uhh! Oh! Uggh! Whew!"
"That will be $..."
"Uhh! Oh! Uggh!"

Eager to shed its outdated image, the new massage profession has wasted no time in cutting a path for itself as a serious preventive health care option. No longer using the titles masseur and masseuse, the modern-day massage therapist is much more than a manipulator of muscles. He or she has probably had extensive training in a variety of massage techniques in addition to a host of other subjects including anatomy and physiology, hydrotherapy, pathology, and injury repair.

Today, massage therapists entering the field find a great variety of career options from which to choose. Some work closely with the medical field, possibly in tandem with a doctor, chiropractor, or physical therapist. Others may work in health clubs, hotels, and resorts. Others may find they like the privacy of working in their homes, or the independence of setting up their own office or clinic. Massage is also making its way into the corporate world. "On-site" massage has become popular with executives who turn themselves over to the massage therapist for a brief 10- or 15-minute stress-reducing break. Possibly the biggest growth in the massage industry has come in the rapidly expanding field of sports massage.

Training in the massage field can take a variety of different forms. There are around 500 schools teaching massage nationwide. However, of these, there are only 55 in the U.S. and 3 in Canada with their curricula approved by the American Massage Therapy Association, the largest professional organization and regulating body for massage education and practice.

Upon completion of their training, massage therapists may be required to pursue state licensure in order to practice. There are currently only 24 states with statewide massage practitioner-based laws. The majority of states have no statewide laws regulating massage practice, while a few others have laws which regulate establishments only. There is also a great deal of variance between states regarding what constitutes proper training.

The questions that follow were provided by the Atlanta School of Massage, an AMTA-approved school in Atlanta, GA. They are similar to questions that might appear on a licensing exam. Questions 1–9 refer to anatomy and physiology, questions 10–25 to massage theory, practice, and history, and questions 26–32 to hydrotherapy. For more information about courses, contact the Atlanta School of Massage at 2300 Peachford Road, Suite 3200, Atlanta GA 30338, tel. (770) 454-7167.

Anatomy and Physiology

1. An inflammation of a vein is known as
    (A) a varicose
    (B) phlebitis
    (C) nephritis
    (D) venules

2. The prevention of the backflow of blood in the veins is caused by
    (A) vesicles
    (B) venules
    (C) valves
    (D) all of the above

3. Muscle action where the muscle remains the same length and increases in tension is called
    (A) isotonic
    (B) isometric
    (C) tetanic
    (D) both A and B

4. What type of joint is between the thumb and hand?
    (A) saddle
    (B) ball and socket
    (C) hinge
    (D) pivot

5. Lateral refers to
    (A) a plane divided between upper and lower halves of the body
    (B) towards the midline of the body
    (C) away from the midline of the body
    (D) movement in a superior direction

6. What muscle originates on the sternum and inner border of the clavicle?
    (A) Splenius capitis
    (B) Scalenes
    (C) Semispinalis
    (D) Sternocleidomastoid

7. The following muscles help stabilize the scapula for movement of the arm:
    (A) anterior serratus and rhomboids
    (B) trapezius and triceps
    (C) rhomboids and gluteles
    (D) levator scapulae and pectoralis major

8. The four basic types of tissue are
    (A) muscle, nervous, epithelial, and connective
    (B) nervous, squamous, muscle, and connective
    (C) simple, compound, complex, and stratified
    (D) none of the above

9. What effect will stimulation of the parasympathetic nervous system have on heart rate?
    (A) It will decrease heart rate
    (B) It will increase heart rate
    (C) It will have no effect
    (D) None of the above

Massage Theory

1. The semimembranosus is located in the
    (A) posterior arm
    (B) posterior thigh
    (C) posterior leg
    (D) hand

2. Through which of the following does lymph drain from the arms and breasts?
    (A) Axillary nodes
    (B) Superficial inguinal glands
    (C) Superficial inguinal nodes
    (D) Submaxillary group

3. What type of effleurage is used to encourage lymphatic flow?
    (A) Light and soothing
    (B) Fast and vigorous
    (C) Alternating fast and slow
    (D) Slow and rhythmic

4. What is the purpose of petrissage?
   (A) To spread lubricant
   (B) To "milk" the muscle of waste products
   (C) To help the patron go to sleep
   (D) All of the above

5. Massage deep into joint spaces or around bony prominences is known as
   (A) vibration
   (B) effleurage
   (C) friction
   (D) petrissage

6. When a client is lying face-up, this position is known as
   (A) prone
   (B) extended
   (C) supine
   (D) none of the above

7. Exercises in which the client does not assist the therapist are known as
   (A) active
   (B) passive
   (C) coordinated
   (D) resistive

8. To whom is the first organized system of massage credited?
   (A) Boll
   (B) Ling
   (C) Johnson
   (D) Kamenetz

9. Which of the following is a contraindication for massage?
   (A) Poor circulation
   (B) Sore muscles
   (C) Severe fatigue
   (D) Severe hypertension

10. When should a massage therapist diagnose clients?
    (A) On the phone
    (B) In the office
    (C) After the massage
    (D) Never

11. Nerve strokes are applied
    (A) with deep pressure
    (B) toward the heart
    (C) away from the heart
    (D) with circular friction

12. The movement of the skeletal structure increasing or decreasing the angle of articulation is known as
    (A) vibration
    (B) palpation
    (C) joint manipulation
    (D) tapotement

13. A continuous shaking or trembling movement is known as
    (A) friction
    (B) palpation
    (C) vibration
    (D) joint manipulation

14. What is the manipulation which involves stretching a joint?
    (A) Flexion
    (B) Circumduction
    (C) Traction
    (D) Chiropractic

15. The best form of heat to produce relaxation prior to a massage is what type?
    (A) electric
    (B) dry
    (C) prolonged
    (D) moist

16. The application of hands and fingers on the surface of the body to detect abnormalities of tissue structure is known as
    (A) vibration
    (B) tapotement
    (C) friction
    (D) palpation

Hydrotherapy

1. Underwater exercises are performed in a
   (A) hydrocollator
   (B) contrast bath
   (C) Hubbard tank
   (D) Russian bath

2. The area of the body for which a sitz bath is used is the
   (A) foot
   (B) pelvis
   (C) knee
   (D) back

3. In Hydrotherapy, the most important effect of water is
   (A) thermal
   (B) sedative
   (C) stimulative
   (D) none of the above

4. The local application of cold produces a condition known as
   (A) hypocontraction
   (B) autoreflex
   (C) vasoconstriction
   (D) vasodilation

5. A medicated pack used externally or internally is called a
   (A) salt glow
   (B) fibre pack
   (C) hydrocollator pack
   (D) poultice

6. What is a chemical pack of silica gel called?
   (A) An atomizer
   (B) A hydrocollator
   (C) A lesion reducer
   (D) A paraffin bath

7. In the early treatment of sprains, contusions, and soft tissue injuries, as well as acute bursitis, the normal procedure is to use
   (A) hot packs
   (B) ice packs
   (C) whirlpool baths in excess of 103 degrees
   (D) exercise

ANSWERS!☞

Anatomy and Physiology

1. B
2. C
3. B
4. A
5. C
6. D
7. A
8. A
9. A

Massage Theory

1. B
2. A
3. D
4. B
5. C
6. C
7. B
8. B
9. D
10. D
11. C
12. C
13. C
14. C
15. D
16. D

Hydrotherapy

1. C
2. B
3. A
4. C
5. D
6. B
7. B

NURSE

National Council of Registered Nurses

So you were right and the nurse was wrong! Congrat-
ulations. With that story, a free cup of coffee and a
warm muffin, you can impress a friend for maybe 20
minutes. Just remember, though, you were right one
time, about one thing, and you knew a lot more details
about that one thing because it was happening to you.

T o pass the NCLEX-RN exam you have to be able to smoke out details that will
let you identify a staggering number of conditions you don't have much time to
do the right thing about. We were pleased to see that the NCLEX-RN exam
requires much more knowledge of people's emotional needs than we would have
thought.

It seems inappropriate to lay an alphabet load like NCLEX-RN on a profession like
nursing. That calling requires that people holding authority be sensitive to other people at
their most vulnerable; it requires the patience to be nurturing. Why does their, of all
people's, acronym look at best like an Aztec adverb and at worst like a modern weapons
system?

The questions in this section are modeled after those in the National Council Licensure
Examination for Registered Nurses, the exam that one must pass in order to become a registered nurse in the United States. The full eight-hour examination consists of about 480
multiple-choice questions administered over a period of two days. The scoring ranges from
a minimum of 800 to a maximum of 3200; a score of 1600 is considered a passing grade in
most states.

We chose most of these questions from the areas of pediatrics, psychiatry, and obstet-
rics/ gynecology because those of us trying patiently to be patients instead of doctors may
have a shot at getting the answers right. Medical and surgical questions have received less
representation because they require an understanding of what technical terms mean when
one is charged with the responsibility of describing the human condition physically, mentally, and where they overlap.

Johanna Pettit, a 34-year-old mother of two children, is brought to the emergency room by a friend after a suicide attempt. She is described by her friend as an "outgoing, highly ambitious, sensitive person who gets along with nearly everyone." There is no known previous history of a suicide attempt. Mrs. Pettit lost her father six years ago, and her brother died of cancer two years later. Mrs. Pettit became very depressed over these losses but recovered spontaneously. She is legally separated from her husband of 12 years and is going through the divorce process. Upon admission she appears disheveled. She has lost 25 pounds over a period of 2 months. Her speech is almost inaudible. She refuses to eat or drink. She sits on her bed, staring at the floor, and refuses to leave her room. She is in constant tears. A thorough physical examination reveals findings within normal limits. Mrs. Pettit's problem is diagnosed as severe depression.

1. Which of the following statements is UNLIKELY to be true regarding depression?
   (A) In its milder forms, depression is a predictable reaction to everyday stresses of life
   (B) The degree and the length of a person's response to stress are always proportionate to the significance of the situation that brought on the depression
   (C) Depression is manifested physiologically and psychologically
   (D) Depression may occur during a joyous occasion

2. In assessing Mrs. Pettit's needs the nurse must bear in mind that
   (A) many of the symptoms of depression are also symptoms of other physical and mental disorders

   (B) depression is a self-limiting problem primarily of persons of Mrs. Pettit's age group
   (C) Mrs. Pettit's depression may have been triggered by a specific life event
   (D) both A and C above

3. In further assessing Mrs. Pettit's present condition, which of the following needs should the nurse be MOST concerned with?
   (A) Her need for socialization with other patients to divert her attention from herself
   (B) Her need to be alone in order to think through her problems
   (C) Her need for constant surveillance
   (D) Her need for nutrition, rest, sleep, and activity

4. In caring for a person like Mrs. Pettit who has made an overt suicide attempt, the nurse should understand that
   (A) suicide attempts do not usually indicate serious suicidal potential
   (B) suicide attempts using nonlethal means do not communicate deep suicidal intentions
   (C) suicidal actions usually indicate a direct cry for help
   (D) one must avoid mentioning the word "suicide" to the person because this will reinforce his/her thoughts of self-destruction

5. Which of the following conditions would probably be considered a risk factor for a successful suicidal action?
   (A) A depressed person's energy level is increasing
   (B) A person is severely depressed
   (C) A conversion reaction has occurred
   (D) A person leaves a suicide note

6. Mrs. Pettit is receiving imipramine (Tofranil). Which of the following are

anticholinergic side effects of this antidepressant that the nurse must be aware of?
(A) Diarrhea, drowsiness, loss of motor coordination
(B) Fever, sore throat, body malaise
(C) Urinary retention, constipation, dry mouth
(D) Hypotension, increased temperature, shallow breathing

Alice Long, a 23-year-old stockroom clerk, fell over a carton at work. Immediately after, she complains of pain in her left leg and is unable to bear weight on that leg. She is taken to the emergency room.

7. Another symptom that. Ms. Long may exhibit that indicates she has fractured her left leg is
(A) shortening of the leg
(B) internal rotation
(C) increased range of motion
(D) flaccidity of the muscle

8. Ms. Long is admitted to the hospital, where Buck's extension traction is applied. What type of traction can Buck's extension be classified as?
(A) Skin traction
(B) Skeletal traction
(C) Intermittent traction
(D) Suspension traction

9. Which of these actions would demonstrate that the nurse understands the underlying principles of traction?
(A) Supplying countertraction
(B) Maintaining the client in a prone position
(C) Maintaining the spreader in contact with the bed
(D) Maintaining the weights in a dependent position

10. Buck's traction has been discontinued, and a long leg cast applied. The integrity of Ms. Long's newly applied, wet cast can BEST be maintained by which of these actions?
(A) Maintaining it in a prone position
(B) Covering it with a blanket
(C) Handling it with both hands
(D) g it on several pillows

11. Which of these measures would be of MOST benefit in the prevention of skin breakdown while Ms. Long is wearing a cast?
(A) Keeping the cast soil free
(B) Maintaining the client in a prone position
(C) Maintaining the cast in an elevated position
(D) Applying lotion to the skin under the edge of the cast

12. Evaluation of Ms. Long for indication of nerve damage should include
(A) checking peripheral pulses
(B) inspecting the toes for color change
(C) noting changes in sensation in the toes
(D) feeling the toes for temperature change

13. Six hours after the cast was applied, Ms. Long complains of pain in her left leg. The appropriate action by the nurse is
(A) to administer an analgesic
(B) to note the type, duration, and location of the pain
(C) to measure the vital signs
(D) to readjust the pillows under the cast

14. When Ms. Long is ambulated with crutches, she is not allowed to bear weight on her left leg. Therefore the gait she will use while crutch walking is
(A) swing through
(B) two points
(C) three points
(D) four points

15. A complication that may occur while Ms. Long is using crutches is
    (A) foot drop
    (B) palmar flexion
    (C) muscle wasting of the lower extremities
    (D) overdevelopment of the biceps
    Elsa Schmidt's first child was delivered, using forceps, 12 hours ago. She is about to breastfeed her infant for the first time since his initial feeding on the delivery table.

16. Before the feeding the nurse discusses the lengths of feedings with Mrs. Schmidt. The MOST appropriate time schedule would be
    (A) 3 minutes on each breast the first day, 5 minutes the second day, 7 minutes the third day, and 10 to 15 minutes on each breast thereafter
    (B) as long as the infant sucks vigorously
    (C) until Mrs. Schmidt develops soreness in her breasts
    (D) 5 minutes on each breast the first day, and 10 minutes thereafter

17. When Mrs. Schmidt feeds her baby for the first time the nurse should
    (A) leave the room so Mrs. Schmidt can interact with her infant
    (B) remain at the bedside throughout the feeding
    (C) assist Mrs. Schmidt to start the feeding and then leave so that she can interact with her infant, checking back at intervals on how they are doing
    (D) take the baby from Mrs. Schmidt at intervals to burp him

18. While assisting Mrs. Schmidt to breast-feed her infant, the nurse tells her to place the brown pigmented area around the nipple well into the baby's mouth. The reason for this is to
    (A) promote erection of the nipple
    (B) minimize breast engorgement
    (C) make the infant feel more secure
    (D) improve the efficiency of the baby's sucking

19. Mrs. Schmidt experiences "afterpains" when she nurses her baby. She asks the nurse whether she needs to stop nursing because of this. The BEST response for the nurse to make is
    (A) "This is a rather unusual complaint, so it may be best to stop."
    (B) "Pain is not a serious complaint, so there is no reason to stop."
    (C) "This will disappear in a few days, so you can postpone nursing until then."
    (D) "Nursing stimulates the uterus to contract and helps it return to its normal size. You should not stop nursing, but I can give you medication if you are too uncomfortable."

20. Mrs. Schmidt asks the nurse how she should adjust her diet while she is breast-feeding. The breastfeeding mother needs an average of
    (A) 2000 additional calories a day
    (B) 500 additional calories a day
    (C) 1000 additional calories a day
    (D) 1500 additional calories a day

21. Mrs. Schmidt is concerned lest her baby catch "germs" from her while breastfeeding. The MOST important measure she should be taught to prevent bacterial contamination of the baby is
    (A) wearing sterile pads inside her bra
    (B) not allowing anyone in the room while she breastfeeds

(C) washing her hands before each feeding

(D) cleansing her nipples with an antiseptic solution each day

Carlotta Tate, a 65-year-old widow, is admitted to a psychiatric hospital. Her personality is described as compulsive, inhibited, exacting, and worrisome. She states that her life is not worth living any more because she is "useless and no good to anybody." Her three children are all married with families. Mrs. Tate has numerous somatic complaints. She is unable to concentrate and has poor memory. She is indecisive, has lost interest in the world around her, and is preoccupied with thoughts of death.

22. Mrs. Tate's symptoms and mental state are MOST probably indicative of
    (A) involutional depression
    (B) mild depressive reaction
    (C) hypochondriasis
    (D) conversion hysteria

23. While Mrs. Tate is severely depressed, the nurse should keep in mind that
    (A) suicide is never committed during a period of acute depression
    (B) Mrs. Tate requires constant surveillance
    (C) Mrs. Tate should be encouraged to keep herself busy at all times
    (D) it is important to leave Mrs. Tate alone in order to give her an opportunity to think about her situation

24. According to Erikson, a major developmental task of the older adult like Mrs. Tate is
    (A) generativity
    (B) shared feelings in heterosexual relations
    (C) occupational choice
    (D) maintenance of identity

25. Maladaptive responses during older adulthood may be manifested by
    (A) despair
    (B) isolation
    (C) somatization

Baby Michael Stein is 8 hours old. His parents started the bonding process with him in the delivery room, and are now seeing him for the second time.

26. The Stems express concern because the baby's head appears elongated. The nurse BEST reply would be that the elongation was caused by
    (A) a collection of blood under the bones
    (B) a collection of fluid under the tissues
    (C) a genetically inherited trait
    (D) the overlapping of bones during birth

27. Baby Michael passes his first stool while he is with his parents. They are startled by its appearance, but the nurse reassures them that it is a normal first stool. The first stool of a newborn is
    (A) brownish and puttylike in appearance
    (B) thick, blackish green, and sticky
    (C) soft, yellow, and well formed
    (D) greenish yellow and soft

28. The Steins ask why the baby jumped when the crib was bumped. The nurse tells them that this is a normal neurological response known as the
    (A) rooting reflex
    (B) dancing reflex
    (C) fencing reflex
    (D) Moro reflex

29. A reflex that may indicate an abnormality in a newborn is a
    (A) positive grasp reflex
    (B) positive Babinski reflex
    (C) one-sided Moro reflex
    (D) positive rooting reflex

30. The nursery nurse does a complete new-born assessment on Baby Michael. When the infant's fontanelles are inspected, which of the following observations would suggest an abnormality?
    (A) Posterior fontanelle smaller than anterior
    (B) Anterior fontanelle diamond-shaped
    (C) Bulging anterior fontanelle
    (D) Posterior fontanelle difficult to palpate

31. Which of the following factors in Mrs. Stein's history would indicate that Baby Michael should be watched carefully for signs of infection?
    (A) Membranes ruptured prior to 24 hours before delivery
    (B) An episode of bleeding during the second trimester
    (C) A urinary tract infection during her third trimester
    (D) Use of Pitocin during labor

George Brown, a 55-year-old bank manager, has been experiencing attacks of chest pain, lasting 3 to 5 minutes, that are precipitated by exertion and relieved by rest. He has had a complete diagnostic workup and been diagnosed as having angina pectoris. He is being treated with medication and modification of personal habits.

32. Which of the following BEST describes the chest pain that Mr. Brown has been experiencing?
    (A) Substernal, radiating down the right arm
    (B) Burning, radiating to the left arm
    (C) Sharp, radiating to the neck and shoulders
    (D) Crushing, located to the left of the sternum

33. Mr. Brown is placed on nitroglycerin. The CHIEF pharmacological action of nitroglycerin is to
    (A) constrict the heart
    (B) stimulate the myocardial fibers
    (C) decrease coronary resistance
    (D) dilate the coronary arteries

34. One day Mr. Brown forgets to bring his medication to work and experiences chest pain. An action he could take to relieve his pain is to
    (A) take deep breaths
    (B) take a rest period
    (C) take sips of water
    (D) drink an alcoholic beverage

35. Nitroglycerin tablets are administered sublingually. The nurse should instruct Mr. Brown to
    (A) place the tablet under his tongue
    (B) crush the tablet
    (C) swallow the tablet
    (D) chew the tablet

36. Patient teaching for Mr. Brown while he is on nitroglycerin should include the instruction to
    (A) place the tablets in a clear bottle
    (B) carry medications only when necessary
    (C) take a tablet before an emotional or exertional situation
    (D) repeat the medication dosage every half-hour until relief occurs

37. Nitroglycerin no longer relieves Mr. Brown's chest pain. Therefore he is placed on long-acting nitrites. Which of these drug fits this category?
    (A) Isordil
    (B) Inderal
    (C) Guinidine
    (D) Amyl nitrite

Joan Harrison, a 36-year-old housewife, has recently been diagnosed as having rheumatoid arthritis. Her chief complaints are joint pain and morning stiffness of both hands.

38. The goal of care for Mrs. Harrison during the acute phase of her illness will be to prevent or minimize further
    (A) cardiac damage
    (B) joint deformity
    (C) kidney obstruction
    (D) systemic effect

39. Mrs. Harrison's fingers are swollen. The swelling of her fingers is due to
    (A) distension of the joint capsule by an increased amount of synovial fluid
    (B) infiltration of pus into the muscle and fibrous tissue surrounding the joints
    (C) collection of blood into the subcutaneous surface
    (D) formation of bony spurs on the articulating surfaces of the joints

40. Mrs. Harrison is being treated with aspirin and prednisone. During the early days of drug treatment, it is essential that she be carefully monitored for adverse effects. Common adverse effects that may be observed are
    (A) gastrointestinal upset and bleeding
    (B) diarrhea and pruritus
    (C) vertigo and tachycardia
    (D) diaphoresis and blurred vision

41. To minimize or prevent adverse effects from aspirin and prednisone, when should the nurse administer these medications to Mrs. Harrison?
    (A) At bedtime
    (B) With meals
    (C) An hour after meals
    (D) A half-hour before meals

42. Mrs. Harrison is receiving aspirin and prednisone because the effect of these drugs is
    (A) anti-infective
    (B) antimetabolitic
    (C) antimicrobic
    (D) anti-inflammatory

43. The physical therapist reports that Mrs. Harrison refuses to do her exercises because she is experiencing too much pain. Which of the following actions would be MOST effective in getting Mrs. Harrison to comply with her therapy?
    (A) Explain to her the importance of cooperating in her exercise program
    (B) Suggest to her physician that the exercise program be cancelled
    (C) Administer pain medication a half-hour before Mrs. Harrrison starts her exercises
    (D) Advise the therapist to continue to encourage her to exercise

44. In teaching Mrs. Harrison to care for herself at home, the nurse should advise her to
    (A) plan her housework to allow adequate rest
    (B) apply cold compresses to her joints
    (C) exercise only when she feels stiff
    (D) wear clothing with buttons

ANSWERS !☞

1. (B) The degree and length of a person's response to stress may not always be proportionate to the significance of the situation that brought on the depression. Some people, no matter how mild the stress, may become overwhelmed by their reactions and may become dysfunctional.

2. (D) Depression is experienced not only by adults but by all individuals, especially during life stages where stress is intensified.

3. (C) Mrs. Pettit's safety needs are most important at this time.

4. (C) All suicidal ideations and actions have a serious potential because they are expressions of a hopeless view of a life situation. Self-destruction is viewed as the last recourse to deal with an intolerable life.

5. (A) This is the time when the patient usually has the energy required to actualize a suicidal plan of action.

6. (C) Urinary retention, constipation, and dry mouth are side effects of imipramine.

7. (A) The left leg should be compared to the uninjured leg for length. Shortened of the affected leg is due to overriding of the broken bones.

8. (A) Skin traction such as Buck's extension is accomplished by attaching pulleys and weights to the skin with Ace bandages.

9. (A) It is necessary to have countertraction (pull in the opposite direction). If counter-traction is not adequate, the patient tends to slide in the direction of the traction, so that the purpose of the traction (maintaining the leg in alignment) is nullified.

10. (D) Flattening of the cast is prevented by elevating it on several pillows. Flattening must be avoided at all costs because it may cause skin breakdown, especially over the bony prominence.

11. (D) Special attention should be given to the areas near and under the cast, with lotion applied daily; these areas are pressure points and are prone to breakdown.

12. (C) Only choice C describes a method of evaluating the extremity for nerve damage/sensory loss. No or lessened awareness of pinprick and light touch is indicative of nerve damage. The other choices are appropriate for the evaluation of circulation impairment.

13. (B) Constant, undiminished pain that is present for 4 hours or longer is a sign of complications. Pain is the main symptom of circulation impairment from a cast. The pain is not localized and is usually burning or cramping in nature. A fractured extremity typically becomes progressively painless once it is properly immobilized. Analgesia/pain medication should not be administered to a patent with a cast until the cause of the pain has been evaluated. Pain is an important diagnostic symptom and should not be suppressed or masked.

14. (C) The three-point gait allows for partial weight bearing or no weight bearing. The crutches and the involved leg are moved forward together, with the weight taken on the wrists and the palm.

15. (B) Excessive pressure on the brachial nerve plexus from bearing weight on the palms may cause damage to the brachial plexus or palmar flexion.

16. (A) If the infant sucks on the breast for a prolonged period to start with, the nipples will become sore and cracked, thereby making the mother uncomfortable with breast-feeding. Her discomfort will be communicated to the infant, who will develop difficulty in feeding. By setting up a schedule of gradually increased feeding times, the nipples have a chance to toughen, and both mother and baby will be happier with the outcome.

17. (C) The new mother needs assistance with breastfeeding, but she also needs time alone with her infant. The nurse should be near, however, in case Mrs. Schmidt needs assistance.

18. (D) This action compresses the lactiferous sinuses behind the areola and draws milk into the baby's mouth when he sucks.

19. (D) This answer gives Mrs. Schmidt an explanation of what is happening and reassures her that it is normal. It also encourages

her to keep nursing and offers a solution for the discomfort.

20. (C) This is the number of additional calories required to ensure that milk production will not deplete the mother's nutritional stores.

21. (C) Organisms are easily transported on the skin to form areas of contamination that have been touched. The hands are a common source of bacteria. The breasts need only normal cleansing to prevent any transport of organisms. Sterile technique is not necessary.

22. (A) Mrs. Tate's presenting history and her behavior indicate involutional depression.

23. (B) Constant surveillance will be required for Mrs. Tate during severe depression because her decision-making ability is grossly impaired and the accompanying vegetative symptoms of depression could precipitate life-threatening physiologic problems such as fluid and electrolyte imbalance and circulatory impairment.

24. (D) Ego maintenance is considered to be a major developmental task of late adulthood.

25. (A) Late adulthood is a period when fear of new situations, caused by illness, loss of income, or death of a spouse, or the inability to adjust to these situations, may trigger despair.

26. (D) Molding, manifested by elongation, is the process by which the fetal head accommodates to the birth canal.

27. (B) Meconium is the first stool passed by the newborn. It is the result of digested amniotic fluid that the newborn swallowed *in utero.*

28. (D) Infants have a variety of neurological reflexes due to the immaturity of their nervous systems. The startle reflex is known as the Moro reflex.

29. (C) A one-sided Moro reflex can indicate brain damage, brachial paralysis, or a fractured clavicle.

30. (C) A bulging anterior fontanelle would indicate increased intercranial pressure.

31. (A) Once membranes are ruptured, the infant's protection from external organisms is compromised. When membranes have been ruptured more than 24 hours, the chance of infection is greatly increased.

32. (C) In angina pectoris, the pain radiates to the neck, jaw, shoulder, and/or inner aspects of the upper extremities. The pain is intense and is located deep in the chest (upper or middle third of the sternum).

33. (D) Nitroglycerin relaxes the vascular smooth muscle, thereby causing dilatation of the coronary arteries.

34. (B) Rest decreases the oxygen need of the heart. Angina pectoris is brought on by inability of the damaged heart to utilize oxygen properly because of atherosclerosis and a lack of collateral circulation.

35. (A) The underside of the tongue is highly vascularized; therefore medication placed there enters the bloodstream quickly.

36. (C) Nitroglycerin taken prophylactically prevents the occurrence of pain caused by emotion or exertion.

37. (A) Isordil is a long-acting nitrite that produces the same general effects as nitroglycerin.

38. (B) The primary objective in providing care for the involved joints is to reduce the pain, stiffness, and inflammation, to preserve function, and to prevent deformities.

39. (A) The inflammatory process causes an increase in the amount of synovial fluid.

40. (A) Both aspirin and prednisone cause gastrointestinal irritation and bleeding.

41. (B) To reduce gastric irritation, aspirin should be taken with food and/or milk or antacids.

42. (D) Aspirin and prednisone are prescribed to reduce inflammation and therefore relieve pain.

43. (C) Mrs. Harrison's refusal to cooperate with the therapist probably is due more to the pain that occurs with exercise than to a lack of motivation. Therefore the most beneficial action would be to administer pain medication beforehand so that she can perform her exercises.

44. (A) Both systemic rest and emotional rest are necessary in treating rheumatoid arthritis. The degree of rest depends on the type and severity of the manifestations at the time.

PILOT: GLIDER, HOT AIR, AIRPLANE

Federal Aviation Administration

*Before you are allowed to adjust the earphones over
your crushed cap and carry on a purposeful conversation with the control tower in soft, laconic, Chuck-
Yeager drawl, you'll have to pass a test with questions
like some of these in it.*

The FAA, under the Department of Transportation, regulates flying in this country unless you can take off by running along the ground. The FAA developed the following questions to be used by FAA testing centers and FAA-designated written test examiners when administering Private Pilot, Airplane, Airship, Hot Air Balloon, Gas Balloon, and Glider exams. The written test is the first step in obtaining a license to fly an airplane, glider, or lighter-than-air craft.

The written exam for Private Pilot is taken by most people who want to fly a small airplane themselves. It has 50 questions and takes two to four hours to complete, though a full day is available. The FAA sells a Private Pilot Question Book (FAA-T-8080-1A), which is available at U.S. Government Publication bookstores. We excerpted the questions below from a Private Pilot Test Guide published by ASA Publications in Seattle, WA. Unlike the FAA publication, this guide provides answers to all the questions.

Among the main areas covered by the questions in the full test are: weather theory and forecasts, FAA regulations, aerodynamics, instruments, engine mechanics, weight and balance calculations, navigation, and manuals.

The test booklet also includes pages of information including the legends for symbols on sectional aeronautical charts, lists of abbreviations, and an excerpt from the Airport Facility Directories published by the Dept. of Commerce for the FAA. Students bring some equipment to the exam: portable flight computer, pocket calculator, and a plotting scale for navigation.

It is a pass-fail test with passing pegged at 70 percent. The results are valid for 24 calendar months, and when you get your score in the mail from the FAA—about two weeks after the test—they explain which areas you did not answer correctly.

Glider

1. What force provides the forward motion necessary to move a glider through the air?
    (A) Centrifugal force
    (B) Centripetal force
    (C) Gravity
    (D) Profile drag

2. In which manner should the sailplane be flown while turning during an aerotow?
    (A) By using a slightly steeper bank than the towplane with the sailplane's nose pointed to the outside of the turn
    (B) By flying outside the towplane's flightpath
    (C) By banking at the same point in space where the towplane banked and using the same degree of bank and rate of roll
    (D) By flying inside the towplane's flightpath

3. What corrective action should be taken, if while thermalling at minimum sink speed in turbulent air, the left wing drops while turning to the left?
    (A) Apply more opposite (right) rudder pressure to counteract the overbanking tendency
    (B) Apply opposite (right) rudder pressure to slow the rate of turn
    (C) Lower the nose before applying opposite (right) aileron pressure
    (D) Apply opposite (right) aileron pressure to counteract the overbanking tendency

4. A pilot unintentionally enters a steep diving spiral to the left. The proper way to recover from this attitude without overstressing the glider would be to
    (A) apply up-elevator pressure to raise the nose
    (B) apply more up-elevator pressure and then use right aileron pressure to control the overbanking tendency

    (C) relax the back pressure and shallow the bank; then apply up-elevator pressure until the nose has been raised to the desired position
    (D) apply more up-pressure and right rudder pressure to reduce the rate of turn

5. What corrective action should be taken, if while thermalling at minimum sink speed in turbulent air, the right wing drops while turning to the right?
    (A) Apply more opposite (left) aileron pressure than opposite (left) rudder pressure to counteract the overbanking tendency
    (B) Apply opposite (left) rudder pressure to slow the rate of turn
    (C) Lower the nose before applying opposite (left) aileron pressure
    (D) Apply opposite (left) pressure to counteract the overbanking tendency

6   What would be a proper action or procedure to use if the pilot is getting too low on a cross-country flight in a sailplane?
    (A) Continue on course until descending to 1000 feet above the ground and then plan the landing approach
    (B) Fly directly into the wind and make a straight-in approach at the end of the glide
    (C) Continue on course until descending to 500 feet, then select a field and confine the search for lift to an area within gliding range of a downwind leg for the field chosen
    (D) Have a suitable landing area selected upon reaching 2000 feet AGL, and a specific field chosen upon reaching 1500 feet AGL

7. The sailplane has become airborne and the towplane loses power before leaving the ground. The sailplane should release immediately,
    (A) and maneuver to the right of the towplane

(B) extend the spoilers, and land straight ahead

(C) maneuver to the left of the towplane, and stop as quickly as possible

(D) extend the spoilers, and land. If a crosswind exists, the sailplane pilot should make a gentle turn into the wind

8. Seatbelts are required to be properly secured about which persons in a glider and when?

(A) Pilot crewmembers only, during take-offs and landings

(B) Occupants during takeoffs and land-ings

(C) Each person on board the glider dur-ing the entire flight

(D) Occupants during flight in moderate or severe turbulence only

9. What minimum upward current must a glider encounter to maintain altitude?

(A) At least 2 feet per second

(B) The same as the glider's sink rate

(C) The same as the adjacent down cur-rents

(D) Greater than the adjacent down cur-rents

10. Which is considered to be the most haz-ardous condition when soaring in the vicinity of thunderstorms?

(A) Static electricity

(B) Lightning

(C) St. Elmo's fire

(D) Wind shear and turbulence

11. What is a recommended procedure for entering a dust devil for soaring?

(A) Enter at low level and circle the edge in the same direction as the rotation

(B) Enter at low level and circle the edge opposite the direction of rotation

(C) Enter at above 500 feet and circle the edge in the same direction as the rota-tion

(D) Enter at above 500 feet and circle the edge opposite the direction of rotation

12. An important precaution when soaring in a dust devil is to

(A) avoid the eye of the vortex because of extreme turbulence

(B) avoid the clear area at the outside edge of the dust because of severe down-drafts

(C) maintain the same direction as the rotation of the vortex for maximum lift

(D) avoid steep turns on the upwind side to prevent being blown into the vortex

13. Under what condition can enough lift be found for soaring under stable weather conditions?

(A) Over steep escarpments or cliffs

(B) In mountain waves that form on the upwind side of the mountains

(C) Over isolated peaks when strong winds are present

(D) On the upwind side of hills or ridges with moderate winds present

Balloon/Airship

1. If an airship in flight is either light or heavy, the unbalanced condition must be overcome by

(A) valving air from the ballonets

(B) valving gas from the envelope

(C) a negative or a positive dynamic force

(D) releasing ballast

2. During flight in an airship, when is verti-cal equilibrium established?

(A) When buoyancy equals the horizontal equilibrium existing between propeller thrust and airship drag

(B) When buoyancy exceeds the airship weight

(C) When buoyancy is less than airship weight

(D) When buoyancy equals the airship weight

3. Under which condition will an airship float in the air?
(A) When buoyant force equals horizontal equilibrium existing between propeller thrust and airship drag
(B) When buoyant force is less than the difference between airship weight and the weight of the air volume being displaced
(C) When buoyant force exceeds the variables between airship weight and the weight of air volume being displaced
(D) When buoyant force equals the difference between airship weight and the weight of the air volume being displaced

4. An airship descending through a steep temperature inversion preparatory to landing will
(A) show no change in superheat as altitude is lost
(B) show a decrease in superheat as altitude is lost
(C) become progressively lighter, thus becoming increasingly more difficult to drive down
(D) probably encounter turbulent air near the ground

5. The lifting forces which act on a hot-air balloon are primarily the result of the interior air
(A) temperature being greater than ambient temperature
(B) temperature being less than ambient temperature
(C) pressure being greater than ambient pressure
(D) pressure being less than ambient pressure

6. What would cause a gas balloon to start a descent if a cold air mass is encountered and the envelope becomes cooled?
(A) A density differential
(B) A barometric pressure differential

(C) The contraction of the gas
(D) The expansion of the gas

7. What action should be taken if the balloon shifts direction abruptly while in the vicinity of a thunderstorm?
(A) Land immediately
(B) Descend to and maintain the lowest altitude possible
(C) Ascend to an altitude which will ensure adequate obstacle clearance in all directions
(D) Ascend in stairsteps to find a wind that will carry the balloon away from any thunderstorms

8. An ideal surface for a balloon launch site is
(A) asphalt or concrete
(B) bare earth
(C) tall, dry grass
(D) lawn grass

9. The minimum size a launch site should be is at least
(A) twice the height of the balloon
(B) 100 feet for every 1 knot of wind
(C) 500 feet on the downwind side
(D) twice the height of the tallest obstacle

10. It may be possible to make changes in the direction of flight in a hot-air balloon by
(A) using the maneuvering vent
(B) operating at different flight altitudes
(C) flying a constant atmospheric pressure gradient
(D) operating above the friction level if there is no gradient wind

11. Best fuel economy in level flight can be accomplished by
(A) riding the haze line in a temperature inversion
(B) short blasts of heat at high frequency
(C) long blasts of heat at low frequency
(D) short blasts of heat at low frequency

12. What action is most appropriate when an envelope over-temperature condition occurs?
    (A) Throw all unnecessary equipment overboard
    (B) Descend, hover in ground effect until the envelope cools
    (C) Turn the main burner OFF
    (D) Land as soon as practical

13. What is a recommended ascent upon initial launch?
    (A) Maximum ascent to altitude to avoid low-level thermals
    (B) Shallow ascent to avoid flashbacks of flames as the envelope is cooled
    (C) A moderate-rate ascent to determine wind directions at different levels
    (D) A gradual accelerated ascent to test the fuel valves

14. Row should a round-out from a moderate rate ascent to level flight be made?
    (A) Cool the envelope by venting just before arriving at altitude
    (B) Cool the envelope by venting and add heat just before arriving at altitude
    (C) Vent at altitude and add heat upon settling back down to altitude
    (D) Reduce the amount of heat gradually as the balloon is approaching altitude

15. What is a potential hazard when climbing at maximum rate?
    (A) The envelope may collapse
    (B) Deflation ports will be forced open
    (C) The rapid flow of air may extinguish the burner and pilot light
    (D) The envelope will cool too rapidly and destroy the efficiency of the climb

16. What is a hazard of rapid descents?
    (A) The parachute effect may put undue stress on the envelope
    (B) The pilot light cannot remain lit with the turbulent air over the basket

    (C) Aerodynamic forces may collapse the envelope
    (D) The mouth may close when passing through shears

17. The windspeed is such that it is necessary to deflate the envelope as rapidly as possible during a landing. When should the deflation port (trip panel) be opened?
    (A) The instant the gondola contacts the surface
    (B) As the balloon skips off the surface the first time and the last of the ballast has been discharged
    (C) After ground contact has been firmly established and the envelope is swinging to the downward side of the gondola
    (D) Prior to ground contact

18. When landing a free balloon, what should the occupants do to minimize landing shock?
    (A) Be seated on the floor of the basket
    (B) Stand with knees slightly bent, in the center of the gondola, facing the direction of movement
    (C) Stand back-to-back and hold onto the load ring
    (D) Hold onto the handles attached to the load ring

19 Which precaution should be exercised if one is confronted with the necessity of having to land when the air is turbulent?
    (A) Land in any available lake close to the upwind shore
    (B) Throw propane equipment overboard immediately prior to touchdown
    (C) Land in the trees to absorb shock forces, thus cushioning the landing
    (D) Land in the center of the largest available field

20. Prior to a high-wind landing, the pilot in command should brief the passengers to
    (A) kneel on the floor facing aft
    (B) crouch on the floor and jump out of the basket on first contact with the ground
    (C) crouch facing aft and jump out of the basket as soon as the basket stops moving
    (D) crouch, hang on in two places, and remain in the basket until advised otherwise

21. What is the procedure for relighting the burner while in flight?
    (A) Open the regulator or blast valve full open and light off the pilot light
    (B) Close the tank valves, vent off fuel lines, reopen tank valves, and light off the pilot light
    (C) Open another tank valve, open the regulator or blast valve, and light off main jets with reduced How
    (D) Open the regulator valve full open, close main tank valve, open the regulator or blast valve, and light off pilot light

22. Which of the following takeoff procedures is considered to be most hazardous?
    (A) Maintaining only 50 percent of the maximum permissible positive angle of inclination
    (B) Failing to apply full engine power properly on all takeoffs, regardless of wind
    (C) Maintaining a negative angle of inclination during takeoff after elevator response is adequate for controllability
    (D) Maintaining a light tailwheel contact when taking off in a light wind with a heavy airship

23. Which action is necessary in order to perform a normal descent in an airship?
    (A) Valve gas
    (B) Valve air

(C) Take air into the aft ballonets
(D) Decrease the engine power

24. To land an airship that is 250 pounds heavy when the wind is calm, the best landing can usually be made if the airship is
    (A) in trim
    (B) nose heavy approximately 20 degrees
    (C) tail heavy approximately 20 degrees
    (D) nose heavy 5 degrees

25. Objects may be dropped from a balloon
    (A) only in an emergency
    (B) if precautions are taken to avoid injury or damage to persons or property on the surface
    (C) if prior permission is received from the FAA
    (D) if passengers are not carried

26. An airplane and an airship are converging. If the airship is left of the airplane's position, which aircraft has the right of way?
    (A) The pilot of the airplane should give way; the airship is to the left
    (B) The airship has the right of way
    (C) Each pilot should alter course to the right
    (D) The airplane has the right of way; it is more maneuverable

27. What conditions does a rising barometer indicate for balloon operations?
    (A) Increasing thermal activity and clouds
    (B) Decreasing clouds and winds
    (C) Chances of thunderstorms
    (D) Approaching frontal activity

Other Aircraft

1. The four aerodynamic forces acting on an airplane are
    (A) power, velocity, gravity, and drag
    (B) power, velocity, weight, and friction
    (C) thrust, lift, gravity, and weight
    (D) thrust, lift, weight, and drag

2. What makes an airplane turn?
   (A) Centrifugal force
   (B) Rudder and aileron
   (C) Horizontal component of lift
   (D) Rudder, aileron, and elevator

3. If severe turbulence is encountered, the airplane's airspeed should be reduced to
   (A) maneuvering speed
   (B) the minimum steady flight speed in the landing configuration
   (C) normal operation speed
   (D) maximum structural cruising speed

4. What is the general direction of movement of the other aircraft if during a night flight you observe a steady white light and a flashing red light ahead and at the same altitude'?
   (A) The other aircraft is crossing to the left
   (B) The other aircraft is crossing to the right
   (C) The other aircraft is approaching head-on
   (D) The other aircraft is headed away from you

5. What is the general direction of movement of the other aircraft if during a night flight you observe steady red and green lights ahead and at the same altitude?
   (A) The other aircraft is crossing to the left
   (B) The other aircraft is crossing to the right
   (C) The other aircraft is approaching head-on
   (D) The other aircraft is headed away from you

6. The most important rule to remember in the event of a power failure after becoming airhorne is to
   (A) quickly check the fuel supply for possible fuel exhaustion

   (B) determine the wind direction to plan for the forced landing
   (C) turn back immediately to the takeoff runway
   (D) maintain safe airspeed

7. If power failure occurs at altitude, the pilot should immediately
   (A) center the pedals
   (B) apply left pedal to correct for yaw
   (C) lower the collective pitch control
   (D) hold the collective pitch control in the neutral position

8. If an airship should experience failure of both engines during flight and neither engine can be restarted, what initial immediate action must the pilot take?
   (A) The airship must be driven down to a landing before control and envelope shape are lost
   (B) The emergency auxiliary power unit must be started for electrical power to the airscoop blowers so that ballonet inflation can be maintained
   (C) Immediate preparations to operate the airship as a free balloon are necessary
   (D) Valve large quantities of helium so that an immediate descent to an emergency landing can be accomplished

9. The most effective method of scanning for other aircraft for collision avoidance during daylight hours is to use
   (A) regularly spaced concentration on the 3-, 9-, and 12-o'clock positions
   (B) a series of short, regularly spaced eye movements to search each 10-degree sector
   (C) peripheral vision by scanning small sectors and utilizing off center viewing
   (D) rapid head and eye movements through a horizontal plane to cover the entire viewing area in a short time

10. The most effective method of scanning for other aircraft for collision avoidance during nighttime hours is to use
    (A) regularly spaced concentration on the 3-, 9-, and 12-o'clock positions
    (B) a series of short, regularly spaced eye movements to search each 30-degree sector
    (C) peripheral vision by scanning small sectors and utilizing off center viewing
    (D) rapid head and eye movements through a horizontal plane to cover the entire viewing area in a short time

11. How can you determine if another aircraft is on a collision course with your aircraft?
    (A) The other aircraft will be pointed directly at your aircraft
    (B) The other aircraft will always appear to get larger and closer at a rapid rate
    (C) The nose of each aircraft is pointed at the same point in space
    (D) There will be no apparent relative motion between your aircraft and the other aircraft

12. A person may not act as a crewmember of a civil aircraft if alcoholic beverages have been consumed by that person within the preceding
    (A) 8 hours
    (B) 12 hours
    (C) 24 hours
    (D) 48 hours

13. Under what condition, if any, may a pilot allow a person who is obviously under the influence of intoxicating liquors or drugs to be carried aboard an aircraft?
    (A) Under no condition
    (B) Only if the person is a medical patient under proper care or in an emergency
    (C) Only if the person does not have access to the cockpit or pilot's compartment
    (D) Only if a second pilot is aboard

14. What action is required when two aircraft converge at the same altitude, but not head-on?
    (A) The more maneuverable aircraft shall give way
    (B) The faster aircraft shall give way
    (C) The aircraft on the left shall give way
    (D) Each aircraft shall give way to the right

15. What action should be taken if a glider and an airplane approach each other at the same altitude and on a head-on collision course?
    (A) The airplane should give way because the glider has the right of way
    (B) The airplane should give way because it is more maneuverable
    (C) Both should give way to the right
    (D) The airplane should climb and the glider should descend so as to pass each other by at least 500 feet

16. Which aircraft has the right of way over all other air traffic?
    (A) A balloon
    (B) An aircraft in distress
    (C) An aircraft on final approach to land
    (D) An aircraft towing or refueling another aircraft

17. According to regulations, no person may operate an aircraft in acrobatic flight
    (A) over any congested area of a city, town, or settlement
    (B) within 5 miles of a federal airway
    (C) below an altitude of 2000 feet above the surface
    (D) when flight visibility is less than 5 miles

18. Except when necessary for takeoff or landing, what is the minimum safe altitude required for a pilot to operate an aircraft over congested areas?
    (A) An altitude allowing, if a power unit fails, an emergency landing without undue hazard to persons or property on the surface
    (B) An altitude of 500 feet above the surface and no closer than 500 feet to any person, vessel, vehicle, or structure
    (C) An altitude of 500 feet above the highest obstacle within a horizontal radius of 1000 feet
    (D) An altitude of 1000 feet above the highest obstacle within a horizontal radius of 2000 feet

ANSWERS!

Glider

1. (C) In an unpowered aircraft, gravity must be used to overcome aerodynamic drag.
2. (C) The sailplane will stay on the towplane's radius of turn if it starts its turn at the same point.
3. (C) Lowering the nose will prevent the glider from entering a spiral dive or stalled condition.
4. (C) The correct recovery from a spiral dive is to relax back pressure on the stick and at the same time reduce the bank angle with coordinated aileron and rudder; When the bank is less than 45 degrees the stick may be moved back while continuing to decrease bank.
5. (C) Lowering the nose will prevent the glider from entering a spiral dive or stalled condition.
6. (D) It is. always necessary to have a suitable. landing site in mind and as altitude decreases; the plans have to get more specific.
7. (A) The glider should maneuver to the right of the towplane. The towplane should move over to the left. If there is a narrow runway, a full spoiler landing should be made as soon as possible.
8. (B) Unless otherwise authorized by the Administrator, during the takeoff and landing of U.S. registered civil aircraft (except free balloons that incorporate baskets or gondolas and airships), each person on board that aircraft must occupy a seat or berth with a safety belt properly secured about him..
9. (A) If a sailplane pilot is to remain airborne there must be an upward air current of at least 2 feet per second.
10. (D) Violent thermals just beneath and within highly developed cumulus clouds are strong and dangerous.
11. (D) At around 500 feet the pilot makes a circle on the outside of the dust devil against... the direction of rotation.
12 (A) The rarefied air in the eye provides very little lift and the wall of the hollow core is very turbulent
13. (D) An ideal slope is about I to 4 with an upslope wind of 15. knots or more.

Balloon/Airship

1. (C) Dynamic force created by movement through the air must be used to overcome any out of equilibrium condition.

2. (D) A lighter-than air craft is in equilibrium when buoyancy equals weight.

3. (D) A lighter-than-air craft is in equilibrium when buoyancy equals weight.

4. (C) As the airship descends into the colder temperature of the in version, superheat increases, increasing buoyancy.

5. (A) A hot air balloon derives lift from the fact that air inside the envelope is warmer and therefore "lighter" than the air around the balloon.

6. (C) As the gas contracts, it becomes more dense and so displaces less air.

7. (A) Thunderstorms are extremely dangerous. They move at great speed and can destroy a balloon in flight.

8. (D) A lawn is level and smooth, reducing damage from snags or friction abrasion.

9. (B) A free balloon will move about 100 feet pet second for every knot of wind.

10. (B) A free balloon has no propulsion and so must take advantage of differing wind directions at various altitudes.

11. (B) The desired envelope temperature for level flight is best maintained by short blasts at high frequency.

12. (D) An envelope over-temperature can seriously degrade the strength of the envelope.

13 (C) It is necessary to determine the wind direction accurately at various altitudes during initial ascent

14. (D) The most efficient round-out is to reduce the frequency of blasts so that the envelope cools to a level flight temperature just as the balloon reaches the desired altitude.

15. (B) The positive pressure on the top of the envelope could force the deflation ports open.

16. (B) Turbulent airflow may extinguish the pilot light.

17. (D) In a high wind landing, the envelope should be ripped just prior to ground contact.

18. (B) By facing forward with knees bent, the body is balanced and the legs act as springs, absorbing the landing shock.

19 (D) Turbulent air implies wind shear and that makes surface winds unpredictable.

20 (A) By facing forward with knees bent, the body is balanced and the legs act as springs absorbing the landing shock. It is important that everyone remain in the basket until the envelope cannot lift the balloon back into the air.

21. (C) The desired situation is to get a large flow of gas to make relighting easier.

22. (B) It is necessary to apply full power at the correct moment during an "up-ship" maneuver.

23. (D) An airship is normally flown heavy and so a power reduction would cause a descent. Air should be taken into the forward ballonets.

24. (C) A heavy airship should be trimmed tail heavy to provide dynamic lift during approach.

25. (B) No pilot in command of a civil aircraft may allow any object to be dropped from the aircraft in. flight that creates a hazard to persons or property. However, this section does not prohibit the dropping of any object if reasonable precautions are taken to avoid injury or damage to persons or property.

26. (B) An airship has the right of way over an airplane or rotocraft.

27. (B) A rising barometer means decreasing clouds and decreasing winds.

Other Aircraft

1. (D) The four forces acting on an airplane in flight are lift, weight, thrust, and drag.
2. (C) First, it should be kept in mind that the rudder does not turn the airplane in flight. The force of lift can be resolved into two components – vertical and horizontal. During the turn entry the vertical component of lift still opposes gravity, and the horizontal component must overcome centrifugal force; consequently, the total lift must be sufficient to counteract both of these forces. The airplane is then pulled around the turn, not sideways, because the tail section acts as a weathervane which continually keeps the airplane streamlined with the curved flightpath.
3. (A) Maneuvering speed (Va) is the best speed for turbulent air penetration.
4. (D) The tail of an aircraft is marked with a steady white light. If the only lights visible on another aircraft are the white tail light and the flashing red anti-collision light, it is flying away from the observer.
5. (C) The other aircraft is approaching head-on because the red light is on the left wing and green light is on the right wing and there is no white light visible.
6. (D) Maintaining a safe airspeed is the most important because nothing else can help if you don't have positive altitude control.
7. (C) Lower the collective pitch control to maintain rotor rpm.
8. (C) An airship without power must be operated as a free balloon.
9. (B) Effective scanning is accomplished with a series of short, regularly spaced eye movements that bring successive areas of the sky into the central visual field. Each movement should not exceed 10 degrees, and each area should be observed for at least one second to enable detection.
10. (C) Offcenter viewing must be utilized during night flying because of the distribution of rods and cones in the eye.
11 (D) Any aircraft that appears to have no relative motion and stays in one scan quadrant is likely to be on a collision course.
12. (A) No person may act as a crewmember of a civil aircraft within 8 hours after the consumption of any alcoholic beverage.

13. (B) Except in an emergency, no pilot of a civil aircraft may allow a person who is obviously under the influence of intoxicating liquors or drugs (except a medical patient under proper care) to be carried in that aircraft.

14. (C) When two aircraft of the same "right-of-way" category converge at the same altitude, the one on the right has the right of way.

15. (C) When two aircraft are approaching each other from head on or nearly so, each pilot must alter course to the right. This rule does not give right of way by categories.

16. (B) An aircraft in distress has the right of way over all other traffic.

17. (A) No person may operate an aircraft in acrobatic flight
    (1) over any congested area of a city, town,' or settlement;
    (2) over an open air assembly of persons;
    (3) within a control zone or federal airway;
    (4) below an altitude of 1500 feet above the surface; or
    (5) when flight visibility is less than three miles.

18. (D) Except when necessary for takeoff or landing no person may operate an aircraft below "the following altitudes:
    (1) *Anywhere.* An altitude allowing, if a power unit fails, an emergency landing without undue hazard to persons or property on the surface.
    (2) *Over congested areas.* Over any congested area of a city, town, or settlement, or over any open-air assembly of persons, an altitude of 1000 feet above the highest obstacle within a horizontal. radius of 2000 feet of the aircraft.
    (3) *Over other than congested areas.* An altitude of 500 feet above the surface except over open water or sparsely populated areas. In that case, the aircraft may not bc operated closer than 500 feet to any person, vessel, vehicle, or structure.

PSYCHOLOGY, ABNORMAL

Hassett & Herman-Sissons

The questions in this section have been selected from tests given to college students taking an introductory course in psychology. Students are tested on a range of 15 different chapters in the course of the year. We chose the chapter for this collection that we guessed our readers would be most familiar with.

T here are three types of questions of varying difficulty: factual, application (requiring that specific knowledge be put to work in a situation new to the student), and interpretive (requiring analytical thought as in comparing research findings). As in most questions with multiple-choice answer alternatives, which psychologists call "stems," the stems are all designed to sound individually plausible, which, of course, makes it a lot more difficult to wing it if one has not done the reading.

We suggest you assign a passing grade to your score based on a curve of scores achieved by others taking this test with you rather than assigning a passing grade to an absolute number of questions answered correctly, say, out of the 85 in this exam. In other words, you could average the number of correct answers given by you and any other people you also ask to take this test, then call that average a passing grade.

Be warned, however, that the average could rise or fall significantly depending on the nature of the group. For example, the scores might well be higher among people who are observed to be standing on their heads munching carrots while taking the test. Conversely, lower average scores might be expected from affluent, young, urban professionals from whom you have withdrawn all possible means of cheating.

1. The first person to develop a formal system for categorizing and diagnosing abnormal behavior was
   (A) Rogers
   (B) Kraepelin
   (C) Wundt
   (D) Freud

2. Crime, alcohol abuse, anxiety, and depression
   (A) are all affective disorders
   (B) we among the most common abnormal behavior patterns in the United States
   (C) are forerunners of schizophrenic disorders
   (D) were first identified by Emil Kraepelin

3. Statistical definitions identify abnormality in terms of
   (A) an ideal mental health
   (B) a person's subjective experience of discomfort
   (C) an individual's inability to make a meaningful contribution to society
   (D) deviations from what most people do

4. One problem with defining abnormality in terms of the violation of cultural norms is that
   (A) it would be unfair to conformists
   (B) it would not diagnose schizophrenics as abnormal
   (C) it would increase cultural relativity ratios
   (D) only conformists would be "normal" and all nonconformists would be abnormal

5. Definitions of mental health both in terms of an ideal of mental health, and in terms of a failure to function adequately,
   (A) are based on the view that personal distress is the single most important criterion indicating abnormality
   (B) are based on a rejection of the medical model
   (C) distinguish between unusual as opposed to abnormal behavior

(D) use cultural norms to identify abnormality

6. Determining what behaviors may be unusual but desirable as opposed to behaviors which may be unusual and abnormal is a problem underlying
   (A) the statistical definition of abnormality
   (B) identification of abnormality as a deviation from an ideal of mental health
   (C) defining mental illness in terms of a deviation from cultural norms
   (D) all of the above

7. Beth was amazed to discover that she is the only person in her class who has never experimented with the use of illegal drugs. By which definition of abnormality is Beth not abnormal?
   (A) By a statistical definition
   (B) In terms of deviation from cultural norms established by her class
   (C) In terms of the social norms of the group to which she belongs at school
   (D) In terms of a person's ability to function adequately

8. Research comparing definitions of behavior labeled in our culture as schizophrenic in several other cultures suggests that definitions of abnormality
   (A) may not be completely arbitrary or completely culture - bound
   (B) are almost completely culture-bound
   (C) are universally determined in terms of cultural deviations
   (D) have little scientific value

9. The medical model holds that abnormal behavior
   (A) is caused by physical disease
   (B) cannot be treated as a physical disease
   (C) cannot be thought of as a physical disease
   (D) is a medical rather than a physical disease

10. The fact that general paresis is caused by syphilis supports the medical model of mental illness because
    (A) it enabled doctors to identify the physical cause of schizophrenia
    (B) it proves that mental patients are not faking their symptoms
    (C) general paresis can be cured through psychotherapy
    (D) it identified a biological cause for what had previously been identified as a purely "mental" problem

11. One problem with applying diagnostic labels to people with behavior problems is that the labels may
    (A) have a dehumanizing effect
    (B) become a self-fulfilling prophecy
    (C) make it difficult for a person to get a job later on
    (D) All of the above

12. The major difference between a neurosis and a psychosis is that a neurosis
    (A) is no longer considered to be a problem while psychosis is
    (B) refers to less serious problems with reality definition than psychosis
    (C) is included in the DSM-III while psychosis is not
    (D) has been displaced by psychosis as a diagnostic category

13. An inflexible behavior pattern or enduring personality trait that interferes significantly with a person's occupation or social life or causes personal distress is known as a/an
    (A) phobia
    (B) affective disorder
    (C) personality disorder
    (D) obsession

14. An example of an enduring personality trait that interferes with a person's functioning, characteristic of personality disorders, would be a person who
    (A) is a transvestite
    (B) suffers from severe bouts of anxiety an(depression
    (C) hallucinates frequently
    (D) continuously neglects her children so they are often not fed or adequately clothed

15. A behavior pattern of violating the rights of others that begins before the age of 15 and interferes with adult responsibilities is characteristic of
    (A) paranoia
    (B) histrionic disorders
    (C) pathological disruption
    (D) antisocial personality disorders

16. Suzanne is now 19 years old and has been shoplifting since she was 11. She has been fired from eight different jobs, but it is a lie when she says she graduated from high school with honors and has been accepted to Harvard. Suzanne may have a/an
    (A) obsession
    (B) organic mental disorder
    (C) hallucination
    (D) antisocial personality disorder

17. A person who has a grandiose sense of self-importance, constantly seeks admiration, and is preoccupied with fantasies of success would be diagnosed as a
    (A) neurotic
    (B) narcissistic personality disorder
    (C) achievement disorder
    (D) paranoid personality

18. A man with a narcissistic personality disorder may characteristically
    (A) be unmarried
    (B) be in the upper socio-economic class
    (C) brag about his supposed unexcelled achievements and/or capacities
    (D) be obsessive about telling the truth

19. Peter, a graduate student in English literature, is a case study of a narcissistic personality disorder because
    (A) he apparently was not going to get married
    (B) he is probably a homosexual
    (C) his sense of self-importance interfered with his completing his work
    (D) men did not like him although women were initially very attracted to him

20. Gary always presented himself as "big man on campus," telling stories of making thousands of dollars overnight on the stock market, going with many beautiful women, and performing as the great hero of the football team. In reality, Gary is failing out of school, has many unpaid debts and no girlfriends. Gary may
    (A) be a narcissistic personality
    (B) be suffering from a somatoform disorder
    (C) have an affective disorder
    (D) be an example of a dissociative disorder

21 Narcissistic, antisocial, and paranoid are
    (A) believed by psychoanalysts all to be caused by problems stemming from the oral stage
    (B) examples of anxiety disorders
    (C) affective disorders
    (D) kinds of personality disorders

22. A psychoanalytic view of narcissism is that it is caused by
    (A) disruptions in the social learning process, usually during the grade school years
    (B) indiscriminate use of reinforcements by the person's mother
    (C) a lack of adequate comfort and emotional support during the oral stage
    (D) a reversal of the life and death instincts

23. A social-learning view of narcissism suggests that it is probably caused by
    (A) a cold mother who gives very little love to her child
    (B) an overly demanding father who constantly criticizes his child
    (C) the indiscriminate use of praise of the child by doting parents
    (D) a school system with low standards for learning

24. A Freudian would hypothesize that a person with a narcissistic personality disorder
    (A) has been spoiled as a child
    (B) is really covering up a deep self-hatred with a veneer of self-importance
    (C) should be ignored in order to nonreinforce offensive bragging
    (D) is usually an extraordinarily gifted individual who has not been recognized by society

25. A social-learning theorist would hypothesize that a person with a narcissistic personality disorder
    (A) is an exceptionally gifted individual who has been frustrated by limited opportunities in the environment
    (B) should be given more reinforcement and praise for his/her accomplishments, even when they are quite small
    (C) will change if the pattern of reinforcement and nonreinforcement he receives also changes
    (D) developed it during the oral stage

26. A cognitive approach to analyzing a narcissistic personality disorder would probably begin by asking
    (A) to what extent a person's view of himself and his world is realistic
    (B) about a person's childhood experiences
    (C) whether the person is unusually intelligent
    (D) about the person's eating and sleeping habits

27. In an anxiety disorder,
    (A) the anxiety is a result of a person's guilt usually related to sexual desires or activities
    (B) severe anxiety interferes with the ability to function normally
    (C) anxiety is converted to hysteria to protect the ego
    (D) anxiety is substituted for a realistic and objective fear

28. Unpredictable and repeated attacks of anxiety and panic are typical of a/an
    (A) hysterical reaction
    (B) obsession
    (C) phobia
    (D) panic disorder

29. Persistent repetitive thoughts which cannot be controlled or behavior patterns that are repeated in a kind of ritual without rational explanation are characteristic of
    (A) obsessive-compulsive disorders
    (B) generalized anxiety disorders
    (C) panic disorders
    (D) phobias

30. An irrational fear of a specific object, activity, or situation is known as a
    (A) paranoid reaction
    (B) generalized anxiety disorder
    (C) phobia
    (D) obsessive-compulsive disorder

31. Freud thought that anxiety disorders are caused by
    (A) unconscious conflicts among the id, ego, and superego
    (B) an underdeveloped superego
    (C) a stunted id
    (D) unconscious paranoid reactions

32. Mary frequently gets attacks of anxiety when she feels dizzy and nauseous, and will sometimes even break into tears without any identifiable reason, experiencing a dread of an unspecifiable danger. Mary seems to have
    (A) a personality disorder
    (B) an obsessive-compulsive disorder
    (C) a phobia
    (D) a generalized anxiety disorder

33. Tasha says that she would be terrified to have to do the kind of ski jumps executed by Olympic skiers. Tasha's anxiety about skiing would not be diagnosed as an anxiety disorder because
    (A) she can identify the precise situation that makes her anxious
    (B) her anxiety is not generalized
    (C) it does not interfere with her normal functioning
    (D) it is not rational

34. Jack's boss told him that he may be fired if he continues to come to work so late because he keeps returning home as many as six different times each morning to make sure he has turned off the gas and locked the doors. Jack's behavior reflects a/an
    (A) panic disorder
    (B) obsessive-compulsive disorder
    (C) affective disorder
    (D) generalized anxiety disorder

35. Shiela quit her job in New York City because she could no longer deal with the panic she felt whenever she had to get into the elevator to go to her office on the 86th floor of the Empire State Building. Shiela has a
    (A) major depression
    (B) phobia
    (C) generalized anxiety disorder
    (D) obsessive-compulsive disorder

36. Karen was sitting in class last week when she suddenly began to tremble and sweat and felt that if she were not able to get out of the classroom immediately she would become hysterical. Karen was probably experiencing a/an
    (A) panic disorder
    (B) affective disorder
    (C) obsession
    (D) personality disorder

37. Because of her fear of cockroaches, which has been growing during the last six months, Ethel is no longer able to sleep at night unless she leaves all the lights on in the entire apartment, in addition, she gets up at least twice during the night and thoroughly searches her bedroom to make sure no roaches are creeping around Ethel seems to have a/an
    (A) simple phobia
    (B) complex phobia
    (C) light phobia
    (D) eragasiophobia

38. A young girl who becomes extremely anxious and agitated if she cannot take at least five showers a day is probably suffering from a
    (A) phobia
    (B) generalized anxiety disorder
    (C) obsessive-compulsive disorder
    (D) depression disorder

39. The view that the greater incidence of depression among women is caused by roles women play in our society reflects a
    (A) strict psychoanalytic interpretation
    (B) neo-Freudian approach
    (C) biological approach
    (D) social learning approach

40. The argument that extreme shifts in hormonal levels in women cause a higher incidence of depression in women than in men
    (A) reflects a behavioral approach
    (B) has been supported by Freud's research
    (C) is specious because depression is more prevalent in men
    (D) reflects a biological approach to mental illness

41. John's mother is 48 years old and for several months has been weeping frequently' is so sad most of the time that she does not have the energy to cook or clean, and does not want to go out, even to events that she used to enjoy. John's mother may be suffering from
    (A) a personality disorder
    (B) major depression
    (C) a bipolar disorder
    (D) generalized anxiety

42. When Jerry failed a course in calculus, he argued that it was because "I didn't study, so even though I'm good at math, I failed this course. Attribution theory would characterize this explanation as
    (A) global and long-term
    (B) specific and external
    (C) specific and internal
    (D) short-term and external

43. When Jane says that she did not get invited to the dance because she is "fat and ugly," her explanation would be characterized by attribution theory as
    (A) global, long-term, and internal
    (B) a defensive reaction against depression
    (C) a result of learned helplessness
    (D) a reality defense

44. Suzanne has just been fired from her job. According to attribution theory, which of the following explanations is most apt to cause Suzanne to be depressed?
    (A) It's my fault I lost my job. I'm no good at anything.
    (B) The economy is bad, the company is going under, and my job is being eliminated as a result.
    (C) The boss has trouble with competent women and fired me because he feels

threatened by the good job I have been doing

(D) It's my fault; I handled this last problem badly and I know better, because I've done it the right way before

45. Drugs which have proven useful in the treatment of severe depression
(A) create a manic reaction in most patients
(B) depress brain activity
(C) reduce activity in the cerebral cortex
(D) increase levels of norepinephrine

46. Research with drugs used to control affective disorders indicates that a person's mood may be controlled partially by
(A) psychic phenomena in the cerebral cortex
(B) the level of norepinephrine in the brain
(C) the level of activity in the cerebellum
(D) levels of lithium in the brain

47. A psychoanalytic theorist is most apt to argue that depression is caused by
(A) an undeveloped superego
(B) anger which the person does not express but instead turns against herself
(C) a discrepancy between the ideal and real self
(D) learned helplessness

48. Schizophrenia is a condition characterized by
(A) obsessive thought processes
(B) fragmentation of thought, perception, and emotion
(C) a split personality
(D) phobias

49. One of the symptoms of schizophrenia is
(A) an increased awareness of objective reality
(B) unusually sensitive and expressive emotional reactions
(C) perceptual distortion
(D) all of the above

50. If a person's thought patterns involve loose associations in which he shifts quickly from one subject to another, and fails to form complete and coherent thoughts, you might expect the person to be
(A) depressed
(B) schizophrenic
(C) phobic
(D) compulsive

51. Suddenly one day your roommate began talking about strange organisms from another planet who visited her and controlled her life and told her what to do. At the mental hospital, she was diagnosed as reactive schizophrenic. What is the likelihood of her quick recovery?
(A) Good
(B) Poor
(C) No way of telling
(D) Less than fifty-fifty

52. A person complaining that there were human beings in her fingers who want to kill her would probably be diagnosed as schizophrenic because the complaint would seem to indicate
(A) some biological disorientation
(B) a bizarre delusion
(C) the depth of the person's underlying anxiety
(D) the presence of a major affective disorientation

53. John has been hospitalized because he hallucinates and thinks "green devils" are coming out of the woodwork to carry him to Russia. He is withdrawn and his thought patterns disorganized. He probably has been diagnosed as having a
(A) dissociative reaction
(B) bipolar disorder
(C) major affective disorder
(D) schizophrenic disorder

54. A person with a delusion
    (A) believes, without rational justification, that something is true
    (B) perceives something that does not exist objectively
    (C) has no feelings about his world
    (D) hears voices that are frightening or bantering

55. The studies investigating the incidence of schizophrenia among twins seem to indicate that
    (A) schizophrenia has no biological foundation
    (B) schizophrenia is inherited only in fraternal twins
    (C) the cause of schizophrenia may have a biological basis
    (D) schizophrenia is inherited only in identical twins

56. Regarding the causes of schizophrenia, research strongly suggests that
    (A) it is caused almost exclusively by environmental conditions, particularly in the family
    (B) biological predispositions play an important role
    (C) the most important factor is how the person was raised as a child
    (D) the most important factor is the level of norepinephrine in the brain

57. The reason why the average stay in a mental hospital now is shorter than it was fifty years ago is primarily due to
    (A) the use of drug therapy
    (B) the fall of moral therapy
    (C) the decrease in the incidence of mental illness
    (D) the efforts of Dorothea Dix

58. The eighteenth-century physician, Pinel, was noted for his efforts to
    (A) bring humane treatment to the institutionalized mentally ill
    (B) develop drug therapies for the mentally ill
    (C) develop a diagnostic system for mental illness
    (D) modernize American mental institutions

59. A psychiatrist is different from a psychologist because a psychiatrist
    (A) treats mentally ill patients
    (B) has a Ph.D.
    (C) has an M.D.
    (D) can both diagnose and treat mental illness

60. One difference between a clinical psychologist and a psychiatrist is that the clinical psychologist
    (A) has a B.A. degree
    (B) has been trained to do psychotherapy
    (C) does not give medical treatment or prescribe drugs for mental patients
    (D) knows less psychology

61. To help clients overcome emotional problems, psychoanalytic therapy emphasizes the therapeutic power of
    (A) love and caring
    (B) learning through conditioning
    (C) insight
    (D) therapist instructions

62. Freud believed that in order to overcome emotional problems, a person
    (A) needs to be clear about his role in his family and career
    (B) must retrain herself to stop acting in an emotional fashion
    (C) needs to experience the intense emotion related to the original conflict which had been repressed
    (D) must gain a clear intellectual understanding of the causes and cures of her problem

63. If a patient in psychoanalysis comes late to therapy and occasionally forgets to come at all, the analyst will probably
    (A) give the patient more unconditional regard
    (B) try some different technique than psychoanalysis
    (C) establish a fear hierarchy
    (D) interpret the patient's behavior as resistance

64. While undergoing psychotherapy, Janet "fell in love" with her therapist. Freud would not see this as true love but rather a necessary process he called
    (A) attachment
    (B) fixation
    (C) transference
    (D) repression

65. A therapist appearing on a TV talk show reported, "My techniques are designed to help the person overcome resistance to remembering anxiety-provoking thoughts and impulses." The therapist is probably a
    (A) psychoanalyst
    (B) client-centered therapist
    (C) psychiatric social worker
    (D) behaviorist

66. Contemporary ego psychologists have modified classical Freudian therapy
    (A) in order to include conscious repression
    (B) to stress the importance of the ego rather than to uncover repressed material
    (C) to deemphasize reality-based processes
    (D) because classical analysis was always so ineffective

67. The type of psychotherapy which applies scientific principles of learning to alter observable behavior is called
    (A) behavior therapy
    (B) psychoanalysis
    (C) client-centered therapy
    (D) cognitive therapy

68. If a young girl wanted to overcome a severe debilitating fear of storms, a behaviorist would probably recommend
    (A) a client-centered therapist
    (B) systematic desensitization
    (C) psychoanalysis
    (D) rational-emotive therapy

69. When Joan had kept a journal for a week monitoring when and where she smoked, she discovered that 85 percent of her smoking was in social situations. She decided, therefore, to reward herself with $1.00 for each conversation she had without smoking, and to penalize herself for each conversation during which she did smoke. In terms of self-control procedures, Joan was
    (A) establishing effective consequences
    (B) using covert control
    (C) applying systematic desensitization
    (D) measuring baseline behaviors

70. Fred would be using covert control to reduce his smoking if he
    (A) analyzed his dreams to understand the underlying causes of his smoking
    (B) gave himself a covert shock whenever he smoked
    (C) asked several friends to watch him, and make him stop whenever he lit up a cigarette
    (D) thought about getting lung cancer every time he was tempted to smoke

71. Behaviorists believe that most behavior can be changed through the application of behavior modification techniques because they believe that
    (A) symptoms of maladaptive behavior are less important than their underlying causes
    (B) almost all behavior is learned through conditioning, and so can be reconditioned
    (C) they have developed techniques such as biofeedback that will recondition the unconscious
    (D) the environment is less important than heredity as a cause of maladaptive behavior

72. One of the earliest studies suggesting that fear can be learned through the process of conditioning was when
    (A) Pavlov conditioned dogs to salivate to the sound of a tuning fork
    (B) Thorndike put cats in a puzzle box
    (C) Skinner taught pigeons to peck at a bar to avoid electric shock
    (D) Watson conditioned Little Albert by ringing a loud bell when a rat appeared

73. The aspect of psychoanalytic therapy that behavior therapists would probably reject most strongly is
    (A) the use of a couch in therapy instead of face-to-face interaction
    (B) the belief that the cause of a person's problem lies in past experience
    (C) the emphasis on uncovering unconscious conflicts in order to cure a problem
    (D) Freud's distinction between classical and operant conditioning

74. Behavior therapy has developed as an alternative to psychoanalysis because
    (A) psychoanalytic theory offers no explanation for so many forms of mental illness prevalent in modern times

    (B) Sigmund Freud and John Watson had an intense personal dislike of each other
    (C) behaviorists believe that disturbed behavior is a result of improper conditioning rather than of repressed conflicts
    (D) behaviorists reject the past as the cause of disturbed behavior

75. A behavior therapist conditions an 8-year-old boy who still wets his bed regularly to wake up at night before the bed is wet. A psychoanalyst thinks that the behavior therapy is not sufficient because
    (A) Freud believed that conditioning wears off too quickly
    (B) behavior modification does not solve the underlying conflict that is causing the bedwetting problem
    (C) the use of punishment to stop bedwetting creates anxiety that later interferes with school work
    (D) research shows that bedwetting cannot be changed through conditioning techniques

76. A client-centered therapist believes that usually the best way for a therapist to help a person solve a problem in therapy is to help the person
    (A) clarify their goals
    (B) clarify their own feelings about the problem
    (C) explore her unconscious motivation springing from childhood
    (D) identify the inconsistencies in the person's thinking

77. Tina is a 26-year-old woman who is exploring whether she should break up with her boyfriend who hit her last night. In response to her question, "Should I break up with him?" a client-centered therapist is probably apt to respond by
    (A) nodding her head but saying nothing

(B) telling the client how much the therapist respected the client

(C) asking Tina to try to remember her dreams from last night

(D) saying "You're trying to decide if you want to end this relationship"

78. Groups that promote personal growth by encouraging participants to focus on their immediate relationships with others in the group are called
(A) sensitivity-training groups
(B) assertiveness-training groups
(C) humanistic-training groups
(D) relationship groups

79. Assertiveness training is based on the process of
(A) classical conditioning
(B) cognitive analysis
(C) observational learning
(D) punishment

80. Linda is extremely shy and reserved and does not know how to talk to people very well. In order to help Linda develop more social skills, a therapist is most apt to suggest
(A) meditation
(B) group therapy
(C) biofeedback
(D) covert sensitization

81. The fact that expectations can influence behavior is called the
(A) placebo effect
(B) double-blind effect
(C) single-blind effect
(D) expectation-bias effect

82. The reason for a double-blind study is to
(A) reduce the effect of expectations by either experimenter or subjects
(B) control for the placebo effect
(C) decrease subject bias
(D) All of the above

83. Despite its great advantages, one of the problems of drug therapy is that
(A) schizophrenics all must stay on the drugs all their lives
(B) they often make people suicidal
(C) relapses occur just as often among patients on drugs as among patients treated through psychotherapy
(D) the drugs often produce quite serious side effects

84. Jean is a 36-year-old teacher whose attacks of anxiety have been so severe that they are interfering with her ability to work. The drug most apt to be prescribed for her would be a/an
(A) antipsychotic drug such as Thorazine
(B) antidepressant such as Nardil
(C) tranquilizer such as Librium
(D) mood regulator such as Lithium

85. Mrs. Mills is in her mid-forties and has been suffering for the last six months with severe depression. The drug treatment she is most apt to be given would be a/an
(A) antipsychotic drug
(B) electroconvulsive shock
(C) mood regulator or antidepressant
(D) tranquilizer

ANSWERS!

1. B	30. C	59. C
2. B	31. A	60. C
3. D	32. D	61. C
4. D	33. C	62. C
5. C	34. B	63. D
6. D	35. B	64. C
7. D	36. A	65. A
8. A	37. A	66. B
9. A	38. C	67. A
10. D	39. D	68. B
11. D	40. D	69. A
12. B	41. B	70. D
13. C	42. C	71. B
14. D	43. A	72. D
15. D	44. A	73. C
16. D	45. D	74. C
17. B	46. B	75. B
18. C	47. B	76. B
19. B	48. B	77. D
20. A	49. C	78. A
21. D	50. B	79. C
22. C	51. A	80. B
23. C	52. B	81. A
24. B	53. D	82. D
25. C	54. A	83. D
26. A	55. C	84. C
27. B	56. B	85. C
28. D	57. A	
29. A	58. A	

REAL ESTATE SALESPERSON

Florida Real Estate Commission

OCEAN FRONT, PRIVATE BEACH Lo-rise condo, 3br, 3bth, ft and rear bal, 2600 sq ft, att fin, pvt w/sec, pool, ex rm, tennis, golf, $240,000.

T hose who aspire to peddle real estate in Florida must be licensed by the Florida Real Estate Commission (fondly called "FREC" in exams and other moments of high frustration; being Yankees , we can't help with its pronunciation) whether or not the land they intend to sell is under water except at dead low tide.

In the state of Florida, the first step in the process of obtaining a Salesman's License is completion of a course of study at a Florida Real Estate Commission-approved institution. The next step is passing the actual Florida Real Estate Commission exam, which consists of questions similar to the ones here. In question 39 the correct arithmetical calculations require some local knowledge. A Florida township is six miles square and is divided uniformly into 36 "sections" of one square mile each.

The state of Florida has a statute on the books that imposes restrictions on the practices of real estate salespeople. It is known in the trade as "Chapter 475," and a salesperson violates its provisions at the peril of his license. The enforcement of that law has pretty well put the kibosh on the old whinny of selling waterlogged Gulf Coast real estate to Yankees who should be old enough to know better.

The gender-sensitive reader will perceive that the male pronoun used in this introduction and the FREC exams, as of this writing, has nothing to do with the reality of which of the two sexes sells more real estate in Florida. It is another anachronism which we have preserved in the wording of the questions in the name of accuracy, and to avoid creating a furze bush of parentheses. In other respects, we make an effort to lead a gender-neutral, editorially hermaphroditic life, as it were.

There is a Broker's License exam, too, for which the questions are different from those for a salesman's license, but first things first. The questions that follow have been selected from the Real Estate Salesman's License course at the Bert Rogers School of Real Estate in Florida. For further information, you may write to them at Dept. BOT, P.O. Box 720, Orlando, FL 32802.

1. When using the cost depreciation approach, value equals
   (A) the reconciled value of comparables
   (B) income divided by the capitalization rate
   (C) vacant land value plus depreciated building value
   (D) gross income times the standard multiplier

2. Which of the following is correct concerning appraisers?
   (A) An appraiser's license is necessary
   (B) They are compensated on a fee basis according to the difficulty of their assignment
   (C) They search for market price
   (D) All of the above

3. When the question of title arises, the broker should
   (A) be sure to base any statement he makes upon his opinion only
   (B) do nothing since brokers have no duty to the prospect because there is no fiduciary relationship
   (C) advise the prospect to procure an abstract to be examined by a competent attorney or obtain title insurance
   (D) tell the prospect to seek the seller's opinion

4. A broker may have a branch office
   (A) near his main office
   (B) anywhere in Florida
   (C) in his home
   (D) All of the above

5. A broker has fiduciary duties because he
   (A) is licensed
   (B) adheres to a code of ethics
   (C) is responsible to his principal
   (D) is bound by contract

6. A broker has a listing for $10,000.00. He obtains an offer of $12,000.00. The broker buys the property for $10,000.00 and resells it for $12,000.00. This is a (an)
   (A) conspiracy
   (B) overage
   (C) illegal commission
   (D) lawful practice

7. A salesperson can have an escrow account
   (A) in the normal course of business
   (B) only with the approval of his employer
   (C) only with the approval of his employer and the FREC
   (D) under no circumstances

8. Which of the following statements best describes the relationship between the broker and his prospect?
   (A) They are dealing at arm's length
   (B) The broker must report any facts or rumors concerning the property
   (C) They are governed by the rule "caveat emptor"
   (D) The prospect can rely upon material statements

9. A salesperson selling his own property
   (A) must have the broker place the ad and need not state that he is a registered salesperson
   (B) can advertise in his own name and need not state that he is a registered salesperson
   (C) can avoid the rule about advertising in the broker's name and advertise as for sale by owner, indicating that he is a registered salesperson and giving his employer's telephone number
   (D) must have the broker place the ad and give the broker's and salesperson's names

10. If a broker wishes to obtain a true option, he must
    (A) pay a definite, valuable consideration
    (B) divest himself of his identity as a broker
    (C) pay a definite valuable consideration and divest himself of his identity as a broker
    (D) do no more than any other purchaser

11. Which of the following is (are) correct?
    (I) A contract for sale of a homestead requires two witnesses
    (II) An individual must file annually for homestead exemption
    (A) I only
    (B) II only
    (C) Both I and II
    (D) Neither I nor II

12. Eminent domain is thought of in connection with
    (A) courts
    (B) the government
    (C) private enterprise
    (D) death intestate with no heirs

13. An encumbrance affects
    (A) existing mortgages
    (B) title
    (C) possession
    (D) zoning

14. The secret sale of more than one-half of a business's assets is prevented by the
    (A) Fictitious Names Act
    (B) Florida Real Estate License Law
    (C) Division of Florida Land Sales
    (D) Bulk Sales Act

15. Which of the following are proof of merchantable title?
    (A) Abstract and survey
    (B) Abstract and title insurance
    (C) Title insurance and survey
    (D) None of the above

16. Which of the following is (are) correct?
    (I) An abstract is an assurance of clear title
    (II) A title search required for closing always takes place on the day of closing; therefore, the buyer is protected when he receives the deed.
    (A) I only
    (B) II only
    (C) Both I and II
    (D) Neither I nor II

17. The mortgage insurance premium for the insurance on FHA 203(b) loans is
    (A) one-half of 1 percent of the remaining principal balance payable monthly
    (B) paid with the annual casualty insurance premium
    (C) one-half of 1 percent of the monthly payment
    (D) paid with the discount at the closing

18. The primary concern of any real estate investment should be
    (A) tax shelter aspects
    (B) depreciation deductions
    (C) economic soundness
    (D) location

19. Which of the following are incorrect concerning mortgages?
    (A) Signed by the mortgagee
    (B) Signed by two witnesses
    (C) Signed by the mortgagor
    (D) Both A and B

20. Broker Brown receives three offers on a parcel of property he has listed. Two of the offers were oral. In order to properly serve his employer, he must
    (A) submit the offers in the order he received them
    (B) submit only the written offer
    (C) submit only those offers accompanied by a binder deposit
    (D) submit all of the offers regardless of form, binder deposit, price, or order in which they were received

21. A contract with a promise of performance on one side is called a (an)
    (A) implied contract
    (B) bilateral contract
    (C) executed contract
    (D) unilateral contract

22. The passage or amendment of rules by the FREC is an exercise of which power?
    (A) Executive
    (B) Quasi-legislative
    (C) Ministerial
    (D) Quasi-judicial

23. Which of the following is probably not real estate?
    (A) A tree
    (B) A refrigerator
    (C) A lease
    (D) A fence

24. Prior to acceptance of the offer, the earnest money deposit is under control of the
    (A) broker
    (B) seller
    (C) broker and buyer-depositor
    (D) buyer-depositor

25. A purchaser signs an offer stating that he wishes to offer $65,000.00 for a home listed for $67,000.00. His offer is accepted and signed by the offeree. Prior to being notified of the acceptance, the purchaser enters into an agreement to purchase another property. Which of the following applies?
    (A) If the purchaser revokes the $65,000.00 offer prior to being notified of the acceptance of the offer, no breach of contract has occurred
    (B) The purchaser has breached the contract because offers must remain in effect for a reasonable length of time
    (C) The purchaser will be found guilty of fraud because this is a direct violation of the Statute of Frauds
    (D) Both B and C are correct

26. If a seller of property did not receive all money due him and did not receive security for that unpaid money, he is eligible for a
    (A) lis pendens
    (B) second mortgage
    (C) mechanic's lien
    (D) vendor's lien

27. Which of the following Florida business organizations can register as a broker?
    (A) Corporation not for profit
    (B) Corporation for profit
    (C) Corporation sole
    (D) Cooperative association

28. Broker A pays $50.00 for a 90-day option to owner Ann. The agreed upon price is $100,000.00. On the 60th day, broker A finds a purchaser for the property at a sales price of $130,000.00. Broker A exercises his option and sells the property for $130,000.00. Which of the following applies?
    (A) Broker A is entitled to a $30,000.00 profit
    (B) Broker A has violated his fiduciary duties
    (C) Ann, the owner, and the purchaser may sue for damages
    (D) Answers B and C are correct

29. The right granted by a property owner to another to enter upon that owner's property is known as an
    (A) encumbrance
    (B) easement
    (C) encroachment
    (D) escheat

30. Real estate salesmen may be employed by
    (A) owners only
    (B) brokers only
    (C) broker or owner-employer
    (D) None of the above

31. A deed warranting title only against claims of the grantor, his heirs, assigns, executors, or administrators, and others claiming by or through him is called a
    (A) general warranty deed
    (B) bargain and sale deed
    (C) quit-claim deed
    (D) special warranty deed

32. Brokers A and B are partners in developing a parcel of land. C, a licensed salesperson, later purchases a share of the partnership. All proceeds from the sale of the developed land are divided according to ownership shares. Which of the following is correct?
    (A) C must be a broker to become a true partner
    (B) The salesperson must be inactive

(C) No registration with the FREC is necessary

(D) This partnership must register with the FREC

33. In order to reduce the risk inherent in originating high loan-to-value ratio loans, lenders require
    (A) increased interest rates
    (B) mortgage insurance
    (C) discount
    (D) all of the above

34. Prior to the marriage, real estate owned by a husband or wife is presumed to be
    (A) in a joint estate
    (B) in a tenancy in common
    (C) in an estate by the entireties
    (D) separate property

35. The mortgagor's right to bring himself out of default by paying money owed to the lender is called
    (A) the assumption of mortgage
    (B) the amortization of mortgage
    (C) the equity of redemption
    (D) strict foreclosure

36. A mentally incompetent person may act as a grantor and deliver title to his own property by signing a
    (A) guardian's deed
    (B) committee's deed
    (C) quit-claim deed
    (D) none of the above

37. A member of the FREC may serve no more than
    (A) four years
    (B) eight years
    (C) ten years
    (D) None of the above

38. A written offer to purchase is submitted to a seller and he in turn changes the terms or conditions, initials the changes, signs the instrument, and sends it back to the offeror. In the law of contracts, this is a (an)
    (A) offer
    (B) binding offer
    (C) irrevocable offer
    (D) counteroffer

39. How many acres are contained in the NI/2 of the SWl/4 of the SEl/4 of the NEl/4 of Section 9?
    (A) 10 acres
    (B) 5 acres
    (C) 2 1/2 acres
    (D) 11/4 acres

40. Negative taxable income is known as
    (A) capital gain
    (B) cash flow
    (C) debt service
    (D) tax shelter

41. During periods of disintermediation in the primary mortgage market, the mortgage money supply
    (A) is unaffected
    (B) decreases
    (C) increases
    (D) either increases or decreases according to demand

42. Under the income approach to appraisal, value equals
    (A) vacant land value plus depreciated building value
    (B) rate times income
    (C) rate divided by income
    (D) income divided by rate

43. A and B form a business in which A is totally liable for any debts which are incurred but B is only liable to the extent of his investment. This is probably a
    (A) corporation
    (B) general partnership
    (C) joint venture
    (D) limited partnership

44. Brokers are permitted to draw leases
    (A) in the normal course of their business
    (B) if power of attorney is granted to the owner
    (C) never
    (D) only if the brokers divest

45. The license of a broker is revoked. Licenses of salespeople employed by that broker are
    (A) revoked
    (B) suspended
    (C) reprimanded
    (D) canceled

46. Which of the following may involve the securities laws as well as the real estate laws?
    (A) Condominiums
    (B) Sales of real estate by transfer of stock of a corporation
    (C) Group investment
    (D) All of the above

47. Finders' fees paid to unlicensed individuals
    (A) violate Chapter 475
    (B) are simply poor business practices
    (C) should be made to stimulate referrals
    (D) are not illegal

48. Qualifying refers to
    (A) lender analyzing borrower and property
    (B) salesperson determining a prospect's needs and capabilities
    (C) broker checking up on past clients
    (D) both A and B

John is a salesperson working for Ann, the broker. John obtains a written offer and a deposit on a property listed with the office. He deposits the money in his own account, indicating that it is to be held in escrow for the buyer. The seller accepts the offer and John writes a check to his broker for the deposit. She deposits the check in her business account. The buyer defaults and Ann divides the escrow deposit with John. Based on this information, answer the next four questions.

49. What should John have done with the deposit money?
    (A) Exactly what he did since the problem is the action taken by Ann, the broker
    (B) Left it in his own escrow account
    (C) immediately turned it over to his broker

(D) held it until the offer was accepted; then turned it over to his broker

50. What should Ann have done when she received the deposit?
    (A) Exactly what she did since the buyer and seller agreed to it
    (B) Immediately deposited it in her escrow account
    (C) Returned the money to the buyer
    (D) left the money in John's escrow account

51. Which of the following is (are) correct?
    (I) John is guilty of conversion (II) Ann is guilty of conversion
    (A) I only
    (B) II only
    (C) Both I and II
    (D) Neither I nor II

52. Assuming that the money had been handled properly up until the time of default by the buyer, what should Ann do upon the buyer's default?
    (A) Return the deposit
    (B) Exactly what she did
    (C) divide the money equally with John and the seller
    (D) divide the money with the seller according to their agreement and divide her share with John according to their agreement

53 A first-degree misdemeanor will be imposed by courts as a result of
    (A) violations of advance fee accounting requirements or false advertising
    (B) payment made from the Recovery Fund
    (C) any violation of Chapter 475
    (D) Answers B and C are correct

54. Owner A lists 1000 acres with broker B, specifying the price and terms he will accept. B discovers that by selling on the price and terms stated, A will be liable for a large amount of income tax. B should
    (A) change the listing for the protection of the principal

(B) tell A nothing because he has nothing to do with income tax

(C) follow the instructions of the principal

(D) advise A of this and tell him to seek the advice of an income tax expert

55. Which of the following shares of real property will a widow with no children receive at her husband's death in the absence of a will?

(A) One-third

(B) All

(C) One-half

(D) None

56. An estate held by two or more parties in which each has equal or proportionate rights as to possession, enjoyment, and the time and duration, having the same or different origin, is being held as a (an)

(A) estate for years

(B) joint estate

(C) estate by the entireties

(D) tenancy in common

57. A seller agrees to deliver to a buyer a perfect record title Examination of the abstract by a competent attorney reveals breaks in the chain of title. The seller would then do which of the following?

(A) Buy title insurance for the buyer

(B) File a suit to quiet title

(C) Get an affidavit from the Clerk of the Circuit Court attesting to his knowledge and belief that the seller's title is good

(D) transfer title by quit-claim deed

58. A broker-salesperson employed by more than one owner should

(A) apply for a multiple license

(B) apply for a group license

(C) Broker-salesperson may not be employed by an owner

(D) None of the above

59. If all rights under a lease are subrogated, the result is

(A) a sublease

(B) an assignment

(C) a violation of Chapter 475

(D) Either A or B

60. A broker may collect a commission when he has negotiated a sale of property with the knowledge and consent of the owner even though no previous express listing was given the broker on the basis that he had a (an)

(A) open listing

(B) true option

(C) implied listing

(D) option which should be treated as a listing

61. If a grantor in a deed is insolvent, a quit-claim deed is as desirable as a

(A) bargain and sale deed

(B) special warranty deed

(C) general warranty deed

(D) All of the above

62. What is the government survey method description of the following property?

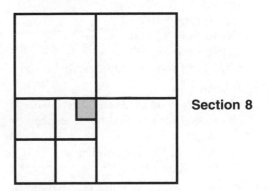

Section 8

(A) NE 1/4 of the NE 1/4 of the SW 1/4 of Section 8

(B) NW1/4 of the NW1/4 of the SW1/4 of Section 8

(C) NI/2 of the NE 1/4 of the SE 1/4 of Section 8

(D) SW1/4 of the NE1/4 of the NE 1/4 of Section 8

63. A violation of Chapter 475 may result in
    (A) imprisonment
    (B) injunction
    (C) suspension
    (D) all of the above

64. The mortgage lien remains in effect until
    (A) the note is paid in full
    (B) defeasance clause is satisfied
    (C) a satisfaction is signed and recorded
    (D) all of the above

65. An exclusive listing
    (A) guarantees the listing broker a commission if the property is sold through another broker
    (B) must be in writing
    (C) is given to only one broker
    (D) All of the above

66. A broker sells a prospective tenant a rental list for $100.00. The prospective tenant inspected all the properties and found them to be occupied. The tenant then demanded a full refund; what action should the broker take?
    (A) Refund $100.00
    (B) Refund $25.00
    (C) Refund $75.00
    (D) No refund should be made

67. A license is
    (A) prima facie evidence of licensure
    (B) issued for a period not to exceed two years
    (C) proof of Florida residency
    (D) both A and B

68. B wants a motel site and salesperson A showed him a good location which was zoned for a motel. A then went on vacation. Upon A's return, B purchased the site with A's assistance. A did not know that while he was on vacation the zoning had been changed and B was subsequently denied a building permit for his motel. Which applies?
    (A) A is guilty of nothing as there was no intent

(B) A is guilty of negligence and may be disciplined
(C) A and his broker are both guilty of fraud and may be disciplined
(D) A is guilty of culpable negligence and subject to discipline

69. When a broker represents two parties in a transaction,
    (A) he must have the consent of both parties in order to collect a dual commission
    (B) he must disclose his agency to both parties
    (C) he may not represent two parties with adverse interests in a transaction
    (D) Both A and B are correct

70. When the license period is about to expire, the licensee should apply for a renewal. The effective date for that renewal will be
    (A) the date the licensee makes the proper application to the department
    (B) the date the department receives the application in proper form with proper fee attached
    (C) the date following the expiration date of the original license
    (D) the date the licensee receives the license

71. When a dispute arises concerning the disposition of escrowed funds and the broker is the escrow agent, the broker's first action should be to
    (A) ask the FREC for an Escrow Disbursement Order
    (B) give the deposit to the seller
    (C) collect his portion of the deposit as damages
(D) notify the FREC

72. Which of the following is (are) correct?
    (I) All officers and directors of real estate corporations must be brokers
    (II) All partners in a real estate partnership must be brokers
    (A) I only

(B) II only
(C) Both I and II
(D) Neither I nor II

73. Paul, a service station owner, has been appointed by a court to appraise another service station. Paul has no real estate license. Which of the following applies?
(A) He may apply to the FREC for a special exception
(B) He may appraise the property only if he is knowledgeable as to its value
(C) He must appraise the property while under the supervision of a licensed real estate broker
(D) He may be compensated for appraising the property

74. Using borrowed money to finance the purchase of real estate is known as
(A) larceny
(B) conversion
(C) leverage
(D) commingling

75. A licensee who appeals a decision by the Florida Real Estate Commission regarding disciplinary decision may have his license privileges restored by
(A) injunction
(B) warrant
(C) the hearing officer
(D) writ of mandamus

76. Concerning the collection of advance fees, the broker should
(A) place 75 percent in escrow to be used for the benefit of the principal
(B) place 100 percent in escrow
(C) place 25 percent in escrow to be used for the benefit of the principal
(D) place 100 percent in escrow to be used for the benefit of the principal

77. In order for a salesperson to become a successful broker applicant, he must
(A) work for one active broker for one year as an active salesperson

(B) complete the required educational course for broker
(C) work for one active broker or an owner-employer for one year as an active salesperson
(D) Both A and B are correct

78 Which of the following is (are) correct?
(I) If the first mortgage is paid off and satisfied, the second mortgage becomes the first (II) Both husband and wife must execute a satisfaction of mortgage when the mortgage is held in the husband's name only
(A) I only
(B) II only
(C) Both I and II
(D) Neither I nor II

79. Broker Alice and broker Bob formed a partnership to provide real estate services for others. Broker Alice converts funds and has her license suspended. Which applies?
(A) Listings held by the partnership have been terminated
(B) The partnership license has been canceled
(C) Salespeople working for the partnership should obtain a reissue of their license under a new employer if they desire to continue operating
(D) All of the above

80. A real estate salesperson wishes to incorporate to buy, develop, and sell real estate. Which of the following best applies?
(A) He must obtain a broker's license
(B) Re must register the corporation with the FREC
(C) No license is necessary
(D) Both A and B are correct

ANSWERS!

1. C	21. D	41. B	61. D
2. B	22. B	42. D	62. A
3. C	23. B	43. D	63. D
4. D	24. D	44. C	64. C
5. A	25. A	45. D	65. C
6. B	26. D	46. D	66. A
7. D	27. B	47. A	67. D
8. D	28. D	48. D	68. D
9. B	29. B	49. C	69. C
10. C	30. C	50. B	70. C
11. D	31. D	51. C	71. D
12. B	32. C	52. D	72. D
13. B	33. B	53. A	73. D
14. D	34. D	54. D	74. C
15. D	35. C	55. B	75. D
16. D	36. D	56. D	76. A
17. D	37. D	57. B	77. B
18. C	38. D	58. D	78. A
19. D	39. B	59. B	79. D
20. D	40. D	60. C	80. C

RESTAURATEUR, HOTELIER

American College of Hotel and Restaurant Management

There's not supposed to be an "n" in Restaurateur. It's French. We can charge more for this book that way.

With the food service industry expected to grow faster and steadier than just about anything else in the U.S. economy into the next century, it's no wonder that more and more people are entering culinary academies and restaurant schools to learn about catering, preparing food, serving food and wine, and managing a restaurant business. Systematic training in restaurant management is strongly recommended not only for those who are interested in seeking a managing position with an existing restaurant or other food service operation, but also—perhaps more importantly, considering whose nest egg may be on the line—for those who want to start their own business. That dream of running your own cozy little tapas bar can quickly go sour if you approach it too naively, that is, merely as a romantic notion and not as a business endeavor. Nothing wrong with romance—it just won't cover the overhead.

Restaurant management programs typically stress not only such hard-core business details as cost control, labor laws, and marketing, but also knowledge which bears on all the other aspects of running a restaurant, such as cooking, dining room service, and wine service, storage, and purchasing. The American College of Hotel and Restaurant Management, which supplied the questions that follow, has courses in all those areas and more—business law, computer technology, and conversational French (so you don't embarrass yourself when offering the customer an *hors d'oeuvre chaud*). As you might guess from the name of the school, ACHRM also has programs in hotel management—another rapidly growing facet of the so-called "hospitality" industry. In fact, you may notice that there are some hotel-related questions sprinkled in with the restaurant ones, just to keep you on your toes. If you're interested in pursuing a study of hotel or restaurant management or in finding out more about the program, you can contact the American College of Hotel and Restaurant Management at 11336 Camarillo Street, North Hollywood, CA 91602, tel. (818) 505-9800.

Multiple Choice

1. The employees of which department are often in a better position to embezzle assets than most other employees?
   (A) The accounting department
   (B) The housekeeping department
   (C) The marketing department
   (D) The personnel department
   (E) The food and beverage department

2. In a well-run housekeeping department, of every dollar spent for floorcare
   (A) .30 goes for labor; .70 goes for equipment and chemicals
   (B) .10 goes for labor; .90 goes for equipment and chemicals
   (C) .85 goes for labor; .15 goes for equipment and chemicals

3. In general, the most productive advertising for restaurants comes from listings in
   (A) local publications
   (B) national publications
   (C) airline publications
   (D) travel guides

4. As the inventory turnover rate decreases for a food and beverage operation
   (A) stock-outs are more likely to occur
   (B) more money is being invested in inventory
   (C) guests may become dissatisfied
   (D) cash becomes available for other purposes

5. If a hotel sold 240 rooms, and the income from room sales equaled $10,636.00, the daily rate would be
   (A) $43.42
   (B) $143.28
   (C) $23.44
   (D) $44.32

6. Which of the following types of chemical poisonings is controlled by washing all fruits and vegetables to be used fresh?
   (A) Lead poisoning
   (B) Copper poisoning
   (C) Antimony poisoning
   (D) Zinc and cadmium poisoning
   (E) Ptomaine poisoning

7. The dollar value used to calculate inventory turnover is taken from the
   (A) requisitions
   (B) physical inventory
   (C) receiving clerk's daily reports
   (D) perpetual inventory

8. An in-house document used by small properties to record informal orders is a
   (A) purchase order
   (B) purchase record
   (C) purchase requisition
   (D) storeroom requisition

9. Which is a major factor in quality grading of beef?
   (A) Amount of marbling
   (B) Outside fat covering
   (C) Conformation of the animal
   (D) Aging of the beef
   (E) Color of the meat

10. The way to find the number of rooms to be cleaned is by
    (A) consulting room attendants' schedules
    (B) doing morning room check
    (C) consulting rooms division
    (D) reviewing the invoices

11. The phrase "X the machine" refers to
    (A) indicating to the manager that the machine needs to be replaced
    (B) replacing smaller bills for larger denominations
    (C) returning the cash register tally to a zero balance
    (D) interfacing the cash register with the companion precheck register
    (E) reading the amount of sale rung on the machine without returning the balance to zero

12. Which of these usually includes three meals a day?
    (A) South American Plan
    (B) American Plan
    (C) European Plan
    (D) Neopolitan Plan
    (E) Family Plan

13. Differentiated marketing means
    (A) positioning a firm in the largest market segment
    (B) trying to attract all market segments
    (C) developing concepts positioned in each marketing segment
    (D) presenting unique, innovative advertising
    (E) learning how to shop for the best prices

14. Which of the following records are to be kept in Housekeeping?
    (A) employee driving records
    (B) invoices for chef's supplies
    (C) lost and found; room histories
    (D) room status
    (E) check-in status

15. The best prospects for direct mail campaigns are
    (A) lists developed by mail houses
    (B) people who have made inquiries
    (C) people recommended by former guests
    (D) former guests
    (E) friends and families of employees

16. The hotel assures the guest that a room will be held until the guest's arrival or check-out time the next day if the guest holds a
    (A) guaranteed reservation
    (B) nonguaranteed reservation
    (C) nonguaranteed confirmed reservation
    (D) confirmed acknowledgment
    (E) same-day acknowledgment

17. Which of the following is an unacceptable method for thawing frozen foods?
    (A) under cold running water
    (B) under refrigeration
    (C) as part of a conventional cooking process
    (D) at room temperature

18. The details of the order placed with a supplier are contained on the
    (A) menu
    (B) food sample data sheet
    (C) standard purchase specification
    (D) information request sheet

19. Pork and pork products are potentially hazardous foods and must reach a minimum internal temperature of _____ during cooking.
    (A) 165°F/75°C
    (B) 150°F/66°C
    (C) 140°F/60°C
    (D) 130°F/54°C
    (E) It doesn't really matter as long as you cook it for 15 minutes or more

20. All of the following information would typically be found on a wine bottle label EXCEPT
    (A) varietal labeling
    (B) name of winery
    (C) vintage date
    (D) type of wine
    (E) blending process

21. A theme weekend is a
    (A) self-contained promotion
    (B) merchandising technique
    (C) full destination promotion
    (D) trip to an amusement park
    (E) none of the above

22. Budgeting exact amounts for promotional spending should be based on
    (A) an established percentage of income
    (B) industry averages
    (C) the job to be done
    (D) the cost of the marketing staff's salaries
    (E) a percentage of the profits

23. The type of hotel that features guest accommodations which consist of a separate bedroom and living room is called a
    (A) resort hotel
    (B) commercial hotel
    (C) business hotel
    (D) suite hotel
    (E) executive hotel

24. Fresh fish should have all of the following traits EXCEPT
    (A) sunken eyes
    (B) elastic flesh
    (C) red gills
    (D) tight scales

25. Seat turnover is calculated by dividing the number of customers who are served in a meal period by
    (A) the number of hours in the meal period
    (B) the number of seats available
    (C) the number of service employees which have been used
    (D) the number of income dollars which have been generated
    (E) the number of employees working

True or False

1. _____Planning and controlling are two of the functional concepts of management

2. _____The possibility of rebooking a convention into a given property or area is in direct relationship to customer satisfaction

3. _____Housekeeping involves management of people, equipment, and supplies; preservation of building, finishes, fabrics, and furnishings; controlling costs

4. _____Since not all crime is preventable, a security program should stress the apprehension of criminals over the prevention of crimes

5. _____Two goals of the hotel's sales promotion effort are to attract more people from the existing market and to motivate new people to try the property's services

6. _____The way a menu looks is more important than the way it is worded

7. _____The process of accounting involves recording, classifying, and summarizing financial information

8. _____There is little relationship between the extent to which employees are involved and whether or not they are motivated to better perform work

9. _____The primary reason many supervisors are ineffective relates to problems with communications

10. _____The hospitality market must be identified before the product image can be developed

11. _____The marketing concept proposes that customer satisfaction is the means to increasing profits

12. _____Satisfying hunger and thirst are the only reasons a guest visits a dining service operation

13. _____Dining room managers are rarely seen by the guests

14. _____If a guest becomes angry during the complaint handling process, the desk clerk should try to match the guest's level of anger

15. _____A key control system is essential to the security of any hotel

16. _____In order to maintain guest relations, the manager should train the host/hostess to underestimate the length of waiting time when guests' names are placed on a waiting list

17. _____If a credit card company will not allow credit to its cardholder, the front desk clerk should immediately summon the local police to the hotel

ANSWERS !☛

Multiple Choice

1. E
2. C
3. A
4. B
5. D
6. A
7. B
8. B
9. A
10. B
11. E
12. B
13. C
14. C
15. D
16. A
17. D
18. D
19. B
20. E
21. A
22. C
23. D
24. A
25. A

True or False

1. T
2. T
3. T
4. T
5. T
6. F
7. T
8. F
9. T
10. T
11. T
12. F
13. F
14. F
15. T
16. F
17. F

SECURITIES

Securities Training Corporation

"But where are the customers' yachts?"

T he securities and commodities industries are governed by specific regulatory bodies. These include the Securities and Exchange Commission (SEC) and the National Association of Securities Dealers (NASD) for securities and the Commodities Futures Trading Commission (CFTC) for commodities. These agencies require the registration of individuals whose jobs involve interaction with the public and those involved in supervision and management of brokerage activities.

In order to obtain registration, an individual must pass a qualification examination. These examinations are divided into two areas: registered representative examinations and principal examinations. The registered representative examinations are for those individuals involved in selling or trading securities or commodities and the principal examinations are for those involved with supervision and management.

These examinations require extensive preparation on the part of the individual. The most efficient way to prepare for these exams is to enroll in a training program designed for the specific exam that must be taken.

The questions that follow were provided by Securities Training Corporation, which offers a wide range of programs to prepare individuals for the various securities and financial industry examinations. Each STC program is available on a classroom or correspondence basis. STC has its headquarters in New York City and has branch offices in San Francisco, California, Fort Lauderdale, Florida, Chicago, Illinois, and Minneapolis, Minnesota. For a schedule of classes and information on in-house programs, you may contact the STC office nearest you or call (800) STC-1223.

1. Two customers ask their account executive to combine an odd-lot order for each of them. They want the orders combined into one round lot of 100 shares and entered on one order ticket in order to save the odd-lot differential. This:
   (A) would require approval of only one of the customers
   (B) would require the approval of both of the customers
   (C) would require approval of the NYSE
   (D) cannot be done

2. An order entered with a brokerage firm will be processed in which order of priorities?
   I.   Cashier's department
   II. Margin department
   III. Purchase and sale (P&S) department
   IV. Wire room (order department)

   (A) I, II, III, and IV
   (B) I, III, II, and IV
   (C) IV, III, II, and I
   (D) II, III, I, and IV

3. The basic difference between an open-end investment company and closed-end investment company is:
   (A) the capitalization of the investment companies
   (B) how the net asset value is computed
   (C) the type of stocks purchased by these investment companies
   (D) the type of bonds purchased by these investment companies

4. How long after a new issue is registered for sale will it be shown on the NASDAQ system?
   (A) On the effective date
   (B) 10 days after the effective date
   (C) 30 days after the effective date
   (D) 45 days after the effective date

5. A customer wishes to create a spread position. This transaction must be executed
   (A) in the cash account
   (B) in the margin account
   (C) as two separate transactions, with the long position in the cash account and the short position in the margin account
   (D) as two separate transactions, with the short position in the cash account and the long position in the margin account

6. Each of the following broker-dealers are violating Rule 15c3-1 except
   (A) a clearing broker-dealer with aggregate indebtedness of $500,000 and net capital of $34,000
   (B) a clearing broker-dealer with aggregate indebtedness of $280,000 and net capital of $20,000
   (C) a fully disclosed broker-dealer with aggregate indebtedness of $16,000 and net capital of $4,000
   (D) a fully disclosed broker-dealer with aggregate indebtedness of $80,000 and net capital of $5,000

7. Which of the following broker-dealers is in violation of Rule 15c3-1?

   I.   Clearing broker-dealer also doing best efforts underwriting with aggregate indebtedness of $100,000 and net capital of $12,000

   II.   Fully disclosed broker-dealer in his first year of operation with aggregate indebtedness of $80,000 and net capital of $8,000

   III.   Broker-dealer handling only mutual funds and variable annuities plus an occasional trade for his own account with no aggregate indebtedness and net capital of $3,000

   (A) II only
   (B) I and II
   (C) III only
   (D) I, II, and III

8. A broker-dealer has a common stock position totaling $50,000. If there are two market-makers in the security, the amount of the haircut is:
   (A) $50,000
   (B) $25,000
   (C) $20,000
   (D) $15,000

9. Fails to deliver for common stock are subject to a haircut if they are
   (A) 5 days or more old
   (B) 10 days or more old
   (C) 15 days or more old
   (D) 30 days or more old

10. A broker-dealer has an aged fail to deliver for a common stock totaling $20,000. The haircut is
    (A) $2,000
    (B) $3,000
    (C) $5,000
    (D) $6,000

11. A trader has a regulated futures account and a securities account at a member firm. The trader receives a margin call in his securities account. There is excess equity in his regulated futures account. The member firm in this case

    I.   could transfer the money from the regulated futures account to the securities account unless the customer gave specific instructions that this could not be done

    II.   could not transfer money from the regulated futures account to the securities account even if the customer requests that this be done

    III.   could make the transfer only by obtaining written consent from the customer each time a transfer is to be made

    IV.   could make the transfer if the customer has signed an agreement that authorizes the firm to make such transfers from the regulated futures account to the securities account

    (A) I and II
    (B) II and III
    (C) III and IV
    (D) I and IV

12. The term "demand elasticity" refers to a situation whereby
    (A) a change in the price will result in a change in the amount of the commodity that is produced
    (B) a change in the price will result in a change in the amount of the commodity that is purchased
    (C) a shortage of the cash commodity will result in a greater production in the future
    (D) the amount of the commodity that is in storage exceeds the amount that is currently being purchased

13. An exporter of soybean oil can effectively hedge against all of the following *except*
    (A) increases in the cost of soybeans
    (B) decreases in the demand for soybean oil leading to falling prices
    (C) fluctuations in the foreign exchange rates in the countries where he sells his product
    (D) increases in ocean freight rates

14. If the price of near futures is below the price of deferred futures and a spreader thinks the spread will narrow, he will buy the near month and sell the deferred month.
    (A) True
    (B) False

15. Included in the term "offer" or "offer to sell" are all of the following except
    (A) a solicitation to buy a security for value
    (B) a solicitation to sell a security for value
    (C) a gift of nonassessable securities
    (D) an offer or attempt to dispose of a security for value

16. A client is in a low tax bracket and desires a conservative investment strategy. The agent recommends the purchase of a municipal bond. This recommendation would be considered
    (A) too risky
    (B) unsuitable
    (C) suitable
    (D) fraud

17. As an agent, which of the following is prohibited?
    (A) Stating facts relating to material inside information to a client
    (B) Stating facts relating to material in a final prospectus to a client
    (C) Stating facts relating to a firm's current financial statements to a client
    (D) Stating facts relating to a market letter published by your firm to a client

18. Which of the following would be considered a prohibited business practice?
    (A) Giving a quote for a security that is not the current market price
    (B) Soliciting orders for unregistered nonexempt securities
    (C) Creating transactions that give the misleading appearance of active trading in a security
    (D) All of the above

19. An "agent" would be considered:
    I.   a trust company, bank, or any savings institution
    II. a sales assistant authorized to accept customer orders
    III. any person other than a broker-dealer who acts on behalf of a broker-dealer or issuer in effecting sales or purchases of securities
    (A) I, II, and III
    (B) III only
    (C) II only
    (D) II and III only

20. An investor writes one XYZ April 35 call at 18½ and buys one XYZ April 40 call at 14¼. XYZ is selling at 50. If the investor does not own XYZ stock, the amount of cash he must deposit would be
    (A) $75.00
    (B) $500.00
    (C) $2,600.00
    (D) $4,025.00

21. An investor has sold stock short at 60. The current market price of the stock is 40 and the investor believes the stock will recover somewhat before going lower. He should
    (A) buy a put
    (B) buy a call
    (C) write a call
    (D) write a straddle

22. An investor who receives a maintenance call may do all of the following *except*
    (A) deposit cash
    (B) deposit stock with a loan value equal to the call
    (C) liquidate the position on which he is getting the call
    (D) request an extension if he has a valid reason

23. A customer who wishes to purchase securities in a restricted margin account
    (A) must deposit payment in advance
    (B) must deposit payment by the next business day
    (C) must deposit payment within the time prescribed for regular-way margin purchases, which is seven business days
    (D) may not purchase securities in a restricted margin account

24. The opening of a discretionary account requires which of the following documentation?
    I.   Written authorization
    II. A limited power of attorney
    III. A full power of attorney
    IV. An account agreement

    (A) I only
    (B) I and IV
    (C) I, II, and IV
    (D) I, III, and IV

ANSWERS! ☞

1. (B). Odd-lot orders on the NYSE can be combined into one round-lot to save the ⅛-point odd-lot differential. The order is entered as one round-lot but each customer will receive a separate odd-lot confirmation. However, this requires the approval of both of the customers.

2. (C). When an order is entered by a customer, it is processed first in the wire room or order room, then in the P&S department, then the margin department, and then the cashier's department.

3. (A). The basic difference between an open-end and closed-end investment company is the capitalization. An open-end investment company can issue only common stock, whereas a closed-end investment company (like a corporation) may issue common stock, preferred stock, and bonds.

4. (A). A new issue will appear on the NASDAQ system on the effective date of the issue. The effective date, which is determined by the SEC upon completion of the registration process, is the first date that the securities may be sold to the public.

5. (B). Spread positions are executed in the margin account. A spread position is created when a customer simultaneously buys and sells the same class of option on the same underlying stock with different series.

6. (A). A broker-dealer must maintain a minimum dollar amount of net capital, depending upon the nature of his business, or a minimum percentage (1/8th or 1/15th of his aggregate indebtedness), whichever is greater.

   The broker-dealer in answer (A) is a clearing firm and therefore requires $25,000. 1/15th of his aggregate indebtedness is $33,333. As he has $34,000, he is in compliance with the rule.

The clearing broker-dealer in answer (B) has only $20,000 of net capital. As he requires a minimum of $25,000, he is in violation of the rule by $5,000.

   The broker-dealer in answer (C) is operating on a fully disclosed basis and therefore requires a minimum net capital of $5,000. As he has only $4,000 of net capital, he is in violation of the rule by $1,000.

   The broker-dealer in answer (D) is operating on a fully disclosed basis and requires a minimum net capital of $5,000, which he has. However, his aggregate indebtedness is $80,000. 1/15th of the aggregate indebtedness equals $5,333. Therefore, he is in violation of the rule by $333.

7. (B). The broker-dealer in answer (I) is a clearing firm and therefore requires a minimum net capital of $25,000. Therefore, as his net capital is only $12,000, he is in violation of the rule by $13,000.

   The broker-dealer in answer (II) is in his first year of operation. His aggregate indebtedness may not exceed 800% (8 times) his capital. As his net capital is $8,000, he may not have aggregate indebtedness exceeding $64,000.

   The broker-dealer in answer (III) is in compliance with the rule as he requires a minimum net capital of $2,500.

8. (C). The haircut on common stock is 30%. However, common stock that has a "limited market" is subject to a higher haircut. A limited market exists when there are less than three market makers in an over-the-counter security. In this case, the haircut is 40%.

9. and 10.   The correct answer for question 9 is (A) and for 10 (D). Fails to deliver represent an asset of a broker-dealer. They represent the dollar value of securities that the broker-dealer owes to another broker-dealer but has not yet delivered. This might

occur because he sold stock short or because he sold stock for a customer and the customer has not yet delivered the stock. When the stock is delivered, the broker-dealer will receive cash equal to the sales price.

If a broker-dealer has fails to deliver for common stock that are over four days old, he is required to treat the stock as he would treat stock that he owned in his own investment or trading account. As common stock is subject to a 30% haircut, the same haircut would apply to fails to deliver that are over four days old.

In question 10, the haircut of 30% on stock with a value of $20,000 would equal $6,000.

11. (C). Transfers from a regulated commodities account to a securities account may be accomplished only if the customer specifically requests that a transfer be made or if he signs the transfer consent form authorizing that such transfers be made automatically.

12. (B). The term "demand elasticity" describes a condition where changes in price will cause changes in the amount purchased. As the price rises, purchases decrease; as the price declines, purchases increase.

The term "supply elasticity" describes a condition where changes in price will cause changes in the amount produced. As the price rises, production increases; as the price declines, production decreases.

13. (D). A user of soybeans may hedge against an increase in the cost of soybeans by the purchase of soybean futures. A producer of soybean oil can hedge against falling prices by the sale of soybean futures. An individual who fears a devaluation of a foreign country's currency may hedge that country's currency in the futures market. However, it is not possible to hedge against increases in freight rates as there are no transportation futures.

14. (A). If a spreader anticipates that a spread will narrow, he will always buy the lower-priced futures and sell the higher-priced futures.

15. (C). An "offer" or an "offer to sell" is any attempt to buy or sell a security for value. A gift of nonassessable securities would not be considered a sale or an offer to sell. Nonassessable means there are no tax ramifications upon disposal. A gift of a security to a charitable organization would be nonassessable.

16. (B). Recommending the purchase of a municipal bond to an investor in a low tax bracket would not be suitable since the federal tax exemption on municipal bond interest income would not have a significant impact on the investor's overall tax liability. Corporate bonds with higher yields would be more advantageous to investors in lower tax brackets.

17. (A). An agent is prohibited from relating material inside information to anyone except his immediate supervisor.

18. (D). All of the choices listed would be considered a prohibited business practice.

19. (D). Authorized sales assistants and individuals who effect transactions for broker-dealers or issuers (normally charging a commission) are considered to be agents.

20. (A). On a call spread, no margin is required if the long position expires at the same or a later date than the short position and the long position has the same or a lower exercise price. If the long position has a higher exercise price, margin is required.

In this question, the long position expires at the same time as the short position and has a higher exercise price. The margin requirement is therefore the difference between the exercise prices ($500) or the margin on the short position, whichever is lower. The short position is in-the-money by $1,500. The margin requirement on the short call is 15% of the market price of $5,000 ($750) plus the premium of $1,850, which totals $2,600. The difference in exercise prices is $500. Therefore, the lower margin requirement of $500 is required. The total dash requirement would be computed as follows:

Margin on the short position:	500.00
Plus premium on long position:	1425.00
	1925.00
Minus premium received on short position:	1850.00
Total cash requirement:	75.00

21. (B). The stock is currently trading at 40 and the investor thinks the price will rise. An investor who is bullish on an underlying stock will buy a call.

22. (D). A maintenance call (as opposed to a Regulation T call) may be met with any type of deposit. A liquidation is also permitted in the case of a maintenance call. The member firm is not required to freeze the account. The only time that the member firm must freeze an account is when an investor liquidates a position to meet an initial Regulation T call, not a maintenance call. An extension may not be requested for a maintenance call, which must be met promptly.

23. (C). A restricted margin account is one in which the equity is below the Regulation T margin requirement. For example, on 50% margin, if an investor has securities with a market value of $10,000 and a debit balance of $6,000, his equity is $4,000. This is less than the Regulation T minimum. There are no penalties associated with a restricted account. An investor could make a new purchase and would be required to deposit cash within the prescribed time in the same manner as a purchase in a nonrestricted account.

24. (C). In order to open a discretionary account, the member firm requires written authorization from the customer granting limited power of attorney to the person exercising discretion. The limited power of attorney grants the person power to buy and sell securities without reference to the customer. An account agreement is required for any type of account that a member firm opens.

STATE TROOPER & RANGER

State Civil Service Commissions

She: "May I see your license and registration, please, sir?"

You (thinking): "What is a good-looking young woman doing in this job where she has to wear that funny-looking hat?" (aloud) "But, Officer . . ."

She: "72 in a 55-mile zone."

You (thinking): "She's right." (aloud) "I must have taken my mind off it for a minute."

She: "The car you're driving weighs over one ton; that's a pretty dangerous weapon to take your mind off of."

You (thinking): "Now what'll I do? I can't afford the points. Maybe, just maybe . . ." (aloud) "When do you get off?"

She: "Exit 16, State Police Barracks, where I'm meeting my buddy. He wears a funny hat just like this one. Wait in your car while I call you in and write it up."

You: "Yes, Officer."

E xaminations for state trooper and ranger candidates vary somewhat from state to state. The questions that follow are representative of those asked in many different states, all of which seek to determine how well an applicant will react to the spectrum of skills the job demands. The questions we have selected test familiarity with criminal procedures that normally fall within the state trooper's domain, as well as more general judgment and reasoning ability. We have left out reading comprehension and reporting questions, even though they could probably be encountered in an actual state trooper exam, because TV cops neglect to mention that aspect of their work. Trashing overpowered sheetmetal, yes. Licking pencil-tips while trying to spell p-e-r-p-e-t-r-a-t-o-r, no.

State civil service regulations govern the appointment of state police officers. Information about specific entrance requirements may be obtained from state civil service commissions or state police headquarters, usually located in each state capital Candidates must pass a competitive examination and meet physical and personal qualifications (see Michigan Physical Skills Test at the end of this exam). It ain't all legs, Jane.

In all states, recruits enter a formal training program for several months. They receive classroom instruction in state laws and jurisdictions, and they study procedures for accident investigation, patrol, and traffic control. Recruits learn to use guns, defend themselves from attack, handle an automobile at high speeds, give first aid, and avoid having to get it.

Police officer recruits serve a probationary period ranging from 6 months to 3 years. After a specified length of time, officers become eligible for promotion. Most states have merit promotion systems that require officers to pass a competitive examination to qualify for the next highest rank. Although the organization of police forces varies by state, the typical avenue of advancement is from private to corporal, to sergeant, to first sergeant, to lieutenant, and then to captain. (See the "POLICE PROMOTION" section of this book.) Police officers who show administrative ability may be promoted to higher level jobs such as commissioner or director.

Good luck, Officer.

1. In taking a statement from a person who has been shot by an assailant and is not expected to live, State Troopers are instructed to ask the person: "Do you believe you are about to die?" Of the following, the most probable reason for this is
   (A) the theory that a person about to die and meet his Maker will tell the truth
   (B) to determine if the victim is conscious and capable of making a statement
   (C) to put the victim mentally at ease and more willing to talk
   (D) that the statement could not be used in court if his mind was distraught by the fear of impending death

2. Which of the following situations, if observed by you while on patrol, should you consider most suspicious and deserving of further investigation?
   (A) A shabbily dressed youth is driving a late model Buick
   (B) A 1968 Dodge has been parked without lights outside an apartment house for several hours
   (C) A light is on in the rear of a one-family luxurious residence
   (D) Two well-dressed men are standing at a bus stop at 2 A.M. and arguing heatedly

3. In one study it was found that attitude toward the law is approximately the same for children in all social and economic conditions whether in city environment or in rural communities and is but slightly different from that of adults. This finding serves most directly to indicate that
   (A) attitude toward the law is primarily a function of economic factors
   (B) persons who differ with regard to social and economic situation do not, in general, differ with regard to attitude toward the law
   (C) the only difference between children and adults is one of chronological age
   (D) social and economic conditions are environmental products
   (E) the attitude of adolescents toward the law is identical with that of adults

4. A TV crime program dramatized a different police case every week, showed the capture or death of the criminal and ended with the slogan "Crime Does Not Pay." It was found that a gang of teen-age boys listened to this program every week in order to see what mistake was made by the criminal, and then duplicated the crime, trying to avoid the same mistake. This case illustrates that
   (A) all criminal minds work the same way
   (B) attempts to keep young people out of crime by frightening them into obeying the law are not always successful
   (C) it is not possible to commit the perfect crime unless care is taken
   (D) crime programs should not be permitted as they lead to an increase in the number of unsolved crimes
   (E) most criminals learn from their own mistakes

5. A young man who was arrested for smashing a store window and stealing a portable radio was asked why he did it. He answered: "Well, I wanted a radio and I just took it." If this answer is characteristic of the behavior of the young criminal, it is most reasonable to believe that
   (A) the young criminal has a well-organized personality
   (B) he sizes up each new situation in terms of his past experience
   (C) his decision to commit a crime is made after careful consideration of its possible effect on his future
   (D) his temptation to commit a crime is an isolated situation, having, in his mind, little relation to his life as a whole
   (E) he hesitates to commit a crime unless he thinks he can get away with it

6. It is generally agreed that criminal tendencies are present in every person. A basic difference, however, between the normal person and the criminal is that the
   (A) normal person, sometimes, commits trivial crimes but the criminal commits crimes of a major nature
   (B) criminal is unable to understand the possible results of antisocial acts he commits
   (C) normal person is able to control his antisocial tendencies and direct his activity in socially approved channels
   (D) criminal believes that he is not different from the person who does not commit crimes
   (E) normal person believes that he is not different from the person who commits crimes

7. It has been claimed that a person who commits a crime sometimes has an unconscious wish to be punished, which is caused by strong unconscious feelings of guilt. The one of the following actions by a criminal which may be partly due to an unconscious desire for punishment is
   (A) claiming that he doesn't know anything about the crime when he is questioned by the police
   (B) running away from the state where he committed the crime
   (C) revisiting the place where he committed the crime
   (D) his care not to leave any clues at the scene of the crime
   (E) accusing someone else when he is captured by the police

8. An escaped prisoner has been wounded and is lying flat on his stomach with his head turned to one side. The one of the following directions from which a police officer should approach the prisoner in order to make it most difficult for the prisoner to fire quickly and accurately at the patrolman is from the side
   (A) directly behind the prisoner's head
   (B) facing the prisoner's face
   (C) facing the top of the prisoner's head
   (D) facing the prisoner's heels

9. A very accurate test by which an expert can determine the distance from a bullet hole at which a gun was fired is called the
   (A) alphanopthylamine test
   (B) diphenylamine test
   (C) benzodine test
   (D) photo-micrograph test

10. A State Police Officer is frequently advised to lie down before returning fire, if a person is shooting at him. This is primarily because
   (A) a smaller target will thus be presented to the assailant
   (B) he can return fire more quickly while in the prone position
   (C) the assailant will think he has struck the patrolman and cease firing
   (D) it will indicate that the patrolman is not the aggressor

11. A trooper observes several youths in the act of looting a gas station vending machine. The youths flee in several directions as he approaches, ignoring his order to halt. The trooper then shoots at them and they halt and are captured. The trooper's action was
   (A) right; it was the most effective way of capturing the criminals
   (B) wrong; extreme measures should not be taken in apprehending petty offenders
   (C) right; provided that there was no danger of shooting innocent bystanders
   (D) wrong; this is usually ineffective when more than one offender is involved
   (E) right; it is particularly important to teach juvenile delinquents respect for the law

12. The principal reason why the courts require that a confession be voluntary before it can be admitted as evidence is that
(A) confessions seldom reveal the whole truth
(B) the information contained in a confession cannot be corroborated by factual evidence
(C) confessions are at best only circumstantial evidence
(D) an involuntary confession constitutes a denial of a person's constitutional right to a fair trial

13. An officer who has been assigned to work with you has a receding chin. It is most probable that he will
(A) be much like the other men in your group
(B) lack will power to a marked degree
(C) be a very timid person
(D) constantly carry tales to you about the other officers

14. A certain committee found that over 90 percent of the murders in the United States are committed by use of pistols. It follows that
(A) almost all murders are caused by the possession of pistols
(B) 90 percent of murders can be eliminated by eliminating the sale and use of pistols
(C) the pistol is a mechanical aid to crime
(D) no information is available with regard to the way murders happen

15. The one of the following which is the most probable reason for the considerably increasing proportion of serious crimes committed by women is
(A) that the proportion of women in the population is increasing
(B) that greater supervision of women results in a greater number of arrests

(C) the success of women in achieving social equality with men
(D) the increasing number of crime stories in the movies and on television
(E) the increasing number of crime gangs in operation

16. It is well known that most criminals in the city
(A) belong to subversive organizations
(B) work at respectable jobs during the day
(C) are professionally trained
(D) come from crowded localities

17. Which of the following means of avoiding identification would be most likely to meet with success?
(A) growing a beard
(B) shaving off the beard if there was one originally
(C) burning the fingers so as to remove the fingerprints
(D) changing the features by facial surgery

18. "Social security cards are not acceptable proof of identification for police purposes." Of the following, the most important reason for this rule is that the social security card
(A) is easily obtained
(B) states on its face "for social security purposes - not for identification
(C) is frequently lost
(D) does not contain the address of the person
(E) does not contain a photograph, description, or fingerprints of the person

ANSWERS!

(See page 381)

PHYSICAL SKILLS PERFORMANCE

The Michigan Law Enforcement Officers Training Council, which is empowered to set employment standards for those entering the law enforcement field in the state of Michigan, has developed two examinations designed to test critical skills required of police officers.

One of the exams is a Reading and Writing Test. The other is a Physical Skills Test designed to measure the strength and agility required of police officers. We've reproduced a description of the Physical Skills Test below.

For more information about the pre-employment requirements of Michigan police candidates, write: Employment Standards Section, Michigan Law Enforcement Officers Training Council, 7426 N. Canal Road, Lansing, MI 48913.

Description of the Physical Skills Test

The pre-employment Physical Skills Test, which is conducted in a gymnasium, consists of six events. The events are:

(1) *Pushups:*
This is a standard pushup where the back and legs are kept straight. The event starts in the up position and the count occurs when the applicant returns to the up position, after having touched an audible beeper on the mat with his/her chest. The applicant is to do as many pushups as possible in sixty seconds.

(2) *Grip:*
Using a hand grip dynamometer, the applicant squeezes the meter while keeping the arm extended parallel to the leg. Both right and left grips are tested and recorded in kilograms of pressure.

(3) *Obstacle Course:*
The total distance for this obstacle course is 90 ft. and it is run for time. The applicant runs 20 ft., crawls 6 ft. through a 2 1/2-ft.-high simulated tunnel, runs 20 ft., climbs a 6 ft.-6 in. barrier with footholds and handholds. The applicant then runs 20 ft. to and around pylons, then back to the barrier which has footholds and handholds on it. After climbing the barrier a second time, the applicant runs 4 ft. to the stop position.

(4) *165-lb. Drag:*
The applicant drags a 165-lb. Life form dummy 30 ft. for time. The dummy is gripped under the arms and dragged backwards.

(5) *95-lb. Carry:*
The applicant lifts a 95-lb. Bag which has handholds and runs 30 ft. with it and places it on a 32-in.-high platform for time.

(6) *1/2-Mile Shuttle Run:*
The applicant runs between two pylons placed 88 ft. apart for a total of 15 round trips for time.

How To Score Your Performance

Raw scores for each event are converted to a scale of one to nine. The converted scores for each of the six events are then added together for a composite converted score. The 1986 conversion table for the physical performance evaluation follows. The minimum passing score is displayed below the table.

To score your performance, first locate the correct conversion table for your sex. For each of the six events you should find your score in each of the six columns, then look to the left in the row for your "converted score." For example, if you are a male and you did 37 pushups, you would find that you would receive a converted score of 6. You do this for each of the six events, then add up your six converted scores to determine your total converted score.

CONVERSION TABLE FOR
PHYSICAL SKILLS PERFORMANCE TEST

FEMALE

Converted Score	Pushups	Grip-total both hands (kilograms)	Obstacle Course (seconds)	165 lb. Drag (seconds)	95 lb. Carry (seconds)	½ Mile Run (minutes & seconds)	Converted Score
9	99	200	00.1	0.1	0.1	0:00.1	9
	27	88	14.1	6.5	4.4	4:08.1	
8	26	87	14.2	6.6	4.5	4:08.2	8
	21	81	15.6	7.1	4.8	4:22.9	
7	20	80	15.7	7.2	4.9	4:23.0	7
	17	75	16.8	8.0	5.4	4:37.6	
6	16	74	16.9	8.1	5.5	4:37.7	6
	12	69	18.6	8.9	6.3	4:54.7	
5	11	68	18.7	9.0	6.4	4:54.8	5
	8	62	21.4	10.2	8.2	5:17.1	
4	7	61	21.5	10.3	8.3	5:17.2	4
	5	57	25.5	12.3	11.9	5:42.2	
3	4	56	25.6	12.4	12.0	5:42.3	3
	3	50	30.5	14.6	17.7	6:12.6	
2	2	49	30.6	14.7	17.8	6:12.7	2
	2	43	39.1	18.7	24.9	6:45.7	
1	1	42	39.2	18.8	25.0	6:45.8	1
	1	1	59.9	59.9	59.9	9:59.9	
0	NP	NP	NP	NP	NP	NP	0

NP = Non-performance
Minimum Qualifying Score = 31 converted points

CONVERSION TABLE FOR
PHYSICAL SKILLS PERFORMANCE TEST

MALE

Converted Score	Pushups	Grip-total both hands (kilograms)	Obstacle Course (seconds)	165 lb. Drag (seconds)	95 lb. Carry (seconds)	½ Mile Run (minutes & seconds)	Converted Score
9	99	200	0.1	0.1	0.1	0:00.1	9
	61	140	10.6	4.1	2.9	3:27.9	
8	60	139	10.7	4.2	3.0	3:28.0	8
	51	131	11.1	4.5	3.1	3:35.6	
7	50	130	11.2	4.6	3.2	3:35.7	7
	44	123	11.7	4.7	3.3	3:43.2	
6	43	122	11.8	4.8	3.4	3:43.3	6
	37	115	12.4	5.1	3.5	3:53.3	
5	36	114	12.5	5.2	3.6	3:53.4	5
	30	106	13.4	5.6	3.8	4:06.5	
4	29	105	13.5	5.7	3.9	4:06.6	4
	25	97	14.5	6.1	4.0	4:19.9	
3	24	96	14.6	6.2	4.1	4:20.0	3
	20	90	16.0	6.5	4.4	4:36.8	
2	19	89	16.1	6.6	4.5	4:36.9	2
	15	82	18.0	7.2	4.9	4:57.5	
1	14	81	18.1	7.3	5.0	4:57.6	1
	1	1	59.9	59.9	59.9	9:59.9	
0	NP	NP	NP	NP	NP	NP	0

NP = Non-performance
Minimum Qualifying Score = 30 converted points

1. A
2. A
3. B
4. B
5. D
6. C
7. C
8. A
9. D
10. A
11. B
12. D
13. A
14. C
15. C
16. D
17. D
18. C

STUDENT vs. TEACHER CHALLENGE

Rutgers New Jersey Bowl

We do not recommend this quiz show format for daytime TV. Most educators without advanced degrees would be disqualified because they couldn't even understand the rules. For the students, though, brought up in the computer age, they were a snap. Have you ever tried to dope out a computer software manual?

The 1986 kickoff of the New Jersey Network's "Rutgers New Jersey Bowl" television quiz show featured a match between four students from past New Jersey Bowl championship high school teams and four award-winning high school teachers. The face-off ended in a resounding victory for the students, who, after a slow start, came from behind to overtake the teachers and win by a score of 220 to 105.

The Rutgers New Jersey Bowl, now in its eighth season, is a single elimination-style tournament consisting of 31 games that run from November into June. Every year, the kick-off show is a special event that is not part of the regular 31-part series. The first 30 episodes are a half-hour in length; the final is an hour long and is broadcast live in June.

The series is produced by Rutgers, the State University of New Jersey, in an effort to promote a sense of pride in the state's educational system and to reward academic excellence—in fact, the show is partially funded by the New Jersey Department of Higher Education. Todd Hunt, a communications professor at Rutgers, hosts the program. The series airs twice-weekly on New Jersey Network, the state's PBS-affiliate.

Thirty-two New Jersey high schools compete in the tournament each year. Each team consists of four members, an alternate, and a faculty advisor. Each of the four members of the championship team receives a $1,000 scholarship, made possible by New Jersey Power and Light Company, a local utility.

The questions that follow are from the 1986 special kick-off episode. The format of the show is roughly as follows: The first round consists of ten-point "toss-ups," that is, as each question is read by the quiz-show host, whichever team hits the buzzer first gets to try to answer it. If one team answers the question correctly, that team gets a "bonus opportunity," which means that it gets exclusive rights to an extra question. There is no penalty for answering a question incorrectly, but hitting the buzzer before the question is read through in its entirety means that important clues in the rest of the question might be missed. The second and third rounds are ten-point "challenge rounds," one for each of the two teams. In each challenge round, one team gets exclusive rights to the questions, but no discussion between team members is allowed. The reward for hitting the buzzer and answering the questions quickly is that the team gets the chance to answer more questions before the end of the round and thus rack up more points. The final round consists of 20-point toss-ups.

In the "Questions" section, we have just included the questions themselves. Turn to the "Answers" section for the correct answers, actual answers given by the contestants, and a running point tally.

Ten-Point Toss-ups with 20-Point Bonus Opportunities

1. What New Orleans-born author of *The Little Foxes* has crafted her dramatic work so as to speak out strongly for social justice?

    _____

2. There have been many attempts on the lives of U.S. presidents, but only four have been fatal. Name the four assassinated U.S. presidents.
    (1)_____
    (2)_____
    (3)_____
    (4)_____

3. Physical stress and stressful verbal interaction are key elements of a widely used method of personality alteration created in 1971 by Werner Erhard. What is its acronym name? _____

4. Some computer terms are acronyms, such as RAM for random access memory. In fact, some computer languages are acronyms themselves. For what do the computer acronyms BASIC and FORTRAN stand? _____
    _____
    _____

5. B. F. Skinner, the noted psychologist, could also be called the father of behaviorism. Identify these works by Skinner:
    (A) This 1948 utopian vision emphasizes operant behavior and instrumental conditioning _____
    (B) This 1971 work broadly applies the vision elaborated in (A) to the whole of culture _____

6. The U.S. has almost ⅓ of the world's known accessible coal reserves. Which nation currently produces the most coal annually? _____

7. Large airports are very busy places, serving thousands of passengers every day. Identify the cities near which the following airports are found:
    (A) Orly _____
    (B) Heathrow _____

8. She debuted as a director with the 1980 film *Fatso*. Her success as an actress can be measured by her Tony for *Two for the Seesaw* and her Tony-Oscar combination in stage and screen versions of *The Miracle Worker*. Name her. _____

Teacher's Challenge Round

9. It prohibited slavery north of latitude 36 degrees 30 minutes and admitted Maine as a free state. Name it. _____
    _____

10. The name of this sport is a curious condensation of the word "association." The game consists of two 45-minute halves of almost constant action between teams of 11 players each. Name the sport. _____

11. They were officially annexed by Israel on December 14, 1981. What two-word name is given to this territory captured in 1967 from Syria? _____

12. It has two heads but no arms. We, however, have one in each of our arms and it allows us to turn a doorknob. What is this important flexor muscle, whose name means "two-headed"? _____

13. *The Diary of Anne Frank* is one of the most touching and inspiring documents to come out of World War II. In what country did Frank live? _____

14. In Europe in 1870, at the outbreak of the Franco-Prussian War, she volunteered to work at the front for the International Red Cross. It took her 11 years, but she finally received presidential authorization to establish the American National Red Cross. Who was this "angel of the battle-fields"? _____

15. They called her box-office poison in 1938 because of her stiff manner, but already she had won the Academy Award for her performance in *Morning Glory*. She went on to win three more Oscars, most recently for Best Actress in "*On Golden Pond*." What is the name of this actress?

_____

16. Its weekly circulation is over five million. Founded in 1926, it has reached the top of its class by emphasizing sensational and off-beat stories. Identify this national tabloid newspaper. _____

_____

17. In 1903, this Russian physiologist won the Nobel Prize for his investigation of conditioned reflexes. What was the name of this famous scientist? _____

Student's Challenge Round

18. When the Yankee Clipper retired from baseball, the Yankees retired his number. Who was this legendary player?

_____

19. After 1965, he became an increasingly vocal critic of the Vietnam War and was the 1972 presidential nominee of the People's Party. His name? _____

_____

20. Patient Randle Patrick McMurphy fights a guerrilla campaign against Nurse Ratched in this 1962 novel by Ken Kesey. What is the title of the novel?_____

_____

21. Established as a singer, he showed himself a gifted comic actor in the "Road" film series with Bob Hope. His name?

_____

22. Believing that the key to most psychoses lies in the personal and collective consciousness, this psychologist broke from the theory of his teacher Sigmund Freud. Who was he? _____

23. The body constantly renews itself through two energy processes. Anabolism is the process of replacing old compounds and making new ones; catabolism is the process of breaking down compounds to free energy. Anabolism and catabolism are two subdivisions of what overall process?

_____

24. He was born on August 29, 1923 in Cambridge, England, the son of a historian. He made his first stage appearance in 1941 in O'Neill's *Ah! Wilderness,* and his film debut the next year in Noel Coward's *In Which We Serve.* As a director, among his first big successes was *A Bridge Too Far,* which shares its antiwar theme with his biggest success, *Gandhi.* Name him.

   _____

25. In Shakespeare's *Julius Caesar*, Brutus addresses the crowd, "Romans, countrymen, and lovers." How does Mark Anthony begin *his* address?_____

   _____

26. On a musical score, it instructs the musician to play the notes of a chord in rapid succession rather than simultaneously. Name this Italian word. _____

27. Many of the signers of the Declaration of Independence were in their 30s or 40s when they autographed that revolutionary document, but one signer was 70 years old. Who was he?

   _____

28. The growth process of common fungus forms enzymes, which makes it useful for making bread rise. What fungus are we talking about? _____

20-Point Toss-ups

29. In 1984 in *The Adventures of Buckaroo Banzai Across the Eighth Dimension*, he played the evil Dr. Emilio Lazardo. His name? _____

30. Everything is bigger in Texas. In terms of population, what is the largest city in Texas? _____

31. Newark-born Joseph Levitch is well known for his charity work and for dozens of films including *Boeing-Boeing* and *Three on a Couch.* By what name is he usually known? _____

ANSWERS!☞

[Note: Jumps in the sequence and unaccounted-for points indicate visual, audio, or spelling questions we have left out.]

Ten-Point Toss-ups with 20-Point Bonus Opportunities

1. Lillian Hellman
   Answered correctly by teachers. Score: teachers 10, students 0

Teacher's Bonus:
2. Garfield, Kennedy, Lincoln, McKinley
   First three answered correctly by teachers. Score: teachers 25, students 0

3. EST
   Answered correctly by teachers. Score: teachers 35, students 0

Teacher's Bonus:
4. (A) Beginner's All-purpose Symbolic Instructional Code
   (B) Formula Translation
   (B) answered correctly by teachers. Score: teachers 45, students 0

Student's Bonus:
5. (A) *Walden Two*
   (B) *Beyond Freedom and Dignity*
   (A) answered correctly by students. Score: teachers 45, students 20.

Student's Bonus:
6. the Soviet Union
   Answered correctly by students. Score: students 50, teachers 45

Student's Bonus:
7. (A) Paris
   (B) London
   Answered correctly by students. Score: students 80, teachers 45.

8. Anne Bancroft
   Answered incorrectly by students ("Patty Duke Astin"). No score change.

Teacher's Challenge Round

9. the Missouri Compromise
   Answered incorrectly by teachers ("the Mason-Dixon Line"). No score change.

10. soccer
    Answered incorrectly by teachers ("football"). No score change.

11. the Golan Heights
    Answered incorrectly by teachers ("West Bank"). No score change.

12. bicep
    No answer by teachers. No score change.

13. the Netherlands
    Answered incorrectly by teachers ("France"). No score change.

14. Clara Barton
    Answered incorrectly by teachers ("Florence Nightingale"). No score change.

15. Katherine Hepburn
    Answered correctly by teachers. Score: students 80, teachers 65.

16. *The National Enquirer*
    Answered correctly by teachers. Score: students 80, teachers 75.

17. Ivan Pavlov
    Answered correctly by teachers. Score: teachers 85, students 80.

End of Teachers' Challenge Round.

Student's Challenge Round

18. Joe DiMaggio
    Answered incorrectly by students
    ("Rizzuto"). No score change.

19. Dr. Benjamin Spock
    Answered incorrectly by students
    ("George McGovern"), who buzzed
    before the host read the information that
    this candidate was from the People's
    Party. No score change.

20. *One Flew Over the Cuckoo's Nest*
    Answered correctly by students. Score:
    students 100, teachers 85.

21. Bing Crosby
    Answered correctly by students. Score:
    students 110, teachers 85.

22. Carl Jung
    Answered correctly by students. Score:
    students 120, teachers 85.

23. metabolism
    Answered correctly by students. Score:
    students 130, teachers 85.

24. Sir Richard Attenborough
    Answered incorrectly by students ("Ben
    Kingsley"). No score change.

25. "Friends, Romans, countrymen"
    Answered correctly by students. Score:
    students 140, teachers 85.

26. arpeggio
    Answered correctly by students. Score:
    students 150, teachers 85.

27. Benjamin Franklin
    Answered correctly by students. Score:
    students 160, teachers 85.

28. yeast
    Answered correctly by students. Score:
    students 170, teachers 85.

End of Students' Challenge Round.

20-Point Toss-ups

29. John Lithgow
    Answered correctly by students. Score:
    students 200, teachers 85.

30. Houston
    Answered correctly by teachers. Score:
    students 220, teachers 105.

31. Jerry Lewis
    No time for answer.

End of game.
Final score: students 220, teachers 105.

TAXI DRIVER

New York City Taxi and Limousine Commission

New Yorkers take pride in knowing what is going on and where it is happening at its best. Getting there, however, is not easy in a town whose street layout has been evolving since the mid-seventeenth century, whose natives rank with the most impatient in the history of the world, whose population nearly doubles in two hours every weekday morning, and whose citizens consider themselves to be either too important or too smart to have to obey its traffic laws

For many immigrants to the United States, driving a cab for a New York taxi fleet owner is one of the early jobs they can get. Full fluency in English is not a requirement, though a working knowledge is. In fact, a stiffer and more appropriate language comprehension test was recently developed in response to complaints from riders that drivers often did not understand their directions. Now an applicant for a T.L.C. license (Taxi and Limousine Commission, in case your eyebrows just shot upward) listens to a tape which states addresses, then circles matching addresses on a list. Only about 10 percent of applicants fail. Prior to this an applicant had only to read and orally explain a written rule to the satisfaction of the examiners. It is not true that applicants were required to develop a Brooklyn accent.

In order to maintain certain standards in the industry, the T.L.C. also requires applicants to attend a course at one of two Taxi Driver Institutes in the New York City area, and to pass an exam that tests students' knowledge of the city's geography and of the T.L.C. Rules Guide. The course, for which an applicant currently pays $75, is open-ended. A student must attend 20 hours' worth of instruction but may continue to attend for as long as necessary to acquire the knowledge necessary to pass the test. Since the purpose of the exam is not to weed out applicants, the 10 to 12 percent of the students who fail the exam have the chance to retake it whether or not they choose to attend the course again. About 4000 students attend each of the two institutes annually.

Should you possess rapier skills in the verbal come-back and put-down, have a command of expletives in at least two languages, have inherited the gene necessary for infinite patience, know your right hand from your left, and be able to make change, you might consider this career. Those who are serious about it should write to: New York Taxi Driver Institute, do Federation Employment and Guidance Service, I 14 Fifth Avenue, New York NY 10011.

Rules and Regulations

1. Which statement is wrong?
   (A) A driver shall not smoke if the passenger so requests.
   (B) A driver shall not operate a taxi while his driving ability is impaired either by alcohol or drugs.
   (C) A driver shall not turn his "Off Duty" light on within the first 8 hours of his shift.
   (D) A driver shall not permit any other person to use the driver's taxicab driver's license.

2. A passenger requests to go to the World Trade Center. On the way downtown, he asks the driver to pick up a friend at a comedy club on University Place. The driver should
   (A) double the fare on the meter for the trip to the World Trade Center.
   (B) pick up the second passenger only if no waiting is involved.
   (C) pick up the passenger's friend.
   (D) explain' to the passenger that pick-ups are not permitted by the TLC.

3. It is the end of the day. The driver is returning to the garage and has entered the time, place, and reason for going off duty on his Trip Record. Re has his "Off Duty" sign on and has locked the rear doors. He stops for a red light and someone asks for a ride in the opposite direction. The driver must
   (A) accept the fare but leave the meter off
   (B) accept the fare with the meter on
   (C) refuse the fare
   (D) accept the fare but charge an extra $1.00 for the inconvenience

4. Which situation is not a good reason for refusing a fare?
   (A) Another passenger is already in the taxi
   (B) Neither the passenger nor the driver knows how to get to the destination
   (C) A hail from another prospective passenger has already been acknowledged

   (D) A radio-dispatched call has been accepted and the driver has illuminated the "On Radio Call" sign and made the appropriate entry

5. A driver is taking a passenger to Nassau County. Which of the following is true?
   (A) The driver and passenger must settle on a price before starting the trip
   (B) The passenger is required to pay double
   (C) The passenger is required to pay the fare showing on the meter when the taxi reaches the City line and double the fare after
   (D) The passenger is required to pay what is on the meter at the end of the trip

6. A taxi driver may refuse to take a passenger to Westchester or Nassau counties
   (A) if the passenger refuses to pay the return trip
   (B) if the passenger does not accept a flat rate
   (C) whenever he wants
   (D) if he has already been driving for eight or more hours

7. A driver at LaGuardia Airport is waiting on a taxi line for over two hours When he finally reaches the head of the line, the P.A dispatcher gives him a passenger who only wants to go to the next terminal building. The driver
   (A) may refuse the fare and ask for the next passenger going to Manhattan
   (B) must accept the fare
   (C) may refuse the fare but must then leave the airport
   (D) may refuse the fare and go back to the end of the line

Geography

1. The water crossing that does not lead from Manhattan to the Bronx is
   (A) Triborough Bridge
   (B) Willis Avenue Bridge
   (C) Third Avenue Bridge
   (D) Macombs Dam Bridge

2. City Hall is located nearest to
   (A) the Brooklyn Battery Tunnel
   (B) the Brooklyn Bridge
   (C) the 59th Street Bridge
   (D) the Lincoln Tunnel

3. All of these Manhattan streets are two-way
   EXCEPT
   (A) 23rd St.
   (B) 34th St.
   (C) 42nd St.
   (D) 50th St.

4. The most direct route to Long Island City in
   Queens from Midtown Manhattan is
   (A) the Brooklyn Bridge
   (B) the Triborough Bridge
   (C) the 59th St. Bridge
   (D) the Williamsburg Bridge

5. A water crossing that connects the Bronx
   and Queens is
   (A) the Midtown Tunnel
   (B) the Brooklyn Battery Tunnel
   (C) the Queensboro Bridge
   (D) the Whitestone Bridge

6. Lincoln Center is located at
   (A) 50th St. and 6th Ave.
   (B) 42nd St. on 1st Ave.
   (C) 31st St. to 33rd St. between 8th and 9th
       avenues
   (D) 65th St. and Columbus Ave.

7. Radio City Music Hall is located at
   (A) 59th St. and Lexington Ave.
   (B) 50th St. and 6th Ave.
   (C) 42nd St. and 7th Ave.
   (D) 34th St. and 5th Ave.

8. The General Post Office is located at
   (A) Times Square
   (B) 31st St. to 33rd St. between 8th and 9th
       avenues
   (C) Houston St. and 3rd Ave.
   (D) 32nd St. and 2nd Ave.

9. The United Nations is located at
   (A) 59th St. and 3rd Ave.
   (B) 42nd St. to 48th St. on 1st Ave.

(C) 14th St. and 1st Ave.
(D) 42nd St. and 12th Ave.

10. Columbia Presbyterian Hospital is located
    in what Manhattan neighborhood?
    (A) Central Park
    (B) Murray Hill
    (C) Harlem
    (D) Washington Heights

11. The Hayden Planetarium is located in what
    Manhattan neighborhood?
    (A) Chelsea
    (B) Central Park
    (C) Lower East Side
    (D) Battery Park

12. Columbia University is located at
    (A) Washington Square Park
    (B) Campus Road & Bedford Avenue,
        Brooklyn
    (C) 116th St. and Broadway
    (D) Fordham Road and Southern Blvd.,
        Bronx

13. The World Trade Center is located at
    (A) Wall St. and Broadway
    (B) 34th St. and 5th Ave.
    (C) Church St. and Liberty
    (D) 56th St. and Madison Ave.

14. Which thoroughfare is NOT in the Bronx?
    (A) Jerome Ave.
    (B) Grand Concourse
    (C) Steinway St.
    (D) Fordham Rd.

15. Which major attraction is NOT in Queens?
    (A) Shea Stadium
    (B) Sheepshead Bay
    (C) Aqueduct Racetrack
    (D) Flushing Meadow Park

Cab Driver's Relationship with Passengers

1. A man in a wheelchair hails your taxi. He explains that he wants you to place the wheelchair in the rear passenger part of the taxi and he will sit in the front alongside you.
   (A) You agree to the man's request and do as he asks
   (B) You explain that you would prefer that the man sit in the rear
   (C) You tell the passenger that you don't care what he wants

2. You see a woman who seems to be in a big hurry. She is frantically trying to get a taxi. How do you react? Before the woman enters the taxi you say,
   (A) "Taxi?"
   (B) "Where do you want to go, lady?"
   (C) "Get in, I'll get you there in a hurry."

3. You stop for a passenger on 56th St. and 3rd Ave. A middle-aged man enters the taxi. He says very loudly, "Broadway and 46th St. Turn off that stupid radio I hate listening to that garbage."
   (A) You explain that you like the music and refuse to turn it off
   (B) You turn off the radio and turn to the man and say, "You don't have to shout, I'm not deaf."
   (C) You turn off the radio and proceed driving

4. After reaching the passenger's destination, you inform the man that the meter reads $13.40. The passenger explains that he has only $10.00. How do you react?
   (A) You lock the rear doors and tell the man to check again
   (B) You ask the man to accompany you to the nearest police precinct
   (C) You park the taxi, turn on your off-duty sign, and tell the man you will wait for him to return with the money

5. You drive a very well dressed young woman to a new and elegant apartment building. The woman, who is very friendly, hands you $8.00 for the fare, which reads $7.20.
   (A) You return $.80 to the woman
   (B) You keeps the $.80 and thank her
   (C) You return the $.80 and tell the woman she can afford to give you a bigger tip

6. You are driving in what you consider a very comfortable temperature for a summer day in New York. You are not using your air conditioner because you feel there is no need to. Your passenger asks you to roll up your window and turn on the air conditioner.
   (A) You explain that you don't think it is necessary
   (B) You inform the passenger that the air conditioner is an additional expense
   (C) You comply with the request and turn on the air conditioner

7. After driving three passengers for a very short trip, you see that the meter reads only $1.20.
   (A) You accept the fare from only one passenger
   (B) You ask each person to pay $1.20
   (C) You complain that you can't make money this way

8. You see a prospective passenger hailing a taxi on the next corner. As you approach the passenger, another person steps between the taxi and the first person How do you respond?
   (A) You ask the two people, "Who was first?"
   (B) You pick up the first person whom you acknowledged
   (C) You pass both people and look for a third person to pick up

9. After waiting in a line for a long time, you finally reach the intersection and see a woman traffic agent who is directing traffic. Just as you are about to cross the intersec-

tion, the traffic agent motions for you to
stop. How do you react?
(A) You yell through your window, "You
idiot! I've waited long enough."
(B) Although you are angry, you stop and
say nothing
(C) You stop and consider whether you
should ignore the woman and continue
through the intersection

10. You are cruising in the midtown area. A
businessman enters your taxi and explains
that he wants to go to Queens via the Midtown Tunnel.
(A) You tell the passenger immediately that
he must pay for the tunnel toll
(B) You wait until you reach the toll and
then ask for the toll money
(C) You decide to add the toll cost onto the
fare at the passenger's destination

11. After you pick up a young man in Chinatown, he asks you to drive him uptown to
the Museum of Natural History. After only
a few blocks, the young man suddenly says,
"Stop. I want to get out here."
(A) You don't stop and tell the young man
that he hasn't reached his destination
yet
(B) You tell the young man that you think
he must be taking drugs to act so
crazily
(C) You stop the taxi and ask the passenger
for the fare on the meter

12. You stop to pick up a family which consists
of a father, a mother, and two small children. When everyone is seated in your taxi,
the man explains that they are tourists and
would like you to recommend a good, inexpensive restaurant where they can eat lunch.
How do you respond?
(A) You tell them where all the taxi drivers
like to eat
(B) You explain that you are not allowed to
make such recommendations

(C) You tell him about a wonderful place
downtown and offer to drive the family
there

13 After a passenger has left your taxi, you
discover that he has left his briefcase
behind.
(A) You cruise the neighborhood and look
for the passenger
(B) You open the briefcase and check for
valuables
(C) You take the briefcase, unopened, to the
nearest police precinct

14. A baker hails your taxi on the East Side,
puts a tray of donuts in your taxi, and asks
you to take the donuts to an address on the
West Side. You should
(A) take the donuts across town
(B) eat the donuts
(C) charge double the amount on the meter
(D) tell the baker that he must ride with the
donuts

15. After you drive a couple from Kennedy Airport to Manhattan, the couple offers to pay
the fare with foreign currency. What do you
do?
(A) You accept the currency because you
know that the value is the same
(B) You tell the tourists that they are making a big mistake and that nobody in
New York will accept their currency
(C) You explain that you must be paid in
American currency

16. Since your brother has recently opened a
business in New York, he has asked you to
hand out advertisements in your taxi to all
of your passengers. What do you decide to
do?
(A) You think it's all right so long as you're
not too demanding
(B) You remember that using your taxi for
such a service is a violation of the rules
and regulations
(C) You tell your brother that you will do it
— but only if he pays you for it

17. A passenger who is very impatient tells you that you are purposely driving slowly in order to make the fare higher. He decides to tell you that you are a thief.
    (A) You tell the man to shut up because he doesn't know what he's talking about
    (B) You explain that you are driving as quickly and safely as possible, and you ask the man why he feels he has been cheated
    (C) You tell the man that NOBODY CALLS YOU A THIEF, and you threaten to hit him.

18. An angry passenger feels that you have overcharged him. The man becomes red in the face and demands to know your name.
    (A) You tell the man that you don't have to give him that information
    (B) You tell the man that if he thinks that you have overcharged him, that's his problem
    (C) You give the man your name and ask him to explain why he is so upset

19. It's a very cold night in New York, so you haven't had many fares. Two men hail your taxi outside a hotel. The men enter the taxi and say they need to be at the airport within 30 minutes. You realize that it is almost impossible to make the trip that fast.
    (A) You tell the men, "No problem. We'll be there in plenty of time."
    (B) You tell tile men that the trip to the air-port is usually a 45-minute ride and that to make it in 30 minutes is almost impossible
    (C) You tell the men that they should have left earlier

20. You are driving a five-passenger taxicab. A group of six teenagers wants to get into your taxi. You explain that you are not allowed to take more than five passengers in your taxi.
    (A) You offer to take them for extra money

    (B) You tell them to get in, but one person has to sit on the floor
    (C) You suggest that they take two cabs instead of one

Matching
Match the Manhattan neighborhood or special area with the numbered description.

Soho
Sutton-Tudor City
Theater district
West Side
Washington Heights
Little Italy
Yorkville
Whitehall
Lower West Side
Greenwich Village
Gramercy
Garment district
Fur district
Flower Market
Harlem
East Harlem (The Barrio)
Inwood
Stuyvesant
Murray Hill
Millinery district
Antique district
Central Park
Bowery
Chelsea
Chinatown
Diamond Center
Civic Center
Upper East Side
Financial district
Lower East Side
Fort George

(1) Midtown East Side
     About 98th St. and Madison, south to 47th St. and north back to 98th St.
(2) East Side
     Houston and Baxter, east to 1st Ave., then south to Canal St., west to Baxter, and back north to Houston
(3) From 5th Ave. and 110th St. to Central Park West, south to 59th St., east to 5th Ave.
(4) West Side
     9th Ave. and 34th St., east to 5th Ave., south to 14th St., west to Hudson St., north to 34th St.
(5) East Side
     Canal St. and Baxter St., east to East Broadway, south to Park Row, back to Baxter
(6) Chambers St. and Broadway, east to Park Row, southwest Ann St., north back to Chambers St.
(7) Midtown 47th St., 5th to 6th Ave. (now spreading out)
(8) East Side
     96th St. and 5th Ave., east to Park Ave., south to 79th St., east to East River, south back to 59th St.
(9) East Side
     14th St. at 1st Ave., south along the East River to St. James Place ("New Bowery") to East Broadway, back up to 1st Ave.
(10) Pearl St. at Brooklyn Bridge, south on Water St., south Whitehall St., then north-west to Broadway back to Park Row
(11) Hudson River at Dyckman St., east to the Harlem River, south to 181st St., north to Dyckman St.
(12) Spreading out, centers around 6th Ave. from about 24th St. up to about 28th St.
(13) 8th Ave. and 28th St., east to 6th Ave., south to about 24th St., west to 8th Ave.
(14) 5th Ave. and about 38th St., south to about 28th St., west to (and across) 8th Ave., back north to 38th St.
(15) 1st Ave. and 14th St., north to about 30th St., west to 5th Ave., then south back to 14th St.

(16) 14th St. and the Hudson River east to Broadway, south on Broadway to Houston St., west to Hudson River
(17) Hudson River at 151st St., east to the Harlem River, along the Harlem River to 5th Ave., then south along 5th Ave. to 110th St., west on 110th St. to St. Nicholas to 125th St., west to the Hudson River
(18) 5th Ave. and the Harlem River, south to 96th St., east to the Harlem River
(19) Hudson River east along the Harlem River (Spuyten Duyvel) to Dyckinan St., north-east to the Hudson River
(20) Centered on 38th St., from   near 5th Ave., to west of 6th Ave.
(21) 42nd St. and 5th Ave., east to 1st Ave., south to 35th St., west to 5th Ave.
(22) 1st Ave. and 34th St., east to the East River, south to 14th St., west to 1st Ave.
(23) 1st Ave. and 59th St., east to the East River, south to 34th St., west to 1st Ave.
(24) About 7th Ave. and 50th St., east to 6th Ave., south to 42nd St., west to 7th Ave. (spreading)
(25) Hudson River at 181st St., east to the Harlem River, south to 151st St., west to the Hudson River
(26) 110th St. and Hudson River, east to Central Park West, south to 72nd St., west to the Hudson River
(27) 72nd St. and Hudson River, east to Central Park West, south along Central Park West (which becomes 8th Ave.) to 34th St., west along 34th St. to the Hudson River
(28) Hudson River at Battery Place, east to Whitehall St., southeast to East River (most of this area is made up of Battery Park)
(29) 96th St. and Park Ave., east to the East River, south to 79th St., west to Park Avenue
(30) Houston St. and Baxter St., south to Canal St , west to Bowery, north to Houston
(31) Houston St. and 6th Ave., south along 6th Ave to Grand St., east on Grand St. to Broadway, north to Houston

ANSWERS!

Rules and Regulations

1.   C
2.   C
3.   C
4.   B
5.   C
6.   D
7.   B

Geography

1.   C
2.   B
3.   D
4.   C
5.   D
6.   D
7.   B
8.   B
9.   B
10.   D
11.   B
12.   C
13.   C
14.   C
15.   B

Cab Driver's Relationship with Passengers

1.   A
2.   A
3.   C
4.   B
5.   A
6.   C
7.   A
8.   B
9.   B
10.   A
11.   C
12.   B
13.   C
14.   D
15.   C
16.   B
17.   B
18.   C
19.   B
20.   C

Matching

(1)   Antique district
(2)   Bowery
(3)   Central Park
(4)   Chelsea
(5)   Chinatown
(6)   Civic Center
(7)   Diamond Center
(8)   Upper East Side
(9)   Lower East Side
(10)   Financial district
(11)   Fort George
(12)   Flower Market
(13)   Fur district
(14)   Garment district
(15)   Gramercy
(16)   Greenwich Village
(17)   Harlem
(18)   East Harlem (The Barrio)
(19)   Inwood
(20)   Millinery district
(21)   Murray Hill
(22)   Stuyvesant
(23)   Sutton-Tudor City
(24)   Theatre district
(25)   Washington Heights
(26)   West Side
(27)   Lower West Side
(28)   Whitehall
(29)   Yorkville
(30)   Little Italy
(31)   Soho

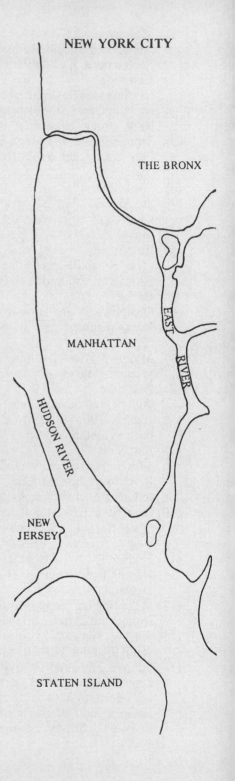

NEW YORK CITY

THE BRONX

MANHATTAN

EAST RIVER

HUDSON RIVER

NEW JERSEY

STATEN ISLAND

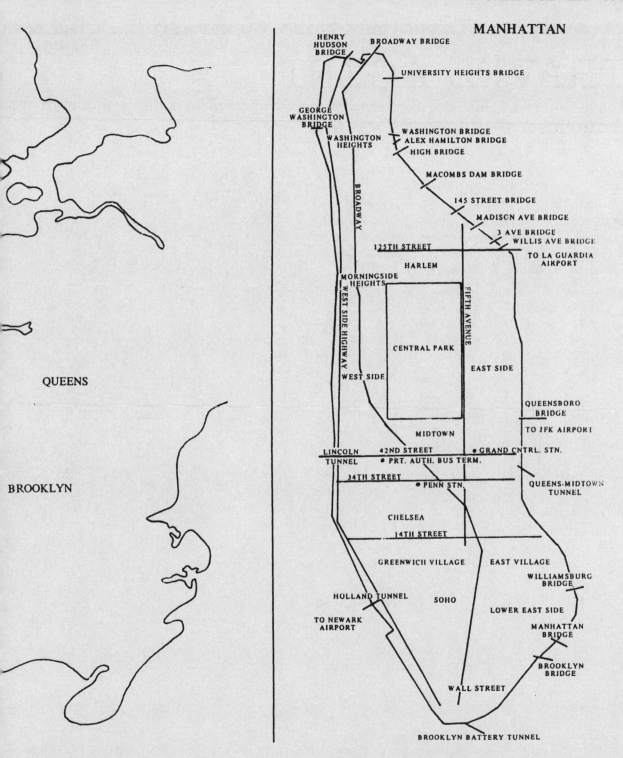

MANHATTAN

TRAVEL AGENT

American College of Travel

"Fly the friendly but incomprehensible skies of PBA—uh—Bar Harbor Airways—un, unnh—Continental—er, ah—that will be $149 for 200 miles, LaGuardia to Hyannis, and $225 for 6000 miles, LaGuardia, San Francisco, LaGuardia. Sir. Please."

I f you have an interest in the varied wonders of the world's cultural, political, and physical geography, you might have considered working as a travel agent, or maybe even dreamed of starting your own agency. In case you think that working in the travel business will satisfy your love of travel and adventure, however, you might want to pause and reflect that travel agents are paid to handle many of the mundane details that carefree vacationers would rather not worry about. That means keeping abreast of the latest fare schedules, memorizing regulations concerning carry-on luggage size restrictions on international flights, and spending long hours on the phone trying to get through to the airline operator. Indeed, the standard warning industry representatives issue to would-be travel agents is, as the American Society of Travel Agents puts it in its informational brochure, that "the travel agency industry is a highly specialized, intricate, and serious business—far from the occasional misconception of being a continuous round of carefree traveling."

Most agencies these days require a formal education in the more arcane aspects of reservation procedures, air travel regulations, the procurement of visas, booking package tours, writing tickets, and securing hotel, car rental company, tour operator, airline, cruise line, and railroad "appointments" from "suppliers" (a prerequisite to collecting sales commissions, the major source of revenue for a travel agency). American College of Travel, the contributor to this section, offers a basic, six-week training course covering the fundamental skills considered necessary for entry into the travel industry, a three-week course in airline computer systems, and a three-week advanced course featuring immersion in case-study situations.

The first set of questions in this section is from a test used by ACT to screen aspiring travel agents before they enter the training course; those who can correctly answer fewer than 75 percent might want to reconsider their choice of career. The remaining questions are from sections of the comprehensive Basic Training course, including Air Scheduling and Pre-Ticketing.

Multiple Choice

1. The Canary Islands are off the coast of
    (A) Spain
    (B) Germany
    (C) Africa
    (D) Madagascar

2. Which is the most visited National Park in
    the U.S.A.?
    (A) Yosemite
    (B) Sequoia
    (C) Bryce Canyon
    (D) Yellowstone

3. Which of these is an American airline?
    (A) SAS
    (B) KLM
    (C) ANA
    (D) TWA

4. Which of the following is not popular with
    cruise ships?
    (A) Dead Sea
    (B) Aegean Sea
    (C) Mediterranean Sea
    (D) Caribbean Sea

5. Which of these attractions is not in
    Europe?
    (A) The terra-cotta army
    (B) The Parthenon
    (C) Big Ben
    (D) The Eiffel Tower

6. "Air tickets cost more money if you buy
    them from an agency rather than from an
    airline."
    (A) True
    (B) False

7. How many degrees does the world turn
    through each hour?
    (A) 24
    (B) 365
    (C) 52
    (D) 15

8. Which of these European cities is west of
    Frankfurt?
    (A) Vienna
    (B) Berlin
    (C) Prague
    (D) Paris

9. In which country is Macchu Picchu?
    (A) Romania
    (B) Peru
    (C) New Zealand
    (D) China

10. To obtain the least expensive round-trip air
    ticket you should
    (A) arrive at the airport two hours early
    (B) buy two one-way tickets
    (C) find three friends to travel with you
    (D) book well in advance

11. Most international travel requires a
    (A) voter's registration card
    (B) letter of credit from a bank
    (C) release form from your place of work
    (D) passport

12. Another name for Eire is
    (A) Iran
    (B) Ulster
    (C) British Virgin Islands
    (D) Ireland

13. Travel insurance protects against
    (A) trip cancellation
    (B) lost luggage
    (C) medical expenses while traveling
    (D) all of the above
    (E) none of the above

14. "Coach class" means
    (A) economy class on an airplane
    (B) steerage class on a ship
    (C) transportation by bus

15. "Airline computers are still an unnecessary luxury for travel agencies."
    (A) True
    (B) False

16. If you leave Santa Monica, California and drive east on Interstate 10, where do you run out of road?
    (A) Chicago
    (B) Jacksonville
    (C) Miami
    (D) Houston

17. "An agency that handles leisure travel cannot make your business travel reservations."
    (A) True
    (B) False

18. Travel agents travel free
    (A) sometimes
    (B) never
    (C) always

19. Which is the highest category of hotel?
    (A) first class
    (B) superior
    (C) tourist
    (D) deluxe

20. Zimbabwe used to be called
    (A) Upper Volta
    (B) British Honduras
    (C) Tanganyika
    (D) Rhodesia

21. "APEX" means
    (A) the highest point reached during a flight
    (B) advance purchase excursion
    (C) associated promotional expertise

22. Which of the following skills do you think is most important in the travel agency business?
    (A) Speaking four languages
    (B) The ability to fly a small plane
    (C) Interpersonal and sales skills

23. Europe and Asia meet at
    (A) Istanbul
    (B) Athens
    (C) Vienna
    (D) The Iron Curtain

24. Which of the following countries is governed by a constitutional monarchy?
    (A) Guam
    (B) Great Britain
    (C) Republic of China
    (D) Italy

25. Which of the following flights is the longest?
    (A) London to Istanbul
    (B) Beijing to Shanghai
    (C) Los Angeles to Honolulu

26. Which of the following cities is a ski destination?
    (A) Davos
    (B) Nice
    (C) Rome
    (D) Dublin

27. Abu Simbel is in
    (A) Israel
    (B) Egypt
    (C) Syria
    (D) Jordan

28. Which is the largest of these airplanes?
    (A) 707
    (B) 727
    (C) 737
    (D) 747
    (E) 767

29. If you cross the International Dateline traveling west, the time is
    (A) unchanged
    (B) the same time one day later
    (C) the same time one day earlier
    (D) none of the above

30. What are the Tropics?
    (A) A hot-blooded tribe in New Guinea
    (B) Daily travel news bulletins
    (C) Belts of the earth on each side of the equator

31. A stateroom is
    (A) an airport waiting room for VIPs
    (B) a cabin on a cruise ship
    (C) a governor's office

32. Which canal was nearly the scene of war in 1956?
    (A) The Suez Canal
    (B) The Isthmus of Corinth
    (C) The Panama Canal
    (D) The Kiel Canal

33. "It is illegal to fly on an airline ticket for which you have not paid."
    (A) True
    (B) False

34. If you cannot use an airline ticket you can
    (A) sell it to any other person
    (B) sell it to a member of your family with the same last name
    (C) either of the above
    (D) neither of the above

35. Which of the following cannot be imported to the U.S.A.?
    (A) Russian caviar
    (B) German World War II memorabilia
    (C) Havana cigars.
    (D) French dairy products

36. Berlin is best described as
    (A) Germany's largest city
    (B) a divided city
    (C) an open port
    (D) a border town

37. Which language is spoken in Brazil?
    (A) Spanish
    (B) Portuguese
    (C) Colombian
    (D) German

38. How many languages are officially spoken in Switzerland?
    (A) One
    (B) Two
    (C) Three
    (D) Four
    (E) Five

39. Which of these languages is not spoken in Switzerland?
    (A) Romansch
    (B) Hungarian
    (C) Italian

40. Thomas Cook was
    (A) the first man to make English food edible
    (B) the inventor of travelers' checks
    (C) the first group tour operator

41. The Renaissance began in
    (A) Heidelberg
    (B) Siena
    (C) Detroit
    (D) Shanghai

42. Where does the Bullet Train run?
    (A) Japan
    (B) Between old Wild West towns
    (C) From New York City to Washington
    (D) On the same route as the Orient Express

43. The Pedernales are a
    (A) South American tribe
    (B) school of Spanish painters
    (C) range of hills in Texas

44. Which country produces the most wine?
    (A) Norway
    (B) Italy
    (C) Saudi Arabia
    (D) Austria

45. "Perpendicular Gothic" signifies
    (A) a romantic novel in hardback
    (B) the family tree of the princes of Gotha
    (C) an architectural style

46. The Michelin guides are helpful for
    (A) choosing hotels and restaurants
    (B) ascertaining current tire prices
    (C) treasure hunting in the Caribbean

47. Where do the Ohio and Mississippi rivers meet?
    (A) Cairo, IL
    (B) St. Louis, MO
    (C) Kansas City, MO
    (D) Cincinnati, OH
    (E) Memphis, TN

48. The Lyndon B. Johnson library is at
    (A) Hyde Park, NY
    (B) Abilene, KS
    (C) Austin, TX
    (D) Dallas, TX

49. Which is the largest of the Great Lakes?
    (A) Lake Michigan
    (B) Lake Baikal
    (C) Lake Windermere
    (D) Lake Superior

50. An autobahn is a
    (A) shuttle between airport parking and terminals
    (B) freeway in Germany
    (C) self-service restaurant in New York

51. The southern tip of South America is called
    (A) The Falklands
    (B) Land's End
    (C) The Cape of Good Hope
    (D) Cape Horn

52. Which Russian city is closest to the U.S.A.?
    (A) Samarkand
    (B) Kiev
    (C) Minsk
    (D) Vladivostok

53. In which region of the U.S.A. is Santa Fe, NM?
    (A) Central
    (B) Southern
    (C) Far East
    (D) Southwest

54. Who were the Medicis?
    (A) A noble Florentine family
    (B) Greek colonial adventurers of the 5th century
    (C) Leaders of the Spanish Inquisition
    (D) Roman proconsuls

55. Travel agents generally earn money from
    (A) service charges paid by clients

(B) commission paid by hotels, airlines, etc.

(C) profits from currency exchange

56. Which is the largest of these islands?
(A) Greenland
(B) Sicily
(C) Iceland
(D) New Guinea

57. Which of these cities is 8 hours "ahead" of Los Angeles?
(A) Moscow
(B) London
(C) Cairo
(D) Tokyo

58. Which city is furthest south?
(A) Tehran
(B) Calcutta
(C) Irkutsk

Matching

1. Match each of the following with its appropriate city
(A) United Nations   (1) Brussels
(B) NATO   (2) St. Petersburg
(C) Mardi Gras   (3) New York
(D) The Hermitage   (4) New Orleans

2. Match the island with its country
(A) Galapagos Islands   (1) Great Britain
   (2) Spain
(B) Shetland Islands   (3) Ecuador
(C) Canary Islands

3. Match these bridges with the towns where they stand:
(A) Golden Gate Bridge   (1) Lake Havasu
   (2) Venice
(B) Tower Bridge   (3) San Francisco
(C) London Bridge   (4) London
(D) Bridge of Sighs

4. Match these countries and currencies:
(A) Mark   (1) Mexico
(B) Guilder   (2) Poland
(C) Baht   (3) Netherlands
(D) Zloty   (4) Germany
(E) Peso   (5) Thailand

5. Match these cities and attractions
(A) Zona Rosa   (1) Cairns
(B) La Scala   (2) Freiburg
(C) Black Forest   (3) Beijing
(D) Forbidden City   (4) Mexico City
(E) Great Barrier Reef   (5) Milan

6. Match these cities and their English-language equivalents
(A) Koln   (1) Canton
(B) Wien   (2) Venice
(C) Livorno   (3) Cologne
(D) Venezia   (4) Vienna
(E) Guangzhou   (5) Leghorn

Short Answer

1. What is the normal rate of commission for
(A) domestic airline tickets
(B) international airline tickets

2. What is a "multiline rep"?

3. What is an "outside sales" agent?

4. What are the new names for the following places?
(A) Upper Volta
(B) Tanganyika
(C) Cyrenaica
(D) Leningrad
(E) Palestine
(F) Rhodesia

5. What is an "override" commission?

6. Where is
   (A) The Caspian Sea
   (B) The Dead Sea
   (C) The Sea of Marmara
   (D) The Aral Sea
   (E) The Black Sea
   (F) The Arabian Sea

7. Where are the following attractions?
   (A) The Blue Mosque
   (B) Amboseli National Park
   (C) The Shrine of the Book
   (D) The Stone Forest
   (E) The Wild Goose Pagoda
   (F) The Hermitage
   (G) The Aswan Dam
   (H) Angkor Wat

8. Which country surrounds Gambia?

9. How many time zones separate 150 degrees west of Greenwich from 105 degrees east of Greenwich?

10. Which mountains are the "backbone" of Italy?

11. What is the capital of Scotland?

12. What languages are spoken in the following countries
    (A) Corsica
    (B) Wales
    (C) Crete
    (D) Malta
    (E) Belgium
    (F) Shetland Islands

13. How many countries border on France?

14. What is American AAdvantage?

15. Which airline(s) would you think of for an itinerary ATL/STL/BUR?

ANSWERS!

Multiple Choice

1. C
2. D
3. D
4. A
5. A
6. B
7. D
8. D
9. B
10. D
11. D
12. D
13. D
14. A
15. B
16. B
17. B
18. A
19. D
20. D
21. B
22. C
23. A
24. B
25. C
26. A
27. B
28. D
29. B
30. C
31. B
32. A
33. B
34. D
35. C
36. A
37. B
38. D
39. B
40. C
41. B
42. A
43. C
44. B
45. C
46. A
47. A
48. C
49. B
50. D
51. B
52. D
53. D
54. A
55. B
56. A
57. B
58. B

Matching

1. A: 3
   B: 1
   C: 4
   D: 2

2. A: 3
   B: 1
   C: 2

3. A: 3
   B: 4
   C: 1
   D: 2

4. A: 4
   B: 3
   C: 5
   D: 2
   E: 1

5. A: 4
   B: 5
   C: 2

D: 3
E: 1

6. A: 3
    B: 4
    C: 5
    D: 2
    E: 1

Short Answer

1. (A) 10%
    (B) 8%

2. A representative of different travel products

3. An agent who sells travel outside an agency

4. (A) Burkina Faso
    (B) Tanzania
    (C) Libya
    (D) St. Petersburg
    (E) Israel
    (F) Zimbabwe

5. Additional commission

6. (A) Iran
    (B) Israel
    (C) Turkey
    (D) USSR
    (E) Turkey/USSR
    (F) Between the Mideast and Africa

7. (A) Istanbul
    (B) Kenya
    (C) Jerusalem
    (D) Kunming
    (E) Xian
    (F) Leningrad
    (G) Egypt
    (H) Cambodia

8. Senegal

9. eight

10. Apennines

11. Edinburgh

12. (A) Italian
    (B) Welsh/English
    (C) Greek
    (D) Italian/Maltese/English
    (E) French/Dutch
    (F) English

13. eight

14. American Airlines' frequent flyer program

15. TWA

WINE MASTER

The Institute of Masters of Wine, London

Enologists who presume to draw the cork on this examination and taste the refined knowledge required of successful candidates for the most prestigious title in the British wine trade are likely to fail.

The high standard this test represents is attested to by this fact: in 23 years from 1953 to 1986, only 130 candidates received a passing grade.

The Master of Wine Examination is the highest qualification open to professionals who have been making their livelihood with the wine trade for at least five years. It is equivalent approximately to a master's degree and has been administered in London since 1953 by the Institute of Masters of Wine which is in turn made up of two prestigious groups active in the British wine trade: the Wine and Spirit Association of Great Britain and the Worshipful Company of Vintners. The exam consists of five written parts covering all aspects of viticulture and wine production, handling, and marketing.

The examination requires four grueling days to complete, including three "Practical Examinations" in which a variety of wines are tasted by the applicant. Since the tasting may take place in the morning sessions (when presumably both palate and mind are freshest), the professional technique of tasting without swallowing becomes, presumably, doubly important.

Here is the four-day examination agenda from a recent year.

15th May: Paper IA: Cultivation of the Vine, 2 1/2 hours, 10:00 to 12:30 PM

15th May: Paper lB: Production of Wine, 2 1/2 hours, 2:00 PM to 4:30 PM

16th May: Practical Examination No. 1 (White Wines), 2 hours, 10:30AM to 12:30PM

16th May: Paper II: Techniques and General Procedures of Handling Wines, 2 1/2 Hours, 2:00 PM to 4:30 PM

17th May: Practical Examination No. 2 (Red Wines), 2 hours, 10:30 AM to 12:30 PM

17th May: Paper III: General Regulations Affecting the Sale of Wine, Marketing Methods, and General Knowledge, 2 112 hours, 2:00 PM to 4:30 PM

18th May: Practical Examination No. 3 (Fortified & Sparkling Wines), 2 hours, 10:30 AM to 12:30 PM

18th May: Paper IV: Essay, 2 1/2 hours, 2:00 PM to 4:30 PM

To get answers to some of the questions, we gave the test to Frank Johnson, noted enophile and author of *The Professional Wine Reference*. Since the applicant is allowed to select specific questions from various groups, we asked Mr. Johnson to compose answers only for those questions that seemed most interesting and within the scope of knowledge of amateur enologists.

Cultivation of the Vine

THREE questions ONLY to be answered. The first question MUST be answered, and carries 400 marks. Any two of the remaining live may be chosen, and carry 300 marks each.

1. In viticulture quantity can only be achieved at the expense of quality. True or false? Discuss in relation to the Rheinhessen, the Napa Valley, and the Côte d'Or.

2. You own a property in the Hérault producing wine that you vinify yourself. So far you manage to break even on the average of one in three years but you are prepared to invest further capital to ensure economic viability within a five-year period. What steps would you take to achieve this?

3. Outline the effects of each of the following adverse weather conditions on viticulture and winemaking, and state the regions around the world where they are likely to occur. Give the measures open to vine growers to combat them.
   Summer drought
   Excessive summer temperatures
   Excessive summer rain
   Cold summer
   Strong winds
   Humid dull summer weather
   Excessive heat at vintage time
   Rain at vintage time
   Cold vintage weather

4. What is meant by training and pruning? Why are they done? Discuss the merits of the different methods used by traditional growers in the Médoc, the Mosel, and the Southern Rhône Valley.

5. It takes about 100 days from the flowering of the vine until the harvest. Describe the stages of this development and the factors that affect it.

6. Describe the annual work cycle month by month at a Bordeaux red wine Château. State if the régisseur has any scope for variation in the timing of each operation and give reasons.

Production of Wine

THREE questions ONLY to be answered. The first question MUST be answered, and carries 400 marks. Any two of the remaining five may be chosen, and carry 300 marks each.

7. Describe in detail the traditional method used in the making of Champagne and any innovations that have taken place in recent years. Explain why the end products can be so different when the same method is employed in other areas using alternative cépages?

8. Describe the process of fermentation. How does it differ in the making of red, rosé, and white light wines?

9. Discuss the changes that can be expected during the course of maturation in cask and bottle of class growth Claret, Old Tawny Port, and quality Fino Sherry.

10. Write briefly about each of the following:
    Chaptalisation
    Paxarette
    Tannin
    Malolaetic Fermentation
    Débourbage
    Seeding
    Carbonic Maceration
    pH

11. What would you look for on your initial visit to the cellars of a potential supplier of inexpensive French red and white wine?

12. How would you set about making a fresh white wine in a hot dry climate?

Practical Examination No. 1 (White Wines)

(A) All questions are to be answered

(B) All wines are in bottles of neutral shape and colour

(C) You must write your examination number and the words "Practical Examination No. 1" at the top of EVERY sheet

(D) You must show clearly to which number wine your answer refers

(E) The answers will not always require a description of each wine

(F) You are also reminded that any faults that a wine may show will be known to the examiners who will expect you to Comment accordingly

(G) You are reminded to read each question carefully before answering

13. Wines 1, 2, and 3 are made from the same grape variety and come from the same country.
    (A) State the country
    (B) State the grape variety
    (C) Identify the origin as closely as possible
    (D) State the vintage
    (E) Place the wines in order of quality (with best last) giving a brief explanation of your reasons for this order

14. Wines 4, 5, and 6 come from the same region and vintage, and are made from the same grape variety.
    (A) State the region of origin
    (B) Identify the district or commune of each wine as closely as possible
    (C) State the grape variety
    (D) Comment briefly on the maturity and quality of each one
15. Wines 7 through 12 are a mixed bag and should be treated individually.
    (A) Describe each concisely, commenting on the quality and maturity
    (B) State the origin of each wine as closely as possible

(The following are the wines actually used in this examination:
    (1) Sauvignon de Touraine 1982 FB
    (2) Vin du Pays du Jardin de Ia France, Cépage Sauvignon, 1982 FB
    (3) Domaine Sancerre 1982 DB
    (4) Puligny Montrachet les Referts 1982 FB

    (5) Chablis, ler Cru, 1982 DB
    (6) Mâcon Viré 1982 PB
    (7) Frascati 1983
    (8) Out of condition White (Mosel)
    (9) Napa Valley Chardonnay 1980
    (10) Liebfraumilch 1982
    (11) Wehlener Sonnenuhr Riesling Auslese 1976
    (12) Coteaux du Layon 1976 DB)

Practical Examination No. 2 (Red Wines)

(A) All questions are to be answered

(B) All wines are in bottles of neutral shape and color

(C) You must write your examination number and the words "Practical Examination No. 2" at the top of EVERY sheet

(D) You must show clearly to which number wine your answer refers

(E) The answer will not always require a description of each wine

(F) You are also reminded that any faults that a wine may show will be known to the examiners who will expect you to comment accordingly

(G) You are reminded to read each question carefully before answering

16. The first six wines are grouped in pairs, 1 and 2, 3 and 4, 5 and 6. Each pair comes from one region; three regions are represented.
    (A) Identify the origin of all three pairs as closely as possible
    (B) State which wine of each pair you feel to be of higher quality, giving your reasons briefly
    (C) Comment on the age and likely development of all six wines

17. Wines 7 through 9 are from the same vintage and region. Identify the vintage and districts as closely as possible, giving your reasons. Compare the quality and state of maturity of the three wines.

18. Wines 10, 11, and 12 are all Vins de Pays. Give your views of their quality and stability. Which would you purchase for resale, and why?

(The following are the wines actually used in this examination:
  (1) Domaine Brouilly 1983 DB
  (2) Beaujolais 1982 FB
  (3) Chianti DOC 1981
  (4) Chianti Classico Riserva 1979
  (5) Côtes du Rhône, Domaine, 1979 DB
  (6) Châteauneuf-du-Pape, Domaine, 1979 DB
  (7) Château Patache d'Aux 1979 CB
  (8) Château de Barbe 1979 CB
  (9) Château Pichon Baron 1979 CB
  (10) Vin du Pays du Card, UK bottled
  (11) Out of condition Vin de Pays (Oxidized)
  (12) Out of condition Vin de Pays (Volatile Acid))

Practical Examination No. 3 (Fortified and Sparkling Wines)

(A) All questions are to be answered

(B) All wines are in bottles of neutral shape and color

(C) You must write your examination number and the words "Practical Examination No. 3" at the top of EVERY sheet

(D) You must show clearly to which number of wine your answer refers

(E) The answers will not always require a description of each wine

(F) You are also reminded that any faults that a wine may show will be known to the examiners who will expect you to comment accordingly

(G) You are reminded to read each question carefully before answering

19. You have three wines of similar style numbered I through 3:
  (A) Identify them as closely as possible, giving reasons for your answers
  (B) Assess the quality of each wine

20. You have three wines numbered 4 through 6:
  (A) Identify the origins of each as closely as possible
  (B) Comment on the quality of each

21. You have three wines numbered 7 through 9:
  (A) Identify the origin and style of each
  (B) Comment on the maturity and the quality of each, giving reasons for your answers

22. You have three sparkling wines numbered 10 through 12:
  (A) Identify the origin of each as closely as possible
  (B) Place in ascending order of quality, giving reasons for your answers

(The following are the wines actually used in this examination:
  (1) Out of condition Fino Sherry
  (2) Fino Sherry
  (3) South African Dry
  (4) Dry Oloroso Sherry
  (5) Bual Madeira
  (6) Tawny Port
  (7) Ruby Port
  (8) 1977 Vintage Port
  (9) 1979 LBV Fort
  (10) Crémant de la Loire Brut
  (11) Champagne 1976 Vintage, Brut
  (12) N.V. Champagne (same house), Brut)

Essay

Candidates are reminded:

(A) That they should head their essay with the title of their chosen subject

(B) That what is required is an original exposition in ESSAY FORM of their own knowledge and ideas upon the subject chosen. These are not questions to which there is a right or wrong answer, but subjects which may be treated in many different ways at the discretion of the candidate.

(1) Wine: The Universal Drink?

(2) The Key to the Successful Selling of Wine

(3) Fine Wine: Asset or Liability?

MASTER OF WINE EXAMINATION, QUESTIONS FROM 1967, 1968, 1969

Cultivation of the Vine

1. Describe the cycle of the year's work in a vineyard in the Jerez area.

2. In a Burgundy vineyard, what is the effect of each of the following?
   (A) A very mild winter
   (B) Hail in April
   (C) Cold wet weather in May and June
   (D) Alternating periods of rain and warmth in July and August
   (E) Exceptional heat in September and October

3. What features of geographical situation, soil, and climate would you consider best for the production of fine dry white wine?

4. The composition of the soil affects the character of the wine. Illustrate from the Burgundy region, including Chablis and Beaujolais

5. Name the main varieties of grape grown in the Médoc, and describe the effect which each has on the character of the wine produced.

Production of Wine

6. How is the maturation of a wine affected by the size and material of the container in which it is stored from vinification to bottling?

7 How and why is added sugar used in wine production?

8. Describe the evolution of the main types of Sherry from the period when they are mostos up to their introduction into a solera.

9. What is Vinho Verde, and how is it made?

10. What methods are used to produce the special characteristics of
    (A) Tavel
    (B) Trockenbeerenauslese
    (C) Madeira
    (D) Château Chalon

11. What are the sources of tannin in wine and what is its value?

The Technique of Handling Wines and General Cellar Procedure

12. Describe in broad terms the natural process of evolution which takes place in the life of table wines. Take as examples a classed growth Claret and a fine Mosel of successful vintages.

General Knowledge

13. Write two or three lines only about each of the following:
    Agrafe
    Balaton
    Dosage
    En Gobelet
    Gumpoldskirchen
    Hunter River
    Kreuznach
    Logroño
    Maderisé
    Nebbiolo
    Plastering
    Première Tranche
    Puttonyo
    Rendu Mise
    Saintes Glaces
    Schist
    Steen
    Via Doux Naturel
    Vinho Verde

ANSWERS!

1. False. In earlier times in traditional. wine-growing areas, production could only be achieved at the expense of quality but this idea is no longer valid. In the past century, winemaking changed from a craft into a science, and in connection with this science came modern viticulture and wine-making techniques to challenge the old notion of quality vs. quantity.

As might he expected Germany is in the forefront of many innovations in wine-growing and winemaking. In the Rhein-hessen area, the shy-bearing Riesling is confined to small sections along the Rhine front, while the more productive Müller-Thurgau, Silvaner, Bacchus, and Huxel grapes grow further inland The Silvaner was formerly the most widespread grape variety in Hessia, but now it has been surpassed by Müller-Thurgau.

Many new grape-crossings were developed in Germany, specifically for the purpose of higher production and more regular yields. The locations for these varieties have been optimized according to soil type; while much wine is used for blending purposes, Rheinhessen wines overall have never been finer than they are today. Yet, for all this, production is many times what it once was.

In the Napa Valley, modern techniques such as clonal selection of more productive varieties, drip-flow irrigation, and advanced vine treatments have boosted output and cut crop losses. In the winery, newer press designs extract more juice from the grapes than older types, and temperature-controlled winemaking equipment assures consistent quality. In addition, there are many more wineries: twenty years ago, there were only a few dozen wineries in Napa; now there are over a hundred, and the quality of what they produce is truly world-class.

In the Cote d'Or, newer clones of Pinot Noir produce several times the crop they did a generation ago, after World War II. While the soil and the climate might not have changed much in 2000 years, wine-growing practices certainly have. For instance, stainless steel winemaking equipment and electronic presses have improved juice extraction and help make more wine. In the vineyards, chemical agents against rot, and advanced fertilizers, are now helping growers in the Côte d'Or to produce more wine, on a more regular basis.

Overall, the quality of wine world-wide has never been better than it is today. The application of a scientific approach toward winemaking, when combined with the right climate and soil type, is far more significant than the notion that quantity can only be achieved at the expense of quality.

4. Training and pruning are methods used in viticulture to regulate the vine's tendencies and direct them toward grape production as opposed to leaf growth. Though they are related, they involve rather different methods.

Training is the application of support systems for the vine. As it grows shoots or "canes" that will later bear fruit, various training methods are used to guide the canes and orient the leaves toward the sun. In many of the world's vineyards, the vines are trained on wires so that as the grape bunches form, they will hang well above the ground and be protected from overexposure by the plant's own leaf canopy.

In the past, the vine was left to stand on its own, and canes spread out of the main trunk at random. More consistent and controllable production can be achieved if the plant is given some sort of support; in the Médoc, the vines are trained low on wires, so that they may be worked in blocks according to how the land is set up at the estate or château. In the Mosel, where steep slopes preclude the use of wire-training systems, the vines are trained individually on stakes. In warmer, drier climates, where water loss may be a problem, the vines are trained very low and the leaf canopies are arranged so that the rate of evaporation is lower. This form of training is still practiced today in the southern Rhône, where summers are hot and dry.

Pruning involves the removal of the vegetal parts of the vine. It corrects the vine's natural tendencies to expend its energies on leaf formation, and directs it toward fruit formation. It is performed during the winter, when the vine is dormant, and the unwanted shoots are removed. Only a few buds are left on the plant, which will later develop into shoots during the growing season.

Pruning is a far more intricate science than most people realize. Since its extent will determine the overall health and vigor of the plant during the growing season, it must be done with great care and with a view to future production. After a series of copious harvests, the vines may have to be pruned back to correct for a tendency to overproduce. Young plants typically require more severe pruning than older plants, because of their vigor and also because their root system is less well developed.

The pruning process ultimately depends on where the vineyard is located, and to what extent local custom and laws require a particular method or type to be used by the winegrower.

5. During the growing season, the vine will direct its efforts toward leaf formation and photosynthesis. Numerous climactic effects will determine the extent to which it will be successful, and weather of course plays a major role.

We will assume that weather during the flowering period has been favorable. Warm, calm weather is vital for proper pollination to occur, and during the next six weeks, as the tiny grape bunches form, the vines must be given a proper mixture of sunshine and rainfall. During July, the weather must be warm but not too hot and dry; occasional cloud cover is in fact beneficial so as to cut down on evaporation and water loss in the vineyard, since in many vineyards irrigation is not allowed.

During mid-August, if July weather has been propitious, the *véraison* will occur. This is the time the grapes change color from green to pale red, and experience has dictated that in many areas the harvest will take place approximately six weeks after the date of véraison. The German term for ripening, *Säureabbau*, when translated into English, is an apt description of the biochemical processes associated with véraison: acid reduction, or the inverse reduction of malic fruit acids associated with the flow of sugar and nutrients to the developing grape bunches.

In early September, the grapes slowly assume their ripe form, and are already delicious to eat, but their sugar content is insufficient for fermentation and they still are high in acid. Now the grapes are ripening a little each day; autumn weather becomes critical. The grower will begin to watch the weather daily; not for rain but for frost, hail, or. warm, humid conditions that could mean an outbreak of rot (checked nowadays by chemicals).

Finally, in the last days of September and the first days of October, the harvest begins. The leaves have performed photosynthesis to their limit, and will now start to drop off. The grapes are high in sugar content and will spoil if not picked. Their sugar is constantly measured by a refractometer, to determine the eventual alcoholic content of the finished wine. Above all, harvest weather must be dry: rain will dilute the must weights by entering into the bunches and being absorbed by the root system.

The plant, meanwhile, has begun to shut down its systems for further growth. Auxins and other forms of vigor in the plant have diminished, and cooler fall weather slows the movement of the vascular systems. As workers gather in the vineyards to prepare for picking, many of the leaves arc yellow or reddish as chlorophyll is lost and autumn colors emerge from within.

In approximately 100 days, or a little over three months, what began as minute specks of pollen, borne by the wind, has evolved into fermentable substances, that will now be shaped by the hand of man into a delicious beverage.

7. The name Champagne relates both to the name of the region where this famous sparkling wine is made, and the name of the wine produced. Since today Champagne is a place-name of geographic origin, there are laws to control the use of this name and restrict it only to wines actually grown in that region in France.

The traditional method used in making Champagne involves several stages: (1) the harvesting of grapes, and initial wine-making; (2) the blending of wines to form the *cuvée* or combination of still wines, with the desired flavor and style sought by the firm; (3) the bottling dosage, or *liqueur de tirage*, which will make the wine sparkling; (4) the *remuage*, or process of riddling, whereby after the second fermentation the bottles are tilted and shaken to separate the wine from the yeast sediment; (5) the *dégorgement*, or disgorging, which removes the yeast by freezing it in a mass at the top of the inverted Champagne bottle; (6) the *liqueur d' expédition*, or shipping dosage, which adds small quantities of sweetened wine to the finished product according to the market where it is to be shipped. Each of these stages is the result of centuries of experience in the making of high-quality Champagne; however, in recent years there have been a few modifications.

During the harvest, Champagne grapes are pressed and the grapes may be given several different pressings. Only the first two pressings are used for quality Champagne. Older presses were constructed of wood plates, pushed down by winches; today, modern press designs facilitate high-quality juice extraction with a minimum of solids.

One of the most significant changes in Champagne is the use of stainless steel fermenters, which permit better temperature control than the older wooden fermenters and are much easier to clean. These tanks have created a wine that is fresher, more aromatic, and more consistent in quality than before, and it is now easier to prepare the ideal cuvée.

Another change in Champagne, now widespread among many houses, is the use of crown caps instead of corks during the second fermentation As opposed to the old corks clamped in place with an *agrafe*, crown caps are much cheaper and essentially do the job just as well.

The most consistent change in Champagne is the new use of vibrating equipment, which automatically shakes the bottles and gets the sediment moving toward the cork without the time-consuming process of *remuage*, all of which formerly had to be done by hand. Much of this new equipment was developed in the United States where many new high quality sparkling wines have been perfected The house of Moët & Chandon has experimented with calcium alginate beads which encapsulate the yeasts and allow them to perform the second fermentation without creating any sediment.

Coincidental to this was the development of automated disgorging equipment: formerly, manual disgorging resulted in considerable waste of product, and was very time-consuming. With the Champagne process speeded up by vibrating and automated disgorging equipment, production may now be increased to suit great world wide demand.

Assuming that these same processes may be implemented in other areas, why is the classic Champagne flavor so difficult to imitate? One reason is the wine itself. The climate, soil, and grape quality are all unique to the area, and the overall chemical and qualitative makeup of the wine are extremely difficult to duplicate in other regions. The northerly location, combined with the particular growing season and soil, assures that the base wines that go into Champagne are unique to begin with, and the fine art of wine production in Champagne goes one step further toward assuring that it is virtually impossible to replicate elsewhere.

8. Alcoholic fermentation can be described chemically as the irreversible process of decarboxylation: the term for biochemical changes brought about by yeasts, as they assimilate grape sugar and convert it into alcohol and carbon dioxide by a complex series of reactions.

The sugar molecule consists of chains of hydrocarbons that when hydrolized in an aqueous solution (i.e., grape must) may be easily altered by the yeasts. Besides the end products of alcohol and carbon dioxide, considerable quantities of heat are liberated during fermentation, which should be controlled if high-quality wines are desired.

Chemically, the process of fermentation in red, white, and rosé wines is essentially the same. Practically, however, there are substantial differences in production according to how the grapes are handled.

White wines are essentially produced without skin contact. The grapes arc pressed immediately, and thc juice is drawn off to ferment on its own, away from the skins. Experience has shown that a brief rest period prior to fermentation (*débourbage*, in French) will allow the heavier solids to sink to the bottom of the fermenting tank: for the best wines, only the top half will be allowed to ferment out to completion.

The manner in which white wines are fermented is significant. Since most white wines will be consumed during their youth, it is important that fermentation be slow and cool — best results are achieved over a period of weeks. Automatic temperature control, either by water-jacketed fermenting tanks or by heat exchangers, assures that temperatures not exceed 55 degrees Fahrenheit. Once the wines have ceased to ferment, either to dryness or to the desired alcoholic strength, they may be bottled relatively early depending on whether they will receive any wood aging.

Red wines owe their color to being fermented in contact with the skins. The initial manner in which they are treated is thus quite different from that used with white wines. First of all, they are picked later in the season than the white grape varieties. To start the winemaking process, the grapes are usually passed through a crusher-destemmer (*fouloir-égrappoir*), where they are crushed and the stems are removed prior to fermentation. In only a few wine regions (the Alto Douro in Portugal, the Sherry district in Spain) are grapes still crushed with the feet.

The crushed grapes are then brought to a fermenting tank, where winemaking will begin as the wine remains in contact with the skins. The time in which the wines remain in contact with the skins (*cuvaison*) determines the degree of color extraction. Light red wines, destined for early consumption, may be either given short maceration (skin contact) or put through a variation on the technique called carbonic maceration. By this method the grapes are not actually crushed but are put into a sealed container, whereby some juice will be extracted under the weight of the mass of grapes. Under a blanket of carbon dioxide, fermentation begins on its own, and after about a week the wine is drawn off. Because only a small amount of color and tannin will be extracted via this method,

such wines are best consumed during their first year.

For red wines suited to long-term aging, the skins remain in contact with the fermenting juice for about three weeks, in accordance with the degree of color to he extracted and the quality of the vintage (deficient years need more skin contact). The skins tend to collect on the surface of the fermenting tank as a mass ("cap"), and occasionally this must be pushed down to assure consistent color extraction. Finally, when most or all of the sugar has been fermented, the free-run wine is drawn off and prepared for further aging in cask. At this time, a little press-wine may also be added, for extra color and body, by taking the remaining lees and subjecting it to a light pressing. Because of its high astringency, this is added sparingly, in small proportions.

A rosé is essentially a light red wine that has been in contact with. the skins only briefly — usually less than 24 hours. Up until this point, the cellar treatments are essentially the same as for red wines, except that for rosé wines, only certain varieties are preferred (Grenache, Cabernet Franc, etc.). These have thinner skins and more neutral flavor than the varieties normally used for red wines, and hence will impart a more subtle flavor to the wine.

The basic difference between red wine and a rosé is one of sweetness: red table wines are almost never sweet, whereas many rosés are. The reason lies in a tannin content: from only limited skin contact, rosés are usually light and fruity, and their aromatic qualities may be enhanced by light sweetness. The more astringent red wines, on the other hand, become dull with sweetness and are much more enjoyable when fermented out to dryness.

One thing I would *not* look for would be long, picturesque rows of casks in this cellar. Inexpensive red and white wine is not suited to long-term aging, and tastes better if released when young and fresh. A short aging period in clean tanks, followed by a relatively early bottling, is better for this type of wine.

In comparison to the market that existed when these questions were originally posed some twenty years ago, there is now a flood of cheap French *vins de table* on the American market; some of them are quite respectable, others much less so. In order for them to be commercially competitive, I would expect an option to market them under varietal labels, because in twenty years the more discerning American public now demands this information on the label.

11. The first thing I would look for upon arrival at the cellars would be Swiss or Belgian license plates on cars parked in the lot. This implies that discerning European palates in other countries have already discovered this supplier and are actively doing business. The last thing I would look for would be Iranian license plates.

The second, and perhaps the most important consideration, would be to size up the cellarmaster himself Since I expect him to be forming his own impressions of me as a potential buyer (i.e., is the bill going to be paid on time), I need to determine what sort of a winemaker he is, his tasting ability, and whether he can be trusted. The French have quite a reputation for tasting you in the good stuff right away, and then shipping you the rest after you order.

In the cellars, I would expect strict cleanliness: stainless steel fermenters, millipore or kieselguhr filtration apparatus, and sufficient inventory on hand for at least a six-month period to achieve continuity. Sterile bottling facilities, while not required, would be desirable. As for the bottles themselves, I would assume some familiarity with the mandatory American 750-ml bottle sizes and the packaging equipment associated with generic or branded labeling. Of course, a container discount based on volume would go along with this type of wine.

Sources

AIR TRAFFIC CONTROLLER/Federal Aviation Administration
Reprinted by permission of the publisher, Prentice-Hall Press, New York NY 10023, from the book Air Traffic Controller by James E. Turner, Ph.D. copyright © 1986

ARCHITECTURE/Georgia institute of Technology
Reproduced courtesy of Professor Frank Beckum Jr., College of Architecture

AUTO MECHANICS
Reproduced by permission of National Institute for Automotive Service Excellence, 13505 Dulles Tech Dr., Suite 2, Herndon, VA 22071-3421. *ASE Preparation Guides to Heavy-Duty Truck Testing and Automobile Technician Testing*.

BALLROOM DANCING/Fred Astaire Dance Studios
Reprinted by permission of Fred Astaire National Dance Association, Inc., Miami FL 33256-0367.

BASEBALL UMPIRE/Joe Brinkman Umpire School
Reprinted by permission of Joe Brinkman Umpire School 1021 Indian River Drive, Cocoa FL 32922.

BIBLE CONTENT/ Presbyteries' Cooperative Committee
Reprinted by permission of Presbyteries' Cooperative Committee, 475 Riverside Drive, New York NY 10115.

BOOKKEEPING & ACCOUNTING/N.Y. State Board C Regents Courtesy of New York State Education Department, Albany NY 12234.

BROADCASTING/ Columbia School of Broadcasting
Reprinted by permission of Columbia School of Broadcasting, 5858 Hollywood Boulevard, Hollywood CA 90028-5619, tel. (213) 469-8321.

BUILDING CONTRACTOR/ American Schools
Reprinted by permission of American Schools

BUSINESS ETHICS/ MBA Students vs Prison Inmates
Journal of Business Ethics 7, pp. 246-7, 1988, Jones © copyright 1988 by Kluwer Academic Publishers. Reprinted with kind permission from Kluwer Academic Publishers

COLLECTOR, DEALER, DECORATOR/American Folk Art Institute Courtesy of the Museum of American Folk Art, New York NY.

COMPUTER COMPETENCY/ Microsoft Certification
Reprinted by permission of The Digital University, 220 Bush Street, Suite 1400, San Francisco CA 94104-3516.

COPYEDITOR & PROOFREADER/Professional Free-lancer's Test Reprinted by permission of the publisher, Harper & Row Publishers, Inc., New York NY 10022, from the book The Complete Guide to Editorial Freelancing by Carol L. O'Neill and Avima Ruder copyright © 1979.

CPA/ American Institute of Certified Public Accountants
Material from *Uniform CPA Examination Questions and Unofficial Answers,* © 1987 by American Institute of Certified Public Accountants, Inc., is reprinted with permission.

ELEMENTARY SCHOOL TEACHER/Texas State Board of Education Courtesy of the Texas State Board of Education, Austin TX.

SUNDAY SCHOOL TEACHER/Educator Certification Council Courtesy of the Presbyterian Church (USA), The Educator Certification Council, New York NY and Atlanta GA.

ENGINEER /Engineer-in-Training and Professional Engineer Licensure Sample Examination Reprinted by permission of the publisher. and copyright by, Professional Publications, Inc., P.O. Box 199, Dept. 280, San Carlos CA 95170, from the following books: Civil Engineering Sample Exam, copyright © 1986, and Mechanical Engineering Solutions Manual, copyright © 1984. both by Michael R. Lindeburg, P.E.; Chemical Engineering Practice Exam Set, copyright © 1984, by Randall N. Robinson, P.E.; Electrical Engineering Review Manual and Electrical Engineering Solutions Manual, copyright © 1983, both by Raymond B. Yarbrough, P. E.

EXECUTIVE ASSISTANT/ Katharine Gibbs School
Reproduced by permission of Katharine Gibbs Schools, Inc., National Headquarters, 52 Vanderbilt Avenue, New York, NY 1017 (212) 885-6900
School addresses: Boston: 126 Newbury Street, Boston MA 02116, tel. (617) 578-7100; Huntington, Long Island: 535 Broad Hollow Road, Town of Huntington, Melville NY 11747, tel. (516) 293-2460; Montclair: 33 Plymouth Street, Montclair NJ 07042, tel. (201) 744-2010; New York: 200 Park Avenue, New York NY 10166, tel. (212) 867-9300; Norwalk: 142 East Avenue, Norwalk CT 06851, tel. (203) 838-4173; Piscataway: 80 Kingsbridge Road, Piscataway NJ 08854, tel. (908) 885-1580; Providence: 178 Butler Avenue, Providence RI 02906, tel. (401) 861-1420.

More great titles from
BrainWaves Books

BUILDING MENTAL MUSCLE

Conditioning Exercises for the Six Intelligence Zones:
Memory, Language & Math, Executive Planning, Spatial Visualization, Social Interaction, Emotional Response. By David Gamon, Ph.D. & Allen D. Bragdon
Hundreds of performance-sharpening tips, exercises, and self-tests
Selected by *Book-of-the-Month Club, Quality Paperback, Money, Prevention.*
Trade Paperback, 320 pp., 2-color, 5 1/2 x 8 1/4
$11.95 ISBN 0-916410-62-5

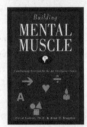

EXERCISES FOR THE WHOLE BRAIN

Neuron-Builders to Stimulate & Entertain Your Visual, Math &
Executive-Planning Skills.
By Allen D. Bragdon and Leonard Fellows
Trade paperback, 128 pp., 5 1/2 x 8 1/4
$7.95 ISBN 0-916410-65-X

BUILDING LEFT-BRAIN POWER

Exercises to Improve Mood, Develop Language and Math Facility, and Build
Uniquely Human Skills. By Allen D. Bragdon and David Gamon, Ph.D
More than 100 tips to improve real-world problem-solving performance.
Trade paperback, 320 pp., 5 1/2 x 8 1/4
$12.95   ISBN 0-916410-63-3

RIGHT BRAIN TEASERS—A Photo-Quiz for the Mind's Eye

Can You Tell What These 75 Old-Time Utensils Were Used For?
By Allen D. Bragdon and Marcia Monbleau. Featured on *Late Night With
David Letterman* NBC-TV. ***"A collector's antique shop & yard-sale handbook
as compelling as a bowl of peanuts"*— Cape Cod Home & Garden.**
Trade paperback, 160 pages, 5 1/2 x8 1/4
$9.95 ISBN 0-916410-66-8

To order the above titles:

Ask your bookseller to order these titles, or to order direct from publisher, list title and
ISBN number, enclose check at prices shown, plus applicable sales tax. Send order to:
BrainWaves Books, Tupelo Road, Bass River, MA 02664. Books will be shipped postpaid
within 48 hours. For quotes on bulk quantities **CALL TOLL-FREE 1-877-8-SMARTS.**

www.mentalmuscles.com